Ian A Anderson
ALIEN WATER
six decades paddling in unpopular music

All rights reserved. No part of this publication may be reproduced, stored in a retrieval system, or transmitted in any form or by any means, electronic, mechanical, photocopying, recording, or otherwise, without the prior permission of the copyright owner and the publisher of this book

Copyright © 2025 Ian A Anderson

The moral right of Ian A Anderson to be identified as author of this work has been asserted in accordance with sections 77 to 78 of the Copyright, Designs and Patents Act of 1988.

Published by Ghosts From The Basement.

First Edition 2025.

Cover design by Alex Merry.

Typeset by Jali Roll Martian.

ISBN (trade paperback) 978-1-0685882-0-4

ISBN (hardback) 978-1-0685882-1-1

ghostsfromthebasement.com

ianaanderson.com

Ghosts From The Basement, Cambridge, CB4 2AW, UK

Contents

	Introduction	iv
1.	**Pre-History : Before Music**	7
2.	**The Great Awakening**	19
3.	**Coming Of Age**	33
4.	**Folk Clubs : A Selective History**	46
5.	**Up And Away**	60
6.	**The Blues Boom**	74
7.	**Changes & The Village Thing**	90
	(Photo section 1)	*97*
8.	**The 1970s : The Gigging Decade**	115
9.	**English Banding In The 1980s**	131
10.	**Folk Festival Life**	147
11.	**The 1980s : The Juggling Decade**	164
12.	**Media Mogul : Magazines & Radio**	181
13.	**Let's Call It World Music**	184
14.	**Tarika & Madagascar Eat The 1990s**	214
	(Photo section 2)	*217*
15.	**The 1990s Otherwise**	239
16.	**Into The Noughties**	256
17.	**21st Century : Live Music Again!**	274
18.	**And The Rest…**	292
19.	**Conclusions & Wig Bubbles**	308

Introduction

When Ralph Vaughan Williams jotted down the song *Lord Allenwater* from my great grandmother in 1904, his hasty scrawl made it look like *Alienwater*. As most of the music I've paddled in since my early teenage years has definitely been alien and off the mainstream to the majority of the British general public, this tome's title seemed apposite.

It may be easier to tell you what this book *isn't*. It's not an academic work with footnotes about traditional folk music, blues, or what got called 'world music' and it's not going to help you with any definitions of such creatures. Nor is it an attempt at a complete history of those movements. Rather, it's a long and winding tale with tangents, about one person's life spent 'doing stuff', deeply embedded in many aspects of those often below-the-radar 'scenes' where those musics were played, developed, promoted and enjoyed over the past six decades. Stories, observations and overviews from that tall bloke wading in the shallows.

Oh, and I have two legs and I don't play a flute or wear a codpiece… I'm not *that* one!

Over those years I've been a full-time musician (speciality: traditional English deathfolk blues and psych-folk world twang, it says here), initially and finally solo but mostly in various duos, trios and bands. Lots of albums were made. I've run clubs, produced concerts and directed festivals as well as sat in many audiences. I've worked as an agent and tour manager for other artists. I've run record labels including 1970s 'alternative folk' imprint Village Thing and '80s world music pioneers Rogue Records. I've broadcast on everything from local radio to a decade on the BBC World Service via BBC Radios 1, 2, 3 and 4, Capital Radio and Jazz FM, and I still produce and present the *Podwireless* podcast. I've photographed, written and designed. Oh, and I co-founded the folk, roots and world music magazine that grew up to be *Folk Roots*, later *fRoots*, and edited it for 40 unbroken years. Some people consider it to have been influential: others may disagree.

What else? I played on the first Glastonbury. I was among the infamous gang who 'invented' world music back in 1987 and I devised the BBC Radio 3 Awards for World Music. I've served my debt to society on Arts Council panels and the National Executive of the English Folk Dance & Song Society. I even appear accidentally to have invented what is now the on-maps name for the area of Bristol where I lived – Clifton Village – in 1970 when drawing up a poster for the legendary Bristol Troubadour club. And loads of other things I've – probably for good reason – forgotten. Mostly done out of a philosophy that if nobody else is doing it (or doing it well) and I reckon it's worth a go, a bit of a creative challenge or an interesting learning curve, fun even, then why not? To paraphrase somebody else's song line, "It's what you can do with what you've got."

In other words a classic Jack of all trades, master of none, though to my surprise and pleasure I've been given some awards for it all by the EFDSS, Folk Alliance International and WOMEX. But it's still possible that I should have learned to concentrate.

Many of those musical scenes and their ecosystems have barely been documented by other people who were involved in them at the time, and certainly not the ways in which they interlocked. So before all my so-called archive probably ends up in the recycling bins after I've croaked, I thought I should write some of it down. Other people's memories, motivations and conclusions may differ, quite possibly widely.

A few parts of this book have been adapted from pieces I've previously written that appeared in *fRoots* (formerly *Folk Roots* and the *Southern Rag*) magazine features, other book and magazine contributions, CD sleeve notes and numerous possibly ill-advised Facebook posts. All used by kind permission of me.

Very little of this lifetime in unpopular musics would have been possible without the support, inspiration, friendship, tolerance, encouragement and contributions of numerous others down all these years. Many are mentioned in the following pages and if I tried to make a definitive list I'd be bound unintentionally to miss some out. But I'd particularly like to thank and dedicate this to two hugely helpful and influential role models, Alexis Korner and Shirley Collins; departed and much-missed Spider John Koerner, Elizabeth Kinder, Al Jones, Dave Evans, Derroll Adams and my mother Sheila Anderson; long-time great friends Ben Mandelson, Maggie Holland and Sarah Coxson; all the long-suffering staff of *fRoots*; and of course my partner Karen and No.1 daughter Cathia Randrianarivo.

Ian A Anderson. Cambridge, 2024.

1.
Pre-History : Before Music

Many friends can recall infinite details of their early years. I've no real idea why I can't: the two schools of thought are either that mine were incredibly boring or that something horribly traumatic occurred. I veer strongly towards the former. People who had siblings, parents who engaged, or have substantial snapshot albums of those years, do a lot better than me as they have the regular triggers to keep memories refreshed. I had none of those. I was the only child of distracted parents in a family that had only passing engagement with an elderly box Brownie. And then in my early teens I got totally obsessed with music…

Sayings like "You can't know where you're going if you don't know where you come from" seem to crop up in cultures the world over. Hampered by that almost total lack of memory of my childhood years, there was a time when I didn't think I even knew who I was, let alone my origins. While I'm still not entirely sure, banging out this story of mine has helped a little, but rest easy, it's not all about *me*: rather, the 'scenes' (as these things were once called) that I was involved in. But first, pre-history…

Luckily my mother kept a 'Progress Book' of my brat years, and as life went on she developed a deep interest and expertise in genealogy, becoming the end repository for photos, tales and paperwork that filtered down the family twig from the time before I was born. So before I get onto my lengthy involvement with unfashionable music, I'll begin with stuff from those mysterious early years and before. Are you sitting comfortably…?

It's on my mother's side of the family that there's the most archaeological evidence of music.

Her great grandfather Thomas Stears, born in 1844, lived on the Isle of Wight, where his older brother Josiah, born in 1823, was a violin teacher and music seller. A schoolmaster in Brading (as well as a constable and eventually Mayor), Thomas married twice. With his first wife Emma he had four children including my great grandfather Alfred Stears. Thomas remarried after the death of Emma, moved to Bonchurch and became the school master there for twenty years until his own death. Clearly an inveterate shagger, he had eight more children including daughters Elizabeth, and Annie who are seen in a photograph from the late 1890s in period morris dancing costume with little sticks and bells. He was obviously interested in folk dance as there is another photo of maypole dancing in the school playground. The school house is still there, next to the church, and nowadays a holiday rental property.

In 1890 his son Alfred Stears married eighteen year old Emily Agnes Ragless, my maternal great grandmother. He worked at various occupations including as a builder and a railway ticket collector. In 1904, folk song collector and composer Ralph Vaughan Williams came to Horsham in Sussex, where they lived, and collected songs from Emily.

I was blissfully unaware of this until the early years of this century when English folk's national treasure Shirley Collins wrote extensive notes for her CD box set retrospective *Within Sound*. It included her version of the traditional song *Lord Allenwater* which, she dutifully noted, had been collected by RVW in Horsham from an "E.A. Stears" (his hasty handwriting of the title makes it look like *Alienwater*.) Not being so up to speed with the Stears family tree at that time, I rang my mother and asked her if we had one of those. "Well, there was an Ernest Alfred," she said. "I'll do some digging."

A few days later she rang back in some excitement. "It wasn't Ernest Alfred," she said. "It was Emily Agnes, it was your great grandmother. I've just talked with your uncle Colin who used to hang out with the old ladies, and he knew the story about when that Mr Vaughan Williams had come to call. I do remember this now – she used to sing some of those old songs you're interested in." "How come, you waited until I was in my fifties to tell me this?" I probably squeaked. She went on to recount how her granny had lived to be 99 – I have very vague memories of meeting her when I was a small child – and, a staunch republican, had allegedly passed away in her old folks' home at that age so as "to avoid getting one of those damn telegrams from the Queen." Ah, so she's where I inherited that tendency from.

My mother, Sheila Elsie Stears, was born in Gillingham, Kent, in 1925. There was no earlier family connection to the county. Her father, Cecil Harold Frederick Stears (mostly known as Fred or, inexplicably, Jim) was born in Horsham in 1899 and left school at thirteen to work for a local dentist. After the 1st World War – for which he'd initially signed up before being booted out again as under age, rejoining in 1917 – he ended up as a dental mechanic in the Royal Navy, initially in Portsmouth but then posted to Chatham Dockyards in Kent in 1922.

In 1929 he was posted to Malta, taking my grandmother and four-year-old mother with him. My mother's time in Malta appears to have been idyllic, other than engaging with education which never seems to have impressed her greatly judging by her school reports which bear many comments of the "could do better" variety (the exception being Art). Her memories of Malta written in later life refer to many picnics and parties among the ex-pat community and the cheapness of silk dresses. There are photos of her as the May Queen.

In 1935 my grandfather was posted back to Chatham where my mother attended school in Rochester, gaining some piano grades in 1937. Her parents lost a second child in 1936 (my grandmother was rhesus negative which was an issue back then) and immediately adopted a new born baby, the aforementioned uncle Colin. They lived there until 1939 when my grandfather was posted again, this last time to the Naval Dockyards in Portsmouth, where the family subsequently remained, living in Southsea.

Shamefully, I have no real idea what my mother did as a teenager during the war years. In 1940 she was in the Lower 5th at City of Portsmouth Southern Secondary School For Girls, and I suspect that she subsequently had some office or secretarial training as she put such skills to good use in later years.

My parents never talked about how they met, but eventually in her old age my mother told the story of how, near the end of WW2, my father was stationed in the RAF near Portsmouth and my mother was working as a telephonist at the local exchange. My father, liking the sound of her voice, had set up a dance date for himself and a friend with my mother and a friend. On the night, neither of the friends could make it but the date went ahead and the rest is history… They got married in Portsmouth on 31st July 1945. He remained in the RAF until he was demobilised in early 1946.

My father, Alexander Gordon Anderson, born in Weston-super-Mare in 1920 and always just known as Gordon, had a two-pronged ancestry. On his father's side they came from Scotland, particularly from around Falkirk.

One of my very vague childhood memories is of a mid-'50s relative-hunting road trip that my parents and I made to Scotland in an ex-Post Office van which my father had skilfully converted into a motor caravan (though in truth its paint job made it look more like an ice cream van). I have no recall where we went or who we met, other than two ancient 'aunts' who lived in a terraced house completely over-run with dozens of cats, and of being taken up a thistle-encrusted hillside, possibly near Largs, and falling into what I was informed was a 'burn'. Breaking the journey, we visited another aunt, my paternal grandfather's sister Emmie, who lived in Lytham St Annes near Blackpool and remains my sole family connection to t'north of England. Yes, we went to see the lights.

On his maternal grandmother's side the family came from the Somerset Levels where they included pub landlords, railway workers and peat diggers, with *Cold Comfort Farm*-esque names like Aquila Durston.

His Somerset grandmother Lyda Jane Norris had come into service in Weston, but had married an upwardly mobile husband, Charles Downes, although at the time they married he was a mere ironmonger's clerk. Lyda seems to have become Ida to go with her married surname… think about it. By the turn of the century they'd joined the respectable property-owning middle class. After his death she re-married a dentist, Mr Taylor, acquiring some more property. The two Downes daughters, Edith (my grandmother) and her much prettier sister Gertrude, continued social climbing and my grandmother became an inveterate snob. She destroyed all evidence of her Somerset ancestry, including photos. My mother, who didn't like her mother-in-law very much, took great delight in digging it all out.

It was only this century that my mother's genealogical research uncovered that a distant member of the Norris family (Charles, my 2nd cousin, 4 times removed) had given songs including versions of *The False Bride* and *Tanyard Side* to collector Cecil Sharp at Shapwick Station on the Levels in 1909, thus bestowing ethno-cred on both sides of my family.

My paternal grandfather Alex Anderson provides one more tenuous ancestral link to music: there are photos of him in local amateur operatic productions of Gilbert & Sullivan in early 1914, before WW1 kicked off. Called up by the North Somerset Yeomanry that August, he was badly wounded in early 1915 at Hooge in Flanders, spending a year convalescing in Cambridge and Lancashire from a big shrapnel wound to his leg. He never fully recovered, though he was well enough to marry my grandmother in 1917. He eventually died from his depleted health when my father was only six. As a result, my father was brought up as an only child by a single mother, including a spell at boarding school on a scholarship: to say he became self-centred would be an understatement.

At some point my father gained interests in woodworking and boats: apparently as a boy he built a canoe and set off across the Bristol Channel from Weston-super-Mare to Wales. It was only on the return journey that he'd become sufficiently tired that he'd accepted a lift from one of the paddle steamers that ran a service from the Old Pier at Weston to Penarth and back. Unfortunately this got reported in the local newspaper and so my grandmother found out about it. In later years she told the tale with pride though this clearly wasn't her reaction at the time. It was not long after this that boarding school came about, oddly enough in Horsham where my maternal grandfather and great grandparents had lived.

Shortly before WW2 my father had joined the Imperial Tobacco Company which his father had briefly worked for as a clerk. He spent the war in RAF ground crew – his eyesight precluded flying – and then returned to the same company for which he worked until retirement. He was much more interested in sailing and woodwork, at which he was very talented. It was the grey late-'40s and '50s. He didn't stand a chance. He didn't socialise, he didn't like music, he didn't like food he could taste. He was typical of a certain type of English bloke of his era. He voted Tory, was borderline racist: we had nothing in common and he always made that clear.

The lives of my grandmother and her sister were considerably entwined, and my father and his cousin Joy – Aunt Gertude's daughter with husband Tom Thompson – grew up in the 1920s more like brother and sister.

A remarkable story up that side of the tree is of my Uncle Tom Thompson – or Commander Thomas Alfred Owen Thompson OBE, to give him his proper name. Born in Weymouth in 1892, he went to sea in the last of the commercial ocean-going square-rigged sailing ships and lived to see men walk on the moon.

He went to naval college at age twelve, doing two years on a training ship at Greenwich. Having failed his navigation exams, he went to sea as an apprentice midshipman on a four-masted barque working from New York to Africa and the Far East. He got stranded in Bombay, so worked his way back as a deck hand on a tramp steamer. Later, in Calcutta, he signed on to a tanker operating around the Indian coast, then sat for his master's certificate and joined the Royal Indian Marines (by now it's 1916 and he wants to see something of the War: he's just 24!) He was given a paddle steamer to take to Basra in Mesopatamia, operating up the Tigris by moonlight, supplying troops and making accurate charts. He was promoted to Captain, mentioned in despatches and given that OBE.

He married Gertrude Downes in 1919: they had first met – for only a few weeks – in summer 1912, and written to each other continually for the next seven years. They soon had a daughter, my aunt Joy. Tom returned to Burma, and Gertrude went out to join him in 1922, leaving Joy with grandmother Downes. But although they enjoyed the privileged European lifestyle with their clubs for swimming, tennis and bridge, Gertrude missed their baby and so eventually, after a year, Tom gave up his well-paid job and finally left the sea.

Back in the UK, they tried various unsuccessful ventures, including running a market garden and distributing Burma cheroots to tobacconists. After this he worked unhappily for an insurance company for five years, and then in 1929 they started a small international language school in Beaconsfield, mainly for the children of diplomats, Indian Princes and Maharajahs. One of the pupils they were entrusted with was the young actor Sabu (*The Elephant Boy*, *The Thief Of Baghdad* etc).

He rejoined the navy for WW2, based in Belfast but going (for the Ministry of Information) on convoys to Russia, Malta, and Normandy on D-Day. When he wasn't away on duty, Tom and Gertrude lived in a cottage at Stone Allerton in Somerset.

After WW2 he became the BBC's yachting correspondent, covering Cowes weeks etc. He wrote a number of Henty-type books – boys-own adventures on the high seas with titles like *Square Rigger*, *Before The Mast*, *The Golden Gryphon* and *Flying Spray*, the latter adapted as a BBC radio play. They lived in various places including in Bristol and in a pair of converted railway carriages in Exmouth (while Tom again taught English to foreign students) before returning to Weston-super-Mare where for a while he operated the ferry boat from Uphill to Brean Down. I remember him as a lovely straight-backed, sparkling blue eyed gentleman, who would occasionally burst into sea shanties at family gatherings, only to suddenly stop and say "ah, ladies present!" The last job I recall him having in his old age when they were, as usual, strapped for cash was as the uniformed doorman on the Grand Atlantic Hotel. He was a good grandfather substitute on that side of the family as I never met my real one.

I've no idea what he and Gertrude made of their daughter Joy marrying jazz trumpeter Chic Mayes – they'd met in Egypt in 1945 when Joy was in the ATS and Chic was the officer in charge of entertainments in Palestine – and them later divorcing, leaving her to bring up my cousins Sean and Roderick as a single parent. Basically they stepped up and took over the parental role. They were, to say the least, a household of total eccentrics.

Another of my hazy childhood memories is of going up into the big attic of a house in Clifton, Bristol, where the family were living. Joy had certainly been a big jazz fan in the '30s and had piles of old 78s that my cousins and I had great fun in breaking over each other's heads. If Joy was upset she never showed it, not in my presence anyway, so I was mortified in my teenage years when I'd learned some jazz history and saw what gems remained unscathed in her collection. I shudder when I imagine what priceless jazz artefacts we may have unwittingly destroyed...

They all seemed proud of Sean, even though having studied Philosophy at Cambridge he promptly went off and joined rock'n'roll band Fumble – later becoming a keyboard player for David Bowie and later still Tom Robinson. The story of that family twig ends in tragedy which I'll come to much later, in chapter 15.

I was born in Weston-super-Mare in July 1947. In my father's declining years he suddenly announced during a family visit that I had been a "mistake," which explains a lot about his distance and irascible attitude to me down the years. I can't say I was surprised, or that my mother kept her silence and didn't dispute it. It would also explain why, when they built their new house in 1953, it didn't have any extra bedrooms to theirs and mine, other than a tiny box room – he clearly wasn't planning for more, or lots of visitors. With hindsight, as an only child he had no experience of being around young children and having been brought up by his widowed mother from the age of six he had no clue how a father might behave.

It was only later on, because when you're a child you accept everything in your life experience as normal, that I realised that I'd never seen any outward displays of affection in our home, either between my parents or towards me. Hugs weren't something people gave. It took me into my twenties to get over that. I remember being amazed when, aged around 21, I was welcomed into households like Alexis Korner's where the children were friends with their father and shared similar interests. I became even more determined not to become like mine.

My parents initially lived in a typical grey limestone two-storey semi on a hillside – indeed it was called Hill Road – on the north side of Weston-super-Mare. I believe it had belonged to my grandmother who then moved into a garden flat in another house that she owned nearby, where she rented out the upstairs flats. One of the first mentions in the Progress Book is that I liked my mother singing Peggy Lee's 1947 hit *Chi-Baba Chi-Baba* – at least I prefer to think it was Peggy Lee's version rather than the smooth, croony Perry Como one: that would never do!

I have only hazy recollections of that house. My bedroom was down the end of what seemed like a long dark landing which constantly spooked me. I remember that it had an interestingly angled ceiling that I found soothing to stare at when lying in bed with the normal childhood illnesses, when I wasn't reading. My school report when I left the local infant school in Milton Road in the summer of 1954 mentions that "his reading age is well above his seven years" and that I "enjoy music" but "find writing difficult, mainly because he finds it hard to take time to write down his words." Hmmm. Meanwhile, the Progress Book noted that the six year old me "shows off like mad, especially in front of little girls."

If there were traumas, the only ones that have stayed with me were caused by the budgie – a standard issue green job. One time it escaped from its cage and took off to the tall trees in the gloomy churchyard located beyond a high stone wall at the top of our longish back garden. Much panic ensued as my mother and my small self took its cage and quantities of millet up there and called its now-forgotten name for some time. Amazingly, it eventually came down and was recaptured. The exercise may have proved fatal though, because I remember that not long after that we were sat at the breakfast table with the bird in its cage when it went into a sudden fluttering frenzy before dropping dead on the cage floor with its legs in the air. For many years I harboured the guilty feeling that I'd pulled a face at it which had brought about its panic and demise, but when I confessed this to my mother in much later life, she was adamant that it never happened. So much for memories. Hers or mine?

I have near-zero ones of that infant school, other than disliking the school dinners – fish pie and the dessert we called "cake and custard" in particular. The fish pie was always foul smelling and made with particularly lumpy potato mash; the dessert cake was always stale and the custard similarly challenged in smoothness. Oh, and tapioca pudding, a.k.a. frogspawn, also lumpy. It was austerity 1950s Britain, after all, indeed 1950s Weston-super-Mare – hardly ideal training to become a foodie.

The only vivid image that comes back is of the very last day of the leaving term when we children were milling around a large room waiting to be united with our collecting parents. A very cute fox terrier puppy came towards me and, when my eyes followed its lead upwards to adult canopy height, I found that it was attached to my mother. It was apparently a birthday present for me but I'm afraid that I have hardly any memories of its subsequent years: we can't have bonded. If it weren't for a few grainy black & white snaps and diary references to taking it for walks, I'd even doubt its existence. Pets and I clearly weren't mutually attracted.

My mother's Progress Book also noted my obsession with reading and writing stories, followed in 1953 by "watching TV". Like many, they'd got a small black & white set to watch the Coronation. I don't remember watching that, but I do recall going to stay with my Southsea grandparents so that we could have a trip around the Fleet lying at anchor for the coronation review, and stay up late one evening to see it all illuminated. "The fleet's lit up!"

As for TV, the standard children's programming of the day – *Hank, Muffin The Mule, The Flower Pot Men* – was OK but I'm not sure how I acquired the response of hiding behind the settee when something scary happened on the occasional adult programmes that I watched. I mean, loads of people reportedly do/did that, but it must have spontaneously happened to many post-1953 – hardly a hereditary human trait. I particularly recall a gate opening mysteriously with no assistance – something tells me it was a production of *Waiting For Godot* – that got me scurrying behind the furnishings in mild terror. Anyway, I'd got well over all that by the time TV was showing things like *Quatermass & The Pit*, though the Progress Book noted that "he does not like watching or listening to any plays or stories where characters are liable to be hurt."

Over the preceding year to leaving the infant school, my parents had been having a new house built in the village of Uphill, at the southern end of Weston-super-Mare, for the princely sum of two grand. It was the first one completed at the far end of a quiet cul-de-sac, and was to be my home for the next decade. We moved there in the summer of 1954: my mother's piano that I vaguely remember her playing in the old house made it down there with us, but didn't last long. My father, apparently, didn't think it was a nice piece of furniture: I imagine its music-making function was of no interest at all, and the fact that the Progress Book records that I enjoyed "banging on it" may well have been a factor too. The contents of her piano stool ended up in the loft, not to be brought down again until old age after my father's passing when she became a fangirl for that "nice young man" André Rieu and liked to read her yellowed sheet music along to his TV extravaganzas.

The timing of the house move allowed me to begin the autumn term in the village junior school. Surprise, surprise, I have few memories of the four years I spent at that school either. Luckily there's a surviving school photo of my class with everybody's name pencilled on the back, so I don't have to wrack my brains to come up with the names of the few boys who were my 'best friends' – Tony Carver, Denis Wright and Tim Clutterbuck (eventually of late '60s/early '70s acoustic duo Mudge & Clutterbuck) – or the very pretty little girl called Jennifer Anderson (no relation) who was my first ever crush, but probably never knew it due to my shyness.

Junior school traumas that I recall: just two. One was the warm summer day when I was sat in the classroom distracted by a wasp circling in the high ceiling, only to suddenly feel its sting impaled in my short-trousered leg. This may explain my life-long hatred of shorts, in later life transferred to the sight of them worn on stage by male folk-rock and ceilidh band musicians of a certain age!

More serious was the Saturday morning in January 1956 when I got knocked down by a van. My mother, no doubt to get me out of the house for a few hours of peace, had decided it would be good for me to go pony riding once a week. I hated it, and probably came up with regular lame excuses why I shouldn't get on the bus ride from Uphill to the stables at Worle at the other side of town. Too much "wolf" had been cried, so the day I actually did feel really sick she packed me off anyway. The woman at the riding school took one look at me and put me straight onto the bus back home. Getting off it in my blurry state, I walked straight into the path of the local odd-job man's little van. I regained consciousness lying on the pavement convinced I had nothing worse than a nosebleed, but in fact I'd slightly fractured my skull, broken my arm and put my teeth through my lip. The van had suffered worse, I proudly claimed, as I'd dented in the radiator grill so far that it obstructed the fan belt and the innocent vehicle had to be towed away. The driver was mortified even though it wasn't his fault.

Returning to school several weeks later with my arm still in plaster, the headmistress, Miss Packer, hauled me up in front of the entire school assembly as an example of how not to obey the *Highway Code*. If I'd known about sticking pins in wax dolls, I'd have been impaling hers for the rest of my time there.

The following December my mother took me with her to Chatham in Kent to stay with an old childhood friend of hers, and every other day we went up to London for my first ever visit. I can vaguely picture the Tower of London and the Science Museum, but it was the West End lights and bustle (and Hamley's toy shop) that most stick in my memory.

My parents, meanwhile, were heavily absorbed in sailing – and in my father's case, his skillful woodwork both on the boat and around the house. After selling an early dinghy with the now deeply un-PC name *Dusky Maid*, and a picturesque old cabin cruiser called *Stormy* that had rust red sails, they'd bought a racing dinghy, of a class called Dayboats. They were also instigators in setting up a small sailing club in the River Axe that separates Uphill from Brean Down, the last land outpost of the Mendips.

As my mother got involved in administration of the Dayboat Association (guess who I got my organisational skills from!) they took to towing the dinghy down to the south coast, Poole Harbour mainly, for meetings and regattas. As I got less and less interested in their nautical activities, I tended to get parked with minders on the beach or in the clubhouses, or increasingly left behind in Weston with my grandmother. I'd already spent most of my summer holidays down in Southsea with my other grandparents.

In the winter months, my mother got into amateur pantomime productions at the Knightstone Theatre, knocking up elaborate costumes on her sewing machine and strutting her long legs as 'principal boy'. Like many post-war women she'd developed her 'make do and mend' skills for clothes making, knitting and embroidery to a high and imaginative standard. It compensated for her complete lack of culinary expertise, though my father's reluctance to eat anything with a hint of herb, spice or interesting flavour no doubt had an influence. We were a meat-and-two-veg household, the latter preferably boiled to submission.

We did occasionally go out for drives in the car, initially a small Morris convertible, later the 'ice cream van'. Probably my strongest memory of those years is climbing up through the bracken thronged with summer-buzzing insects and butterflies to Crook Peak and Wavering Down on the Mendips, gazing out across the ancestral Somerset Levels through the heat haze, or looking down into a tiny hamlet called Compton Bishop that nestled in a sun-trap fold on the south side and I thought would be paradise to live in. I never could afford the dream cottage, but it's a climb and view that I've constantly revisited throughout my life. If I have ashes, they'll get scattered up there.

Left to my own devices, I'd often ramble off around the village environs, nearby hill and surrounding fields with one or two of my school pals, exploring hedgerows, ditches and rhynes, often falling into the latter in our quest to fill jam jars with unfortunate newts, minnows, sticklebacks and tadpoles. We 1950s children weren't so protected and home-encased as those nowadays. As long as you got home in time for tea, nobody seemed to bother. So my other enduring childhood memory and an experience that I like to revisit whenever possible is lying on the grass in a meadow listening to the silvery sound of many skylarks burbling above – a lifelong thrill.

And that was childhood. At the very end of junior school I got heavily into my second hobby, following the predictable stamp collecting, of building and flying free-flight model aeroplanes. This occupied most of my spare time into my early teenage years, and indeed brought my first attempts at journalism with a couple of simple glider plans published in *Aeromodeller* magazine. Then the two great distractions – music and girls – took over and dictated a future in which most earlier memories faded through lack of exercise. Use it or lose it, they say.

2.
The Great Awakening

I must have done a lot of homework at junior school – I think I may have been a nerdy swot as the Progress Book records that I was never lower than 2nd in my class. The Eleven Plus exam seems to have been a doddle – unsurprisingly I have no recall – which had unforeseen results when it propelled me into a strange educational experiment that greatly influenced life-thereafter.

In the late summer of 1958 I went off in my smart new school blazer and cap to the local Boys' Grammar School. For some reason that in later life my parents could never explain how it was justified, the school took some fifteen entering pupils who they considered had the best all-round 11-Plus results and put us straight into the second year. I'm sure my parents thought it gained some status points at the time. The ill-defined plan was that in the first twelve months we'd catch up with the other boys in our class who'd already been there a year, and then… what? In my case, with a birthday in July, I was put in with classmates, some of whom were up to two years older – which is a big difference when you're eleven. Though very useful when you're older and they can drive you to gigs in far-off exotic places like Bristol and Taunton…

Not only did I grow older fast, I had to pick my O-Level subjects the following year, aged twelve rather than the normal fourteen. I had to discard music, art and geography – of all things – to concentrate on 'important' subjects like science and maths. Luckily I was allowed to retain English and history. In truth I didn't take to all this, and I never did so well in school results again. At least one of the other boys in the experiment had a complete breakdown and had to leave the school. Meanwhile I slowly got obsessed with music as a buffer against reality.

I suppose it had crept up on me in junior school days. On the odd occasion I was ill in bed with measles, chicken pox and those other common childhood ailments, my mother would put the radio into my bedroom as the BBC Light Programme churned out *Housewives' Choice*, *Music While You Work*, *Family Favourites* and the like. I was subjected to much crooning and praise for everything from doggies in the window to Davy Crockett so it didn't honestly have great appeal: indeed, a fortnight's 1955 exposure to daily blasts of

Eddie Calvert's irritating *Cherry Pink And Apple Blossom White* brought about a trumpet-phobia that lasted into the 1990s, only undone then by the Cuban roots music boom and favourite American rock band Cake.

Things began to change around my last year in junior school with the advent of TV shows like *Six-Five Special* and *Oh Boy*. Gruesome and lame they may seem in retrospect – the sole aim of the music industry back then being to tame skiffle and emerging British rock'n'roll by putting it into suits and pointing it at 'Variety' – but after Perry Como, Patti Page and up against BBC TV's *Billy Cotton Band Show* they were breaths of fresher air. Showbiz suits would corrupt Tommy Steele, Lonnie Donegan, Cliff Richard and many others up to and including the early Beatles with their neat jackets and haircuts, but it was all we had on the two TV channels of the day. The window opened a little.

When I was around seven my mother had befriended another couple, the Podds, who had two young daughters around my age, on the pebbly beach at Southsea. Their two girls, Diana and Rosalind, and I had got on very well – in later life I reasoned that this was the point when I'd dimly begun to realise that women were much better, more empathic company than blokes – and our parents had stayed in touch for some years. Anyway, for my tenth birthday the girls were invited over to Uphill to stay and party, and as a treat after the jelly and cake we all (my school friends Denis and Tony too) watched *Six-Five Special*. By coincidence, it featured fifteen-year-old Paul Anka's teen weepie *Diana*, on its way to million-selling chart domination of the year. The effect on our Diana was impressive!

Music just wormed its way in. On TV, 1959 saw the launch of another long-running national institution, *Juke Box Jury*, where an often deeply unhip panel of 'celebrities' chaired by one of the BBC's seemingly endless supply of smarmy, well-spoken middle-aged arbiters of teenage taste, David Jacobs, pontificated on the likely hit status of the latest 'platters'. Occasionally, as it went into the early 1960s, it defeated low expectations, but it reached the pits with a December 1964 edition where long-since showbizzed skiffle survivor Lonnie Donegan, recent 'Bond girl' Shirley Eaton, moustachioed elderly comedy actor and failed Tory candidate Jimmy Edwards, and TV announcer Polly Elwes, gave the thumbs down to a single by Chicago blues legend Howlin' Wolf, who was then produced from the wings as the surprise guest. I still shudder to think about the embarrassment of it, and quite possibly that was the last edition I ever watched.

A month before that 1957 *Six-Five Special* revelation, the BBC Light Programme had begun a radio show called *Saturday Skiffle Club*, featuring the likes of The Vipers Skiffle Group, Chas McDevitt and Johnny Duncan & His Bluegrass Boys, introduced by the avuncular voice of Brian Matthew. It somehow became a fixture in the house – I imagine my father would have taken himself off to the moorings or his workshop – and of course I had no idea that several decades later I'd regularly play with Vipers washboard star John Pilgrim who often became an extra Hot Vulture.

It evolved the following year into simply *Saturday Club*, two hours following Uncle Mac's *Children's Favourites*, and survived for more than a decade, even for several years after the Light Programme was euthanised by the creation of Radio 1. Over the years *Saturday Club* moved on from skifflers and Britain's limp would-be-rockers like Cliff, Terry Dene, Adam Faith and Eden Kane (and the occasional credible ones like Johnny Kidd and Duffy Power) and the trad jazz craze of Bilk, Ball & Barber. Relatively bigger budgets to match a listenership in millions by the early '60s, allowed sessions by visiting Americans like Eddie Cochran, Gene Vincent, Duane Eddy, Bo Diddley and the Everly Brothers. Eventually, it would have been the first place where the average person might have heard the Beatles, the Rolling Stones and other major names of early 1960s youth culture as they emerged, often via studio sessions as plays of new releases were restricted by the Musicians Union's 'needletime' regulations.

And then there was Radio Luxembourg, whose variable signal on 208 MW wafted in and out on the night-time air, also listened to by millions of British teenagers, frequently under their bedding after lights-out. Our generation probably thought that this commercial station, with its programmes consisting entirely of records and sponsored by the labels, was specially created just for us but I later discovered that it had begun as far back as the 1920s.

In the earlier 1950s it was apparently still presenting comedy and drama programmes, sometimes formats that had been dropped by or escaped from the BBC, but as the audience for that kind of content migrated to the comfort of TV, they slowly changed to solidly music on records. The shows sponsored by Decca for their London American label, and DJs like Tony Hall and Jack Jackson, were my preference. The nation learned how to spell K-e-y-n-s-h-a-m via Horace Bachelor's famous adverts for his Infra-Draw Method to win the football pools.

My musical tastes developed slowly. You liked odds and ends from what you got given, until you found out how to go digging off the mainstream. No internet, Google or YouTube back then. One advantage of being dumped into the second year at the Grammar School was that I was among older boys who had learned more of the byways of pop music and started to acquire record collections. Some even had older brothers and sisters to give them pointers. One lad seemed bizarrely old-fashioned in his devotion to Elvis Presley and Little Richard, who we considered yesterday's dinosaurs, but then he did maintain as much of a quiff as the school allowed. Mind you, he also owned a copy of Jackie Wilson's *Reet Petite*.

I was just 13 at the dawn of the '60s and briefly succumbed to the charms of pop starlets like Helen Shapiro and Louise Cordet. But it was instrumental groups which comprised most of my early singles buying, something I'd discover a few years later that I shared with songwriter friend Al Stewart. Back then we could nerdily quote catalogue numbers at each other ("*Saturday Nite At The Duck Pond* by the Cougars – that'd be Parlophone 45-R 4989.") The first record I ever bought with my own money was by twangster Duane Eddy, soon augmented by the likes of the Piltdown Men, Johnny & The Hurricanes, The Flee-rekkers, the space-suited Spotnicks (who would later make a great proto-folk-rock single of *The Midnight Special*), B. Bumble & The Stingers and Booker T & The MGs as well as the more obvious Shadows and Ventures.

By this time pop music on TV was represented by ATV's *Thank Your Lucky Stars* (famous for teen pundit Janice Nicholls and her "Oi'll give it foive" catchphrase) and over in our part of the country, TWW's *Discs A Go Go*, which very occasionally featured non-mainstream American touring artists like Mose Allison or Jesse Fuller as the decade expanded. Later still of course we got the best of and most influential of the early '60s TV shows, *Ready Steady Go*, but the weekend didn't start there until the summer of 1963. Slowly but surely, though, often via Radio Luxembourg, I discovered black American vocal groups like the Coasters, Drifters and Chiffons, and soul singers like Arthur Alexander, Ben E. King and Solomon Burke. And around this time I'd begun one of my lifetime obsessions, buying the music press.

As the '60s wound onwards, Britain was the envy of the world for its range of weekly music papers, with different ones representing the musical zeitgeist of a short era or a particular musical tribe at any point. Before getting addicted to *Melody Maker* I was first directed to *Record Mirror* by school friends and persuaded my mother that this would be a good addition to my parents' order in the local newsagents, alongside the weekly *Weston Mercury* (featuring Lola Archer's column *Over The Teacups*, which was mainly about her later-to-be-infamous young son Jeffrey) and the dismal *Daily Express* that my parents took. Even then, with nothing to compare it with, I sensed that the latter was tripe, other than the splendid Giles cartoons which I'd enjoyed and often bought the annuals.

Years later, one of Bristol's earliest folk club organisers, Ken Cotterell, who had known Giles in Fleet Street days, told me the amusing tale of how he'd once bumped into the great cartoonist who was brandishing a copy of that day's paper and exclaiming in great glee "It's in!" Apparently for years he'd been hiding a discarded condom in the small details and it had been the job of a sub-editor to find it in the artwork and apply a different kind of rubber. On this day, whether through incompetence or weariness on behalf of the sub who may have reasoned that if he let a particularly well-concealed one through then Giles might stop, the non-offending item finally appeared concealed in a pile of leaves. And he did indeed stop. But I digress…

I became an inveterate list maker and filled exercise books with notes of interesting LPs and 45s that I'd spotted in the press and in the record catalogues that I used to send off for, or blag from the local retailers, Boots and WH Smith's record departments or an alluring back-street shop called Audio that also sold guitars and amplifiers – more of that later. And my "personal hit parade" from things heard on the radio, and later lists like my top 10 British R&B groups. Nerds-r-us.

As a 15 year old in Weston-super-Mare – i.e. pre-drinking age, which for me began not much more than a year later as I was tall and hung out with older people – the only place to go for organised entertainment in town was the Winter Gardens on a Wednesday night, where they held the weekly Teen & Twenty dances. These were the days of beat group frenzy, and a couple of bands would be featured each time. The best local ones were Dave Whitfield & The Rapids and, later into the R&B, era the Iveys. From Bristol (that was the big city – London was too far away for one-nighters) came the popular Pete Budd & The Rebels and Mike Tobin & The Magnettes. Pete Budd in those days was a lean, leather-trousered Gene Vincent wannabe: it's hard to credit that he's now the chubby, rosy-faced yokel fronting the Wurzels.

Most popular from a bit further away were the sensational (to us) Mal Ryder & The Spirits from Oxford whose live version of the much-covered *Slow Down* by Larry Williams would trounce all later tries by the Beatles, the Jam etc, in my memory glow anyway. And very rarely we'd get genuine visiting Americans, peaking with Johnny & The Hurricanes and Gene Vincent & The Bluecaps, both in the early months of 1963. It subconsciously grew on me that I wanted to learn guitar and be in a group...

And girls. Imagine what the pent-up hormones did to us young teenagers with both the Boys' and Girls' Grammar Schools sharing the same building, but walled up the middle inside, and the playing fields separated by a central drive. Some five metres either side of the drive were lines creosoted on the grass over which crossing by pupils was strictly forbidden, even if an errant ball rolled over. Never the twain could meet. Surreptitious notes were hurled over to objects of one's distant desire, full of now-forgotten acronyms of passionate phrases, but if one was lucky to accidentally meet one's infatuee by the bike sheds in Broadoak Road, despite the deliberately staggered leaving times, tongues were often tied. School uniforms and sniggering friends didn't help.

But at the Winter Gardens on Wednesday nights, fueled by the devil's music, things progressed much better and closer acquaintance could be made. My snobbish grandmother had always warned me not to befriend people from the nearby council estate and Secondary Modern school (this was in pre-Comprehensive days) so naturally I completely ignored her advice.

At that age, there really wasn't much else to do of an evening, other than trek out to the Old Pier where the café had quite a decent juke box selection (a hearing of the Everly's *Cathy's Clown*, Eddie Cochran's *C'mon Everybody* or Louise Cordet's *I'm Just A Baby* never fails to bring back the nostalgia). If your luck was in you might even enjoy a little exploratory snog. Or watch the Sunday night cabaret: at this time, Wales was 'dry' on Sundays so Welsh drinkers would flock over on the paddle steamers to Weston for their tipple. Inevitably the more inebriated ones would be seen stumbling, holding each other up, along the pier in the desperate hope of catching the last ferry home which left around 10pm. I was startled when my father once enquired of me where I'd been late-ish on a summer holiday Sunday and I'd told him the story, only for him to say "Oh, is that still happening? We used to go and laugh at them in the 1930s." A tradition, no less, now lost to relaxed licensing laws.

Cycling everywhere certainly kept me fit, as did chasing errant model aeroplanes around the countryside. I wasn't the slightest bit into sport, which at school consisted of rugby in the winter and cricket in the summer, both of which seemed inherently risky and being involved in a team with people unlikely otherwise to be your friends. So I took the offered alternative, cross country running. Whereas others would get as far as the sand dunes near the beach and bunk off for a smoke, I really enjoyed stretching out on my own with my thoughts and the skylarks and would always do the full course. Nobody could have been more surprised than me when I came second in my year on the annual school run, though.

I took my O-Levels in summer 1962 and did OK, but the school continued its misjudged demolition of my academic career. Having prevented me from following music, art or geography beyond the age of 12, my best O-Level results were in English language, English literature, history and French. You'd have thought... but no. How I was persuaded, and doubtless my parents too, that the only future lay in me doing maths and physics to A-Level, is now a mystery. I wasn't the slightest bit engaged with either subject and the teachers were uninspiring. Sixth form, which I began that September, was drudgery and just something I had to do between getting more involved with music.

I don't think I'd paid much attention to news and current affairs up to that point, hardly surprising in a household that took the *Express* and in the days long before rolling TV news, but I can clearly remember the events which changed that. October 1962 saw the 'Cuban Missile Crisis' when charismatic American President John F. Kennedy had stared down that nasty bald Russian proto *Bond* villain Khrushchev – as we were indoctrinated to regard these two world leaders – and prevented impending World War 3 and nuclear armageddon. It went on for a fortnight and we were all scared witless. I remember waking up one morning in a nightmare brought on by the sound of an aeroplane going overhead, probably doing nothing more threatening than taking early tourists on a trip around Weston Bay, convinced by having seen too many war films that the bombing was imminent.

I wish I could pin down the date but it must have been around the end of 1962 or the early part of 1963 when I was still 15. Championed by Guy Stevens (who'll re-enter my story later) and Norman Jopling in *Record Mirror*, I was already well-aware of what was then called R&B – Chuck Berry, Bo Diddley, Jimmy Reed, John Lee Hooker – and had begun buying the singles by Diddley and Howlin' Wolf on Pye International's iconic new red & yellow labelled R&B series. And I'd run across the name of Alexis Korner via radio broadcasts (maybe on the BBC's posh Third Programme) and his band's influential mid-priced *R&B From The Marquee* LP with Cyril Davies and Long John Baldry, released around then. I'd maybe even clocked that some of the songs on it were learned from somebody called Muddy Waters.

One Friday lunchtime, and this I can remember clearly like yesterday, I walked into a school physics lab where the weekly sixth-form record club was held. Everybody was a year or two older than me, as had been the case from the moment I joined the school. As I entered the room and put my bag down, somebody – I have no recollection as to his name, even though at that moment they single-handedly and profoundly changed the direction of the rest of my life – put on a record that totally thrilled, mesmerised and transported me. It was an EP called *Mississippi Blues* on French Vogue Records with a pink cover, by that man Muddy Waters, with Little Walter on harmonica and notes, I discovered later when I got my own still-treasured copy, by Alexis Korner. The first track was Muddy's iconic *I Can't Be Satisfied*, recorded in Chicago just the year after I was born, with cutting electric guitar but in all other aspects the same kind of country blues played before the war by Son House and Robert Johnson. Of course, I didn't know any of that back then: it was simply the rawest, most urgent sound I'd ever heard and my flabber was 100% ghasted.

I'm not sure if I grabbed the owner by his lapels but I certainly mobbed him and interrogated him about what this music was, where it came from, and where I could hear more of it and meet other people who were into this sort of thing. He gave me a bit of an outline which I barely absorbed, and suggested that I should pay a visit to a place called the Swahili coffee bar up in the town. They had lots of interesting records there, he said, and people who knew all about them. I could barely wait to sprint home from school at the end of that day's lessons, get out of my uniform and into casual clothes, jump on my bicycle and pedal furiously into town… and hardly left the place for the next couple of years.

The Swahili had the arty beatnik vibe of the day: subdued lighting, a vaguely African decor, permanently steamed-up windows and coffee served in those little wide Pyrex cups that were the fashion. I was probably wide-eyed like a tourist visiting New York and seeing the skyscrapers for the first time, but I don't think anybody paid me much attention at first. I certainly clocked the denizens though: it was not far from the art college and many of them turned out to be its students. Blokes with beards and wild hair or some of them proto-Mods; girls with long hair and lots of dark eyeshadow; plenty of denim, corduroy, Breton tops. And there were some guitars and a banjo. I'd found my tribe.

I have no idea if every seaside town with an art college had an equivalent scene, indeed I'd be surprised if places like Brighton didn't, but even if Weston and the Swahili weren't unique I was unbelievably lucky.

The revelation that would dawn over the next few exhilarating weeks, though, was the music. My theory is that once you've taken your first curious steps off the mainstream, every subsequent one is easier. The Swahili didn't have a juke box, it had a record player behind the counter and a big pile of well-thumbed LPs that, it turned out, regulars would bring in and leave there for a while. I, and a growing little cohort of my friends who I'd immediately persuaded into making this our 'scene', had our education sorted in the following months.

Not only did we hear plenty of blues – Muddy, Big Bill Broonzy, Sonny Terry & Brownie McGhee and Lightnin' Hopkins among them – but proper traditional and modern jazz (from King Oliver and Jelly Roll Morton to Charlie Parker and Lambert, Hendricks & Ross), folk (the Davy Graham/Alexis Korner *3/4AD* EP, Carolyn Hester, Joan Baez, and Bob Dylan's first LP, fresh in from the States where somebody apparently had a sister who sent them records), and even my first ever African music on a Miriam Makeba album.

English folk hadn't found its way in there, mind: I had to discover that for myself in the future. The 1963/4 UK TV folk series *Hullabaloo* would give a few pointers – oh look, there's that Davy Graham – though in truth I only occasionally watched it because it had guest appearances by Sonny Boy Williamson, Cyril Davies and Carolyn Hester. It was a while before I really cottoned on to Martin Carthy, after his debut LP appeared in 1965, while the likes of the Spinners already seemed too heartily aimed at older people, and Peter, Paul & Mary with her doing that self-conscious flicky hair thing felt way too 'commercial' – opinions formed of my own free will that never changed down the years!

From the moment I found the Swahili I never looked back. Hence my early years memory loss. This was re-set day zero, where everything began again. Over the next eighteen months or so, the number of hours I spent in there or umbilically connected to its scene and the music it introduced me to, must have only been exceeded by those inflicted by school, and probably not by a major margin!

In spite of diving off the mainstream and quickly becoming a bit sniffy about really commercial pop music, I still kept up to speed with what was happening and, I like to think, judged things on merit. My notebooks of what looked interesting in the new release lists just included a lot more obscure country blues and folk among the likes of the Pretty Things and Downliners Sect and not a lot of chart hits. But I'd still watch *Ready, Steady Go* – didn't everybody? – and the Wednesday nights still beckoned. There simply wasn't an alternative – though the girls who were part of the art school crowd now seemed much more interesting, and liberated, than the tidily dressed pop fans who danced together in little groups in their neatly coiffed hair and smart little dresses.

The latter were the ones who bunked off school en-masse for a week in July 1963 when the manager of the Weston-super-Mare Odeon cinema had pulled off a major advance booking coup and secured the Beatles for six nights. I didn't go, nor did I in August '64 when he'd secured a night on a Rolling Stones tour: by then I'd seen them anyway.

It was around this time in the sixth form that I made my first attempt at being an event organiser. Just as in more recent years with international famines and disasters, there was something which had pricked the national consciousness and I decided to do a fundraiser for the Freedom From Hunger campaign. Somehow I persuaded the school that we should be allowed to put on a charity dance and thanks to the lucky coincidence that one of my earlier model aeroplane flying friends, Dave Christopher, was now the bass player in the most popular local group, the Rapids, I was able to persuade them to do it.

Normally, the partition wall that separated the main halls of the Boys' and Girls' Grammar Schools was only opened once a year for a joint official assembly, but we were allowed to have it wound back for the evening and the dance rapidly sold out. This was great for the finances but not so good for security. We were woefully innocent and unprepared, with just a few staff and prefects as stewards. We'd over-ambitiously sold tickets outside the school and incoming local youth ran amok. Fire extinguishers were set off in the changing rooms, alcohol was consumed, fights broke out and a window was smashed. None of this impinged on the fun going on in the hall itself, which was deemed a huge success and gave me much kudos on both sides of the creosote lines, but my name was mud with the headmaster the next day. It was a good thing we'd raised a lot of money for the charity or my punishment might well have been terminal...

Over the years I'd fed my hobbies from pocket money, odd regular jobs like mowing my grandmother's lawn, the occasional paper round and the financial generosity of relatives at birthdays and Christmases. Luckily, after my mother had gone back to work when I'd started secondary school, extra levels of funding emerged to pay for my record and music press buying addictions and my slowly growing social life. She managed a small secretarial services bureau which produced a lot of parish magazines in particular. I got roped in to crank the handle of the duplicating machine, collate pages, staple them together and stuff envelopes, a skill set that would be very useful later once I'd got involved with running folk and blues clubs and touting for gigs. I even learned how to pretend to be amused every time one local clergyman bounced in to pick up his magazines and would announce with great glee "I'm the Bleadon vicar!" Every time.

But as 1963 progressed I was desperate for a guitar and got myself a summer holiday job doing menial tasks in the local High Street Littlewoods store to fund it. Everything from breaking up and baling cardboard boxes, cleaning maggots off pork carcasses and operating the potato peeling machine in the back, to clearing tables in the cafeteria, where I gained a cynical view of the great British holiday-making public who would allow their unappealing children to fill the ash trays with gravy. I paid my dues to get my first axe, maaan...

My friend Tony Watts who lived out at Worle got a guitar first, after we'd both learned absolutely basic chords on an old seven-string banjo that had apparently belonged to his grandfather, re-strung with six and in guitar tuning. It was an interesting instrument: the seventh string being the equivalent of the high-tuned fifth on a 5-string, but threaded into a little tube at the fifth fret to re-appear at the headstock. Once he'd got a cheap electric guitar, a second hand Hofner Colorama II (for £20 – they now sell for over £700!) I attempted to play clanking bass parts on the lower strings of the banjo until my first guitar – a cheap Italian job – allowed me at least to do it with some tone. My first stumbling steps in my guitar ownership had been Duane Eddy's *Peter Gunn* on those same bass strings: I don't believe I was unique in that! Our pal Roger Chillcott hit things and got a few basic bits of a drum kit.

It must have been an awful racket: we were going to be a band called The Blues Disciples and even had our friend Dave Hart take some pouty photos, slouching around the Marine Lake at the end of the sea front that November. Luckily we got too distracted by impending A-Levels, and Tony getting a small motor bike that we christened, unoriginally, The Banger. On my first outing as a pillion passenger, he got stuck in some railway lines while trying to turn at a junction by the gas works, and slowly topped over, gashing my leg. I never liked motor bikes much after that.

I saw my first proper-job rock concert on a Friday night in October 1963, courtesy of one of those school friends who had a brother with a car. If my parents had any concerns about 16 year old me going off on the 30-odd miles down the A38 to faraway Taunton Gaumont in a car full of excited lads I don't remember it. Excited we were, for it was the first UK tour by Bo Diddley, on one of those Don Arden packages with the Everly Brothers and Little Richard. Both the latter were by then considered a bit old-fashioned as the beat groups, often inspired at least partly by them, had taken over the popularity of the rock'n'roll stars of a mere five years earlier.

Down the bill, but still above Mickie Most and others, were the Rolling Stones on their first national tour. This was not long after their debut single and they were still playing small London club venues like Studio 51 and Eel Pie Island up to this point. But they'd been on *Thank Your Lucky Stars*, the girls had learned to scream loudly and so we didn't gain much of an impression during their very short set of maybe four songs other than that they were probably pretty exciting, but seemed exhausted from several dozen previous one-nighters on pre-motorway Britain's winding roads. We were there for Bo who was magnificent and for us could have played all night, but he didn't.

The following month the outside world impinged again. I'd been over to Tony's house for our usual Friday evening twanging and banging and was just packing up to leave when his shocked-looking mother came in and told us she'd just seen that President Kennedy had been assassinated in Dallas. It's a cliché for people of my generation that everybody knows where they were when that happened, and I'm no exception. I jumped on my bike and rode like the wind back to Uphill, to find that my parents already knew too. It was the beginning of the souring of the romantic American lifestyle myth that had been believed in and aspired to by many Brits throughout the 1950s, hitting an accelerating downhill path leading to Trump and beyond in the next century. I loved American music, but with awareness growing of the ongoing civil rights struggles too, the country was now showing less attractive characteristics.

It was hardly surprising, then, that Bob Dylan's hard-hitting songs gained so much appeal in the Swahili circle, and soon increasingly to aware mainstream UK youth. I'd been hooked by his first LP, mainly because it seemed like a gutsy white blues album (and it remains a lifetime favourite as that), but then that person's sister had sent over *Freewheelin'* in the summer of '63 and by the time that was barely assimilated we'd all dived on *The Times They Are A-Changin'* in the spring of '64. It's impossible for anybody who wasn't contemporary to appreciate how extraordinary those songs seemed, and sense the rapid evolution and changes between those early albums, the first seven of which came in quick succession, two a year up to *Blonde On Blonde* in 1966. You had to be there, in the time, totally absorb each one and then get the knockout punch of the next.

Still restricted by having to attend school in Weston-super-Mare, I was effectively cut off from all the alluring musical scenes happening some 140 miles away to the East in that London. We could only read about it with dreams and jealousy in the pages of *Record Mirror* and increasingly *Melody Maker* which had begun to gain our allegiance. So it was with great excitement that we spotted that Dylan's first proper UK concert (he'd briefly visited and floor-spotted London folk clubs in the company of Martin Carthy back in 1962) was to be at the Royal Festival Hall on a Sunday afternoon in May 1964. This could be done by day return on the train, so off a little gang of us went. He didn't disappoint and our fandom was cemented as his solo acoustic set ranged through the familiar songs from *Freewheelin'* and *Times* and even a few like *It Ain't Me Babe* and *Chimes Of Freedom* which would appear later that summer on *Another Side Of...*

It must have been a school day the next day but I have no recall!

Eleven days later, nearer to home in Bristol's Colston Hall, we thrilled to another of those package tours, this time much more satisfactory. The stars were Chuck Berry, backed by impressive Liverpool band Kingsize Taylor & The Dominoes, *Blue Suede Shoes* rockabilly legend Carl Perkins backed by the Nashville Teens, and the Animals. Chuck was every bit as showmanlike and guitar blistering as we'd hoped, firing off all the hits, doing his famous duckwalk and, as we eagle-eyed fans in the third row noted, playing with a red plectrum which clearly was part of his secret formula! Perkins was great too, but the big surprise of the night were the Animals. Their house-shaking, Hammond organ-powered versions of two songs from that first Dylan album, *Baby Let Me Take You Home* and their imminent but then still unreleased epic *House Of The Rising Sun* blew our socks off. And that was a school night. Did we care?

My musical education, if not my academic one, had continued apace during 1963 and into 1964. Alongside binge reading Jack Kerouac's obligatory *On The Road* and getting hooked on John Wyndham novels, I'd discovered that the public library in Weston-super-Mare had a good selection of books on blues and jazz. I devoured, and later acquired my own copies of pioneering classics like Paul Oliver's *Blues Fell This Morning*, Sam Charters' *The Country Blues*, Big Bill Broonzy & Yannick Bruynoghe's *Big Bill Blues*, Mezz Mezzrow's *Really The Blues*, Alan Lomax's *Mr Jelly Roll*, Sidney Bechet's *Treat It Gentle*, Robert Reisner's *Bird* and many more.

I'd got my own fix of Bird when I discovered several ultra-cheap LPs of Charlie Parker's early Dial recordings in a rack in a gent's clothing shop in a back street in Weston while looking for an acceptable pair of jeans: I couldn't yet afford the status symbol Levis and Lees that the older, hipper Swahili users got from a shop on Christmas Steps in Bristol and then shrank to fit in the bath, legs turning blue in the process – that came later. I still thrill to those same Parker recordings in much better sound on CD to this day.

The local music shop, Audio, not only sold me lots of records that they would get to order. In due course they were the source of my second, better guitar, a Swedish-made España Spanish model that I promptly converted to steel strung and lasted me up until 1968, and music books too. Little did I know when I bought the *Penguin Book Of American Folk Songs* in 1964, edited by Alan Lomax, that some many decades later I'd get to meet him and others of those American folk legends. Many things were catalysed by walking into the school record club on that life-changing day.

Needless to say, I was ill-prepared and minimally motivated for my A-Levels in June 1964, which marked the end of my engagement with the education system.

3.
Coming Of Age

My A-Level results were as marginal as I expected. Somehow I just scraped enough to get offered a place at Bristol University to study, of all things, economics with accountancy, but I wasn't having any of that. I'd been let down and mis-directed enough by the system. At this point my father took a brief interest in my future, no doubt urged by my grandmother who was probably worried about what the neighbours might think, and suggested to me that if I didn't want to go to university I could still get a good qualification for a Proper Job by becoming an articled clerk in a firm of Bristol accountants at which he knew one of the partners through sailing. I think I realised that I could do this for the time being to keep everybody quiet, but my heart was set on a life in music.

Meanwhile my cousin Sean, a year older than me but who I'd caught up with in the system because of the school experiment, had got a place to study philosophy at Cambridge. Much family pride to compensate for their disappointment in me. Little did they know that, a talented classical pianist, he'd blow his first year's grant on an electric organ and join a rock'n'roll band, taking up disreputable music as a career immediately after graduating.

That summer of 1964 I'd written to all the record labels asking what jobs were available but had got nothing but polite, duplicated rejection letters. I pleaded with my parents for a few months of respite so it was decided that I'd begin the office job in mid-September, and meanwhile I could get another summer gap one in Littlewoods to pay for that better guitar. That suited my parents as they had a busy summer going away regularly on their boating activities, and as I'd just turned 17 I was now considered old and responsible enough to be left untended. If only they knew… They had an account in the local village store on which I could buy food, so on a diet of mostly Vesta curries, toast, black coffee and tins of minced beef and onions, I was sorted for my two months of relative freedom.

I'd recently discovered where the older Swahili regulars went on Friday and Saturday evenings. The pub just across the street, the London, had a back room where impromptu music sessions happened, and there was a separate door into it down an alleyway so you didn't have to traipse though the bar. People gathered with guitars and banjos, plus the occasional saxophone and even an old boy with a phonofiddle. I got slowly more confident at brazenly ordering under-age drinks at the bar from Lil, the friendly landlady. Cue her explosion a year later when people were celebrating my 18th and she realised she'd been hoodwinked, though I'd never actually lied about my age as she'd never asked. Luckily my expulsion only lasted 24 hours.

My initial attempts at learning the guitar had been fairly hit-and-miss. I never had a single lesson, nor could I read music (what do you mean, you can tell?!) There had been a few good players in the Swahili crowd, particularly a classical guitarist called Dave Stanley, but none I could pick anything up from until one day across in the London when I was startled to encounter the local musician, Terry Wiltshire, who everybody called 'Beetle'. Here was somebody who could play the guitar like Big Bill Broonzy and sing in a big, bluesy voice. What's more, he'd apparently played in a skiffle group who had appeared on *Six Five Special*. Of such things are heroes made. He often led the sessions and I sat in close eyeshot to him as he rattled off things like *Keep Your Hands Off Her*, *The Glory Of Love*, *San Francisco Bay Blues* and *The Midnight Special*. I absorbed as much as I could to take home and misremember on my own box, and apply to things I was trying to learn off Dylan and Sonny & Brownie LPs. Then a foghorn of a voice slowly emerged from me, too, as much to my surprise as everybody else's when I eventually dared open my mouth in the sessions.

After the pub closed on Saturdays, we used to head round the corner to the JL Club, where our local R&B heroes and answer to the Downliners Sect, the Iveys, played regularly, or to a late-opening café up the street called the Continental – always referred to as "the Cont" – for omelettes and blathering. I felt quite grown up by then. The Iveys' Des Henly and Mario Ferrari (a great rock'n'roll name, and really his) were sometimes part of that social scene. A few years later they'd join with my cousin Sean and the drummer from his Cambridge band to form rock'n'roll revivalists Fumble.

That August, with my parents away much of the time, I was left to my own devices once I'd finished my day's labours in Littlewoods. A couple of friends had cars by now: it was summertime, and the living was indeed easy. I was determined to earn respect as something hipper than a middle-class schoolboy. Not realising how close I was to disaster, I threw a party on a Saturday night in my parents' house. Bring your own booze usually meant taking a car out to a nearby cider farm and getting a large container filled, finding the cheapest bottles of wine in the local off licences, or if a bit flush, something called Russian Stout which had an improbably high alcohol content akin to the Belgian trappiste beers we'd discover in the '70s. Thirty or forty people, some of the usual crowd, some I didn't know, descended and we had a right old time. A few crashed overnight. Very drunk and not in command of my senses, I rather inexpertly lost my virginity in my parents' double bed to one of the art school girls who I never saw again.

Come the morning when the last stragglers had limped off, I surveyed the wreckage as well as a hangover. Empties and ash tray contents could be disposed of, every drinking receptacle washed, the carpets hoovered and every window in the house left open to fumigate it, but who knew that spilled cider left overnight could be such an effective varnish stripper on the wooden tea trolley my father had crafted? I had a few days before their return, so I obtained some French polish, stripped the top completely and set about refinishing it: luckily I had reasonable skills from my model aeroplane building past. It wasn't quite the same colour stain as before, but it looked good and, having explained it away as an accident, I think my father was more impressed at my efforts to right it than angry. If they'd noticed the misuse of their bed after much airing of the sheets, they never commented.

I'd actually got off lightly. Around then I'd been slightly infatuated with an art school girl called Helen. If I'm remembering correctly she bore a resemblance to Suze Rotolo off Dylan's *Freewheelin'* cover and, really, she was out of my class. Not long after this she also hosted a party out in a nearby village. She came off far worse: the place was trashed, the TV stolen and the police called shortly before her parents arrived home to find the aftermath. We didn't see her around for a while...

My diary records that on 19th August my friends and I were glued to the TV for a broadcast of the *Blues & Gospel Train* programme, filmed that May on a rainy Manchester railway station with Muddy Waters, Sister Rosetta Tharpe and Sonny Terry & Brownie McGhee. It was the first moving pictures we'd seen of any of them, and the clip of the fur-coated Sister Rosetta rocking out *Didn't It Rain* with scalding electric guitar riffs has become legendary and much re-broadcast to this day. Years later when I got to know American record producer and self-made eminence gris Joe Boyd, I discovered that his first visit to the UK, where he'd eventually take up permanent residence, was as tour manager for that package.

Friends' cars came in useful again in early September when we headed up to Bristol to catch Long John Baldry & The Hoochie Coochie Men (featuring Rod the Mod) at the Chinese R&B Jazz Club, held every Wednesday at the Corn Exchange, my first experience of the Bristol night life that I'd increasingly get drawn into.

Freedom was about to be somewhat curtailed though. I was kitted out with a suit and delivered to the accountants' office just off College Green in Bristol, which was to be my albatross for the next few years. I was truly but unwillingly to become a 'weekend beatnik', only marginally relieved some years later when I discovered that both Robert Plant and the Incredible String Band's Mike Heron had suffered the same early career indignity before escaping the clutches of the accountancy profession. For the next year before I left home for good I would commute to Bristol daily with my father in his car, unless posted away by work duties to faraway places like Plymouth, Tewkesbury or the outskirts of London, only to resume my alter-life in evenings, at weekends and on holidays.

Within a week or so I'd ventured up the hill in office lunch breaks and discovered Rayner's record shop which was well stocked with blues, folk and jazz records. It became an occasional haven away from the lunchtime pub where the half dozen other articled clerks went to discuss sport, cars and women (in terms that even back in those days seemed somewhat demeaning to me – I don't think the word 'misogynistic' was in anybody's vocabulary back then). I clearly didn't fit in and I immediately knew that a career in the company of such people wasn't for me, not that I had any intention of pursuing it anyway.

That October the third of the annual American Folk Blues Festival package tours found its way to Bristol's Colston Hall, their first visit to the city which then became a regular stop-off for the rest of the decade. Organised by German promoters Horst Lippmann and Fritz Rau, who used Chicago blues' chief songwriter Willie Dixon as their local artist finder and fixer, over the years they brought the absolute cream of living black blues artists over to Europe. With the exception of Mississippi John Hurt it's hard to think of anybody major who never made it over during those years, and as well as the concerts there were multiple albums recorded and released and well-staged TV specials filmed, many still available on DVD in the digital era. Any musician with the slightest interest in the genre made sure to catch them and their influence was profound, a major catalyst for the late 1960s UK 'Blues Boom' and the '70s rock bands who grew out of that, taking it back home to a whole new white audience in America.

We were beside ourselves in Bristol. On that year's show we saw Howlin' Wolf with his longtime guitarist Hubert Sumlin, harmonica giant Sonny Boy Williamson, the astonishing one-man boogie of Lightnin' Hopkins, country blues legend Sleepy John Estes with his harmonica player Hammie Nixon, energetic young soul blues singer Sugar Pie DeSanto and a near unknown rediscovery, John Henry Barbee, who had recorded once in the '30s. Barbee was clearly unwell but delivered one of the deepest, most heart stopping performances of the night. Not long after this show he was diagnosed with advanced cancer and returned early to the USA where he spent his tour proceeds on buying his first car. A week later he accidentally hit and killed a man with it, dying in jail after a couple of days, aged only 58. The album he recorded during the tour remains even more poignant in that knowledge.

Estes meanwhile appeared to be the oldest person it would ever be possible to see on stage performing. Blind, frail and intensely wrinkled, the photos shared of him with a battered acoustic guitar using a capo made from a pencil and rubber band seemed to represent the epitome of a hard life in the blues. It's astonishing to look back now and realise he was only 65 at the time, and lived another dozen years. His high voice was still instantly recognisable from his old 1930s recordings and I certainly know why the great English folk singer Bob Copper had fallen on them with such joy back when they were first released.

"I came across a 78 of Sleepy John Estes in a second-hand shop in the 1930s," he told me much later. "I played it until it wore clean through. All my contemporaries just said 'what's that bloody row, then?' Somebody once said he cried the blues. Well, I was transfixed when I heard Sleepy John. I just never heard anything like it in my life! The prickles were all down the back of my neck and down my spine. I thought, God, it's so full of expression. It's wonderful stuff, and it comes from the heart. It was crying, and speaking so clearly and decisively... I've always felt there's a great tie between the blues and our stuff. Not on the surface, because they're so vastly different, but somehow there's a great link... there's a great bond there. It's a feeling more than anything... more of a spiritual thing."

An extra factor came into play that autumn to distract me from the career gloom. Hardly had I commenced my daily commuting when a tall and very attractive red-haired girl started coming to the Swahili, fresh to the art college. We got chatting and soon clicked: it turned out that she also lived in Uphill only a few roads away from me, new to the area. We shared a sense of humour and a quest for music. Unexpectedly, after a long series of brief but leading-nowhere pursuances, I suddenly had a proper girlfriend. Sheila – coincidentally my mother's name too of course – fell in easily with my friends and we hung out together inseparably every weekend and a few evenings in the week too, if I wasn't sent away as a poorly paid lackey on auditing work. I'll hand it to my mother – I don't know what she thought we were doing upstairs in my bedroom 'playing records' on Wednesday nights, maybe just that, but she never disturbed us. Which was just as well…

All went wonderfully for around six months, until I made the mistake of briefly re-engaging with my model aeroplane flying, fixing up a neglected glider and power model. Sheila came with me when I went off to a rally one Sunday in the following spring and seemed quite taken by it all. It turned out that she was actually taken by another of the lads there, a GPO telephone pole erector (enough with that smutty chortling). Within a fortnight she'd dumped me and vanished off the scene. The next time I glimpsed her was some seven or eight months later. She'd dropped out of college and was at work behind the counter in a local baker's shop – heavily pregnant and looking defeated. He'd managed to do what I'd luckily avoided. I was gutted. I never saw her again, and that was also the last time I flew model aeroplanes.

So I'd lost my first real girlfriend, but I was about to discover one of my great lifelong musical heroes, and eventually friends. In 1964 John Lennon had told the *NME* that his favourite album at the time was Elektra's *Lots More Blues, Rags & Hollers*, the second outing by white American blues stompers Koerner, Ray & Glover. I'd already spotted it reviewed and had it on my 'to investigate' list, so Rayner's ordered it up for me and I wasn't disappointed. When Spider John Koerner's first solo album *Spider Blues* came out in 1965 I got it on the UK release day and from then on started trying to see his gigs wherever and whenever I could.

Koerner was one of the key figures of the 1960s American folk boom, an influence on the young Bob Dylan, as well as admired by the likes of Lennon. Koerner, Ray & Glover, who put out a series of those *Blues, Rags & Hollers albums*, were a loosely structured trio with 12-string guitarist Dave Ray and harmonica player Tony Glover, more often than not featured as soloists or duos. They never toured over here – I'd eventually catch them in Canada in the 1990s – but from 1965 Koerner did regularly.

Getting a bit ahead of my chronology here, I first saw him at the Bristol University Folk & Blues club (more on that in due course). He was staggering: all long, lanky legs that stretched on forever until terminating in a pair of banging army boots, fingers that seemed to somehow bend back on themselves as he frailed impossibly complex rhythms out of one of those wondrous Gretsch flat-top guitars with a plectrum-shaped soundhole, like Ramblin' Jack Elliott used to play in the '50s, but converted to be an 8-string. He mostly wrote his own songs in a very original take on the old country blues styles rather than slavishly copying old records as many of us did back then, and was genuinely inimitable (trust me, I tried!).

Over the next couple of years, Koerner regularly toured the UK and I saw him perform on numerous occasions. I never tired of his early 'hits' like *Crazy Fool, Creepy John, Good Time Charlie, Whomp Bom, Good Luck Child* and *Ramblin' And Tumblin'*, and especially his trio of 'epics', *Duncan And Brady, Hangman* and *Rent Party Rag*, which he would spin out into free-association tall-tales lasting 10 or 15 minutes; never, I swear ever, even remotely similar two nights in a row. He was the only one of that era's American white bluesmen who was really seriously admired by us chaps on the late '60s British country blues scene like Jo Ann Kelly, Mike Cooper and myself.

Before I'd even seen him live, I'd read *Little Sandy Review* editor Paul Nelson's descriptive notes to *Spider Blues*. "Spider John Koerner, six feet of legs, his Belmondo cap tipped back, his long legs, those incredibly long spider legs... unrolling... like strands of yarn spilling out to meet his boots... Spider John Koerner, good friend, film aficionado, blues singer, songwriter, unique and original personality..."

And I'd absorbed Koerner's own comments on there: "You know that the white guys are not the same as the old blues guys and if you think they are, you're crazy, but you still want to make good swinging music. Okay, once you have figured that out and start fooling with the music so that you don't think so much, then you are doing some stuff, maybe even your own stuff. You start thinking about little rhythms – boombachika – and like that. You start thinking about little notes and chords that really work and you think how good it feels to snap the strings with your fingers and it's a treat to beat your feet on the upbeat and put 'em together and what have you got – bipity bopity blues and you know that's right." Bipity bopity blues! Eureka! Hero!

Anyway, where were we? Ah yes, it's the spring of '65 and I'd just been dumped by my beloved. After a few weeks of acute woe-is-me worsening the daily drudge in a suit, I got back to pursuing the weekend nightlife and being a music obsessive. Alongside my growing record collection I'd added to my *Melody Maker* habit with subscriptions to *Blues Unlimited* and *Jazz Journal*, and on a work trip based in London I'd used an afternoon off to hit the West End, paying my first visits to the two key specialist shops of the day, Dobell's blues, folk & jazz shop in Charing Cross Road and Collett's folk shop in New Oxford Street.

The only good thing about these enforced audit trips was that you got a very generous expenses allowance, so if you avoided eating much you could turn a decent profit. Thus it was that I came home not only with some otherwise hard-to-find records but also a selection of my first folk magazines, copies of England's *Folk Scene* and *Sing*, and mind-boggling American imports like *Sing Out!*, the *Boston Broadside* and *Little Sandy Review*. I'd embarked on my lifelong habit as a magazine junkie.

There was another memorable trip to London around about that time. I'd been taken under the wing of Beetle by then, and he drove a trusty Morris Traveller. Some of the Swahili regulars had moved up to the capital and had sent word back about a big party they were throwing one Saturday night just off the Kilburn High Road. Bring your own booze… Somebody had discovered that an off-licence in Weston would let you have the big boxes holding collapsible plastic containers from which they'd sold draft sherry, once empty. A couple of these were obtained, taken to the cider farm at Sandford and filled with cheap scrumpy: job done, on a budget.

Off went a car load of us to London. The party was actually memorable for two very different reasons. The good one was that in the course of it I first heard two massively important, influential and lifetime favourite albums that had very recently been released – Davy Graham's *Folk, Blues & Beyond* and his experimental duo one with Shirley Collins, *Folk Roots, New Routes*. Graham's guitar playing was out there, way ahead of anything I'd been used to hearing, the father of that whole subsequent British acoustic guitar movement later headed by Bert Jansch and John Renbourn.

I was also struck by how the singing of both of them was… weird. I wasn't sure about the way they sang American songs without adopting the accents. It took me some years before I realised it wasn't them who was weird, it was everybody else, and Shirley would turn out to be a major influence on my life.

There were other discoveries too. I heard Jimmy Giuffre's iconic *The Train And The River* (as featured in that great film *Jazz On A Summer's Day*) for the first time, and a hip American comedy record by what I mistakenly assumed to be a black raconteur, doing the story of Jesus as *The Nazz*, in beat speak. It would be some years before I found out that it was another eventual hero, Lord Buckley.

It's amazing that I remember all that so clearly, because the other thing about the party wasn't so good at all. Whoever had got those sherry containers from the off-licence had failed to check that they were empty or wash them out. One or both of them had probably still contained a good amount of sherry. Rough cider and sherry are not an advisable mix, so as the evening wore on a lot of us started to get very sick. I'd gone outside to get some fresh air, had curled up in the back of Beetle's Traveller and passed out, only to wake up finding him careering around Hyde Park Corner about 3 am, singing loudly. Luckily we weren't spotted by the fuzz. I persuaded him to stop before I emptied my stomach into the gutter. To this day, I've never been able to drink cider again – just the smell makes me queasy. God knows what colour I was when I limped into the office that Monday…

Some other audit work trips, with their welcome expenses bonanzas, took me for a couple of weeks at a time to Plymouth, where I'd spotted in *Blues Unlimited* that there was an excellent establishment called Pete Russell's Hot Record Store. It was here that I first discovered the serious hardcore American blues imports of the day, the first Columbia Robert Johnson LP, those on the Origin label like *Really! The Country Blues* and a set by Charley Patton, and more on Blues Classics – by Memphis Minnie, Blind Boy Fuller and the *Jug, Jook & Washboard Bands* compilation.

Over a couple of such trips, my immersion in pre-war country blues began in depth, along with crucial sources for later repertoire. It was almost worth the stultifying boredom of cross-checking massive dot-matrix computer printout ledgers at the South Western Electricity Board, and suffering the trains home on Friday afternoons which were often packed with sailors and squaddies going on leave with their bulky kit bags. It was them first, women and children (and auditors) last, and my opinion of 'our brave boys' never really recovered.

My folk education continued apace too. In April 1965 yet another package tour hit Bristol Colston Hall, titled the *International Folk Festival*. As with many things, 'international' just meant that it had a couple of Americans on it, but the two of them were most impressive: young blues revivalist John Hammond Jnr, and already-veteran banjo player Derroll Adams, my first introduction to somebody who'd become a good friend in the 1970s and record probably his best album for my Village Thing label.

The other revelation was my first sighting of English folk great Shirley Collins who I'd recently discovered via that LP with Davy Graham. It was one of those concerts that did two shows, so we rushed out in the interval of the first house and bought some tickets for the second one. In spite of seeing them twice on one day, I have no recall of billtoppers the Ian Campbell Folk Group or the rest of the cast, so impressive were Adams, Hammond and Collins. I asked Shirley about it in more recent years and she can't remember it at all!

Meanwhile, around May 1965 in the back room of the London, things were slowly coalescing into an informal outfit that we'd eventually call the Backwater Jook Band. Beetle on guitar and vocals, of course; me on a ramshackle one-string oil drum bass and kazoo (and occasionally a bit of guitar and voice when the others took pity); a school friend called Bob Summers on washboard and harmonica; a random selection of guitarists, banjoists and mandolin players depending on who was around (Alan Iggulden, Tim Clutterbuck, Adrian Bastin), and various others including a new recruit called Terry Silver, stationed at the local RAF Locking, who was a hot shot tin whistle and soprano sax player. Terry would go on to become a well known folk scene character nicknamed 'Leadfingers', a stalwart of Sidmouth Folk Festival sessions for many years.

But before the BJB had its brief moment of fame, somebody mentioned that this weekly thing called a 'folk club' had opened in town. I'd heard of these through the magazines I'd started reading but never experienced one, so it was suggested that Bob and I go along that spring and see if we could do a spot.

I think it was organised by local head librarian, Geoff Rye, who I discovered much later was an important figure in the English Folk Dance & Song Society and one of the founders of the excellent Halsway Manor Folk Centre on the south side of the Quantocks. I don't know what I expected but the reality wasn't at all to our taste. They were very serious, and a number of the audience appeared to be little old ladies knitting. (Remember, when you're 17, anybody over 30 is 'old'.)

We did our floor spot, me on guitar and singing, Bob on harmonica, a thrashed version of *San Francisco Bay Blues* and a localised parody of Pete Seeger's *Little Boxes* called *Little Tourists*, mocking Weston's hordes of holiday makers, which we thought hilarious and almost certainly was nothing of the sort. We were young and bumptious and they hated us, and showed it. Worse was to come: the guests were the Yetties, portly and deeply uncool yokelly blokes in jumpers and beards with a piano accordeon, who we also thought were old but were probably barely in their twenties. They went on to become an institution, even providing the theme music for *The Archers*, but I never saw them again.

I thought the whole thing was an enormous practical joke that had been played on me, and vowed that I'd never ever go to a folk club again...

That August a few of us decided to have an economical summer holiday by going 'on the road' – all very Kerouac, not. We packed tents and sleeping bags and got the paddle steamer across to Barry in South Wales, stuck out our thumbs and headed for Fishguard, some 100 miles away. Amazingly we got there the same day and got another ferry across to Rosslare in Ireland. If that wasn't adventure enough, the first lift two of us got in Ireland was a rubber-tyred pony-drawn flatbed cart with milk churns on the back. I could probably have walked faster, but it was an engagingly rustic form of transport and saved carrying the gear. It also gently ran over my foot.

We were heading for Waterford but never made it that far. We managed the first twelve or so miles as far as a field just outside Wexford, pitched the tents, discovered a great local pub with music and real Irish draught Guinness like we'd never experienced before. A combination of indolence and inertia prevented us from moving on. Five or six days later we summed up the energy to pack up and return the way we came. Apart from a gig in Dublin in 1969 it remains the only time I've ever been to Ireland. From what I remember, it was lovely.

Back in Weston-super-Mare, I was now 18 and had reached the end of the time I wanted to spend living at home, let alone the daily commute in the company of a father with whom I had hardly anything in common. In September 1965 I found a very cheap garret at the top of a house in Redland Road, Bristol, two rooms and a kitchen/bathroom. Bob Summers – by now a dental student at the University – and I shared it. Cue a chilly winter where a fair amount of my diet consisted of white bread and margarine.

For a while I went home every other weekend which allowed me to continue being part of the Weston music scene where the Backwater Jook Band now had a regular Friday night club/session in another pub with an actual audience. And it got the washing done, and a supply of provisions.

I had, however, broken my vow never to go to another folk club. A new, short-lived girlfriend had implied that if I didn't go to the Bristol Ballads & Blues club at the Bathurst Hotel down by the docks with her, then my chances of favours were minimal. So I tagged along. The first time I went, it couldn't have been more different from the Weston experience. Many of the audience were younger and lively, student age. The residents included local hero Fred Wedlock and a fine guitar/fiddle duo called Bev & Rich Dewar, and I struck gold on my first go as the featured guest was Tom Paley, the great American old-timey guitar and banjo player who was not long ex- the legendary New Lost City Ramblers. I was hooked, became a regular and they at least seemed to tolerate my floor spots.

The girlfriend didn't last, but she probably did me one other favour. I'd been told that I ought to wear glasses all the time, not just for reading and TV, but was too vain. Some months later I was descending Park Street and failed to recognise her until the last blurry moment. Distracted, I walked into a lamp post, to the great amusement of passers-by. After that I got an acceptable pair and became a lifetime 'four-eyes'. It was less embarrassing.

And at the end of the month when the students had come back, Bob got me into Bristol University Folk Club. They got so used to seeing me over the next couple of years that the Union jobsworths never ever asked for a Students Union card. I struck lucky again. The academic year 1965/66 was the peak of the post-Dylan folk boom in the UK, and the University Folk Club was reportedly the biggest event society within Bristol Uni that year, with attendances that often dwarfed the Saturday night rock gigs – quite often getting audiences of over 500.

That particular year they booked the biggest names on tour in the UK including Tom Paxton, Phil Ochs, Spider John Koerner, Julie Felix, Mike Seeger, Buffy Sainte Marie, Bert Jansch, Pete Stanley & Wizz Jones and The Watersons. They did so well that they kept making a profit, so they kept reducing door prices lower and lower each week, even offering multi-artist bills, in an attempt to spend their grant allocation or they wouldn't get one again the next year.

On the night when Spider John played at Bristol Ballads & Blues, it turned out that the club had (as folk clubs often did, and probably still do) forgotten their obligation to provide him with accommodation, so I dutifully kidnapped my hero and gave him a bed for the night. It was the one and only time in my life that I ever slept in the bath...

So what if I had to put a suit on and slouch off to an office to earn a meagre pittance for the next eighteen months or so. I was grown up (I thought) and free and could indulge myself in music to my heart's content.

4.
Folk Clubs : A Selective History

Folk clubs, then. When I started going to them regularly from 1965 they were less than a decade into their evolution and had only really boomed in the previous five years. Over the next few they bred like bunnies, and some estimate that there were well over a thousand in the UK at their peak. It seemed like every town, large village even, had one, as indeed did most of the colleges. Bristol had clubs every night of the week, plus those at the University and various other educational establishments.

They'd grown up via various routes. One was that the mid-1950s skiffle craze slowly fizzled out but the people involved either got electric instruments and formed beat groups or burrowed down into acoustic roots musics to get hooked on everything from country blues to British regional traditions. Some became hardline evangelists for their chosen speciality, others enjoyed what was an underground anything-goes open stage. Some were actively engaged in the fledgling CND and class warfare, some were developing their own personality cults with rules that rivalled religious equivalents, some just were in it for community entertainment – an ethnic variant on music hall and working men's clubs. And some confessed to it all just being a good way to get stoned and/or laid.

Artists learned their 'trade' through a wide variety of routes and experiences. Some busked in Paris and then hitched to Cornwall in UK summers. Some headed for London where there was a denser population of early clubs. Others created scenes and communities in Liverpool, Manchester, Birmingham, Bristol, Edinburgh or Glasgow that slowly joined up via the underground grapevine. Little magazines sprang up.

The English Folk Dance & Song Society (EFDSS)'s heart was more in social dancing back then, with a membership dominated by people who'd come in via a 1940s/'50s square dance craze which even captured the Princesses Elizabeth and Margaret, the latter becoming the Society's president. But it also had the Vaughan Williams Memorial Library containing the early 20th century collectors' notes and manuscripts and much else besides as an invaluable resource, plus activists like Peter Kennedy who promoted the music and song side via events and recordings.

Other people's tales about those early years before I jumped in can be found in the late JP Bean's book *Singing From The Floor* (Faber), an oral history of admittedly subjective first-person anecdotes and views from many of the performers, activists and audiences of the day. It's fascinating stuff, even if you get the impression that the whole UK folk scene up to about 1962 consisted of only around a hundred key people who performed or got things done, much like the punk scene of the mid '70s. There are probably as many people who claim to have been at the King & Queen for Bob Dylan's first UK folk club drop-in spot as who say they were at the 100 Club for notorious early Sex Pistols gigs.

I heard directly about those earlier years from the tales of people I knew who'd been there, like *Sing* magazine editor Eric Winter who later kindly gifted me his archive going back to the mid '50s when he retired, or musician friends, heroes and survivors of those days like Wizz Jones and Martin Carthy.

I'd have loved to have witnessed Alexis Korner & Cyril Davies' club at the Roundhouse pub in Soho where artists like Ramblin' Jack Elliot, Derroll Adams and Big Bill Broonzy performed. I think I'd have been much less enamoured of the clubs run by Ewan MacColl who seemingly demanded that everything be run in his image and, one gets the impression, desperately wanted to cling on to his role as folk dictator, getting more and more unpleasant as control slipped from his hands. It was only in later years that it struck me how there were similarities between the personality traits of turn of the century English folk collector Cecil Sharp and MacColl, although they came from entirely different social backgrounds. Both were self-mythologising, authoritarian gatekeepers who brooked no criticism or differing views. Both did really important work but are hard to admire.

It's interesting to compare the US and UK's folk scenes of the late 1950s and '60s. In both cases, those times are widely known as the 'folk revival', so widely that we don't ever think about those terms and the implications carried within them. But is that really what they were?

In the USA, probably yes. American rural folk music had been widely documented on commercial recordings in the 1920s and '30s, partly as a way to sell gramophones. So had the political song movements of the pre- and immediately post-war years. With the legendary early 1950s Harry Smith *Anthology Of American Folk Music* LP box on Folkways and Pete Seeger's circle as catalysts, a lot of what happened in the USA was indeed a straightforward revival of and evolution from those earlier forms. And achieved considerable success.

But in the UK? We had hardly any equivalent repertoire of commercially released recordings to reproduce and develop. We hadn't really had a topical song tradition since the days of broadside ballads a century earlier. Yes, some people set out to become clones of the remaining elderly unaccompanied traditional singers, but few caught the public's imagination.

The key instrument of the British folk movement of the late 1950s and '60s, the guitar, hadn't been part of any folk tradition here at all. Far from reviving anything, the English had to invent something new. People like Davy Graham and Martin Carthy had to create local ways of playing that worked (and, like the English people, were mongrels). Others evolved original and uniquely English ways of playing American music – sometimes accidentally, by conspicuous failure to copy their sources. Even the Rolling Stones did that.

True, old songs and tunes were rediscovered but the way they were performed began from year zero. It was actually a complete folk re-imagining, a re-invention. Perhaps we should get into the habit of calling it that, rather than a folk revival.

By the time I began in folk clubs in Bristol, respect for MacColl had waned and he'd already become a bit of a laughing stock to some, other than as a deservedly respected songwriter.

Whatever your preference, you could usually find a club that suited it. If there wasn't anything at all, or you didn't like the one already there, and you were keen and organised enough, you could start your own. There were notable exceptions, of course, but the great majority of 1960s and '70s non-college clubs were held in the back or upstairs rooms of pubs or occasionally skittle alleys, often a room that they'd share on another night of the week with a jazz club or meetings of the Royal Antediluvian Order of Buffaloes, a more benign version of the Freemasons. Many a folk club guest would perform in front of a set of buffalo horns mounted on the wall. Because folk music did good business back then and gained an early and perhaps unfortunate reputation for 'beer swilling', pub landlords would often give successful clubs their room for free because of the bar turnover they'd create. They were a fabulous underground movement, unique to those times.

Many of those pub rooms were a bit seedy, under-ventilated, very smoky, and often probably a fire hazard with limited exit too. It's extraordinary that there were no major tragedies. If there wasn't enough seating, people sat on the floor or lined the walls. Any sensible capacities were often exceeded – we sometimes crammed upwards of 150 people into rooms that these days would carry a legal limit of 70 or 80 – and the landlords turned blind eyes except when overloaded floors began to bounce up and down to the alarm of normal people down below. Many couldn't have existed with modern day health & safety requirements.

Atmospheres were sometimes electric but the music was almost entirely acoustic. Virtually none had microphones. When PAs began to be carried by artists in the '70s, it turned out that many pubs' electrical systems were hazardous too, frequently unearthed. Often there were no stages either, the artists playing from a preferably (but not always) well-located area of floor. And certainly no stage lighting. If you were lucky, there were good acoustics, people listened intently and there was no bar in the room to accompany everything with crashing glasses and a ringing till. Faced with bigger, noisier rooms holding 100 plus, you quickly learned how to project or you died, which artistically wasn't always best suited to more subtle music and possibly contributed to the relative lack of young women artists. But a small folk club with 50 or 60 crammed in could be heaven, the best place to play and hear the music ever.

We loved these clubs. We were young, and the ones not dominated by shouty bearded blokes in cable knit sweaters were hip and bohemian and the sort of places that our parents' generation would be thoroughly alarmed by – if they knew. They were our community centres, our musical universities, the places where we could meet and bond (and maybe more) with people of like minds. They were where nervous, aspiring musicians and singers could have their first go at performing in front of a generally tolerant audience, slowly honing their skills, and sit at the feet of some of the many truly remarkable giants or innovative new artists who were emerging, apparently in their droves in those peak years. Whether your tastes were for unaccompanied traditional ballads sung by ancient Scottish travellers or for guitar wizardry coupled to a new style of songwriting, there were places for you – with a bit of searching.

Their importance for giving people who were serious about 'doing music' a safe place for an apprenticeship can't be overstated. The only down side was that they were sometimes a little too safe. Many people found out the hard way that, aside from stage confidence, they mainly taught you how to play in folk clubs held in smaller rooms, which have their own special expectations. Thrust onto a big stage, perhaps supporting a rock band, even the most confident folk club performer might have to rapidly relearn their approach when confronted with shouts of "get on with it" during what they thought was an amusing or interesting but long-winded song introduction. Horses, courses, etc.

Many clubs were started by artists, to give themselves a ground base and add to a circuit of clubs run by other performer friends who mutually supported each other with bookings. The folk scene back then was a real community where word of mouth really counted. Forty years before social media, a recommendation from another singer or musician was often all it needed. In those days, the opposite of now, there were far more clubs than bookable artists. And those clubs didn't book very far ahead, so a recommendation, or dropping in to do a 'floor spot,' could easily result in a gig within a month or two. If the clubs couldn't or wouldn't or forgot to provide accommodation, you could always – often preferably – count on a musician friend in that part of the country to give you hospitality.

The ones that weren't just informal singarounds pretty soon fell into a formula that everybody recognised wherever they went. Some opening spots by the resident singers (often a vital key to a club's success) and maybe a few 'floor spots' from visitors dropping in. Then a half hour of a booked guest, an interval where there was usually a raffle to raise extra funds, followed by a repeat of the first half format and probably a big chorus sing-up to close and send everybody home happy. You'll find many of the surviving clubs are just like that to this day except that the audiences, which have remained stubbornly of the same generation if not the same people, are now often predominantly in their seventies. This ageing process has been a cause for alarm in folk circles since the late 1970s and may soon reach the inevitable end.

Less common after the early Soho skiffle days of the 1950s were clubs that met in unlicensed premises like coffee bars, unlike the American folk scene in New York's Greenwich Village or the Boston/Cambridge area that thrived almost entirely in coffee houses. So a down-side was that there was a disincentive to younger participants in the UK due to the licensing laws. And to some visiting American performers who underestimated the strength of our beer compared to what they were familiar with back home!

There were even a few folk clubs, or small circuits of them, that were succesfully run by people as a living in the mid-to-late 1960s, such were the attendance levels, the relative cheapness of artist fees and room hire.

The few that had their own premises and were able to open all week round as a business were unlicensed. Oldest of those surviving at the time I discovered it all were London's Troubadour in the Old Brompton Road and Bunjies Coffee House in Lichfield Street, on the Soho/ Covent Garden border, both dating to the early 1950s. They were added to in 1965, my folk club year zero, by the opening of the legendary Les Cousins at 49 Greek Street in the heart of Soho.

The premises used by The Cousins, as everybody called it (we never knew who this bloke Les was!), had a previous life in the 1950s as The Skiffle Cellar. In 1964 the Matheou family who then owned the restaurant upstairs tried to open it as a discotheque, as was then fashionable, but when that didn't work and with 'folk' as a buzzword in music circles, it began operating as a folk venue in April 1965.

Al Stewart, who at that time had a residency at Bunjies, remembered those early days in a 2013 *fRoots* interview. "I was talking to Noel Murphy," [a popular Irish entertainer making his name in folk clubs at the time] "and he said there was a brand new folk club just opened up a couple of blocks away which turned out to be Les Cousins. So Murphy said 'do you want to go over and check it out?', so I said 'fine'. I went over with Noel, I went down the stairs – there were maybe twelve people down there and they were all crowded round one guy playing the guitar, and that of course was Bert Jansch..."

"So I'd work at Bunjies and then I'd go over and hang out at Cousins and watch the people. I think it did all-nighters very quickly which is actually where I got my first gig, because Phil – who used to run it before Andy Matheou – by about three o'clock in the morning he'd basically had it and wanted to go home, so what he was looking for was someone who'd basically put people on and off. I got the gig as the compère of the Cousins which I had for a couple of years. It was my job to put people on and take them off which meant that round about 4 o'clock in the morning when everyone was asleep I could get up and start doing my own songs!"

The venue took off very quickly. Not only did it have an adventurous booking policy and a growing in-crowd, but it also had all-nighters on the weekends. For many like myself, hitch-hiking up to London to see all these amazing artists who were being advertised in the *Melody Maker Folk Forum* each week and enjoying growing fame nationwide, it wasn't only a musical honeypot but the cheapest hotel in London. And once you'd become accepted as a performer, you even got in for free.

The room was an elongated rectangle with the entrance, accessed down a steep staircase from the street, emerging next to a small stage half way down one long side. It had hard wooden benches, a coffee bar and toilet at the far end and a dark space at the other where it protruded under the street above. It held maybe 100 when crammed, from memory.

Unlike most small clubs of the day, it had a microphone plugged into a fairly decent hi-fi amplifier that fed the house speakers behind the stage. I have a theory that the Cousins mic was single-handedly responsible for the performing posture of many of the 1960s singer/ songwriter/ guitarist legends. Look at photos of Bert Jansch, John Renbourn, Al Stewart or Michael Chapman from those days, and they're likely to be hunched on a stool over their instruments, bringing mouth and sound hole as close as possible together. This was before the advent of pick-ups in acoustic guitars – the early Barcus Berry transducers didn't become ubiquitous until the start of the next decade – so you needed to direct everything into that one microphone, as closely as possible. We all got rather adept at it.

Andy Mattheou's widow Diana has his pocket diaries and address book for the Cousins years and they make mind-boggling reading for people familiar with the burgeoning folk scene of the day.

"April 1966: Al Stewart £3. Diz Disley half the door. Trevor Lucas £8. Davy Graham £15. Long John Baldry £15 for the all-nighter. Sandy Denny, John Foreman… Spider John Koerner £25! (I was probably there for that, 10th April 1966)… Mox & John Lemont. Tuesday 26th, Van Morrison £3. Wednesday 27th, Jo Ann Kelly £6. Malcolm Price, Gerry Lockran, Sandy Bull (the American equivalent to Davy Graham), Bert Jansch, Sandy Denny…" what a week!

"June 1967. Friday, Tom Rush; Diz Disley for the all-nighter. Saturday, John Renbourn; Long John Baldry for the all-nighter. We go through to the following week… Friday 9th June, Sandy Denny in the evening, Cliff Aungier doing the all-nighter. Saturday 10th, Bert Jansch; all-nighter Noel Murphy and Wizz Jones. Friday 16th, Indian music. Saturday 17th, Alex Campbell in the evening, Davy Graham on the all-nighter. Friday 23rd, Roy Harper evening, Al Stewart all-nighter. Saturday 24th, Young Tradition evening, Alexis Korner the all-nighter."

Jumping forward, "October 1968: Friday 4th Michael Chapman and Saturday 5th, Jackson C Frank and Ron Geesin. Saturday 12th Young Tradition, Mike Cooper and Peter Sarstedt. Thursday 17th October – Al Jones and Ian Anderson" (beginning a residency! Yay, there you go!). "Saturday 19th October Al Stewart, evening; John Martyn on the all-nighter – Al Stewart was up to £20 by then! Gordon Giltrap, Sally Oldfield, The Strawbs, Andy Fernbach…"

Mike Cooper remembers that "the all-nighters on a Saturday were a trial by fire of stamina and patience both for audience and performers. Leaving there on Sunday morning we would stagger bleary-eyed into a Greek Street being hosed down and swept clean, ridding all trace of the previous night's reveries, and going for what was sold as coffee in glass cups at the Pollo Bar around the corner in Old Compton Street. But when you played Les Cousins you had joined 'the scene'; been acknowledged, made it, whatever that meant at the time. It was the Vatican and Mecca and Jerusalem of the folk scene."

You never knew who would turn up to play on an all-nighter. The singer-songwriter just introduced as Steve, who grew up to be Cat Stevens. A short American who Noel Murphy would stick on at 4am to try out some remarkable song he'd just written was called Paul Simon. A wonderful set from another American who'd come across to experience Cambridge Folk Festival but we already had his records: Eric Andersen. Later on a really nervous, undistinguished singer-songwriter called Nick Drake who sent the allnighter audience to sleep. I have fond memories of when Spider John Koerner put Al Jones and myself on for a small-hours floor spot and Davy Graham got up and played bongos with us; of other blues allnighters hosted by Alexis Korner (on which Jimi Hendrix sat in), and of Ron Geesin disembowelling the piano, passing bits of it out into the pews while playing, searching for an elusive sound. And of transporting music from the Third Ear Band...

Andy Matheou's booking methods were delightfully ramshackle. Once he liked and trusted a performer, they'd be booked every few weeks. I remember when I was living in London over the blues boom winter of 1968/'69 I'd get the tube in from Notting Hill every Wednesday lunchtime to get a *Melody Maker* at the news stand at Tottenham Court Road tube station, hot off the press. That was how you found out if you'd got a gig at the Cousins that coming weekend. But you didn't mind because not only was it a great gig, those listings were pored over by folk fans and organisers all over the country and if you were listed there, you'd made it. It was a guaranteed career boost.

The following year, October 1966, the Bristol Troubadour opened in Waterloo Street, Clifton. Already a city with a healthy folk scene, there were at least half a dozen well-established clubs, most notably the Friday *Poetry & Folk* and Saturday *Ballads & Blues* at the Bathurst Hotel and the massive term-time Bristol University Folk & Blues club at the students' union.

Founder Ray Willmott recalls the lead up to the opening. "I had gone to Australia at the age of sixteen and planned to stay for a couple of years before coming back to Bristol to attend Art College. I didn't return until 1966. I was twenty two, recently married and needed a job or a business. I decided after visiting several folk clubs in and around Bristol that a club run on commercial lines was badly needed and I then set about finding premises. My decision to locate the club near to a university proved to be the right one as the students of the area formed probably eighty percent of the audience. The other decision I made, that all of the singers I spoke to thought would ensure the club's immediate and definite failure, was that I would not have it licensed – in my experience all the licensed clubs were far too noisy and difficult to hear the artists. I then announced that it would be open at least five nights a week. Well, that was it, those same singers agreed that my idea would definitely not work!"

"In order to subsidise our now rapidly diminishing savings my wife Barbara and I secured work at Bristol Zoo, Barb working in the gift shop and I was one of two keepers looking after the birds. After work, and sometimes before, my father and I laid a new concrete floor in the basement, rigged up old kerosene lanterns as light fittings, put in archways, two toilets, the coffee bar and rough plastered all the walls. I found a fellow who could make me twelve tables from solid pieces of elm and the benches were made from 12" x 2" solid lengths of pine which came from the lining of the hold of a ship carrying flour. Six tables upstairs and six in the basement was the original layout giving seating for ten per table."

Rumours of Ray's total folk naïvety were unfounded, it turns out. "It has often been said that I didn't know anything about folk music when I opened the club but that isn't strictly true. During my time in Australia I'd regularly visited the Folk Attic and the Troubadour Folk Club in Sydney where Trevor Lucas, later of Fairport Convention fame, and Martyn Wyndham-Read were regulars. Both later appeared at The Bristol Troubadour."

Ray's diaries record that the opening night included Fred Wedlock, Anderson Jones Jackson (yours truly, Al Jones and Elliot Jackson), Bob Stewart and the Crofters.

Within what now seems like a few months, the Bristol Troubadour became one of the hippest places in town and built a reputation that soon spread nationally. Ray established good relations with the other clubs around the city, making sure not to book artists who clashed, and gained a loyal band of top class resident artists and MCs. Pretty soon a two-way musician axis formed between the Troub (as it became affectionately known) and Les

Cousins, with artists like John Renbourn, Al Stewart, The Watersons, Bert Jansch, The Incredible String Band, Sandy Denny, Jackson C Frank, Ralph McTell, Martin Carthy & Dave Swarbrick, Tim Hart & Maddy Prior, Shirley Collins, The Young Tradition, Michael Chapman, John Martyn, The Strawbs, Noel Murphy, Mike Cooper and many more, all appearing on its tiny stage. Later, into the '70s, you could see early gigs by subsequent mainstream names like Jasper Carrott. For some, especially Al Stewart who immortalised the club in his song *Clifton In The Rain*, it became a second home.

Many, many memories flood in. Of the first 'big guest' John Renbourn, who Al Jones and I had persuaded Ray to book, wandering scruffily up Waterloo Street, where the queue waiting for him stretched round the block into the Mall, with a really cheap guitar bag slung over his shoulder, looking like one of the floor singers. And being such a success that the next time he came back a few months later he was booked for three nights, same queue every night – so he stayed with us and taught us how to boil guitar strings. And pointed me at Dock Boggs.

Memories of seeing people like the Incredible String Band close up, literally at their feet, at the height of their creative powers and wiggy eclecticism. Or of a later night when Noel Murphy, his banjo playing sidekick 'Shaggis' (later better known as Elton John's guitarist Davey Johnstone) and Strawbs bassist Ron Chesterman had spent too much time in the Somerset pub nearby in the interval. Murphy's second set launched into *Dublin In The Green*, proceeded to *The Wild Rover*, then started into *Dublin In The Green* again as he slowly folded forwards onto his guitar on the front table, and passed out. The other two continued playing, apparently unaware. Needless to say, the next time he was booked there was another of those queues around the block.

The Troubadour stage was cramped with anything more than a trio. Nobody looking at the building now – not even those of us who were regulars and in my case even lived for a while in the flat upstairs – can work out how the tiny premises at 5 Waterloo Street, Clifton, now occupied by a beauty clinic, can possibly have held what it did. It has a blue plaque though.

Entering the front door, past a little pay desk and through a curtained archway, you'd find the stage immediately on your right, with a big cartwheel propped at the back of it. Those wooden benches and tables filled a roughly plastered, white painted room enhanced by artist photos, posters and a few 'ethnic' props. At the back was a small coffee bar. If you're familiar with London's current, award-winning Green Note café, the music room beyond that venue's own curtained archway is nearly identical – except that once the Troub's was unbearably full, a cramped rear staircase led down to a similar capacity cellar with more benches and another stage.

On full nights, artists had to rotate between floors, duplicating their sets. For most of its first year, until the Fire Brigade insisted that a fire escape was installed, the only way out of the basement was the way in. 21st Century Health & Safety would have a fit, especially as audiences smoked back then! "Most of the time, the tables sat twelve at a squeeze, additional people stood wherever possible, and sat on the floor in the aisles which gave us a maximum audience of around 160 to 180," reckons Ray.

Ray and Barbara eventually sold up and returned to Australia in April 1969, leaving the Troubadour sold as a going concern to local nightclub owner Peter Bush, who put musician John Turner and later Tim Hodgson in as manager. This coincided with the start of a glorious couple of years when the club hit its best-known era on the national stage. The fact that it was open five nights a week, stayed open until the small hours, and didn't have a drinks licence or PA meant that it had an amazingly beneficial effect on the local scene – a place where under-age music fans could be inspired, where musicians could try out new material or play with others, and you could drop in to socialise and unwind after a gig elsewhere.

Musicians from all over the country started relocating to Bristol because of the scene centred on the club; others began professional careers there. Eventually some dozen Troubadour resident artists had nationally-released albums, including Keith Christmas, Shelagh McDonald, Al Jones, Steve Tilston, Dave Evans, Fred Wedlock, the Pigsty Hill Light Orchestra, Sally Oldfield (with her younger brother Mike, later of *Tubular Bells* fame, as The Sallyangie), Hunt & Turner and myself.

Those illustrious residents were an asset on many occasions, especially in the final years when the second owner was demanding more profits. Everybody went on a rota of playing Friday nights for no fee to boost the cash handed over. But one memorable night (not in a good way) was when John Martyn was showing the early signs of becoming the noxious person he turned into. He was so objectionably stoned and drunk, effing and blinding in earshot of the audience, that Ray Willmott decided to get rid of him, pay him his fee, put him in a taxi and send him back to the station. I was MCing the night and drew the short straw, getting up on stage and telling the capacity audience that John Martyn wasn't going to perform but lots of others from that residents list would. If anybody wanted their money back, just ask. Nobody did, which pissed Martyn off even more.

I poured him into the taxi and went off to run the evening which was wildly successful, of course. I was told a few days later that Martyn had gone to the Cousins allnighter, got up on stage and declared "I hate fucking Bristol and I hate that fucking Ian Anderson. I knocked him out and left him lying in the road." News to me!

On another occasion I was in the Cousins when he'd just returned from America, recording the first John & Beverley LP, bragging to his little gang of acolytes about how they'd gone to tea with Bob Dylan. Years later, reading Beverley's deeply upsetting autobiography *Sweet Honesty*, it turns out that the real story was that Dylan had taken a shine to Beverley and invited them over, but Martyn got jealous and beat her up, so they never went.

One of the frustrating things about the 1960s is the rarity of live photographs taken in the clubs and private gatherings. There are a fair few from the Bristol Troubadour, largely thanks to local photographer Jo Gedrych, but hardly any from the Cousins. Over in America things were very different, so that for example the legendary folk scene in New England got a whole book bursting with them in Eric Von Schmidt & Jim Rooney's fabulous *Baby Let Me Follow You Down*. When Joe Boyd was writing his book *White Bicycles* about the 1960s, he had a fruitless search for photos from the Cousins. I had to explain to him that compared with his native USA, camera ownership in the UK was low at that time, partly because we were still suffering from the long grey tail of 1950s post-war austerity. There was a reason why cartoon images of American tourists often showed them festooned with cameras.

Brian Shuel, the great English folk photographer who shot publicity and album photos for many of the Cousins regulars, has a different take on it. It was he, after all, who'd shot the iconic pictures of Bob Dylan doing a London folk club floor spot in 1962 in front of an unimpressed Ewan MacColl. "About Les Cousins: I did go there once or twice but was put off by it being pitch dark and visibility was zero due to pot smoke." Aha...

The Cousins and the Bristol Troubadour both made it into the early years of the '70s before closing. The pub and college clubs thrived for longer but then became victims of their own idiosyncracies. Many of the successful '60s folk clubs had been broad church, hosting what was then called 'contemporary folk' alongside the traditional music revivalists. Al Stewart and the Young Tradition appeared together on nights at the Cousins, the Incredible String

Band and the Watersons were equally appreciated at the Bristol Troubadour, and the latter booked visiting American blues artists at their club in Hull. But then, partly because most clubs were run by amateur organisers at their own risk, booking policies began to centre on those organisers' own sometimes narrow tastes and prejudices. You can hardly blame them, but for every club whose organisers thought guitars were the instruments of the devil, there was another who reckoned that traditional music was really boring and they only wanted 'entertainers'. The middle path shrank.

Regardless of type, they all looked on in horror at the punk generation in the mid '70s. I remember going on stage in a folk club around 1976/'77 just as the door opened and a little gaggle of newly minted baby punks with their safety pins, freshly made mohicans and torn bin bags stuck inquisitive heads in the door, maybe attracted by the poster advertising something called Hot Vultures. Before we'd finished our first song the organiser had shooed them away. The folk club scene lost a whole generation of potential converts like that, luckily gaining a few back later into the '80s.

The mid '70s, especially in the colleges, saw the dominance of people who became the forerunners of the alternative comedy circuit. Some were outrageously and naturally funny – I remember actually falling down the stairs at the back of the Bristol Troubadour laughing at Jasper Carrott. Some stayed closer to folk music, with a higher ratio of songs to jokes, others less so. Quite a few, like our Bristol hero Fred Wedlock, eventually and deservedly had hit records. Others like Nottingham's Dave Turner and Brighton's Alan White should have but missed out. Billy Connolly emerged from the Scottish folk clubs to become a national treasure.

Unfortunately a minority had big, unpleasant chips on their shoulders at not being taken seriously as musicians, and some were as racist and sexist as it was apparently OK to be back then. The localised humour of some of the northern ones didn't translate to the south (and no doubt vice versa), and some chose to blame that on class. By the time fashion and careers had moved on, many people who preferred an evening of musical inspiration to belly laughs in folk clubs had drifted away.

In the tradition of artists running their own clubs, in winter 1974/'75 Maggie Holland and I had a brief stab at running one at the Star in Guildford, the *Guildford Troubadour*. Unfortunately that October, between the first and second weekly meetings, the IRA blew up two other Guildford pubs, killing five and injuring sixty five. It wasn't the best time to be trying to coax audiences into local pub rooms, but we persevered and ran a winter season including memorable gigs by Alexis Korner, Michael Chapman, The Dransfields, Peter Bellamy, Jo Ann Kelly, Davey Graham, Derroll Adams, Wizz Jones and lots more. Audiences picked up, but in the end it got too complicated when we needed to be away on tour to make a living, so we called a halt early the next summer. It was fun while it lasted. Later, we mucked in and helped with Fleet Folk Club in North East Hampshire whenever we could.

Lots of us who didn't fit in either the very traditional or so-called 'entertainer' factions spent the middle years of the 1970s touring in mainland Europe as a result – Belgium, Holland and Germany in particular – until the hardline clubs began to relax, take the corks out of their arses, broaden their musical horizons again and actually became really nice, receptive places to play. Luckily, the inspiration of the '80s golden age for roots musics was just around the corner...

5.
Up And Away

Back to 1965 then. With my newly found freedom I was out more evenings than I stayed in. Fridays and Saturdays were usually the two folk clubs, but other regular haunts included Henry's Bootblacks' club at the Ship at St Mary Redcliffe (a crazy, exhilarating vintage jazz big band based on the era of King Oliver and Jelly Roll Morton), and the Chinese R&B Jazz Club at the Corn Exchange. It feels like things were less tribal back then.

Great gigs came thick and fast. Not long after moving, on 12th October '65, the inimitable Jesse Fuller came to the Corn Exchange. Aged sixty nine at that time, he was a one man band and blues songster, the writer of that folk blues standard *San Francisco Bay Blues* as well as *You're No Good* that Dylan covered on his first LP, and one of the early influences on that man Spider John. I already had one of his LPs featuring his extraordinary set-up of 12-string guitar, harmonica and kazoo on a neck rack, a hi-hat cymbal operated by one foot and his famous 'fotdella' – a self-invented six-string bass instrument operated by pedals from the other foot. Had to see *him* then!

The Corn Exchange doors opened late, and as we entered the star of the show was to be seen on his hands and knees on the stage hitting the fotdella with a hammer, mumbling and cursing loudly. It seems that earlier in the evening he'd recorded his spot for *Discs-a-Gogo* at the local TV station and a technician had managed to break the contraption, necessitating those last-minute repairs. It was the very first time I (and probably most of the audience) had ever heard the word "motherfucker" used! But he went on to be brilliant, driving along like a well-oiled if primitive machine, at least once jumping up to do a bit of buck and wing dancing.

But the next event, a big one, came just eleven days later on the 23rd of October. The annual American Folk Blues Festival tour reached the Colston Hall, and on this one alongside John Lee Hooker, J.B. Lenoir, Buddy Guy, Big Mama Thornton and another one-man band, Dr. Ross, I first saw the legendary Fred McDowell.

He'd been 'discovered' by Alan Lomax and Shirley Collins on their epic 1959 *Southern Journey* recording trip, though the way Shirley tells it he brought about his own discovery by wandering into their recording session. He took the breath of blues afficionados away by being, at age fifty five, a uniquely original and amazingly driving 'bottleneck' guitar player. His first proper LP in his own right was recorded by Chris Strachwitz for Chris's Arhoolie label and released in 1964, one of those I'd found in Plymouth: the graphically ambiguous artwork for the title *Mississippi Delta Blues* led people to believe his name was billed as Mississippi Fred McDowell, which stuck. The opening song, *Write Me A Few Short Lines*, would become a standard in the repertoire of late '60s English country bluesers: everybody had a version.

He was the exciting revelation of that year's concert series, and another life-changer for me. I'd heard him and others play bottleneck guitar on record – that's the generic name used for any form of glass or metal tube slide fitted over a left hand finger – but it was the first time I'd ever seen it done live. It blew me away, and somehow I'd had a 'lightbulb moment,' realising that to do it the guitar had to be open tuned, to a chord. I went back to the garret, figured out from a key on the record what the tuning must be, looked around for some piece of metal tube, spotted my landlord's brass curtain rail and took a hacksaw to liberate two inches of it. I stayed up all night working out how to play his *61 Highway*.

After hearing the milkman outside, I rang in to the office and pulled a sickie, slept all day, got up and practised some more, and in the evening went up to the University Folk Club where the guest was American singer-songwriter Phil Ochs. I was given the last floor spot before he went on, and finished it with my new bottleneck party piece. As I walked off through the audience with applause ringing, Ochs was coming up to play and as he passed by me he said "Great, man!" At that point, receiving such praise from a big star, I decided then and there that I really was going to do music full time, no more doubts. It took me another 18 months or so but the die was cast that night.

Apart from expenses wrangling there was just one other beneficial side to the office lark. On Fridays we got day release to go to the College of Commerce for lectures. Sat in the back row one week, studiously ignoring the lecturer, I was reading my new subscription copy of *Blues Unlimited* inside my text book when I glanced across to the bloke at the next desk. To my great surprise, he was doing the same thing. Naturally, in the next break we pumped each other for information and it turned out that as well as being a blues fan with similar enthusiasms, he was also picking up playing blues harmonica. His name was Elliot Jackson and over the next three years he'd be my trusty musical sidekick on gigs and my first records.

My time of slipping back to the Weston scene was coming to an end, but not before the Backwater Jook Band had its 15 minutes of fame. Our Friday night sessions had been reported in the *Weston Mercury*, and the presenter of TWW's early evening TV magazine programme *TWW Reports*, Guy Thomas, had spotted this and got in touch thinking we'd be an entertaining novelty item. So off went six of us to TWW's Bristol studios one morning in December 1965 to film three songs, good old *San Francisco Bay Blues*, *Louisian-i-a* and Big Bill Broonzy's *Keys To The Highway*, plus a rather earnest interview with me by posh-voiced Guy Thomas about the origin of jug bands. A lo-fi fourth generation recording exists (a CDR burned from a cassette dubbed from an acetate disc cut from the copy of the master tape they'd given to a band member on the day!) which show us to be jovially robust in a post-skiffle sort of way, but sadly no moving pictures survive.

They showed two of the songs that day and the third the following week. We were a blink-and-you-missed-it micro-sensation in Weston and got a couple of gigs in the following month as a result before fading to the obscurity we deserved. The most remarkable thing about it was that this, my first ever paid gig, got us the then-massive fee of £75, £12.50 per head. This at a time when, if you played your cards right, you could book Paul Simon at your folk club for £5 plus expenses, and the most money I'd earn from one gig for another three years or so.

In spite of the day job, 1966 was the year I slowly learned the ropes, musically (and lifestyle) speaking. I'd figured out how to hitch-hike, which was so normal back then as to be unremarkable, and so reliable that you could get a bus out to the edge of Bristol to thumb up to London on the old A4 in those pre- motorway days, via Chippenham, Calne, Marlborough, Newbury and Reading (the names are still ingrained in my mind) and be pretty sure what time your final lift would drop you somewhere convenient in the West End. Ditto in reverse after getting the tube out to Chiswick Park before thumb-out for the return.

One memorable lift was the final part of a journey from the outskirts of London into the middle, perched in the back of an open-top sports car with my guitar case and girlfriend, and being dropped right in Piccadilly Circus surrounded by all the advertising lights. Yay, swinging London!

I must have gone up there at least one weekend a month that year on average, visiting places spotted in *Melody Maker*'s *Folk Forum* like the Witches' Cauldron at Hampstead, where I enjoyed regular blues duo Mox &

John LeMont. Harmonica player Mox was a well-known London 'face' with his waist-length red hair who, a few years later, would briefly join my Country Blues Band: nobody knew how old he was but it turns out we probably guessed higher than reality. John LeMont was a guitarist who was rumoured to have spent some time at Her Majesty's pleasure, I discovered later, but not before he'd relieved me of a that España guitar which he never paid me for...

Pretty soon those weekend routines revolved around going record and magazine shopping to Dobell's or Collett's or a bit of Soho clothes buying. Then it was on to the allnighters at Les Cousins, where British acoustic guitar styles were being evolved from the Davy Graham wellspring by John Renbourn, Bert Jansch and all those who followed in their own wakes. I think I'd come across Renbourn a few weeks before I heard Jansch, when his *There You Go* duo album with wonderful black American singer Dorris Henderson was released just ahead of his own debut. I'd slowly got to know people like Al Stewart who were beginning to make their mark, and hesitantly approached Alexis Korner who had already played such a role in my musical awakening. It soon became unremarkable that you could just go up and talk with such legends in clubs like they were normal people.

My favourite shop for those occasional clothes buying treats was the famous Lord John in Carnaby Street, from where I slowly acquired a small selection of then-trendy floral shirts, and a black cape with a red lining and fake gold fastening chain. My father had put his woodwork skills to good use and made me a coffin-shaped plywood guitar case, originally in varnished mahogany, later painted matt black. It had a double lid so that the top part could hold song words, my kazoo rack, a few LPs I might want to carry, spare socks etc. I may have alarmed a few people wandering around Clifton at night in my cape, carrying that case. It eventually vanished in 1968 with John LeMont and that guitar: every now and then I wonder if it's still out there in somebody's attic...

More big stuff happened that May. On the 10th, the Bob Dylan tour on which he'd controversially 'gone electric' with The Band, as they became known, came to the Colston Hall. It was all very bizarre: he'd already done electric tracks on his great *Highway 61 Revisited* LP the previous year and his appearance with the Paul Butterfield Band at the 1965 Newport Folk Festival had been widely reported, so it was hardly a surprise. But duffel-coated earlier Dylan fans went along wanting to show that they were shocked and outraged that he'd 'gone commercial'. In truth it was an exciting gig in spite of the disgruntled Folkistanis, the only possibly justifiable thing to complain about apart from their heckling being that in those days of primitive PA systems, his vocals and therefore the all-important words got a bit lost in the mix. So the audience got somewhat tribal, though the 'fors' definitely won out over the 'againsts'.

And that would be the last time I ever saw Dylan live. I never wanted to spoil the memories of the twice I'd caught him. Years later when I was living in North London, I could hear the distant thud of one of his gigs in Finsbury Park from my back garden, within walking distance, but wasn't tempted to go. My 18-year-old self would have thought I was bonkers!

Later that same month, the BBC showed a fascinating, gritty documentary film called *Travelling For A Living* about Hull-based traditional folk group The Watersons – siblings Norma, Lal and Mike and their cousin John. It's possibly even more enthralling now, released on DVD, as the UK it depicts in stark black & white is from a bygone age – the housing grim and run down, the travelling up and down a less traffic-congested England in a cramped old van is tiring, and everybody smokes, especially the audiences in those folk club rooms. But the wild unaccompanied harmony singing was earthy and glorious and the youthful, hollow-cheeked group in their '60s haircuts could easily pass for a '90s Britpop band. Small wonder they became the darlings of the emerging traditional folk scene, or that not much later they'd quit, exhausted.

Suddenly, English folk music had new standard bearers, along with their friend Anne Briggs, who all had a bit of alluring wildness to beat down its twee image. Later that year a trio called the Young Tradition would carry all that much further. The two group's attacks for a capella harmony have hardly ever been bettered since.

Also recorded in May that year was the debut album by a truly original multi-instrumental group whose myriad influences from many traditions and none, coupled with unique songwriting, invented their own un-named genre. The Incredible String Band had been developing away up in Scotland before, with albums produced by Joe Boyd, bursting fully formed onto a startled English folk scene. Within a couple of years they were in the proper album charts (not just the specialised folk ones published in *Melody Maker*) and appearing at major festivals internationally, Woodstock even. It's a mark of how conservative the folk scene has become in the 21st century, and how much the mainstream has lost interest in it again after a brief flirtation at the millennium, that there is absolutely no chance so inspiringly different a group could make much headway today.

By this time, spring 1966, I'd moved on from my initial garret as I'd got wind of a house share in Grove Road, right on the junction with Blackboy Hill, the main thoroughfare down past Clifton to the University area, Park Street and the city centre. The slim town house, adjacent to a shop on the corner, was nearly derelict, and John who'd leased it had done so on the basis that a very low rent would be charged if the tenants renovated it. We had a living room and kitchen on the first floor (where I finally learned to cook a little more adventurously), two bedrooms on the second floor and a third one at the top opposite an enormous bathroom. There were also more rooms above the shop next door and a cellar below it that could all have been added to John's lease, but we never got around to taking those on in the time I was there. Nowadays it's all been well done up and gentrified and mysteriously changed from No.2 as it was back then to No.3 now.

It became a great community, almost an open house for musicians and friends, and by the following year, the famous 'summer of love', gained a rainbow painted front door (which had quite different implications back then to what it does nowadays) and the nameplate *Freak House*. We regularly put up visiting guests for the Troubadour, especially those like John Renbourn, Al Stewart, members of the Incredible String Band and the Watersons who were occasionally booked for more than one night. There were epic all-night sessions playing Monopoly with Al Stewart every time he came – boy, did we know how to live! – and he reckons, probably correctly, that he always won. But once again I'm getting ahead of myself.

One evening early in that summer of '66, Elliot Jackson and myself had been sitting in the Somerset pub on Park Row, a known social hangout for musicians (sadly, since become a blacked-out karaoke bar) when the door opened and an interesting-looking guy with a large nose, curly hair, scooter gear, and a guitar case slung over his shoulder walked in. This turned out to be our first sighting of Alun Ashworth-Jones, better known simply as Al Jones, fresh in from Saffron Walden in Essex to an electronics job in Bristol. We struck up a conversation and instantly got on really well. Eventually he opened the case and got out a 12-string guitar which he proceeded to play with the agility of a 6-string picker, which generally isn't easy, or indeed possible. We were impressed, amazed, and subsequently liked to joke that we'd immediately realised we couldn't beat him so the best thing to do was join him. As we shared lots of musical enthusiasms, we very soon decided to form a group. And so Anderson, Jones, Jackson were formed, to become Bristol's answer to Koerner, Ray & Glover. Sort of...

That August I went to my first ever folk festival. Apart from the long-running Sidmouth which at that time was still mainly a folk dance and folklore display event, there were very few established ones. In 1966, Cambridge and Keele were both in their second years and were to be joined by what was pitched that year as Britain's answer to the big, long-running Newport Folk Festival in the USA. I tossed up and unfortunately picked that one, Beaulieu World Folk Festival (meaning Brits & Americans!) down in Hampshire. My memories are mainly of hitching there and back with a girlfriend and it absolutely pissing down with rain.

On the way there on the Friday we slept in a hedge before the rain began; on the way back we found a barn and slept in the haystack. The romance of youth (well, not very romantic, she dumped me straight after!) From a contemporary Robin Denselow review and a listing for a TV film which seems to have been made but I never saw, it seems that the Dubliners, the Spinners, the Settlers, the Ian Campbell Folk Group, the Watersons, Cyril Tawney, Phil Ochs, Tom Paxton, Ramblin' Jack Elliott, John Renbourn and Martin Carthy all played. Once again I have no recall of the Campbells (I detect a pattern!) or any other of the 'mainstream' groups, indeed I only remember Renbourn, Ochs and the Watersons as I think we spent a lot of time huddling in shelter and left early. Peter Paul & Mary, the Clancy Brothers and Julie Felix were also listed on the original flier but there was no sign of them on the day.

The event was never repeated. If anything would emerge as an 'answer to Newport' it would eventually be Cambridge down the years. And I was subsequently determined to never, ever, camp at festivals!

Although Anderson, Jones, Jackson were slowly becoming a thing, I was still doing local folk club spots solo or with Elliot. By this time I was edging heavily into being heads-down authentic blues whenever I could. One night, I'd hauled a tiny amplifier, a borrowed electric guitar and probably Elliot down to the *Ballads & Blues* to do a spot of pretending to be Muddy Waters. The Ballads crowd were usually pretty broad minded, but this was too much for them – maybe they'd been at that Dylan concert – and they hated it and showed it. As we snuck to the back of the room with our metaphorical tails between our legs, I spotted Paul Carter (an early director of traditional folk's most respected label, Topic Records) and his wife Angela Carter (who had not yet become the famous novelist she would later) at the bar. They ran what was reputed to be a hard-line fundamental traditionalist club, *Folksong & Ballad* at the Lansdown in Clifton and if anybody was guaranteed to hate what we'd just done, it would be them. So imagine my surprise when they greeted us warmly, said how much they'd admired the integrity of what we'd just done, and invited us to do a spot at their club. To my everlasting regret, I never dared...

At that point it didn't seem to be absurd that a white teenage English boy from Somerset could change out of his office suit and become a geriatric country blues guitarist from Mississippi. After all, with ancestors who'd been peat diggers on the Somerset Levels and Sussex farm hands, what was so different to Mississippi cotton pickers, went the failed logic...? It seemed perfectly reasonable to want to become one. There had been a noble tradition of English musicians starting out by trying to reproduce the work of obscure American artists that they'd only heard on records and, in the process of failing to do so, creating music that – looking back all these years later – was accidentally a British thing instead. In more exalted circles Lonnie Donegan did it with Lead Belly and the Rolling Stones with Bo Diddley, and in the mid-1960s a little gang of artists did the same with those old country bluesmen. More of that in the next chapter though.

More clubs and venues opened in Bristol that autumn, not just straight folk clubs but bistros who liked to have some live music. At some point, Fred Wedlock invited three solo artists he'd seen doing floor spots in local clubs to be a triple bill at a folk evening he was organising at a teacher training college in Redland: myself, Sally Oldfield and Keith Christmas. For all three of us, I believe it was our first ever paid, advertised solo gig.

The Bristol Troubadour opened on Friday 7th October and was satisfactorily packed on that opening night, and onwards. There's some debate about who actually played the opening set, but it might well have been Anderson, Jones, Jackson. We got surprisingly popular quite quickly, with a repertoire that included some of Al Jones' originals alongside the blues. We added an occasional jug player, Noel Sheldon, aka King George VI, which was good for variety, and would often chuck in some daft throw-aways. Al was famous for being able to pull medleys of requests for old pop songs out of the air, from Buddy Holly to the Beatles, and I was known to drop in the odd funny Shel Silverstein song like *It Does Not Pay To Be Hip* or *Folk Singer's Blues*.

We'd just occasionally push it too far and come unstuck. Winging it one Saturday, I'd suggested a Watersons-style a capella version of Brian Hyland's pop sob song *Ginny Come Lately*, which went down well, but then we followed that with the Fugs' Appalachian country spoof *My Baby Done Left Me*. Many of the audience laughed uproariously at lines like "I feel like heifer fucking" and the chorus "I feel like home-made shiiit," but Barbara Willmott didn't and Ray showed us the door!

The Troub, as it was affectionately known, was actually very welcoming and you never knew who might show up looking for a gig or just wanting to play a drop-in spot. There were far too many to mention but from quite early on I remember a hilariously original duo from Coventry called the New Modern Idiot Grunt Band, Rod Felton & Rob Armstrong, who instantly earned themselves a gig. Armstrong became a well-known luthier: his beautiful girlfriend who didn't sing that night, or indeed a little while later when I ran into them again at Les Cousins, grew up to be June Tabor.

Another drop-in was Robin Dransfield who eventually, with his brother Barry, had one of the biggest selling folk albums of the early '70s. He was at teacher training college up in Malvern after they'd disbanded their Yorkshire bluegrass band The Crimple Mountain Boys – seriously! – and he created quite an impression. We became good friends.

Luckily our ban was brief and by early in 1967 we'd been voted Bristol's most popular contemporary folk group in the Troubadour poll. In late December '66 we'd trooped out to local label Saydisc's improvised studio in the Friends Meeting House at Frenchay on the outskirts of Bristol, gathered around the big iron pot-bellied stove to keep warm, and pointed our music at one Reslo ribbon microphone plugged into a bulky mono Ferrograph tape recorder. The resulting 5-track 33rpm EP came out early in the new year, imaginatively titled *Anderson Jones Jackson*, one of those 99-copy editions that were very common back then as Purchase Tax only kicked in if you pressed 100 or more. It sold out quite quickly.

After that we slowly drifted in different musical directions, though Al and I remained lifelong friends and would often play together down the years whenever the opportunity presented itself, even reforming the trio for a concert in 2002 that marked the 30th anniversary of the Troubadour's eventual closure. We might have continued it longer because, having sent him the EP, we'd been offered an album recording session by early Fleetwood Mac/Chicken Shack producer Mike Vernon at Decca – but it was one of those mirage deals that never actually came off. Al was getting into prolifically writing his own very individual songs, and was also regularly going to London, becoming part of the Les Cousins scene at John Renbourn's instigation. Meanwhile my time of living a double life was at an end.

1967 was to be one of those big creative years in what became known as the counter-culture, the underground, and I was finding more excuses simply not go to the office. I'd already grown a Manfred Mann-esque beard that had gained me the nickname 'the beatnik auditor' and they knew I wanted out. I'd started getting just about enough gigs to scrape a living and knew I could do better if I concentrated on it full time. Weekends up in London where temptations now extended beyond Les Cousins to venues like Joe Boyd's recently opened *UFO* club were not going to be sustainable if I had to go home Sunday night.

(A weird UFO aside: I definitely remember going there on one occasion because Spider John Koerner was playing: I can't for the life of me recall who was the main band among all the light shows and whatever, it may even have been the early Pink Floyd. UFO's Joe Boyd, who produced them, was also running the London office for Elektra, Koerner's record label and doesn't remember him playing there at all. But then I have a copy of John's ultra-rare UK Elektra folk rock single *Don't Stop/ Won't You Give Me Some Love* which came out at that time and Joe doesn't have any recall of that either. When I finally met Ray & Glover in Canada in the mid '90s, KR&G archivist Tony Glover was astounded that I had a copy as, even though he played on it, he never knew it had actually been released!)

Although the paperwork to cancel my articles to the accountancy firm wasn't finally concluded until May, I'd effectively left by April, which allowed me to head up to London for one of the big counter-culture events of the year, the *14-hour Technicolour Dream* at Alexandra Palace. This was a bonkers affair with two main stages, sometimes with bands playing simultaneously, and lots of dancers, poets, performance artists on a smaller stage, light shows, smoke machines, a helter skelter and a complete battering of all senses. Headliners Pink Floyd didn't appear until around dawn, leaving the night to the likes of the Crazy World Of Arthur Brown, Soft Machine, the Deviants, the Pretty Things, underground stalwarts like Third Ear Band predecessors Giant Sun Trolley, Ron Geesin and a massive further cast including apparently Alexis Korner and Noel Murphy, though I never spotted either of them. That was 1967 set in motion.

The country blues scene was beginning to crank into serious action, too, and the players were accepted as an element of the underground as well as the folk clubs, but the story of the blues evolution is for the next chapter. I may have been determined to turn into Charley Patton, performance wise, but I couldn't ignore the other music roaring into focus at that time. I went to loud Bristol gigs by the Who and Jimi Hendrix, and became an early adopter of John Peel's *Perfumed Garden* on pirate station Radio London, which inspired purchase of LPs by US West Coast bands like the Grateful Dead and the Mothers Of Invention. I tried really hard to break my resistance to the Beatles when *Sergeant Pepper* was released in May, but never quite managed it.

In Bristol, oddly enough, while *Sergeant Pepper* was No.1 on the album charts nationally it was held off the top spot by local hero Adge Cutler's debut LP for several weeks. One could put up a decent argument for Adge being the Hank Williams of the West of England. Many people knew and loved his localised dialect songs long before he and the Wurzels got around to recording them, and can burst into favourites like *Thees Got'n Wur Thee Casn't Back'n Asn't*, *Virtue Et Industrial* and of course *Drink Up Thee Zider* to this day. Anderson, Jones, Jackson even did a support gig to them at Weston-super-Mare Winter Gardens early that year, one of my more incongruous billings.

That summer I briefly tried to run a better folk club in Weston-super-Mare. My theory was that since the summer ones in Cornwall like the legendary Folk Cottage did so well out of the tourist demand, there might be a killing to be made in Weston. Turned out that the sort of people who holidayed there were profoundly disinterested in folk music and my 8-week summer season's programme including Tim Hart & Maddy Prior (pre-Steeleye Span), Robin Dransfield, Fred Wedlock and Mike Cooper only just broke even. But it did introduce me to a then-unknown singer called Shelagh McDonald, just down from Scotland and pointed at me at short notice by agent Sandy Glennon when somebody else cancelled. A couple of years later, she'd move to Bristol and become part of the illustrious selection of Troubadour residents with albums out. And Mike Cooper and I, full of 1967 flower power daftness, cleaned Weston's Woolworths out of strings of beads the morning after his gig: a right pair of twerps we must have looked on the bus up to Bristol, me in an old embroidered kimono that my mother had dug out of the depths of her wardrobe.

Fanning out from gigs in the easy 50 mile radius of Bristol, I started to pick them up around the country, from South Wales to Yorkshire, Teeside, Surrey and even the hardest to break into, London. Once the distance was too far to hitch reliably, it was by train, or a little circle of friends with cars, who were also obliging when we wanted to do something like go over to Swindon Folk Club to be blown away by the Young Tradition for the first time.

One of our circle, Mike Blann, had a mini-van and I remember him getting a bit tired and lost while driving cross country in the middle of the night, back to Bristol from a gig in north Hampshire. No SatNavs then of course. At one point he literally screeched to a halt inches from the bank of a village duckpond, with a small gaggle of awakened fowl paddling furiously away in the headlights. A while later he became the personal road manager for Mick Taylor after he'd left John Mayall's band and joined the Rolling Stones... but no reports of duck-related rock star incidents ever emerged.

Probably my most memorable gig of that year was for sociology students at Aston University Students' Union in Birmingham in December. Being 1967 it was a 'happening' and I was on with sound, visual and performance poet Bob Cobbing and his tape recorders, a light show and something – I can't remember the actual title but it was pretentious – that was otherwise referred to as "the eating, drinking, pissing and shitting film". Exactly that, in full close-up detail including up-toilet-bowl shots. So a white youth banging out 1920s country blues wouldn't have seemed odd at all. Apparently there was a major scandal about this event in the university the following day and the organisers got severely chastised, but I was long gone.

I'll swiftly drift into early 1968 before looping back. There was a brief point when sufficient gigs weren't coming in and at the same time I'd allowed my attraction to a girl called Lynne get the better of me. Since I was skint and her lorry-driver father deeply disapproved of my self-employment, I applied for a job in the civil service. I got accepted, turned up on the Monday morning which I spent reading up on the regulations, went out to lunch and never returned: the last time I ever had a proper job. All four hours of it.

Meanwhile, it was pointed out to me that I'd actually paid sufficient 'stamps' during my time at the accountants that I was legally entitled to sign on for benefits for a month, so I trotted off down to the Labour Exchange and did just that, the only time in my life.

Some weeks later, gigs had looked up again so I did the proper thing and signed off on a Friday. That Sunday night I returned late and tired from a folk club gig up in Gloucester. The next morning my housemate Ian Osborn, who had the room above mine, dropped a smouldering cigarette end into his waste paper basket when leaving for work. I was awoken by a fireman shouting at me to get out fast. Somewhat bewildered, I pulled on some clothes and legged it down to the pavement outside where I was collared by a reporter from the *Bristol Evening Post*.

Later that day it carried the great front page headline *Singer Sleeps On As Blaze Rages* over a report saying "Bristol folk singer Ian Anderson (20), tired from a late night engagement, slept on as a fire raged in the room above today. He was awakened by the police. The fire happened in a top floor bedroom at 2 Grove Road, Redland. Bristol firemen wearing breathing apparatus soon had the blaze under control and damage was confined to the one room. 'The first I knew of the fire was when I heard someone outside saying he is in there sleeping. I wondered what I had done for a minute,' said Mr Anderson. 'Then a large policeman with a torch came rushing into my room and said there was a fire above me. I quickly got dressed and salvaged a few of my belongings – my instruments first and then my records and then my clothing.'" I clearly had my priorities right…

The report exaggerated. The fire wasn't actually that serious, just smoke damage, but somebody among the Troubadour regulars who worked in the dole office told me that this report had been spotted and queried: if I hadn't signed off correctly I'd have been busted. It taught me the lesson of the Bob Dylan line "to live outside the law you must be honest", and provided a great title for my third Village Thing album a few years later.

And just to keep linked tales together, Ian Osborn later went off to work in HM Customs & Excise, stationed in Dover, which we used to go through regularly for continental touring as Hot Vultures in the '70s. We found it quite useful to casually ask if he was on duty – though he never was – which smoothed our way with customs officers who knew him. But at some point in the mid-'70s, arriving in Dover at silly a.m. after a night ferry from Ostend, the clearly half-awake and just-on-duty customs man barked "switch off your windows and wind down your engine." We laughed. Mistake!

Next thing, we were pulled over and made to empty out the entire contents of our VW bus, since he wanted to seem on the ball, and the Osborn ploy didn't work. He was blearily checking items off the equipment list as we brought them out and put them down at the kerb in front of him: "One bass amplifier" Check. "One PA speaker" Check… He failed to register that I took out a large box of 100 copies of our first LP released by Belgian EMI and deposited it right at his feet, proceeding to "one Guild guitar" and so on. Then we had to load it all again. One little smirk is not worth losing an hour of your life when you really just want to get home to your bed after a month on the road!

Oh dear, did I just confess to a technical smuggling offence more than 50 years ago? What's the statute of limitations…?

6.
The Blues Boom

It was early in 1967 that I ditched the small amount of non-blues material from my performing repertoire and for the next couple of years concentrated on initially covering and then working up heavily influenced originals from old 1920s and '30s sources. There'd been an accepted blues presence in folk clubs since the early days, but until around this time songs tended to be drawn from the more popular blues entertainers like Big Bill Broonzy, Sonny Terry & Brownie McGhee, Josh White and Lead Belly.

It wasn't until the beginning of the 1960s that the Origin label compilations, the Columbia (CBS here) Robert Johnson set, and Blues Classics re-issue LPs by 1930s artists like Blind Boy Fuller and Memphis Minnie had begun to show up in the specialist import shops and be seized upon by young British musicians. Unlike younger American musicians, we really weren't aware of the 1952 Harry Smith *Anthology*, which put white artists like Dock Boggs, Dick Justice and Frank Hutchison in the context of the early black players. Few copies of it found their way over here then, though it would materialise later.

Now we suddenly had a rush of re-issues of rarer early stuff, and the excitement of researchers in the USA going out and rediscovering older, semi-retired artists from those days. Artists like Son House, Mississippi John Hurt, Skip James, Sleepy John Estes and Bukka White were performing and recording again and most eventually came to the UK on tour.

It would be the powerful Mississippi players like Charley Patton, Son House, Willie Brown and their associates, slapped bass strings and all – the musical ancestors of 1950s Chicago electric innovators like Muddy Waters and Howlin' Wolf – who most drew my attention. I was also drawn to ragtimey East Coast players like Blind Boy Fuller, and particularly to the pre-blues songsters like Texan oddball Henry Thomas and Memphis legend Frank Stokes, who'd both been born in the 1870s. The latter would have a slow-burning but lasting influence on me. Half the time I had no idea what they were on about, and it embarrasses me now to think of lyrics that I sang unthinkingly back then which were in fact profoundly sexist, violent and culturally inappropriate. But of course that was then and this is now and it took a while to wake up to such things.

It's remarkable to think that in the mid-1960s, most of those records were around thirty five years old, but they seemed to come from another mysterious time far away in the distant past as well as from an exotic culture. At the time of writing, the blues records that I and my contemporaries made in the later 1960s are now nearly sixty years old... I do occasionally wonder how impossibly far away in an alien past *they* may seem to late teenagers stumbling across them now.

Learning from those re-issues of degraded old 78s wasn't easy. Working out mumbled lyrics full of slang, dialect and unknown cultural references was only part of the problem. Transcription of the originals with the technology to clean them up for re-release was in its infancy and none of us had sophisticated hi-fi equipment to play the results on. I swear that the first Blind Lemon Jefferson re-issue LP I heard back then, he might as well not have had any bass strings on his guitar. They suddenly appeared with more clarity in the 1970s when better-equipped labels like Yazoo had a go at them, and nowadays with digital technology working its magic for CD re-issue such artists can sound like they're playing in the same room as you. Back then, though, all you could do was repeat-play the LP as the vinyl slowly turned grey from wear and hope to come up with an approximation that satisfied you, from which you could evolve your own version, and all I had was a basic Dansette-style record player.

Small wonder then that the pulsating, if complicated guitar part that I worked out for my take on Garfield Akers' classic *Cottonfield Blues* was even possible since, undetected by my ears, there were actually two guitars playing on the original. It became my party piece, appeared on my own first EP *Almost The Country Blues* in January 1968 and has subsequently been reissued several times, but once I found out the truth about those two guitars which I'd unwittingly tried to ape as one, I gained a mental block on being able to play it any more. Of course, recent digitally remastered CD versions of Garfield Akers' & Joe Callicott's 1929 duet have no such aural confusion.

It was only in more recent years that I caught up with the research which had uncovered the facts that Akers had been an earlier musical side-kick of my Memphis guitar hero Frank Stokes, and that Stokes had been a live influence on the great country music pioneer Jimmie Rodgers whose songs would be integral to our later Hot Vultures repertoire. It all joins up!

I'd had inspiration from young white Americans like Spider John Koerner and John Hammond, but I'd had no inkling that there were others out there in England getting into playing the same music. Everybody's hero Alexis Korner was by then well into electric R&B with jazz influences. But then it fell out that one Saturday night in 1966, arriving early at the Bristol Ballads & Blues to get a floor spot, I encountered a hip-looking bloke wearing a fur coat and a sea-green satin shirt. He opened his guitar case to reveal a shiny National Tri-cone guitar, which back then were iconic things only seen in 1930s photos of obscure bluesmen. Crikey! It turned out that he was Mike Cooper, over from his home town Reading to do a floor spot that might get him a gig (it did) and a dab hand at channelling Blind Boy Fuller. Naturally we got talking, became friends and have remained so ever since.

Cooper had apparently found his National in a junk shop in Reading for a fiver: he claimed that they'd had two, but by the time he'd got back with the cash for the other one it had already been sold. Meanwhile I then struck lucky, almost literally on my doorstep. Returning home to Freak House late one night, I found that the hairdresser who lived above his shop next door was moving out, with lots of possessions piled up on the pavement by his car. Sticking up in the middle was a guitar neck. I enquired what it was and he replied that it was some strange thing he'd had hanging on the wall. "Have a look," he said, so I picked it up, turned it round and was astonished to see a wooden bodied, single resonator National-style guitar. "I don't want it," he said. "You're a guitarist: give me five pounds and you can have it." I don't know how I managed to bluff lack of interest with a straight face, but somehow I said "Oh, I don't really need it. How about two pounds?" To my further astonishment he agreed, and that's how I got my first 'National'!

It became apparent that blues was becoming quite a thing over that winter, so in March 1967, around the time I finally escaped from the day job, we convinced Ray Willmott to let us launch a dedicated country blues night on the first Sunday of each month at the Bristol Troubadour, booking Mike Cooper for the first one. Anderson, Jones, Jackson supported, as well as Mac Tresler, a Midlands player brilliant at Blind Blake covers who had first shown up at the club in the duo Mac & Mick. The other half of the duo, Mick Strode, had gone off to join Robert Plant's early Band Of Joy.

The night was a great success, and Cooper told us about some other players he'd recently met in London, particularly someone called Dave Kelly. So we took his word and booked Dave for the next one, by which time word had got round and it was packed. With an interesting adaptation to his acoustic guitar – the top plate off a harmonica sandwiched between the bridge and the strings to give a loud metallic sustain – he took out his bottleneck and roared into Fred McDowell's *Write Me A Few Short Lines*, a selection of Robert Johnson numbers and other Delta blues classics. The place erupted and we knew something special was happening. We had kindred spirits!

After that, within a couple more months the Troubadour was too small for the audience. We moved the club, by then called *Folk Blues Bristol & West*, to the upstairs room of city centre pub the Old Duke. Within a year we were fortnightly and in a room at the Full Moon in Stokes Croft that held 250. We were regularly packed with a queue around the block.

Dave Kelly had told us about his big sister, the late and much-missed Jo Ann Kelly, so she became our first guest at the Old Duke. Booked on trust, I had no idea what to expect when I went down to meet her off the train at Bristol Temple Meads station, but it certainly wasn't a charming small blonde woman in spectacles, with a cheap-looking 12-string guitar when she removed it from a soft case. I was a bit nervous when I introduced her to the packed audience, and I could see a few suspicious looks. We needn't have worried. From the moment she opened the set with an astoundingly intense version of Charley Patton's *Moon Going Down* and proceeded on to Memphis Minnie's lively *Nothing In Rambling*, she had us captivated. In Bristol, a star was born…

Something was in the air nationally, via the success of bands like John Mayall's Bluesbreakers, Chicken Shack and Fleetwood Mac (who were a blues band at their beginning) and anything involving Eric Clapton. Blues soon became big business in Bristol. Young local electric blues band, The Deep, gained a big fan following, often supporting those top national blues bands and sometimes playing rings around them. Their more curious audiences started turning up in our club too. Sadly, The Deep, who had a residency at the Dugout Club in Park Row (subsequently famed as the home of trip-hop and the 'Bristol Sound' of Massive Attack), never recorded as their musicians kept getting headhunted. They provided players for the John Dummer Blues Band, the Groundhogs and my own later trio, and their Pete Emery eventually married Jo Ann Kelly.

I occasionally got asked to sing with them, which usually involved ace guitarist Adrian 'Putty' Pietryga burning into an early '50s riff in the style of Howlin' Wolf's Sun Records guitar ace Willie Johnson, and their rhythm section of bassist Bob Rowe and drummer Ken Pustelnik hitting a groove, while I just adapted some Mississippi delta blues lyrics. It was great fun and meant I actually got to play the Corn Exchange and under the big glitter ball at the New Bristol Centre.

We also had the thrill of that year's American Folk Blues Festival at the Colston Hall in November '67, including Son House, Skip James and Bukka White on the one bill. We were sat at the front of the balcony overlooking the stage, and I remember Son House being led on, looking frail, sat down on a chair and handed his heavy steel National guitar. He sat there gently rocking forwards and backwards for a few moments and my heart dropped, thinking "he's too old, he can't do it any more." And then – wham! He struck the guitar, the bottleneck tore up the neck and he launched into one of his epic pieces like *Death Letter Blues*. The audience physically gasped. At the end of that first song, the applause nearly brought the building down and I turned to look at my girlfriend sat next to me. She'd been a bit of a blues agnostic up to that point but now her hands were tightly gripped, knuckles white, on the balcony rail and tears were running down her face. That year's tour was epochal in the late '60s blues boom.

Afterwards we all got to go backstage to meet them...

By now, a grapevine had started and musicians began to crawl out of the national woodwork. Following our Bristol model, Mike Cooper had started a club in Reading, the Kellys began one at the Elephant & Castle in London. People began to turn up like Simon Prager & the late Steve Rye, who played a supercharged version of the Terry/ McGhee style with lacings of Gary Davis and the first Sonny Boy Williamson; the Missouri Compromise, a very wild trio of approximately 17 year olds with a black singer who sounded not unlike Tommy McLennan; and the Panama Limited Jug Band who (in their first incarnation) had really got to grips with the authentic sound of the Memphis Jug Band, Gus Cannon and others..

At the beginning of 1968, with all the main artists regularly appearing at the Bristol club, Mike Cooper and I took an idea to Gef Lucena of Saydisc. We'd both made limited edition EPs through him which had sold out quickly, so we suggested he start a blues label which would be called Matchbox. Over the next few months, both of the Kellys, Cooper, myself, Prager & Rye, the Panama Limited and Missouri Compromise went out to that echoing Quaker Meeting House on the outskirts of Bristol. Gef set up that big old Ferrograph and once again we huddled around the microphone and the old iron stove, recording tracks.

The time was just right. In March '68, Alexis Korner had written a major piece about British blues in *Melody Maker* where he mentioned us acoustic players alongside the electric bands who were already achieving vast cult followings. I was so thrilled to personally get a name check from him! Around then, most generous and supportively, he'd come down and played our club for the door to help give us a boost. Soon DJ Mike Raven was playing tracks off our EPs on his Radio 1 blues show. Gigs had taken off and I was travelling the country, earning an average club fee – still mostly folk clubs at that time – of £10 a gig which actually went a long way in those days.

Late that spring there was an unseasonal heatwave. One Thursday afternoon, the phone rang: it was the man from the local BBC TV in Bristol. "Could you come down for tomorrow evening's *Points West* and do a song about sun?" So Elliot and myself quickly slung together all those blues verses about "the sun's gonna shine in my back door some day" and "I hate to see the evening sun go down" to a standard country blues tune and presented ourselves at the allotted hour. To find an improvised studio set consisting of a large parasol and a 'model' in a bathing costume who then proceeded to bounce a large beachball completely out of time with the music behind us. We got 14 guineas (again, a princely sum in those days).

It was pre-VHS days, let alone digital boxes and the like, so there was nobody to capture this no-doubt cringe-inducing episode. But all these years later, I sort of hanker to see it. Sadly, it doesn't seem like the BBC kept copies. Considering all the other far more valuable stuff that they dumped or wiped, I suppose it's hardly surprising.

When the first Matchbox LP, *Blues Like Showers Of Rain*, appeared in July '68, everything went silly. I'd got into the habit of occasionally going up to London on a Sunday where there were afternoon blues sessions at Studio 51 (a.k.a. Ken Colyer's jazz club) in Great Newport Street, and Sunday evenings hosted by Jo Ann Kelly at nearby Bunjies. I took a box of 25 copies of *BLSOR* up the week we got them and sold the lot in minutes.

Seeing what was coming up the track I realised I needed to be in London full time. I reluctantly gave in my notice at Freak House and put the running of Folk Blues Bristol & West into the capable hands of Elliot and photographer/ designer Jo Gedrych who had been documenting the local scene along with writer David Harrison.

I spent my twenty first birthday trudging the streets with a copy of the *Evening Standard*, found a second floor maisonette in Chepstow Road on the edge of Notting Hill – which was a cheap area then – and moved up the following week. Although cheap, I still needed a flat mate to share the rent and luckily High Wycombe blues promoter Ron Watts then said he wanted a London flat too, so I was sorted.

Ron was a colourful character for whom the description 'larger than life' could have been coined. Completely lacking in inhibitions, he later fronted a notorious college circuit band called Brewer's Droop that included the pre-Dire Straits Mark Knopfler, all the while promoting weekly gigs at Oxford Street's legendary 100 Club. These progressed from blues at the beginning of the '70s to him being one of the only promoters who'd book the Sex Pistols as they rose to notoriety. Sharing a flat with Ron, sadly no longer with us, was a lot of fun.

John Peel, by then on Radio 1 after the closure of the pirate stations, was always the first to spot something good happening at the roots. He played tracks from *Blues Like Showers Of Rain* regularly and had most of the artists guesting on his show that summer. Mine, my first Radio 1 session, was recorded on 14th August 1968, for which I took along Steve Rye on harmonica and among the songs I debuted was a good-timey, Koerner-influenced one called *(My Babe She Ain't Nothing But A Doggone) Crazy Fool Mumble*. It was to play its part in my nearly assassinated recording career the following spring and has remained a fun thing in my repertoire ever since.

I'd also by then got a proper steel National – an utterly beautiful and very rare one, which I paid a decent price for from singer Mike Absalom, who'd in turn got it from an excellent London singer called Lisa Turner. She can be seen in several episodes of that early '60s UK TV show *Hullabaloo* singing *In The Pines* with Martin Carthy and Davy Graham, though not playing that guitar.

At that time, nobody knew much about Nationals. This one had the name "Don" engraved on the hand rest over the bridge and I'd just assumed that was the name of somebody who'd once owned it. Long after I'd reluctantly sold it again because I needed a good wooden guitar more suited to what I was later playing, it turned out that the *Don* had been the very top-of-the-range limited edition model back in the '30s. It was immaculately nickel-silver plated with beautiful, intricate engravings, a mother-of-pearl faced headstock and, unusually, was 14th fret to body. No wonder it sounded so good and played so well. Since the '80s they've fetched name-your-price telephone number figures. Too late!

The really sad ending to this story is that some five years after I'd sold it, it was offered back to me after having been through several more owners. One of them had been a member of pop group The Tremeloes who had roughly cut a hole in the top to instal a pickup and badly worn the fingerboard. I was so distressed to see it in such a state that I turned it down. It still occasionally surfaces out there, in worse and worse condition.

Melody Maker went to town on the country blues scene revealed by the album, followed by the rest of the music press and even national newspapers. In September, the new National Blues Federation (in which flatmate Ron Watts was a prime-mover) held the first of two annual National Blues Conventions at Conway Hall in London and people from all over the country and even the USA – players, collectors, experts and fans – got to meet each other and enthuse or come to blows. Major record companies descended in swarms, datesheets filled solid. We were off and running! I even got offered a *Blues In Britain* page in *Blues Unlimited*, the authoritative magazine of the day, that I contributed throughout the following winter and spring.

The only fly in the ointment was that one of the big hits of that year's National Jazz & Blues Festival, the forerunner of Reading Rock Festival, was reported in *Melody Maker* to have been a band who had recently changed their name from Jethro Toe to Jethro Tull. Apparently their frontman had the same name as me, but that surely didn't matter as I was already reasonably well-known now, wasn't I? Eventually that November, *Melody Maker* had a full page headlined "Presenting The Two Ian Andersons", so that was alright then, wasn't it?

I'd had to miss that autumn's American Folk Blues Festival tour as I had a gig of my own in London the same night as its Hammersmith date. But I popped in backstage during the afternoon. I got to meet legendary old country blues man and musical hero Big Joe Williams, writer of blues classic *Baby Please Don't Go*, covered by everybody. He seized on my beautiful National and clearly wasn't ready to let it go, and he wasn't a character you'd want a dispute with. So I picked up his famous 9-string guitar – a monster of a thing unplayable by mere mortals with impossibly high playing action (the height of the strings above the neck), ultra-heavy gauge strings and bits of razor blade under them at the bridge to make them buzz and rattle – and bravely said "Well, Joe, I've got to go to my own gig now so if you're going to hang on to my guitar I'll have to take yours." Luckily, he grumpily agreed to swap back and off I went. Phew!

Moving to London did open up a lot more places to play. The Cousins remained my main home-from-home, whether I was booked or not, but I also picked up a lot more gigs around town, including long established folk venues like the original London Troubadour. Not far away from where I was living, the tail end of the 1967 hippy underground still existed on weekly nights at All Saints Hall in Notting Hill, light shows and all. It became apparent very quickly how playing bottleneck guitar, where your fingers don't feel the frets, was very difficult under a fast-flashing strobe light.

I'd picked a good area to live in, as it turned out. It was within reasonable walking distance of Paddington station and in those days, as long as you got back through the barrier at the other end before midnight, you could travel to gigs on a cheap day return – even if the actual train home didn't leave until 3am. So I spent a lot of time on platform benches, which was when I gained a massive addiction to Sci-Fi and fantasy paperbacks. Drawbacks included being threatened with a rusty knife by a drunken Irishman on Birmingham New Street station, demanding "would you be after letting me have a go on your banjo?" before some fortuitously arriving policemen hauled him off. Better was walking home along Westbourne Grove, sometimes at dawn, where you could get a hot container of curry and rice and freshly baked Greek Cypriot *koulouri daktylia* – sesame-covered loaves – from the all-night shops for a few shillings.

More to the point, it was very near Queensway where Alexis Korner and family lived in a first floor flat. Alexis was very hospitable and you never knew who you'd find around there. At this time his daughter had a bass-playing boyfriend, Andy Fraser, who Alexis took under his wing and, in typical fashion, made introductions for and soon the band called Free emerged with Andy in. Alexis was a mentor to so many, myself included. He became my lifetime role model for the principle of offering a helping hand to people: if you can, why wouldn't you?

He would sometimes call me up when he was going off on a solo gig and ask me if I'd like to come along. I think he liked company on drives in his famous Citroen Safari, but he also never missed an opportunity to help other musicians if he could. So I'd get to do a floor/ support spot and might get a gig out of it myself. This sort of thing wasn't so unusual back then. Al Stewart also did the same for me sometimes, resulting in mildly terrifying drives in his favoured sports cars, and John Renbourn had been very helpful to Al Jones. It was really appreciated.

One of Alexis' other long-time mentees was re-emerging as an acoustic blues soloist at this point, often playing Cousins allnighters. Duffy Power had been one of late 1950s rock'n'roll manager Larry Parnes' protegés alongside the likes of the more successful Marty Wilde and Billy Fury. Like all of Parnes' stable, he'd been given a new stage name to replace his birth one, Ray Howard. Duffy had an extraordinary voice and presence, and of all the white blues players I ever saw live and knew, he was the one who most gave the impression that he had a hellhound on his trail.

There were two young sisters, Val and Lori, among the Cousins regulars and Val took Duffy under her wing. They eventually got married and she somehow coped with Duffy's severe mental health problems and periods of depression right up to his death in 2014. Back then, Duffy and Jo Ann Kelly were world class singers and it's a huge shame that neither achieved the mass recognition they deserved.

There was a friendly race between the Kellys, Mike Cooper and myself to see who could be the first on the country blues scene with an album release. I got approached by several producers and accepted an offer from Sandy Roberton, who was then working as an in-house producer for publishers Chappell Music. His previous project there had been an album by the Liverpool Scene, which included poet Adrian Henri and guitarist Andy Roberts, and their famous song *I've Got Those Fleetwood Mac, Chicken Shack, John Mayall, Can't Fail Blues*.

We both wanted something a little punchier than a solo voice/guitar LP, so I co-opted bass guitarist Bob Rowe from Bristol's The Deep, and extraordinarily wild and talented harmonica player Chris Turner from The Missouri Compromise, to make a trio. It was Al Stewart who came up with the elusive but then obvious solution to call it Ian Anderson's Country Blues Band...

On a Saturday in November 1968, we went into the studio, inviting pianist Bob Hall (then with the Savoy Brown Blues Band) and three of the Panama Limited Jug Band to join us. I borrowed Al Jones' 12-string to add to the range of textures, and five or six hours and a fair amount of drink later, we'd recorded all of *Stereo Death Breakdown*, mostly in first takes. Listening now, Chris Turner's playing seems extraordinary, inspired.

That autumn, with us both living in London, Al Jones and I had a weekly residency at the Cousins. A couple of weeks before the recording session, a slim young woman in her late teens, who sometimes worked behind the coffee bar, had got up to jam on harmonica. She was a good player, but when she opened her mouth to sing, everybody was astonished. I immediately asked her to come and sing a track on the album and that's how 'Harmonica Annie' – Annie Matthews – got to be featured on *Lonesome Day*. I hope she took it as a compliment that many mistakenly assumed the name was a nom-de-disque for Jo-Ann Kelly.

The following months were mayhem. The trio started gigging extensively, though as Chris Turner didn't want to turn professional we had a succession of other fine harmonica players, the best of the day, rather at the rate Spinal Tap went through drummers except none suffered from bizarre fatalities. From Cousins regulars we'd grabbed Paul Rowan, who'd often sat in with Spider John, or sometimes the enigmatic Mox, whilst on the next (and final) Country Blues Band studio session in April '69 it was Oxford's Dave Jeffs.

This was my first proper experience of banging up and down the land in clapped-out vans. That winter the trio or me solo began to play some of the bigger underground rock venues like Mother's in Birmingham. I wore a groove up the M1 since, for some reason, I got a lot of gigs in the Leeds area, at one time six within a few weeks. Apart from the strain on my repertoire this was fine, except quite often the support was an outstanding local player called Steve Phillips, who was a difficult act to follow. Years later he'd join Mark Knopfler and Brendan Croker in that occasional band called the Notting Hillbillies.

Returning to London from Brighton one night our roadie hit a patch of ice and in slow motion (it seems in my memory) his van slid off the road and overturned into the ditch. Nobody was injured other than a few bruises and it was driveable when we righted it, but it was one of those vans with the battery between the front seats and I was only vaguely aware that battery acid had spilled over me. It was rather more alarming the next time I put my clothes into the launderette and everything came out full of holes, including my underpants! Meanwhile, the next day, in best tour routing style, we were due in Glasgow so we had to take all the gear on the train. Luckily harmonica players have spare hands…

Not long after finishing *Stereo Death Breakdown*, Sandy Roberton brought the good news that it had been licensed to the hippest of big independent labels of the day, Island Records, for whom the legendary Guy Stevens was then doing A&R. Him being a long-time blues fan back to the *Record Mirror* days of my early teens, we got on really well. I was sent off to do a cover shoot, and all seemed set for the LP to be released to coincide with a February 1969 tour we were to do supporting Mississippi Fred McDowell. This was the first big project of the National Blues Federation and I'd managed to book Fred's dates from the payphone in the hall of our flat!

Somehow in amongst all that blues boom madness, I'd got together with a lovely girlfriend, Liz, sharing nights between my place and hers in Camden. She and her flatmate Cyndy both also regularly worked behind the coffee bar at the Cousins, and Liz's company and support were definitely great help in getting through that epic winter of 1968-'69 in the big city. Cyndy eventually married singer-songwriter Tom Yates and they ended up back in the Manchester area, running a folk club which later used to book Hot Vultures in the 1970s. Between Liz and Cyndy they introduced me to the Chinese oracle the *I Ching*, which had a fair old influence on my life for a while. In the words of the song I was later to write titled *Book Of Changes*, I kept on throwing No.42. Years later, I wondered if that was also the influence on Douglas Adams for his famous "answer to life, the universe and everything."

Liz came with me on the shoot for the cover of *Stereo Death Breakdown*, which was done by John Peel's photographer housemate Pete Sanders – the band rendezvoused at their place in Upper Harley Street, by Regent's Park. An acceptable if odd colour photo of me standing self-consciously in a floppy hat and fur coat near their fire escape appeared on the front, an inexplicable black & white one of a squirrel eating a lump of chocolate on the back. As was the way with record labels, I never saw the rest of that shoot until forty years later, shortly after (isn't that always the way, too?) the album masters had been unearthed and re-issued on CD. There were lots of nice shots of us all that could have ousted that squirrel!

A little while later, the hound of fate intervened as it so often would do down the years, just as something special was about to come to pass. I got a call to show up in Hyde Park early one freezing Friday morning because Island had the bright idea of putting out a cheap-price compilation LP of all their current artists, and they wanted a 'school photo' of everybody for the cover. Lots of bleary-eyed musicians from all the bands like Free, Fairport Convention, Traffic, Spooky Tooth, the earlier UK band called Nirvana, and more, arrived grumpily, including Jethro Tull, which was the one and only time I ever met my namesake. He clearly wasn't well pleased, or maybe he just had a hangover. Photographer Po Powell, of the emerging Hipgnosis design partnership, stood on a stepladder and apparently only managed to grab one roll of film before musicians started to mutiny and wander off.

Regardless, and the stories have varied down the years, it seems this was the first time that anybody from the Jethro Tull camp knew that my record was signed to Island. And whoever instigated it (I later became good friends with Jethro Tull's first guitarist Mick Abrahams when I supported his next band Blodwyn Pig a few times, and he gave me a pretty good clue), the next thing I heard was that I was being dropped by Island. Jethro Tull's manager Terry Ellis – who had earlier been the famously uncomprehending 'science student' in the Bob Dylan *Don't Look Back* film – allegedly went to Chris Blackwell, the boss at Island, and said words to the effect that "There can't be two Ian Andersons on Island Records. It will confuse things and ruin their chances of becoming the next Beatles. Either he goes or we do," which was possible since Jethro Tull were on a lease deal from Chrysalis, not actually signed to Island.

I can hardly blame Blackwell. It was a no contest when choosing between an unproved country blues oik or a band who by then had a chart record. It probably only took him a few seconds. But Guy Stevens, bless him, was furious and went on a mission to find another placing for my LP, which soon went to the excellent Andrew Lauder, newly head of A&R at Liberty/United Artists. So that ended well, except the delay meant that the album release missed the Fred McDowell tour and Cooper and Jo-Ann Kelly beat me to the post in the race to be first with debut albums.

Also it was too late for Island to re-do the photo shoot so their iconic compilation, *You Can All Join In*, came out with me on the front, in dodgy self-inflicted fringe and fur coat, with Stevie Winwood peering over my shoulder and my nemesis grinning away at the back. There was an old Spencer Davis track where mine had been. So I missed out on being part of a best-selling LP, but that track, *Crazy Fool Mumble*, eventually made the Top 30 on Liberty's own *Son Of Gutbucket* sampler, technically remaining my 'greatest hit'…

It was Andrew Lauder, very generous at gifting musicians on the label with LPs when visiting his office, who revealed to me who that extraordinary American raconteur was that I'd heard reciting *The Nazz* at that party in Kilburn some years before. He gave me a copy of *Lord Buckley's Best*, along with all sorts of other goodies he was releasing by US bands like Creedence Clearwater Revival, Canned Heat, Johnny Winter and UK outfits like The Famous Jug Band and Cochise, my first encounter with English pedal steel maestro BJ Cole. Some 40 years later it would be via BJ that I'd re-make contact with Liz, who had gone to work as Andrew

Lauder's secretary at that time. I was very content to be amongst such a roster on *Son Of Gutbucket*.

The Fred McDowell tour was brilliant. A little posse of us including Ron and Alexis went out to meet him at Heathrow. The previous time he'd toured in the UK he'd looked like the Mississippi farm worker he'd been, playing a battered old f-hole acoustic guitar. He emerged from Arrivals in a smart overcoat with shiny patent leather shoes and a slimline guitar case. Opening it revealed a gleaming red electric guitar. "What happened to your old acoustic, Fred?" "Oh, I gave it to some hippie at Newport Folk Festival."

Not long after he arrived there was a reception for him at the Two Brewers in Covent Garden. Somebody had the good thought to invite Shirley Collins who had 'discovered' Fred with Alan Lomax a decade before, which had launched Fred's international career. They hadn't met again in the intervening years, so I remember a very emotional greeting – not a dry eye in the house! This must have been the first time I met Shirley too, having only seen her on stages before then: little did I know how much effect she'd subsequently have on my life.

Before the first date, Alexis entrusted tour manager Gareth Hedges with his own little tweed-covered Fender amplifier for the duration. Fred claimed that he'd been sitting in with Chuck Berry and Buddy Guy and was impressed by how they'd attracted all the girls, figuring out it was the red electric guitar which did it. But throughout the tour he always began with his catch-phrase "I do not play no rock'n'roll" before launching into his driving, burning bottleneck riffs that would put most rock bands to shame.

And as for the girls, many of the dates were in venues not unlike big folk clubs in format, where there was very little separation between performers and audience. The first few times that he was mobbed by white, student-age female fans who just wanted to give him a big hug, he initially recoiled – but soon got very used to it! We realised that where he came from, physical contact with a white female might well have got him strung up from the nearest tree.

It was an absolute pleasure to have Fred as our house guest in London whenever he wasn't out on the road and my trio were thrilled to support him on a fair few of the dates. Among the bigger ones were two London concerts at the Mayfair Theatre where Fred invited Jo-Ann Kelly up to sing with him, luckily recorded and later released, and the final one promoted by Ron Watts in High Wycombe with Alexis, Jo-Ann, Mike Cooper, Duster Bennett and us on the bill.

All through the tour he'd asked musicians to join him on stage, particularly our harmonica player Paul Rowan, but we'd had to tactfully explain that there were these strange people called 'purists' who would only tolerate the 'real thing'. But on the celebratory last night, why not? For the finale, everybody was invited up for a jam, only to find a local (white) accountant in a grey suit jumping on stage, trying to push the likes of Alexis off, shouting "white trash, get off" before he himself was removed. Accountants, eh?

By the time *Stereo Death Breakdown* was released around May, it was already over for the Country Blues Band. Still only 21, I was exhausted, at a dead end with what I was doing musically, fed up with all those endless 'Can blue men play the whites?' remonstrations, and totally disillusioned with the music business. Oh, and I had split up with Liz. Little did I know that life's often like that...

I'd had a major 'lightbulb moment', musically, which is where the next chapter will go, and I went through some sudden and sizeable changes (not all of them as predicted by my well-thumbed *I Ching*). For the previous three or four years I'd been totally obsessed with playing old country blues, making as authentic noises as I could, but now I had an identity crisis.

I was ready to be outta there. At this point I was with Blackhill Agency, having previously been taken on by Al Stewart's agent Julia Creasy at Folk Directions, who had moved over to them. As well as running the big Hyde Park free concerts in the summers, they represented a lot of the key 'underground' bands, some of whom by then were very overground. This meant I'd occasionally go out on bills with the mesmerising Third Ear Band, for example, but you can only do so many supports to the likes of the Edgar Broughton Band before you lose the will to get out of bed. "Out Demons Out!" Out Ians out! There was camping space going in the flat above the Bristol Troubadour, which was still second only to London's Les Cousins as the nation's most happening folk venue. So I hopped it back West to where I'd left the year before. It felt great.

My last real brush with the blues scene came that September when soon-to-be *MM* and later *Sounds* writer Jerry Gilbert put on a blues festival in the park in Farnham, Surrey. Also on the bill were Duster Bennett, Jo-Ann Kelly, Andy Fernbach's Connexion (which my Country Blues Band's bassist Bob Rowe had joined), Blue Horizon Records signing Gordon Smith and a duo called Blue Blood who were discoveries of the MC – Radio 1 blues DJ and part-time Hammer Horror films actor Mike Raven.

By then I was trying out a whole new repertoire of self-written stuff, one of which was a thing called *De 12-Bore Blues* which took an affectionate rise out of all the unthinking clichés and attitudes of less-discriminating British bluesers. The audience loved it and were baying for more. I could hear Mike Raven stomping around behind the screen shouting "Fuck him, get him off." I didn't take much persuading to leave all that behind.

7.
Changes & The Village Thing

There was no particular road to Damascus moment that brought about my directional swerve in 1969. It was just an accumulation of influences and prods at a time when I was having both a cultural identity crisis and my first rough ride from the big bad music business. Surely there must be something else, I was slowly realising?

Back at the beginning of the year Guy Stevens had given me a pre-release white label copy of *Kip Of The Serenes*, the Joe Boyd produced debut LP by Dublin trio Dr Strangely Strange. Wikipedia describes them as 'experimental folk' which is as good as anything for a band without a genre, other than a kinship with the Incredible String Band. I was fascinated by their whimsical rule breaking and literary bent, and played it a lot for pleasure. When the album was released I went out and bought a proper copy with a sleeve, and binned the white label. Little was I to know that by the '80s copies would change hands for approaching a grand. When I told the Strangelies' Ivan Pawle this in the 21st century, he informed me that he'd done exactly the same around that time with a white label of Nick Drake's first album!

There was a weekend in June 1969 that was oddly symbolic of my transition, when I was invited to Ireland to play for the Dublin Blues Society and also had an impromptu gig added at the club run by the Strangelies at Slattery's. And that was my other visit to Ireland.

I had been a regular customer at Collett's Folk Shop in London, where I'd quite often run into the Young Tradition's Peter Bellamy. He and Collett's co-manager Hans Fried would point me at what two decades later would be called 'World Music' albums on labels like Lyrichord, Folkways and Nonesuch and I accumulated a small, esoteric selection of LPs of things like Egyptian oud, Chinese pipa and Bauls from Bengal.

I remember having a conversation on a train platform with Shelagh McDonald where I was fantasising about getting players of such instruments into the last days of the country blues band, but lamenting that I had absolutely no idea where to find such creatures. I wouldn't find out about SOAS (London University's School of Oriental & African Studies) until the '80s and it would be three decades before everybody's little helper, Mr

Google, came along. So my chance of being well ahead of my time never got off the fantasy drawing board.

Something was in the guitar air too. In what was then called 'contemporary folk' there was a movement away from the more delicate, intricate, mid-'60s 'folk baroque' school of guitar playing associated with Bert Jansch & John Renbourn. That summer I reluctantly traded my steel National for a regular wooden guitar and, along with other acoustic guitar player friends of the day like Michael Chapman, Keith Christmas and Al Jones, tried to evolve a bigger noise. My way was using the open tunings, heavier strings and the chunky thumb pick and finger picks I'd retained from my blues playing. Indeed to this day I'm still using the same, now very worn but still serviceable, set of nickel silver fingerpicks that I bought in Ivor Mairants Music Centre around 1968.

From Leeds via Hull, Michael Chapman had dropped in to Bristol clubs on his way down to the Cornish folk scene in 1966, and I'd booked him for our Folk Blues Bristol & West club. From Cornwall via Les Cousins he quickly gained a cult following nationally, evolving a highly original guitar and songwriting style from blues and jazz roots. It was a fuller, heavier sound utilising power chords in open tunings which became very influential: it was only half a century later when re-listening to some of my recordings from those days re-issued in a CD box set that I realised how much I'd taken on board too. Via his early albums like *Rainmaker* and *Fully Qualified Survivor* for EMI Harvest, his songs became as ubiquitous around contemporary folk clubs, especially those in colleges, as Jansch's and Al Stewart's.

In those days before English handmade guitars that ring like pianos, we stripped the heavy lacquer off the fronts of imported Gibson J45s and Yamaha FG300s, refinished them with light coats of button polish, and replaced plastic bridge pins with brass ones, all in attempts to squeeze more volume and bigger tone out of them. Some journalists called what we played 'heavy folk'. Very little of it was actually folk at all in the traditional sense. But then Martin Carthy had already laid down the foundations of another English guitar playing school for just that…

And words. Once I was no longer lyrically restricted to blues culture, they came tumbling out. Within a matter of months I had a completely new, self-written repertoire. A lot was influenced by reading far too many Sci-fi and fantasy paperbacks for a healthy mind, and listening to all the other music that was happening. I'd also begun to wake up to the world around me. Up to this time I'd generally been politically unaware and uninvolved but now I began to tangentially tackle – somewhat clumsily– subjects like the environment, the nuclear threat and societal pressures on young people.

In spite of several massive culls in subsequent house moves, I've still got hundreds of those books that I'd collected and read on the road from then through the '70s. I'll occasionally re-read things like Kurt Vonnegut's *Sirens Of Titan*, Ursula K Le Guin's *The Dispossessed*, or some Philip K Dick, Michael Moorcock, Harry Harrison or Jack Vance (a particular favourite). Many are timeless. Some from my old blues circles were outraged by all this but there seemed to be a different and growing audience and I was soon completely immersed in my newfound direction.

That August I got my first passport and set off for my first couple of gigs in what would become a home from home over the next decade, Belgium. In spite of breaking a toe on the overnight ferry by carelessly stubbing it on the iron frame of a deck bench, I had a wonderful time for the next few days. Met off the ferry by organiser Al De Boeck, who soon gained the nickname 'Al de bookings' for his sterling work arranging early Belgian gigs for English twangists, my first stop was a hotel room to catch up on some of the hours of sleep missed by using the cheap rate overnight ferry.

Then later that day, my first ever gig to a non-Anglophone audience, at a big festival called Kick '69 in a town square in Ostend itself. I'd already worked out that many people there actually spoke good English so I just had to remember to speak clearly, not use unfamiliar words and construct sentences simply. Turned out I was quite good at that, as I was often told down the years I was over there in Europe.

I suspect that in crediting the inspiration for some of my new songs I must have done some good PR for author Michael Moorcock, because a few years later I read in a Belgian magazine that I'd started a Belgian cult following for him on that festival. I've no idea if this is true but it's a nice story that I regaled him with some years later, the only time we met, at an exhibition by artist Rodney Matthews. I gained a raised eyebrow! Turns out that Moorcock himself had been active on the London post-skiffle folk scene in the late 1950s, editing a folk fanzine called *The Rambler*. It had contributions from fellow folkie Sci-Fi writer John Brunner, who had written songs like *The H-Bomb's Thunder* for the fledgling CND to sing on their Aldermaston marches.

Apart from that Belgian trip, which also included the big Bilzen Jazz & Pop Festival, and a continuing run of gigs up and down the UK, I spent three or four months that summer camping above the Bristol Troubadour. In my year away, original founder Ray Willmott and his wife Barbara had sold up and returned to Australia. The buyer, local night club owner Peter Bush, had initially stayed at arm's length, putting musician John Turner in as resident manager.

It was the perfect venue in which to try out new songs in relaxed surroundings with a familiar audience. I must admit that some got over-familiar since my mild dose of celebrity on the national level had briefly made me inexplicably interesting to young women. I was just 22, single, and much as I ought to be ashamed now, I wasn't complaining at the time.

I still had unfinished business with the record industry though. I was contracted to Chappell Music for a second LP, but Sandy Roberton had left to go independent. In the meantime I'd introduced him to Al Jones, whose debut he produced, licensing it to Parlophone. Al had pointed him at Keith Christmas, and Keith had then done the same for Shelagh McDonald, with their debuts appearing on RCA and B&C respectively. So this whole chain of albums emerged in the next year from artists associated with the Bristol Troubadour.

I had to move back to London for a couple of months that autumn while I sorted all this out, so I got myself a bedsit not far from my previous flat and across the street from Blackhill's office. My first call was a summons to see Chappell's director Teddy Holmes. An old boy who had been with the company since 1917 and had hobnobbed with the likes of Noel Coward, he was clearly baffled about me and actually asked "Now what exactly is it that you do?", Prince Phillip style.

I was given another eight hour studio session to make the second album, which I did that October, summoning up a motley crew of Al Jones on guitar, Mox on flute, John Turner on double bass and Keith Christmas on bongoes! It was an unsatisfactory, rushed session that I wasn't happy with. Then Teddy Holmes told me it wasn't going to Liberty/UA like *Stereo Death Breakdown* as I expected, but to unfashionable Fontana with whom Chappell's had recently done a first-refusal deal on their in-house productions. Alarm bells began to sound.

This was quickly followed by a second trip to Belgium, to hit the club scene in the company this time of Dave Kelly and Al Jones, and to discover Belgian beer… There's a truly dreadful live cassette of us all somewhere in my archive which basically proves that drinking and gigging aren't the best companions. It's hand-labelled "The Great Geel Disco Fiasco of '69…"

My battered pocket diary tells me that as soon as I was back it was off to Windermere Folk Club, from which I have a really clear memory of being rowed across a millpond-smooth Lake Windermere in the early morning mists to catch a train – you don't forget things like that – and on to Cockermouth and then Aberystwyth University Arts Festival on a bill including Martin Carthy and Shirley Collins. Life wasn't dull.

By December I was back in Bristol where a proper room of my own had become available above the Troubadour. Meanwhile, Fontana fixed a photo shoot in London for the album cover, which was to be titled *Book Of Changes*, so I went up on the train for it. The photographer's bright idea was to hire two models, one white and one black. On the front there'd be a black and white shot of the back of me, facing away, posed between those two as they looked towards the camera in front of a derelict building. On the reverse there would be a colour pic of me looking outwards through the back views of the models who had swapped coats, in front of a modern building. Changes, eh? Oddly, there's no photographer credit on the resulting cover.

It got worse. Early in the new year the postman brought a test pressing and a proof of the resulting cover. It was just awful. The pressing was really lacklustre and had lost any of the minimal sparkle from the studio, as was often the case with vinyl. But the cover was the final insult. The front photo had been tinted sepia ("shit brown" as somebody unkindly but accurately described it) and the layout had been done by somebody with low Letraset skills and little familiarity with the principles of typography. They're not credited either…

Singer/songwriter Ralph McTell had stayed over from his Troubadour gig and commiserated, saying I should go to Fontana and make my feelings known. So I jumped on the London train with him and headed for Fontana's offices, only to be told "What's that got to do with you? You're only the artist." I walked out, vowing to have nothing more to do with it.

As it turned out, I got cosmic revenge. The week in March 1970 that it was eventually released, Fontana's parent company Philips changed to computerised distribution which promptly fell over and some three weeks of releases were effectively lost. It deservedly sank with very little trace. Phew!

Ralph McTell figures in another tale from around then. The artists booked for the Saturday evening at the Bristol Troubadour would sometimes be playing the allnighter at Les Cousins, so somebody with a car would offer to drive them back to London, and we'd pile in for the ride. On this particular occasion, Ralph was the booked artist, and John Turner the driver.

We were bowling up the old A4 around midnight, on a beautifully clear summer night. Half way between Calne & Marlborough there's the Beckhampton roundabout, then you pull up a rise towards mysterious Silbury Hill on the left. As we did that, the car's engine just cut out completely and we coasted into the layby just before the hill. Ralph and I were in the back, and as we got out each side we both looked up at the starry sky. I immediately saw an intensely bright light that seemed to recede very fast. "Did you see that?" I asked Ralph. "Yes, wonder what that was."

We became distracted by another car that had pulled into the same layby and its driver was also looking under his car bonnet. John set off walking back to the roundabout to find a phone box, and joined the other driver doing the same thing. The AA duly came to the rescue, got both cars towed into the local garage, and both were fixed quickly – by weird coincidence, the same electrical part had burned out. So we then set off, breaking all speed limits, to get Ralph to his gig, and forgot all about it.

About a decade later I opened the *Observer* one Sunday to find a big piece on UFO sightings and the phenomena connected with them. One of those, apparently, was electrics burning out on cars. I picked up the 'phone and rang Ralph. "Hello, it's Ian Anderson here…" "You've just been reading the *Observer*, haven't you?" he says. "Yup. Do you remember…?" "Of course I do." It was later still that I became aware that the region around Avebury, down to Glastonbury, was heavily associated with UFOs, crop circles etc.

A less authentic UFO experience happened one night in the Troubadour flat. John Turner, Al Jones and myself had been up late partying when one of us noticed a really bright light in the early dawn sky. We convinced ourselves that it was moving, hovering, so John decided to ring the local police station. "Where is this light, sir?" John gave co-ordinates. There was the sound of large boots receding, a door being opened and closed. A few minutes later the boots returned. "Would you say it's in the east, at about 20 degrees?" "Yes, yes, that's it. Can you see it too?" "We can, sir. We think it's Venus and that you should go to bed." We did…

Back in Bristol in the dying days of 1969, it was the habit of us Troubadour flat residents, after late nights, to take our hangovers and whichever girlfriends or club guests had stayed the night across to Splinters coffee house in nearby Clifton Down Road for late breakfast. One day, over strong coffees and Sally Lunn tea cakes, John Turner and I were wondering what would be the best for his band the Pigsty Hill Light Orchestra's recording career and for my own future one in the light of recent experiences. We'd already started using the term 'Clifton Village' for the area on the club's posters – it later caught on and is now an actual thing, on maps and all – and we dreamed up this concept of an agency and record label where we could all be in complete control of our own destinies, without the interference of uncomprehending 'suits'. So our concept was this... thing... this... ahah! The Village Thing! The agency idea came first, followed by the label after we'd roped in Gef Lucena of Saydisc as business partner.

The first half of 1970 was a whirlwind of constant gigging, breaking in all this new material, at the same time as planning for the label launch at the end of the summer. Meanwhile the Troubadour's new owner Peter Bush had realised that it wasn't the cash cow he'd been led to believe and fired John as manager. Luckily, around then, student friends of mine who had a flat around the corner in Royal York Crescent were leaving, so we were able to take it over. We initially ran the new organisation from there but later, as it grew, we moved into offices in Park Street that we shared with local rock promoters Plastic Dog and their design studio. This included the brilliant, subsequently award-winning fantasy artist Rodney Matthews whose early works graced some Village Thing covers.

To complete the Troubadour saga, when he'd fired John Turner, Peter Bush had then installed a friend of his called Tim Hodgson as manager, who came from the business world where he'd been a debt collector, wore a suit, drove a big old Jaguar and knew nothing about folk music. But the incredible happened. In a very short space of time after an early stand-off, Tim fell in love with the whole Troubadour ethos and the music, became a devoted friend of all the musicians, changed sides, grew his hair, and continued the attempts to keep the Troubadour going by any means possible. As mentioned earlier, between us and a rota of the 'big name' resident artists who played packed Friday nights for free to boost the takings, we all managed it for another year until Peter Bush finally lost his patience and closed it without notice in summer 1971.

We just had time to liberate the club's trusty Gestetner machine which continued to do sterling service duplicating press releases and newsletters well into the 1980s. And an eagle-eyed regular spotted that all the artist photos which had decorated the walls had been dumped in a skip outside and brought them round to Royal York Crescent. So they survived too, along with many, many memories.

The beatnik auditor, 1966

Elliot Jackson, IAA, Noel Sheldon, Al Jones. Bristol Troubadour, December '66.

From the Royal York Crescent LP session 1970: Lee, Andy Leggett, Janet, Tim Hodgson, Jane, Ian 'Heavy Drummer' Turner, Eve, Maggie Holland, IAA, Pat Roche, Ian Hunt.

Recording at Saydisc, 1968, with the National Don.

At Rockfield Studios, 1972, with the Guild 12-string.

First Glastonbury Festival, September 1970. IAA on stage with 'Heavy Drummer'.

IAA & Maggie Holland, Hot Vultures, with the trusty VW bus – Farnham 1974.

Hot Vultures & friends: Maggie Holland, Martin Simpson, Chris Coe, Pete Coe, IAA, 1979.

The English Country Blues Band with guest Martin Carthy: MC, Maggie Holland, Rod Stradling, IAA. Farnham Maltings, 1981.

Tiger Moth's late night ceilidh at Bracknell Folk & Roots Festival, 1989. IAA, Maggie Holland, John Maxwell, Jon Moore, Rod Stradling, Ian Carter and an idiot dancer!

Rodney Matthews, Michael Moorcock & IAA, late 1990s.

At the Village Thing 40th anniversary celebration, Cecil Sharp House, London, 2010. Dave Evans, John Turner, Maggie Holland, Tucker Zimmerman with IAA in front.

Photo: Judith Burrows/fRoots

IAA in Tiger Moth at the Big Chill, 2006: the infamous mariachi trousers.

Joe Strummer, Cathia Randrianarivo and IAA at the Awards For World Music 2002.

IAA, Spider John Koerner and Tom Paley at the Roundhouse, London, 2010.

Blue Blokes 3 2008: Lu Edmonds, IAA, Ben Mandelson.

IAA in the fRoots Office, 2008

Hot Vultures in the Cellarful Of Folkadelia at Sidmouth Folk Week 2016, with guest Tymon Dogg: IAA, TD, Maggie Holland.

False Beards: Ben Mandelson, IAA, 2012

Alex Merry as Crow Jane, and IAA. Wardrobe Theatre, Bristol, 2019.

Dave Kelly, IAA, Paul Jones. Folk House, Bristol, January 2017. Solo gigging began again…

CHANGES & THE VILLAGE THING

Village Thing was literally a cottage industry: its official headquarters were at Inglestone Common, a tiny hamlet in the wilds of South Gloucestershire where business partner Gef Lucena and his wife lived. Some of the initial recordings were indeed done in Gef's cottage, others in the Royal York Crescent flat. Later, we were able to set up in the familiar Quaker meeting house at Frenchay on the outskirts of Bristol where Gef's parents were wardens. Equipment was good but basic – at least one album was recorded with a pair of mics plugged straight into a Revox tape recorder, and the maximum was a pair of Revoxes, multi-mics through a small mixer and a simple reverb unit. Anything more complicated than that, on the few occasions when it was needed, we took over to record at Rockfield near Monmouth. It was also very much a family of artists and musicians, as will be apparent from the way that names crop up on each other's recordings.

Subtitled 'the alternative folk label' (decades ahead of the coining of 'alt.folk', let alone 'psych folk', 'acid folk' and all the other bewildering terms that get showered on it these days), Village Thing eventually released two dozen albums and a few singles between 1970 and 1974. With immediate strong national press and radio support, we initially prospered with our unique and hard-to-pin-down mix of established names and newcomers, original singer/ songwriter/ guitarists, a few visiting Americans, and folk entertainers. It was the contemporary folk scene's complement to the more traditionally-based recordings being simultaneously released by Bill Leader's wonderful Trailer label, and soon both were being manufactured and distributed by the folk 'major' of the day, Transatlantic.

I got cracking on my first Village Thing LP, *Royal York Crescent*, out at Inglestone Common. To differentiate myself from my troublesome namesake I'd inserted the middle initial A into my solo billing, in good Sci-fi author tradition, and I'd teamed up for gigging and recording with superb local acoustic guitarist Ian Hunt.

Talk about changes! It was released barely eighteen months after the appearance of my country blues band album, but it had heavy Sci-fi and fantasy themes (Michael Moorcock, Kurt Vonnegut and H.P. Lovecraft got namechecked, and there were guitar instrumentals named after E.R. Eddison's *The Worm Ouroborous* and Philip K. Dick's *The Man In The High Castle*), a fantasy suite featuring some *Kip Of The Serenes*-esque recorder – recorder! – by Andy Leggett, and a piece called *Goblets & Elms* accompanied by birdsong...

Ian Hunt helped us create a distinctive twin guitar attack, aided by bassist John Turner and the pattering bongos of hirsute Ian Turner – wittily a.k.a. 'Heavy Drummer' as his name was just too confusing among the other two. But not everything was entirely serious: *Mr Cornelius* may have been named after a Moorcock anti-hero but the song was a retaliation against sociology students who regularly pestered for details of deep meaning in lyrics. That one had absolutely none whatsoever, but I didn't let on.

The photo on the back cover, taken in the summer of 1970, told a tale. It's one of a series by Jo Gedrych showing lots of the Troubadour/ Village Thing gang and girlfriends. My activities in the latter department had got irresponsibly over-complicated. John and I had got together with a pair of very attractive young women, Eve and Janet, who were club regulars and they'd begun to stay over. But I'd also met Bristol University Folk Club organiser and singer Maggie Holland, who was clearly a soul mate. Both are in the photo! It marks the day I made the decision to get my life in order. Sorry Janet. Maggie promptly moved in: we got married that December and she immediately became an indispensable part of the Village Thing team.

In spite of its reputation for singer/ songwriter/ guitarist albums, some of Village Thing's best sellers were by popular folk club entertainers like Fred Wedlock, jug band kings Tight Like That and the anarchic Pigsty Hill Light Orchestra. We kicked off with the latter, who'd been a smash hit at that summer's Cambridge Folk Festival and were embarking on a frantic schedule of folk club gigs, with a chest full of improvised instruments (most famously Andy Leggett's 'ballcockaphone') and a zany repertoire mostly of 1920s jazz classics. Their debut *PHLOP* ("Pigsty Hill Light Orchestra Presents...") was studio recorded and in retrospect didn't capture the full essence of the band, so we followed it up the next year with the live *Piggery Jokery*.

Immediately highlighting the intended diversity of Village Thing, the other in the label's first pair of LPs was the sole album made by a couple from Cardiff, Graham & Anne Hemingway, who went under the name The Sun Also Rises. They clearly inhabited the same musical zone as the Incredible String Band and Dr Strangely Strange and had impressed us with gigs in South Wales and at the Bristol Troubadour. They briefly blazed, with *Sounds* calling their self-titled album "the most original record of the year" and claiming they'd "opened up a new dimension into which British music can blossom," before they slid into obscurity.

Those first releases were in September 1970: the launch gig at the Troubadour was the night before the very first Glastonbury Festival, to which many of us then trooped off the next day. That first one – originally called Pilton Pop – luckily enjoyed an Indian summer weather spell so lying on the grass in T-shirts was fine. Though that might have been the extent of the luck that farmer/festival promoter Michael Eavis got that weekend. I don't know how many ticket-buyers he was hoping for but none of the photos I have seem to show more than a few hundred.

I'd been booked for this unknown festival with Ian Hunt. Various bods from the music press like Jerry Gilbert and Andrew Means, and artist friends like Al Stewart had come down from London for the Friday night launch. So the next day a whole horde of us – some rather the worse for wear – piled into vehicles and pointed ourselves south to check it out.

The only festival that we were really used to back then was Cambridge Folk Festival which had been running for a few years with several stages and well-organised bars and catering. Glastonbury's sole stage was – well – some wobbly planks on some scaffolding in a field, with canvas covering in case it rained. Luckily it didn't. As shown by Jo Gedrych's suite of photos, the PA was minimal, there were no stage monitors for the musicians (though that was what we were used to in those days anyway), but all was perfectly fine for a small event. The security fence in front of the stage was a few strands of farm-like wire between wooden posts. I have no recall of the state of catering or loo facilities, so they may have been OK.

Those photos show our lot lounging on the grass like everybody else, as was the hippy habit in those days, and watching whoever came on. I'm not entirely sure that those appearing on the day bore much relation to the poster which had advertised the Kinks and Wayne Fontana, neither of whom materialised. Quintessence, Amazing Blondel and Stackridge (several times) came and went.

When it was time for my set, I did some solo things, then brought up Heavy Drummer and Ian Hunt. We kept getting frantic signals from the wings to keep going, allegedly because headliner Marc Bolan was, probably wisely, unwilling to go on until he'd been paid. Eventually, when we finally got the sign to finish we dragged up most of our horde – musicians, girlfriends, writers from *Melody Maker* and *Sounds*, hangers on – in a ramshackle attempt to summon up some 'Woodstock Spirit' with Ian Hunt's version of Country Joe's *Fixin' To Die Rag*.

Decades later, Al Stewart was fêted in a BBC Glastonbury broadcast for having "appeared at the first Glastonbury": that was the extent of it, the cheeky blighter! Re-written history now also wants to record that it was the 'other' Ian Anderson who played in 1970. No it wasn't.

Michael Eavis was once quoted in the *Guardian* as saying "Marc Bolan was late arriving, and I was quite worried, but Ian Anderson saved the festival. He knew I couldn't pay him, but he played a great set that got everybody in the right mood." That was nice to know. I never did see Bolan – we were knackered from the night before, and all needed to get back to the Troubadour for that night's guest appearance by singer/songwriter Steve Tilston who we'd soon sign for Village Thing. Of course we had absolutely no idea of what it would turn into over the years. And, perhaps strangely, I've never been again since. Never was asked...

Royal York Crescent was released shortly after, in November 1970. Coinciding with it was the arrival on the label of folk blues guitar legend Wizz Jones. Wizz, a contemporary of Davy Graham, was a major influence on '60s artists from Bert Jansch, John Renbourn and Ralph McTell to Eric Clapton, Keith Richards and Rod Stewart. He, like me, had previously been with UA/ Liberty and we were very happy to put out his self-mockingly titled *The Legendary Me*. He then nipped off to do an album for CBS before returning for his second VT album *When I Leave Berlin*. The title track was covered live, years later, by Bruce Springsteen of all people. Many consider those two albums to be among Wizz's finer works.

It was either Wizz or Ralph who recommended Steve Tilston – originally from Liverpool and by then in London – to point himself in our direction. A very talented 21year old guitarist and songwriter, he impressed us mightily, came to Bristol and produced the simple but striking debut *An Acoustic Confusion* that the *Daily Mail*, of all things, promptly made one of its records of the year. Rod Stewart bought a box of them to give to all his mates for Christmas!

Tilston's debut served another purpose: it introduced us to the amazing Dave Evans who came to Bristol to play on Steve's sessions and promptly moved there. With his own debut *The Words In Between* he produced one of Village Thing's towering treasures, a criminally under-acknowledged classic of the day. He followed it up a year later with the excellent *Elephantasia*.

Dave, with his totally unique and often mind-boggling guitar playing, self-made instruments, utterly delightful songs and madcap tunings, became a great friend. He, his then partner Barbara and charming, gluttonous labrador called Corey, were mainstays of our Bristol social scene, not to mention expert introducer to Indian cookery which he'd learned from Indian crews during a time spent in the merchant navy. He was one of those impressive people who seemed to be able to turn his hand to any creative pursuit: just before coming to Bristol he'd been working in a Devon pottery turning out unique pieces. Unfortunately, like many creative people, his ambition and organisational skills were in inverse proportion to his other talents, otherwise his musical career could have been huge.

It's perhaps unfortunate that 21st century journalists and record label PRs have such lack of imagination that they almost always feel the need to make comparisons with Nick Drake whenever Dave's name comes up. In truth, hardly anybody had heard of Drake back then, nobody listened to his records and they certainly weren't known in our circles. Dave's LPs sold much better on our small independent than Drake's did on a major, but he didn't have any link with London-based folk rock royalty and lived a long and hugely productive life, failing to die of an overdose, so he didn't have a tragic back story to propel him to cult fame.

George Peckham, then at the Beatles' studio Apple, was our cutting engineer of choice for Village Thing LPs. When I took Dave's *The Words In Between* in, he put on the tape and exclaimed "Wow, how did you get that great acoustic guitar sound?" "Well, it was really simple, just a couple of good AKG condenser mics plugged straight into a Revox in a room in my flat with nice acoustics and a wonderful guitar that Dave made himself..." He jabbed on the intercom button and summoned in the engineer from the main multi-track recording studio, and started the tape up again. "Wow, how did you get that great acoustic guitar sound?" asked the engineer. "Tell him, Ian, tell him," crowed George. And after I did, he said to the engineer "See, I told you all that expensive crap you've got in there just gets in the way of a good sound!", poking the engineer's chest with a finger!

It took a fair bit of persuasion to convince local folk club hero Fred Wedlock to make an LP. We recorded his debut *The Folker* in my living room: it went on to sell some 20,000 copies, easily the label's biggest. We'd anticipated trouble from Paul Simon's lawyers over the title track, his classic spoof on Simon's *The Boxer*. That never came, but the ladies at the EMI pressing plant objected to another track containing the line "Prince Phillip is the queen in drag" so we had to do a swift re-edit. That debut included a few of the traditional songs that had been a regular part of his club repertoire.

By his second LP *Frollicks* (like the PHLO's second, also recorded live to more capture the essence) he'd completely concentrated on his inimitable comedy, which stood him in great stead from then on, culminating in his top 10 single a decade later, long after Village Thing had expired.

For my second Village Thing LP, *A Vulture Is Not A Bird You Can Trust*, I wanted a bigger production. We took ourselves over to Rockfield Studios near Monmouth, where we got good deals. They often found that their daytime hours were quiet as rock star clients like Dave Edmunds and Hawkwind preferred to record overnight. "Don't touch the sugar bowls," engineer Kingsley Ward would warn us on mornings after Hawkwind sessions.

Ian Hunt handled acoustic lead guitar duties again, and resident at the studio were a band called Spring, who Michael Chapman had recommended. I was pleased to use their bass and keyboard players, and drummer Pick Withers, later a founder member of Dire Straits, as the session team. Notable among the heavier tracks was my total failure at emulating Nostradamus on the track *The Survivor* which confidently predicted the end of the world in 1979. Among the worst things to actually happen that year was the coming to power of one Margaret Thatcher…

What it *wasn't* was 'folk rock' (since what I was doing clearly wasn't folk songs). I'd been a Byrds fan and loved the early electric Dylan era, but apart from liking the early Steeleye Span line-up with Martin Carthy and no drummer, and the raw and basic sound of Mr Fox, I was never quite drawn to the British version of the day. It always seemed to me that it was a forced fusion because the folkies largely didn't understand the dynamics and techniques of rock music and the rock musicians – Richard Thompson excepted – had no feel for traditional music, especially the ubiquitous battered jigs & reels. So it really wasn't very good at either. Over the years the clichés descended into a hamfisted pub rock with plodding rhythm sections, until the '80s – post-punk and the new wave of English country dance bands – when certain people like the Oysterband and Jumpleads found different angles.

By 1971 I was regularly touring in Belgium and Germany and on those travels – notably at a festival in Osnabruck – I met a couple of Belgian-based American exiles. One of those was Tucker Zimmerman who had come to Rome on a scholarship, and ended up in England in the late '60s where his first album was produced for Regal Zonophone by Tony Visconti, allegedly becoming one of David Bowie's favourite LPs. After moving to Belgium, he'd built a strong following in Germany, where they called him a 'song poet'. His second, home-recorded album had been released on a small German label and we were happy to pick it up for UK release, the only Village Thing album we didn't originate.

The other Belgian-based American was already a legend. Zen banjoist Derroll Adams had come over with Ramblin' Jack Elliott in the '50s and never gone back. Resident in the UK, he'd become a major guru for the young Donovan and people like Ronnie Lane of the Small Faces. Eventually alcohol had got the worse of him – as witnessed in the Dylan *Don't Look Back* film's hotel room fracas – and he'd had to get out of England, to France and then Belgium where he was miraculously taken care of and nursed back to drink-free health by a dedicated young woman, Danny.

In due course he made a triumphant return to stages. I'd been billed with him and Alex Campbell on a Belgian festival as far back as '69, and he later came over for the 1972 Cambridge Folk Festival. Soon after this we brought him back to record his wonderful *Feelin' Fine* LP along with Wizz Jones, Belgian hero Roland Van Campenhout and others.

His UK tour to support the album release included a launch gig at the Shakespeare's Head in London's Carnaby Street, where Wizz accompanied him for part of the set. Long-time fans Rod Stewart & Long John Baldry showed up to see him, but to avoid distracting the audience, they'd considerately waited in another bar downstairs, intending to slip in quietly at the back once the gig had started. Unfortunately, the door was at the front of the room right next to the stage, so Rod Stewart's appearance in a canary yellow silk suit and six foot seven Baldry's in a one-piece beige woollen jumpsuit had quite the opposite effect. And Rod then proceeded to win the raffle…

My own third and final VT album also got recorded that summer of 1972, partly at Rockfield with Mike Cooper's short-lived electric band The Machine Gun Company, and partly – the acoustic tracks – back at Frenchay. The Sci-fi content was on a lighter level, and one prescient song, *A Sign Of The Times*, seems to have retained currency as a swipe at dumbed-down culture. "It's a sign of the times that the simpleton's the winner and the wise man is banished to his cell." And they wouldn't invent social media for many years to come. The album finally found a use for that 1967 newspaper headline, *Singer Sleeps On As Blaze Rages* as title, with another Rodney Matthews cover.

I've owned too many nice guitars over the years (yes, it's possible!) but the only ones I really regret not being able to afford to keep were that beautiful National Don that I'd played in my Country Blues Band and my lovely

Guild 12-String which got its recording outing on this album (as well as being borrowed by both Wizz Jones and Dave Evans, for tracks on the Derroll Adams LP and Dave's second one, *Elephantasia*, respectively.)

Leo Kottke was a bit of a role model for playing bottleneck 12-string, especially on his version of *Pamela Brown*. Kottke once let me play his Bozo 12-string in his dressing room. I wondered why it was so heavy. "Look inside," he said. There was a towel folded up in there. "Eh? Why...?" Apparently without that it was so loud that it overloaded most microphones of the day.

We also took jug band superstars Tight Like That, led by bouncing good-time blues guy Dave Peabody, over to Rockfield to record their one LP – possibly the only time that iconic rock studio ever housed a jug band. Peabody would later record his first solo LP *Peabody Hotel* for the label in its final years.

By 1972 my gigs were increasingly in colleges and rock venues, where I supported bands like Fotheringay and was even supported by the Average White Band one bizarre night in Manchester. Our agency regularly put little double bills – Dave Evans and myself, for example – and Village Thing 'packages' out on tour. Work in mainland Europe continued to increase, with lengthy tours of Belgium – where we'd regularly begun to stay with Roland Van Campenhout and his partner, Catherine Mattelaer, in Gent – and across Germany. Catherine was (still is) one of Belgium's top models and had our undying respect for the way she could stay out drinking and eating with us until 3am and then re-appear looking utterly beautiful (if a trifle grumpy) at 8am to go off for something like a *Vogue* shoot in Paris.

By 1973 my great friend and early musical partner Al Jones had also been through a thoroughly disillusioning experience with the music biz. His Sandy Roberton produced debut on Parlophone had barely registered, and then another one for Bill Leader's Trailer label remained uncompleted. He'd retired semi-hurt to Cornwall but I prised him back out to record *Jonesville*. Sessions in the Quaker meeting house involved a drummer encased in a box made of mattresses! Al really was an original, both in his oddball lyrics and crafty chord structures and his album, along with Derroll's and the first Dave Evans remain the three Village Thing releases I'm proudest of having recorded.

Probably the most sought-after Village Thing album of all by collectors came from New Zealand singer/ guitarist Chris Thompson. He'd spent time in Ireland where he'd recorded some initial tracks; rumour and radio tapes from Belgium (again) had reached us and I eventually bumped into him in a London club where he was visiting with Wizz. We got him to Frenchay with tabla player Keshav Sathe and among the tracks we recorded to complete his album was the extraordinary flight of *Her Hair Was Long*.

Chris's eponymous album later got into the silly money stakes for collectors, but that's partly because sales were so low. This wasn't through any musical faults of his own, though, but entirely because faltering distributors Transatlantic eventually had to find a creative way of disposing of massive over-pressings of Pentangle's post-*Basket Of Light* albums. Thus their vans curiously acquired a habit of being stolen and the contents – which naturally were bound to include a certain amount of other Transatlantic-distributed stock as well, to be convincing to the insurance company – were lost or destroyed (by fire, or dumping into a canal...). Many low-selling albums end up among the stock of cheap deletions out there depressing the market, but not Chris Thompson's or his label-mates Lackey & Sweeney.

We probably met the latter, a couple of rambling Americans, at that Derroll Adams gig at the Shakespeare's Head. Billy Lackey & Kathy Sweeney were from Tucson, Arizona and doing that classic 1970s thing of seeing Europe while living in a Volkswagen Microbus full of instruments. Their *Junk Store Songs For Sale* became one of the last in the Village Thing catalogue and, as with Chris Thompson's and for the same reasons, it never got the circulation it deserved.

Meanwhile, the closure of the Bristol Troubadour had a devastating effect on the local folk scene's sense of community. Other clubs opened but the social side suffered. Maggie Holland and I decided to move to Farnham in Surrey. It was close to her family as she'd grown up in the area, it was somewhere I knew well from regular gigging, and it was within striking distance of London for keeping an eye on Village Thing Records business while it lasted, which, as it turned out, wasn't to be much longer. In the end I pulled the plug as I was tired of getting the blame from artists for Transatlantic's failings beyond my control.

The Troubadour's last manager Tim Hodgson, who had been an invaluable supporter of Village Thing as well as the club, had to do a quick runner to Cornwall to avoid the plod as he'd previously allowed his name to be put as figurehead licensee on another of Peter Bush's rather suspect clubs which had then been raided and closed down. He got a job as the cook on a fishing boat out of Newlyn, eventually getting his 'first mate' qualification and some years later was to be found ferrying interesting people and cargoes on a yacht around the Caribbean. He lost a leg in a motorcycle accident in Cuba, and ended up running a casino in Costa Rica with a local wife and daughter before passing away. That's what getting involved with the Bristol Troubadour could do for you.

Plastic Dog took over running the Village Thing Agency. I had another of my lightbulb realisations, losing interest in being a sci-fi singer/songwriter and wanting to return to playing roots music. Something called Hot Vultures would emerge from the wreckage…

8.
The 1970s : The Gigging Decade

A couple of months before we left Bristol my paternal grandmother in Weston-super-Mare had died, so we went down for the low-key funeral. By this time my cousin Sean Mayes was in what would become rock'n'roll revival band Fumble and had flown back specially from Switzerland where they had a club residency. It was nice to catch up with him and the other surviving members of that side of the family, though his brother Ricky was nowhere to be seen: we were told that he'd gone off travelling with friends some weeks before and couldn't be contacted. As it turned out, this far-from-unusual family event would come back to haunt in the future.

In June 1972 we enlisted the services of a Bristol prog-rock band's Transit van and three trips later were in a first and second floor maisonette in East Street, Farnham, Surrey, which was to be my rented home for the next sixteen years. Both already familiar with the area, it took no time at all before we gained a really good and mutually supportive social circle. Prominent among them at the outset were Keith Calton (then beginning the R&D on his famous Calton instrument cases) and his girlfriend Caroline, later to be a *Folk Roots* co-founder and long-time staff member – plus lots of local musicians, journalists and general scene-makers.

In the months immediately after we moved to Farnham I did the first of a number of Cambridge Folk Festivals that I'd be billed on, we commuted to-and-fro to Bristol and Monmouth to record Derroll Adams' Village Thing LP, my *Singer Sleeps On As Blaze Rages* album and Al Jones' *Jonesville*, and we soon became well-embedded with the local folk scene. Indeed, not long after our move we'd gone over to Farnborough Folk Club to let them know we were now local, and to check out their guests, a band called Oak – Rod & Danny Stradling, Peta Webb and Tony Engle.

They were one of the first outfits on the folk club scene to adopt a repertoire of specifically English traditional tunes and songs, which they did with robust attack. It was the first time I'd ever heard people playing music sourced from those traditional players like Scan Tester, Walter Bulwer and Oscar Woods and found it revelatory and exhilarating. Of course I wasn't to know that eight years later that man Stradling would become a willing conspirator in a band...

There were occasional diversions, as when Gef Lucena of Saydisc heard I was going to Cornwall for some gigs. He asked me to take a Village Thing tape machine and some mics and go and record the instruments in the West Cornwall Museum Of Mechanical Music at Goldsithney. Everything from disc-driven music boxes to early electrified café organs via player pianos – with mandolin, violin or xylophone attachments – driven by perforated discs, planks of wood with nails in or rolls of punched paper. So I spent two days listening to where the sound came out of these contraptions, placing a stereo pair of good mics and adjusting recording levels accordingly. More common sense than skill. I was astonished when one of the resulting LPs won an award from the mechanical music press (who knew there was such a thing?) as the best such record of the year. One wonders what the worse ones were like…

For the next year, when not dealing with the death throes of Village Thing Records, I continued on the road as the solo performer I'd been since 1970. Maggie had long-since dropped out of University and taken on the role of my driver – I didn't take my driving test until the early '80s – while we did ridiculous amounts of travelling, not just around Britain but increasingly long and gruelling tours in Belgium and Germany. It can't have been much fun having to listen to me night after night while we fought with keeping old vehicles in working order – a rusty little blue Ford van and then a Vauxhall estate – and the wolves from the door. Maggie's diaries from that time paint a grim picture of our financial state.

My 'career' was often complicated by having a certain namesake, or several even! On one occasion I rolled into Bolton for a gig at the Octagon that had both a music venue and an art gallery, to find a large poster saying "Today: folk/blues from Ian Anderson. In the gallery, exhibition of sculptures by Ian Anderson." People attending clearly assumed I was multi-talented, so I had explaining to do! And as well as the mono-legged flute botherer, there were others. Luckily I don't think anybody confused me with the footballer or, far worse, one of the National Front leaders, but people who can't spell did occasionally think I had a radio programme in Scotland…

With the polarisation of English folk clubs into 'trad' or 'entertainers' with little middle ground, a higher percentage of my bookings in the UK at this time were in colleges. These were generally well – and reliably – paid but you never really knew what they'd turn out to be like. Often they could be an actual folk club with an intelligent, interested audience, though the differences in reactions to stage repartee from students in a domestic science teacher training college in the West Midlands to those in a Cambridge college were quite noticeable… But you might otherwise find yourself being ignored like a juke box in the corner of a rowdy students' union bar, or opening for a rock band on a Saturday night gig, which could go either way. And the organisers changed from year to year, so an efficiently run event one academic year might be a nightmare shambles the next. And vice versa. From that point of view, life was never dull.

In Europe, gigs tended to be in music bars or 'youth houses', with longer playing sets and generally much better pay than English folk clubs. They were often fun and energetic, though also tended to be extremely smoky, so much so that on one gig in a Belgian bar with a high stage and no ventilation I came very close to blacking out. Like anywhere, they were unpredictable, particularly in Germany where they might either be wildly enthusiastic or occasionally ignore you completely, with very little middle ground.

The German touring experience reached an early low when, after struggling in our sick Vauxhall estate through rain and fog along the appallingly pot-holed 'corridor' from West Germany to Berlin, Maggie got us to the Steve Club to find a sign on the door saying words to the effect that "We are sorry, the Ian Anderson appearing tonight is not the Ian Anderson of Jethro Tull as advertised." It was a scam. The promoter had known this all along, but also knew that once people had made the effort to come out on a winter evening in partitioned Berlin, they'd stay out. To say that the audience that evening – the first of a 3-night residency – were initially hostile would be accurate. But, miraculously, quite a lot warmed to me, I sold loads of LPs, and some of the people who came on the first night returned with friends on the third. It became a win of sorts.

And then poor Maggie had to coax the expiring car the 500+ miles all the way to Brussels the following day, including along stretches of autobahn that had *minimum* speed limits. One of our closest near-death experiences was when a truck pulled out in our path going up a hill, Maggie's emergency deceleration causing the engine to stall and refuse to re-start. There we were stopped in the second lane with a wall of trucks hurtling towards us up the hill with their headlights full on. Miraculously, a motorway patrol van appeared from nowhere with its hazard light. The men on board jumped out and helped push us onto the shoulder. I still get nightmares about that…

It all got very wearing. Travelling could be tiring and stressful, playing conditions wildly variable (especially the sound), you never knew what accommodation you were going to get, if any, and the relatively small fees of a solo artist just weren't enough for a couple to live on, pay the rent, eat and clothe ourselves. When it was good, which was quite often, the lifestyle was wonderful – after all, we were young and reasonably healthy – and it certainly beat working for 'the man.' But the appeal got dented by things like nursing a misfiring van with broken windscreen wipers through yet another long overnight drive home, all the while I'd try to stay awake to keep Maggie alert at the wheel with sparkling conversation, because the club organiser's idea of 'accommodation' had been a dirty sleeping bag on his living room floor.

In the spring of 1973, we hatched a plan to become an actual duo and eventually bury my confusing name. Maggie already played guitar well and, partly inspired by the remarkable pairing of Michael Chapman and bassist Rick Kemp who made far more music than seemed possible for two people, she thought that taking up bass guitar would suit her. And after that, the higher fees that a duo could command would be going into one household. It wasn't accident or fashion that dictated the number of married duos like John & Sue Kirkpatrick, Pete & Chris Coe, Dave & Toni Arthur, Richard & Linda Thompson and more who were common on the 1970s folk club scene. Of course, while Maggie became pretty much unique as a woman bass guitarist around the clubs back then, it's not at all unusual now.

I had a big tour of Germany coming up and reckoned that the fees and LP merchandising proceeds from it, with a bit of help from the bank, should just about cover getting a bass and amplifier, a small PA system and a better vehicle. But the hound of fate struck again, just as it had done with my Island Records deal and Village Thing. The big German tour in the diary from an agent for May 1973 suddenly vanished, a mirage. Another lesson that if you want something done properly, you do it yourself. From then on I would do most of the booking and contracting myself, direct with the venues, for European tours if possible. But here was a big income-free hole in our diary and seemingly the dashing of our duo dream. I did something that I'd never wanted to do since leaving home eight years earlier and asked my parents for help.

My grandmother had left the proceeds of her estate solely to my father, with the express wish that any remaining should eventually come to me on his passing (it was her less-than-subtle way of saying she didn't want it going to my mother!) He'd pretty soon realised that he didn't like the responsibility of being the landlord of her flats, so he'd recently sold them. My mother, bless her, pointed out to him that since I was supposed to get some of it eventually, it wouldn't be a bad thing to help us out with what we needed at that point, especially as it would be a good investment for our future. Thanks to her intervention, since he always seemed resentful that I'd managed to carve out a life from something I enjoyed doing whereas he had one of commuting to an office job when he'd rather have been sailing or woodworking, he agreed.

That summer of 1973 we bought Maggie's first bass, replaced fairly quickly by a proper early '60s Fender Precision. I replaced my touring-worn Yamaha acoustic guitar with a new Guild F40, and we bought a decent small HH PA system and mics. We also found a second-hand left-hand-drive VW Microbus which I set about converting for our needs. I installed a double bunk in the back which meant that not only did we always have somewhere comfortable to sleep if needed, it also concealed all the equipment, instruments and merchandise that could be stashed away underneath.

We rehearsed up a fair bit of new repertoire, my own songs from the previous albums slowly being replaced by our own versions of old or traditional folk and blues material, often from the 1920s and '30s (old-time duos and pre-blues songsters a speciality) or songs by friends like Derroll Adams, Tucker Zimmerman and Al Jones. It had taken me nearly a decade at that point, but by then I think my playing and singing had evolved to sound like me rather than any residual influences, so 'covers' were definitely not copies.

When I'd first started out as a teenage wannabe Mississippi bluesperson, I unthinkingly sang in a fake American accent. Probably no stranger than what anybody else did and still does and most people think is normal but one day I heard one of my records and thought "Why do I do that?" Martin Carthy once told me how he'd also had a shock revelation when hearing back one of his '70s studio takes and realising he'd become a prisoner of unintelligible folkie singing mannerisms, so had to work really hard to rid himself of them. I spent the early '70s deliberately trying to sing the way I spoke – the way that Nic Jones, Shirley Collins or Davy Graham's singing voices were the same as their speaking voices, with no artifice – until it seemed to become natural and I didn't have to think about it any more.

Not everybody approved. "Why do you sing blues in a posh accent?" enquired a singer in a North Eastern folk club who had just sung in a straight imitation of a Texan one. "That's not posh, it's the local accent where I come from. Why don't you sing in yours?" Needless to say, the idea of a Lightnin' Hopkins song sung in a Geordie one was greeted with derision.

Meanwhile Maggie's emerging bass style was pretty unique from the outset, being more akin to the kind of melodic lines that a flat pick guitarist in an old-timey band might play than the four-square thump of a folk rock bassist. We just did songs that we liked and they all came out sounding like us. We never theorised about it, but I felt that this wasn't unlike what many traditional musicians had always done – sometimes to the irritation of folk song collectors.

We did our first live trial runs in late August when we and Al Jones booked a couple of village halls local to where Al and his wife Lesley were living in Padstow, Cornwall, and promoted our own shows to summer tourists. With the confidence from those, Hot Vultures were then off and running and everything from the end of the following month was turned into a duo gig. Though I say so myself, we'd got pretty good quite quickly.

The PA made such a difference, giving consistent sound wherever we went, even though it was a pain hauling it all up pub staircases. We learned to indulge in subterfuge, getting to folk club rooms really early, well ahead of the organisers, so that by the time they turned up we'd got everything tidy, covers and cases away, leads neatly gaffa-taped down, speakers up on their stands, less distracting. We still regularly encountered reluctance as PAs were unusual and often frowned on in folk clubs back then, but we were using it for clarity of sound and balance rather than excess volume, and to allow us to play and sing at a natural level in bigger rooms rather than have to shout and thrash.

More often than not at the end of the night the organiser would say something about how they'd expected it to be horribly loud but it just made everything better. Since we'd always offer the use of it to the residents and floor singers, they were generally well pleased too (though that meant that I had to sit and mix the sound for them). Later on we started to carry some small spotlights as well, since folk club rooms often had to have either all the lights on or all off, and club organisers were often astonished how it made the atmosphere better by focussing attention on the music. In these small ways we did our bit to help haul folk clubs' presentation into the real world...

The autumn of 1973 into early 1974 was a steep duo learning curve, during which we did what turned out to be a Village Thing swansong tour, a fun triple-header of us with Al Jones and American duo Lackey & Sweeney. I also did my last two Village Thing production stints, on Wizz Jones' second VT album *When I Leave Berlin* (which featured his new band

Lazy Farmer and a guest appearance by Bert Jansch) and finally on Noel Murphy's *Murf*. All had associations with the early days of Les Cousins and later the Bristol Troubadour, both now closed. It felt like the end of a lot of eras when I sent Gef Lucena my resignation letter from the label.

That winter saw the Heath government's 3-day week, rolling power cuts, petrol rationing, a national 50mph speed limit and TV transmissions halting at 10.30pm. This was all in the name of conserving energy during a miners' strike and the Arab countries' oil embargo following the Yom Kippur war between Israel and Egypt. There were shortages in the shops (why is it always loo rolls first?), the IRA had begun following the earlier lead of the Angry Brigade by letting off bombs in London, and 'comet of the century' Kohoutek flew close by. There was a 'vinyl crisis' too. It wasn't exactly the end of days, but it was a depressing time. Gigs dried up, of course, so we just hunkered down among our excellent social circle and sat it out as best we could. By February, Heath had been ousted in a snap election by the return of Harold Wilson as PM.

On Friday nights when we weren't out gigging we'd take a car load over to the nearby village of Crondall where a folk club had started up, though it was tempting to stay in the warmth of the pub's bar. "Feel my biceps," said our charmingly eccentric friend Damien, an officer in the Army Education Corps, to one of the assembled young women in our circle. "Crikey"… and then a little head and forked tongue appeared from his jacket sleeve. We all held out hands as a python emerged and gently slithered around from person to person before disappearing into the coat of our friend Caroline. Damien gently removed it, restoring his pet to its original warm place. Later, he went into the folk club to do a floor spot, for which we all trooped in. One could feel rather smug knowing what the rest of the audience don't, that the artist performing has a python inside his shirt…

Having missed out on cross-channel touring in 1973, the first year that entering and leaving had got easier after Britain joined the EEC, we got out of the wreckage of the UK quite often in 1974 with two German tours and one each in Belgium and Holland. This pretty much set the pattern for the next five years, helped by a network of friends to stay with in the gaps and on days off. Homely hospitable housing was often provided by Roland and Catherine around Gent, Tucker Zimmerman and his wife Marie-Claire in their forest cottage over towards Germany near Liege (where Tucker would ply us with demo tapes of wonderful songs, which is why we ended up doing so many), and Bristol photographer Jo Gedrych and his wife (also Jo) who had moved to Venlo in the Netherlands. This was all much better than our early experience of the Zeemans Huis (seamen's hostel) in Antwerp which had introduced me to my first encounter with marauding armies of cockroaches...

We did our bit for homely house providing back in the UK too, of course. Musicians always helped each other out, and if we were around when somebody was touring in our area, they'd often prefer to base themselves with us. Much fun would be had in scurrilous late-night post-gig unwinding conversations.

In one lengthy Euro-touring spell that stretched from November 1975 to February '76 we didn't even think it was worth returning to the UK for Christmas, so to avoid outstaying our welcome with friends we rented a small, cheap, unfurnished apartment on the edge of Antwerp, moved the bedding, camping gas cooker and utensils from the VW bus indoors and happily camped there for the break while we greatly enjoyed Belgian hospitality, food, beer and general craziness. Belgium was always our favourite touring place: we must have played every youth house and music bar in Flanders over those years.

We had more of a suspicious relationship with touring in Germany. For sure the good gigs well outnumbered the dodgy ones and generally audiences and promoters were very friendly, hospitable and enthusiastic. But you just never knew if you were going to hit a rowdy youth house in Duisburg where a drunken thug would lurch onto the stage and try to grab Maggie's bass, or the entire 'audience' would completely ignore us when we were introduced to play in Kiel ("I-on Anderzon mit frau!") to the extent that we stopped mid-song, took their photograph with flash, and resumed again without them apparently noticing. Or the fans of Irish music – it was big in Germany at the time – who shouted at us because we were English and look what we (personally?) were doing in Ireland with the H-Blocks so we couldn't criticise Germany for concentration camps any more, could we? Don't mention the war!

Even in the company of friends you might come undone. Somewhere on the road in Germany we had a night free between dates in the south and north, so we stopped off in Göttingen, booked into a hotel, and then rang up a wonderful German promoter friend who lived there, to see if we could take him out to dinner as a 'thank you' for past help. Turned out he was promoting a concert in the University that night by Britfolk's self-appointed royalty, Ewan MacColl & Peggy Seeger. Would we like to join him and them for dinner and then see their gig? Ah, er, well – we could hardly say that wasn't the convivial way we'd looked forward to spending our one night off, so we had to accept.

We'd never met MacColl & Seeger before, and they made it abundantly clear to our friend that they'd never heard of us, asking where we normally played with sniffy, barbed remarks like "Oh, so don't you do Arts Council tours?" And "Ah yes, Bert Jansch, I think my children have some of his records." The great socialist ordered the most expensive dish on the menu (piquant duck, as I recall), barely toyed with it, never offered to share, and then proposed that we split the bill equally. We were, to heavily understate, not impressed.

The concert was mild torture. In an overheated lecture theatre with all the lights on (which of course meant that we couldn't sneak out), MacColl pompously pontificated, posed and bigged himself up while sat on his characteristic backwards chair with hand cupped to ear. They made a point of marketing their magazine, *New City Songster*, which they announced contained the best songs being sung around all the British folk clubs by the best songwriters. When we leafed through a copy on the merch table, we'd barely heard of any of the writers or their works: it was apparently just their cronies and acolytes. We were very glad to escape back to our hotel and use all its facilities to wash away road grime and weariness. As it turned out, I never met either of them again. It's quite possible this was deliberate on my behalf...

Back in the UK that spring we'd begun to work up a Hot Vultures circuit of friendly clubs who'd book us regularly over the coming years, no more so than the Saturday night one held in the upstairs room of the Rising Sun in Tottenham Court Road, London. Run by a lovely black poet called Raggy Farmer, the rest of the evening would be taken up by an unpredictable array of floor spots.

Quite often in the '74/'75 era these drop-ins would include amazing fiddle-singer Tymon Dogg, after his brief period of attempting not to become a pop star and before his solo career, sitting in with the Clash and much later membership of Joe Strummer's Mescaleros. At this time he was a busker in Tottenham Court Road tube station, and living in a squat. Years later he pointed out to me that the bloke he used to regularly bring to our Rising Sun gigs was the young Strummer, pre-Clash and 101ers, who was 'bottling' for him (collecting the money) while busking, and learning guitar.

I'd actually first met Tymon when running the Cambridge Folk Festival club tent a few years earlier. He'd signed up for a spot. "Who are you?" "Me." "Er, but what name would you like to be introduced by?" "Me." Difficult one to pull off as MC! There was another occasion when we were doing a gig at Redcar Folk Club in the North East and he showed up, so we blagged him a spot just before ours. He attacked his violin and the stage with such ferocity, probably showcasing one of his high energy masterpieces like *Locks & Bolts & Hinges*, that the entire audience rapidly shuffled back a metre or so! But I digress…

We also started getting regular bookings in Southend at a club run by a fine blues singer called Mickey Jupp who would sometimes sit in with us. We weren't aware of his status, or his cult earlier band Legend, until later when he got signed by Stiff Records. There was an amusing incident when Hot Vultures were appearing at Loughborough University folk club and the *Be Stiff* package tour was on in the main hall. We'd just started our first set when the door opened and Mickey led a crocodile of the Stiff Records stars in – Wreckless Eric, Jona Lewie, Lene Lovich, Ian Dury and himself – to stand and watch us for 10 minutes before going off to their own show. The folk club were astonished.

In retrospect, Hot Vultures clearly had appeal outside folk gigs, but we never realised this or knew how to explore it. Possibly we were happy enough in the folk world anyway. We were always on good terms with the *Melody Maker*'s folk writers of our era – Andrew Means who had married American singer Sara Grey and eventually emigrated, and his replacement Colin Irwin from 1974 onwards. Colin remained a great friend, eventually writing for *fRoots* through most of its existence. But they could only put us on the folk page.

There was a memorable pair of micro-brushes with the rock world one day in the spring of 1974 when we'd been back at Apple sitting in on the mastering of one of the final Village Thing albums. George Peckham showed us into a gloomy side room where there was a dusty, neglected pile of instruments and equipment, including old Vox amps and a black Rickenbacker electric guitar with rusty strings. I picked it up and had a twang, though it was close to unplayable. Hang on, could this be? Yup, the gear the fab moptops had used on their last gig at Shea Stadium, complete with a fading handwritten set list and packet of pills taped to the back of an amp, dumped and not touched since. Sometimes I wish I could have been brazenly light-fingered! Sadly, no John Lennon mojo dust transferred itself to my fingers.

Later that same day we had a Hot Vultures gig at the White Bear in Hounslow, a venue which had housed everything from the folk club run by the Strawberry Hill Boys, when they were a bluegrass band before evolving into the Strawbs, to the Hounslow Arts Lab when such things were fashionable. (David Bowie ran another one in Beckenham which I'd been booked at in 1969). We were in the habit of opening our set with a version of Jimmy Reed's *Baby What's Wrong?* which I always credited as being inspired by London R&B band The Downliners Sect's frenetic version from a decade earlier. In the interval, the gig organiser, Mick O'Donnell, revealed himself to be none other than the deerstalker-wearing Downliners leader, who'd used the stage name Don Craine. Awe!

Also in 1974 we did a couple of support spots to American blues veterans Sonny Terry & Brownie McGhee at the 100 Club, courtesy of my old flatmate, promoter Ron Watts. Both gigs were well received and Brownie took quite a shine to Maggie (not reciprocated!). On the second one, my cousin Sean came and invited us along to the Dorchester Hotel where his band Fumble were to be the late evening hooligan element on some society ball.

Ushered down from the suite that served as the band's dressing room, via the kitchens, we stood by the stage and watched as the spectacle unfolded. Chinless wonder Guards officers cavorted with drunken debs, with much tipping of ice cubes down cleavages. ("Good grief," said our friend Damien who'd come with us, "I have to teach English to some of these chaps – they're as thick as two short planks!"). One inebriated specimen stood up in front of Des, Fumble's singer, and demanded "I say, bandleader chappie, can you do *Wock Awound The Clock?*" Another drunken old geezer kept complaining it was too loud and made a lurch for the mixing desk, only to be picked up by the lapels by Fumble's impressively muscular roadie and dumped unceremoniously back onto the dance floor. He was later seen crawling across the stage to try grabbing the drummer's cymbals: his knuckles suffering contact from a firmly struck drumstick. How the other half lives, eh?

After eighteen months on the roads as a duo and three years since my last solo LP, we really needed to release an album – people were constantly asking, and by now merchandising was becoming a vital part of any artist's gig income. We didn't want to sign to a major record label after my early experiences, so decided to produce our own masters and see if we could licence them, retaining ownership. For our debut, we booked into London's Riverside Studios in April 1975 and recorded with engineer Barbara Blyth.

Because it was so normal for people to jump up and join us on gigs, we enlisted some of those reliable friends for the sessions. Al Jones was on extra guitar, of course. Dave Griffiths on fiddle and mandolin and Dave Peabody on harmonica came from Tight Like That who'd recorded for Village Thing. On washboard was John Pilgrim, once of 1950s skiffle hitmakers The Vipers, who always rocked up with his washboard when we played in the North West around Manchester and helped bring evenings to a fine and rowdy climax.

I still have a fine sheaf of rejection letters from bigger labels of the day like WEA, UA, Virgin, CBS, Polydor, Phonogram, A&M, Rocket, Anchor and more, but their inability to understand what we were all about just increased my belief that we were doing something right. Within two years, punk and its myriad indie labels would begin to burst their bubbles anyway. But as luck would have it, we were approached by EMI Belgium who already had our pal Roland Van Campenhout and a subsequent Derroll Adams album which we'd participated in, so we licensed the LP, *Carrion On*, to them. It came out there in 1975 and, many hundreds of Belgian copies imported to the UK later, we put it locally with our UK agents' small label Red Rag the following year where it thrived once more.

And so the 1970s years rolled on, usually averaging well over 120 gigs a year, wearing out two engines on the trusty VW and going though many hundreds of sets of strings: sweaty venues usually meant changing them on several guitars after every gig.

Somewhere in there, Maggie discovered her real voice. At the beginning it had been quiet, high and breathy, but a combination of Martin Carthy poking her in the diaphragm and instructing "Sing from there," and singer Frankie Armstrong's explanation about what she called the "Hey!" voice (imagine you're shouting "Hey" at somebody across the street: where you produce that voice from is where to sing from) had enabled her to get a much more powerful singing style. Even better, she could do the break between her old voice and her new one, which meant she could blue yodel, like Jimmie Rodgers.

This emerged not long before we recorded our second album, 1977's *The East Street Shakes*, so Rodgers' *Hobo Bill's Last Ride* on there was a pointer, a clue to the future. We recorded this one at Riverside again, this time with John Gill as engineer. It began our association with a young whizz-kid guitar and banjo player we'd fallen in with called Martin Simpson, who had recently burst onto the scene with his debut LP *Golden Vanity* for Bill

Leader. We also called in Reading duo Simon Mayor on mandolin & fiddle and Hilary Jones on harmony vocals – later forced to change her professional surname to James because of Equity union rules which don't allow two members with the same name.

There was always some weirdness about though. One time in 1976 we arrived back from another of our lengthy Euro-tours to find that Britain was rife with flu and, having contracted it, our old friend Fred Wedlock had been forced to cancel a gig not that far from where we lived. We were asked to step in. During the evening (I worked this out later) in two separate song intros, I'd a) joked that we'd brought back the flu epidemic in order to clean up on other people's gigs and b) that the Holy Modal Rounders song *Low Down Dog* that we were doing at the time was an advert for a secret organisation called Canine Lib. In both cases, the clearly undiscerning audience laughed heartily.

A few days later there was a ring on the doorbell from a man with a briefcase from (something like – can't precisely remember now) the Ministry Of Agriculture's Animal Diseases Inspectorate. Somebody in that folk club audience had reported us to the authorities as saying we were part of a shady organisation dedicated to smuggling diseased dogs in from Europe. To give him his due, the man from the ministry (having previously questioned our elderly downstairs neighbours and been assured we'd never had any pets) did agree that you couldn't make this story up. Except some humourless twerp actually did. Briefcase man went off with a report that the only creature he could spot in our flat was a large soft toy vulture – depicted among the artefacts on the cover of *The East Street Shakes* – that my mother had made.

Slowly but surely the more traditionally inclined UK folk clubs and festivals began to discover us and recognise kindred spirits. Maggie's Jimmie Rodgers songs never failed to charm older traditional singers like Willie Scott or Walter Pardon, since it was often the music of their youth. And she soon took up old-time frailed banjo, when it wasn't so popular on the UK folk scene as it has become since the millennium. I was more than happy to do less of the singing and take pleasure in slide guitar accompaniments to older songs. By 1979 our diaries show us doing the folk club at Cecil Sharp House, home of the English Folk Dance & Song Society, and the Copper Family's club in Peacehaven, Sussex, on consecutive nights. Where we discovered that Bob Copper was a closet blues fan. "Do you do any Son House?" he asked. "Well yes!"

That relentless, over-fast jigs'n'reels thing that the 'Celtic' bands did had never particularly appealed to me, other than in the more subtle hands of people like Ireland's Planxty. But when English roots music came into the ascendant through the 1970s via bands like Oak, the Old Swan Band and New Victory Band – more on that next chapter – I'd got thoroughly engaged. It wasn't just records and live music either: magazines like *Traditional Music* were publishing things like Keith Summers' epic *Sing, Say Or Pay* double issue full of inspiring research into what was now commonly being called 'English country music' ('country' as in rural, not 'and western'!) in Suffolk.

And so it was that when we came to recording our third and final Hot Vultures LP, *Up The Line*, in 1979, we enlisted the NVB's Pete and Chris Coe on melodeon and hammered dulcimer. We wanted to give a specifically English flavour to what we were doing. We'd also been doing trio gigs around then with Martin Simpson as the Scrub Jay Orchestra, so he was naturally involved again too. Our first gig under that brand name at Staines Folk Club was a riot: there's an absurd photo of the finale where June Tabor, Dave Peabody and Dave Evans joined in on a version of *Got My Mojo Working*: what the photo doesn't show was that Labour Party leader Neil Kinnock and TUC general secretary Norman Willis were in the audience joining in the chorus.

Also involved again on *Up The Line* was engineer John Gill, except this time we went up to Bill Leader's studio near Halifax where John was now resident. My cousin Sean Mayes lent us the money to make it from his David Bowie world tour fees, soon repaid. It was in this very studio that John would engineer Leeds post-punk band The Mekons, turning them on to the legendary *English Country Music* LP of field recordings of old traditional players from East Anglia, re-issued around then by Topic Records. John would eventually join the Mekons himself, as well as being one of their members who later moonlighted in Edward II & The Red Hot Polkas. Little did I know how many connections there'd be with those Mekes down the years.

To our amazement, after years of having been looked at a little in askance by the UK folk scene's establishment, *Up The Line* got lots of enthusiastic reviews, including being made Album Of The Month by veteran folk/rock journalist Karl Dallas in his *Folk News* magazine. Even more astonishingly it was picked up by an American label for US release in 1980, something that rarely happened with English folk records in those days.

Just at the right time we were very grateful and privileged that Al Stewart, now ensconced in Los Angeles following his platinum-selling success with *Year Of The Cat* but missing his old UK folk scene friends, generously sent us tickets to go over and stay for a couple of weeks, which allowed us to do some radio promo while we were there.

It was fun doing rock-starry things with Al, ushered through the velvet rope at the Whisky a Go Go to catch an XTC gig ("Anybody heard of Swindon?" shouted frontman Andy Partridge, to be somewhat startled by the yelps of agreement from the VIP area). But the most unforgettable night was when we guested on Roz & Howard Larman's famous *Folk Scene* show on KPFK Santa Monica. The helpful local McCabe's guitar shop loaned us instruments.

The format of their programme was that for the first hour you'd play live, interviewed perceptively by Howard, and then for the second hour play records and talk with people who 'phoned in. In the first part we'd done our version of *The Lakes Of Pontchartrain*. In the second, a man called in from somewhere called Barstow to tell us that he'd really enjoyed it, saying that he'd once seen Hank Williams sing that song live. It suddenly dawned on me that Barstow was a town namechecked in the iconic song *Route 66*. Here was somebody who lived on that famed road, who'd seen Hank Williams, ringing in to a Californian radio station to tell us they liked us and our strange English twist on American music. (One US review of *Up The Line* had gone so far as to suggest that my accent might be caused by a speech impediment!)

I thought I'd died and gone to heaven, confirmed later that evening when, having linked up with our old friends Lackey & Sweeney who were now living in the Valley, I sat on the steps of Billy Lackey's Airstream trailer (just like the one on the cover of Ry Cooder's first LP) and heard my first freight train whistle in the balmy night air. I have to say that all subsequent visits to the USA were culturally hard to match after that.

Back home our folk club demand had greatly increased as a result of *Up The Line*. But somewhere around the end of the 1970s Maggie had bought me one of the new-fangled pocket calculators for Christmas. For some anorak reason I sat and worked out the number of hours we'd spent unproductively in the previous year – driving along roads, killing time waiting to perform or between gigs when forced to stay away. It was shocking: it added up to a ridiculous number of days, and brought the realisation that one of the finite things we have in life is time. Meanwhile Maggie had started an Open University course and I'd co-founded a small regional folk magazine called *The Southern Rag*... more on that later too.

We both wanted less time on the road, so took a decision to limit gigs, other than festivals or major concerts, to a maximum of 100 miles from home. Maggie had also added a Guild acoustic bass guitar to our growing armoury of instruments – also expanded in late 1979 by my getting a wonderful pair of custom made acoustic guitars by luthier Nigel Thornbory, one for regular picking, one for slide – which have remained my main instruments ever since. We reverted to playing completely acoustic wherever possible, 'unplugged' as became the fashionable term a decade later, which was strangely liberating as well as time-saving. By then, many clubs had their own PAs if needed for the room.

And then there was an event at the 1980 Loughborough Folk Festival which set everything off in a new direction…

9.
English Banding In The 1980s

The 1980s were a decade during which I juggled wearing an unfeasibly large number of music-related hats as the folk and roots music scene in the UK blossomed into a diverse golden age. In order to make any sense out of those times I'd best house that headgear in separate chapter boxes and mess with chronology for a while. I'll get playing music out of the way first.

A quick backwards look to begin. UK folk scene history of the 1970s has mostly been re-written, by people who weren't there or only in a peripheral way. Of course it's reasonable that tales are constantly retold and uncovered about the high profile, well-selling and influential bands of the day like Fairport Convention, the Incredible String Band and Steeleye Span. But strange cult status has grown up around some other artists and bands who, partly through their back stories, later achieved much greater acclaim or cult followings than they ever did when they recorded. Few people were that bothered at the time about many of those whose old vinyl has sold at unfeasible prices in the 21st century and whose stories have got the column inches. Often they only have a reputation from back then because they'd been picked up by a major label who advertised their LPs in *Melody Maker* and *Sounds*, and more recent writers have fallen on them out of context.

Hot Vultures got plenty of coverage on the folk pages of the 1970s music press and had a decent number of sessions broadcast on BBC Radio 1 and Radio 2 throughout the decade. We did well over eight hundred gigs via which we sold a huge quantity of LPs. But in the subsequent historical record we may as well have not existed. Mind you, I probably shoulder a lot of the responsibility for this due to having been the publisher of the main folk magazine for the four decades since those days. A self-imposed reluctance to encourage writing about your own history comes with the territory, or ought to. So it goes…

If received history has overblown the relative significance of certain songwriters and folk/rock explorers, it has nothing on the cruel hand dealt to most of the exponents of traditional song and music of those days. For a while, most of the popular and innovative artists playing traditional music around the folk club circuit of the early '70s who didn't record for Topic were on Bill Leader's Trailer label, or other smaller independents. Bill's labels operated on pretty much the same shoestring and with similar basic equipment as we did with Village Thing, and with the same distributors. Beginning just before us in 1969, by 1973 his catalogue included wonderful albums by Nic Jones, Pete & Chris Coe, Tony Rose, Dave Burland, Bob & Carole Pegg, Dave & Toni Arthur, John Kirkpatrick, Alistair Anderson, Robin & Barry Dransfield (whose debut made *Melody Maker* folk album of the year and reputedly massive sales for a folk album), Lal & Mike Waterson's *Bright Phoebus* and many more.

Many of these artists have also been pretty much written out of history, hardly appearing in any literature, neglected by trend-defining journalists, their reputations only living on in the memories of older folkies and their musical offspring who grew up with their parents' record collections. This was the era when things had moved on from the stern so-called 'folk revival' of the Ewan MacColl days and to a great extent, along with the earlier recordings of Shirley Collins and Martin Carthy, set the stylistic foundations for younger folk performers into the 21st century – particularly Nic Jones.

This is not unconnected with the fact that in the late '70s Bill Leader sold his label, all the masters, to another company. Later still – with no reference to Bill – it was sold on again to an organisation called Celtic Music in Harrogate, run by the late Dave Bulmer. For reasons that seem totally inexplicable to everybody who has ever heard the story, the famously litigious Bulmer sat on his treasure hoard, declining to re-issue anything other than on badly packaged CDRs, or to license it to others who could do a much better job. Disappointingly, his heirs have continued this.

'Celtic music' itself was an all-conquering concept in the 1970s and '80s, especially on festivals and over in Europe and America. This was partly because many Scottish and Irish bands had worked out that the formula of playing everything clap-along fast and loud and creating a hard-drinking image was exciting to live audiences. Legend even had it that the after-hours behaviour of some of those bands had made it impossible for promoters to book hotels in certain German cities if they admitted that the guests were folk musicians! (Hot Vultures once experienced sharing accommodation in a Dutch youth hostel with the Tannahill Weavers: the warden is probably still suffering from PTSD, and their mid 1970s album title *Are Ye Sleeping Maggie?* seemed particularly apposite!). And then there was the worldwide phenomenon of the 'Irish Pub', not to mention the vast Irish diaspora itself.

More to the point, we English had been encouraged to ridicule our own folk traditions, whereas in Ireland and Scotland they remained much prouder of theirs. In Ireland in particular, their Comhaltas organisation was and remains in receipt of a high level of government funding to support Irish culture worldwide, whilst Arts Council England only really began any serious funding of the EFDSS after the millennium.

I remember somebody (possibly Bill Leader) saying that unlike in America where mobile recording units went to the regions in the 1920s to record local artists in order to sell not only records but the gramophones on which to play them, this didn't happen in England. They sent units to Scotland and Ireland but just assumed there was no English regional music to record or that the public wouldn't have been interested in buying it. Wrong in the first case, probably right in the latter.

England had of course lost many of its 'tradition bearers' during the two world wars, and the glossy, all-powerful American entertainment industry had obliterated everything in its path. And then celebrating English identity became linked to the extreme right and football hooliganism and you can see why people would distance themselves from it.

In a Facebook discussion about all of this in 2020, Steve Rowley probably hit the nail on the head. "In the first half of the 20th century there was a strong government emphasis on being British," he wrote. "Our arts institutions were focused on making us the best world player. In their eyes we should have the best orchestras, opera, ballet, etc. Arts education was developed to establish that. Music education was entirely built on creating excellence in classical playing. There was definitely a snobbery around any music that did not fit in to that paradigm."

"Scotland and Ireland, and to a certain extent Wales, had much smaller pots of funding for cultural development, and they partly used it to focus on national distinctiveness. They would not be able to compete with the huge classical resources, so they used it to promote their own voice. To not be subsumed in the British cosmopolitan culture."

"To that extent, Scotland became more Scottish in its cultural policy, Wales more Welsh and Ireland more Irish. In the meantime England was stuck with being British. There was no strategy for English culture apart from having great international orchestras that could play Beethoven or Mozart along with the best of them."

One could add that whilst Scotland in particular had its own radio and TV folk programmes to put a local focus on their culture, English listeners only got national "British" programmes.

Folk song continued to be explored by a small number of academics and enthusiasts, but with a few exceptions it wasn't really until the 1970s that English musicians started digging into and becoming proud of their instrumental folk traditions to any great extent, especially those played for dancing. They had a lot of catching up to do.

A very influential 1970s and '80s phenomenon that's invariably left out of folk scene histories, from books to BBC4 TV's much-repeated *Folk Britannia* series, was the flowering of the 'New Wave of English Country Music'. [If you'd like an in-depth study of that, hunt out the 2004 Topic CD *Stepping Up* which I compiled.] I mentioned early in the last chapter how I'd first encountered Oak, whose tunes played on melodeon, concertina, fiddles and percussion drove along like nothing I'd heard before. In 1972, Rod & Danny Stradling from Oak moved to Wiltshire and the quartet ceased. Rod & Danny set out to inspire young Cotswold musicians with their vast tape collection of tunes by traditional players and moulded them into The Old Swan Band.

In other parts of the country, the idea was catching on too and by the mid '70s, through sessions at festivals like Sidmouth and Loughborough, many others were being turned in the same direction. The Free Reed label debut albums by The Old Swan Band and London's Flowers & Frolics resulted in other bands springing up country-wide, often copying the repertoires from the Old Swan and Flowers albums in their entirety. The Albion Country Band, formed by folk rock refugees specifically to get involved in more English music, made an LP where they were joined by two traditional players, Dartmoor accordeonist Bob Cann and the South Coast-based hammered dulcimer player Jimmy Cooper.

Further north, one of Jimmy Cooper's dulcimer pupils, Chris Coe, her then husband Pete Coe, and three other couples evolved into The New Victory Band who determinedly hunted out a repertoire of tunes from Midland and Northern sources. Their first LP soon added to the repertoire pool. Also Midlands-based were Umps & Dumps, the outfit which included squeezebox maestro John Kirkpatrick (a regular member of Richard Thompson's bands of the day) and his wife, hammer dulcimer/oboe player Sue Harris.

Suddenly, ceilidhs or barn dances – nobody ever came up with a satisfactory new and more English name for them – became all the rage as dancers discovered how the lift given to the music by these melodeon-led bands was so much more exciting than that they'd been used to hearing from the strict-tempo EFDSS piano accordeon bands. To me, it did the same thing to my feet as the backbeat of early Chicago blues. Lightbulb!

In May 1979, shortly before recording *Up The Line* and trying out some of its songs, Hot Vultures appeared at Epping Folk Festival with Martin Simpson and Pete & Chris Coe. Also on the bill were the Old Swan Band who we'd already loved on record. We all checked each other out and mutual fan clubs emerged.

For a few years we'd regularly been going to Loughborough Folk Festival, the main event in the British traditional music calendar, just to enjoy the music. When it came to the 1980 one though, with tastes expanding and relaxing all round, director Roy Harris gave us a large free room on the Sunday to do whatever we'd like with. We consulted with others, put a sign on the door saying "An English country blues band?" and awaited the results.

And so it was that Hot Vultures led a packed session that included Rod & Danny Stradling, John Kirkpatrick & Sue Harris, Pete & Chris Coe, Nic Jones and others, through a raggedy jam on blues, old time traditional songs, early country and more. Everything from Frank Proffitt's *Going Across The Mountains* to the Drifters' *Save The Last Dance For Me* via Jimmy Reed and Jimmie Rodgers. A glorious if lo-fi cassette survives. It was the talking point of the festival. I think this festival was also the one where we encountered the Smith family of travellers, including son Derby who had written a song for the English gypsies in the mould of Jimmie Rodgers. *(Will There Be Any) Travellers In Heaven* soon became an English country blues staple.

Inevitably, not long afterwards, we said to Rod Stradling "Let's form a band". And so, in the coming months, The English Country Blues Band emerged, with Sue Harris on hammered dulcimer and oboe joining the core trio for bigger gigs. Hot Vultures soon went onto the back burner.

There was another 1979 reason for that. Twixt the decision to launch *The Southern Rag* magazine and the first issue arriving from the printer, there'd been a general election and a certain Margaret Thatcher's regime had come to power. One of their first actions was to massively increase the VAT rate, and its effect on artists' expenses, particularly petrol prices, meant that every folk club artist's costs were increased at a stroke by an average of £5 per gig. That may not seem much now, but back then a folk club fee for a duo was around £30 – £40 including expenses, and dates were already contracted up to a year ahead. Then she set about destroying the Student Unions by withdrawing grants, so the college circuit collapsed. Much career rethinking went on at that time. It wasn't as cataclysmic as Brexit or Covid in the far future, but it hurt.

Back in those folk clubs, many were initially bemused – what was 'arch traddie' Stradling doing with these noisy, bluesy reprobates? Luckily lots started booking us or coming along to find out. The answer was having a lot of fun and letting the musical elements – much more compatible than many imagined – find their own way. Why shouldn't *John Barleycorn* work to the tune of *Stagger Lee*? Why couldn't slide guitar be an effective underpinning for dance tunes? Why couldn't *The Nutting Girl* be powered along by old time banjo, slide guitar, hammered dulcimer and melodeon? The Old Swan Band's debut LP had been titled *No Reels*, so it was a no-brainer to call the English Country Blues Band's debut *No Rules* when we recorded it for Dingle's Records in autumn 1981, with most of those who'd taken part in that original Loughborough session guesting.

Predictably, the many reviews were divided. The (majority) positive ones tended to gush and shower it with superlatives, as if hailing new messiahs. The negative ones were savage – very savage – as if we had committed some crime against good taste. Folkies, eh?

It didn't harm the live demand and much pleasure ensued, with others often wanting to take part. In the tradition of the regular jammers we'd always had with Hot Vultures, I have great memories of Martin Carthy joining in one night at Farnham Maltings playing whichever out of Fender bass or 5-string banjo that Maggie Holland wasn't on at that particular moment, and of Peter Bellamy jumping up on a London gig to add some harmony vocals. And of much amusement being caused by Rod arriving at the first gig of a weekend tour-let to find that he only had his slippers, which he liked to drive in, as footwear. Did we mention this to the audience? Mercilessly! Rod adopted those slippers as gig uniform henceforth: eccentrics-r-us.

That particular time when Carthy sat in, he was staying with us for a few days between his own gigs, and it coincided with a brief period of anagram madness instigated by Lawrence Heath in *Southern Rag*. His *Borfolk* cartoon strip often had his inventive anagrams of artists' names – famously, Peter Bellamy had become Elmer P Bleaty, which Pete loved. The magazine held an anagram competition, which produced many gems (including The English Country Blues Band as The Rubbishy Song And Tune Cell!) and we and Martin sat up until the small hours with Scrabble letters spread out on the sitting room carpet. At some point I guffawed and pointed at what I'd made up from Ashley Hutchings. Maggie and Martin peered over and ended up rolling around in helpless mirth. Yah, Such Thin Legs! It stuck...

Less fun was our one gig for the long-established Herga Folk Club in Wealdstone. I'd been in hospital having all my wisdom teeth removed, but of course it would be OK to take a gig four days later, wouldn't it? I mean, I'd been to the dentist before... What I didn't realise was that the operation involved dislocating my jaw under full anaesthetic, and an overnight stay. When I awoke my face looked like a yellow hamster and my severely painful gums were stitched up. To say I was under par for the gig is an understatement. The front row of the audience were even less impressed than the rest since I burst my stitches singing and showered them with blood. Oddly enough, they never re-booked us. They hadn't expected the folk Alice Cooper...

By the end of 1981 there were hardly any Hot Vultures gigs in the diary – we'd almost completely morphed into the ECBB. Meanwhile, as I'd got more involved with magazine work and other activities – an agency and running ceilidhs, a festival from 1982: see later chapters – Maggie had begun doing increasingly successful solo gigs. And in our 'spare time' we'd got involved in local pub sessions where we really learned how to play English dance tunes in a scratch band called the Hollybush Hoboes.

My second label Rogue Records – more about that later too – started in January 1983 and apart from Maggie's debut solo album, one of the initial things we decided to do was have a crack at some singles. The first of these was by an augmented English Country Blues band, adding drummer John Maxwell from Milton Keynes ceilidh band Cock & Bull (via a short stint in the Albion Band), on the Tex-Mexy ballad – well, it became that in our hands – *Don't Take Love*, written by Des Henly of Fumble.

Then that August I had another of my occasional daft wheezes. All the English dance bands of the day were playing a version of what was considered the proper national anthem tune among English country dance music fans, *Speed The Plough*. I reckoned we should do a single of it, as close as possible to the magic three minutes of all the classic pop instrumental hits of the turn of the '60s. And to achieve this we should expand the band.

By now Sue Harris had needed to retire from ECBB commitments because of pregnancy, so Chris Coe had slipped back into the hammered dulcimer seat. As well as fully involving John Maxwell we brought in electric guitarist Jon Moore, from Oxford band Jumpleads who had recently become Marmite to folkniks because of their poppy, post-punk approach to folk rock. Jon and Rod Stradling cooked up a glorious, snappy, key-changeful version of *Speed The Plough* and the recording session was a blast. Celebrating down the pub afterwards, a discussion about what to call the band produced Tiger Moth. And so it began.

Recording the single had introduced us to an excellent local studio, Chestnut at Churt, and its engineer Paul Travers who seemed to have an affinity with what we did. A couple of months later we took the English Country Blues Band back there to record the second album, *Home And Deranged*. John Maxwell guested again and Jon Moore co-produced. Released at the end of the year, it once again became (mostly) a critical favourite and stout seller in folk terms.

However, it was around this time that I began to notice a tendency: the people who didn't like the fast-growing success of the magazine I edited would aim their knives at the band, most unfairly to the others. It's a scenario that has been an occasional downer on any subsequent music I've made. Personally, I'd rather my music making be judged on its own actual merits (or lack of) than pre-judged through the lens of a grudge because your mate's record got a poor review by another writer in a magazine that happened to have my name on its contents page. But as Tucker Zimmerman's song *So It Goes* (that we recorded on the first Hot Vultures LP) says, "You can't win 'em all." When I returned to solo gigging in the next century, whenever a club or concert MC asked me how I wanted to be introduced on stage, my only request was not to mention the magazine as it was a day-job hardly relevant to the music I played.

The Tiger Moth single didn't trouble the charts – realistically it never stood a chance – but it did get a decent amount of airplay, and set the English ceilidh micro-world into a brief tizz. To our great surprise there were lots of requests, mostly from festivals, as to whether Tiger Moth were available for ceilidhs. And lots more enquiries as to when there would be a whole album. We decided that if we were going to take gigs, we'd better put on a couple of own-promotions first to try it out.

Rod circulated tune tapes to everybody and we swapped ideas, probably by semaphore in those pre-internet and text message days. If we had an actual rehearsal, I have no memory of it. Later on, I'd tease people by saying "There's a type of music where everybody is familiar with the tune repertoire, so you call up players of the standard instruments for that music and put together a scratch band for a Saturday night gig, where everybody improvises. What's that music called?" Everybody would naturally answer "Jazz". But that pretty much described a good wedge of the English ceilidh world, and definitely Tiger Moth.

We were inordinately proud of never rehearsing, evolving initial arrangements live that were largely thought up by Rod and Jon, and where the motto was "the last one playing the tune's a cissy," and then keeping the best bits. As long as, importantly, it kept being in the right format for the particular dance – a 16-bar hornpipe or a 48-bar polka, say – and at a good speed for the dancers, all was well.

Tiger Moth's first live outing was at Farnham Maltings on 4th February 1984. We arranged to have the hall early for a long sound-check and play – I suppose that might count as a 'rehearsal'. For me it was my first time playing electric slide guitar in public since that embarrassing spot at the Bristol Ballads & Blues back in 1966.

Nigel Thornbory had made me a special black Telecaster copy with a wide, flat fingerboard and high action for that very purpose. Some years later, I remember singer/songwriter Bill Caddick standing and watching me intently at a Tiger Moth festival gig and then coming up and saying "I know what you're doing." "Please tell me," I probably quipped, "as I haven't a clue!" "You're playing trombone parts," he announced. And, by crikey, he was probably right, since in the band I tended to play slide parts on the lower strings with a thick tone. It wasn't intentional, but that was indeed the purpose it served and sort of how it sounded.

The event was, to our happy surprise, completely sold out in advance, with a waiting list. As friends were putting up the ticket table at the entrance to the hall, a couple entered in full EFDSS folk dancer uniform – her in felt dirndl skirt, him in check shirt and neckerchief. In spite of being told it wasn't open yet, I could see them remonstrating with our helpers and him being pointed in the general direction of me, as we were playing away warming up a tune. He marched the full length of the hall, tugged on my trouser leg and shouted "Is it going to be this loud?" He wasn't amused by my response, "Probably louder!" He marched back to the door and demanded his money back, which they were only too pleased to give as there was a small queue waiting for any returns. The first person into our first gig! It always was a badge of honour, that one. And the night was a roaring success…

We tried one more warm-up gig where Rod lived in Cricklade and again it went well. Then we put ourselves out there for hire. But that also meant recording a Tiger Moth album...

Before we did that, an Italian label who'd been recording many of the survivors of the late '60s British country blues boom decided that as the only ones they hadn't grabbed were Mike Cooper and myself, and since we'd recorded together before, why not do so again? In summer '84 we went into Gateway Studio in London with a decent budget, each contributing five songs to the project. Mike brought in Geoff Nichols on drums, Tim Hill on saxophone and Mike Messer on guitar: I came with Maggie on bass and Dave Peabody, who co-produced with us, on harmonica. And we winged it. Mike's version of Son House's *Preachin' Blues* had our unfeasible number of slide guitar overdubs and his take on Blind Willie Johnson's *Dark Is The Night* contained some superb alto sax improvisation from Tim. I got to lead on some enjoyable Chicago-style blues, a Chuck Berry cover even, and to accompany Maggie singing a couple of beauties. The resulting album, appropriately titled *The Continuous Preaching Blues*, isn't greatly known – we didn't do any promotional gigs – but I'm quite fond of it.

Engineer for the sessions was Pascal Gabriel who was to evolve into a major record producer and songwriter (Google up his Wikipedia page), and this was a stroke of luck because he showed me how to handle recording loud electric guitar. This was invaluable when it came to Tiger Moth's imminent studio work.

In the following month the 6-piece Tiger Moth re-convened twice at Chestnut Studio to make the first album, imaginatively titled *Tiger Moth*. Rod and Jon cooked up arrangements for thirteen tunes, aiming as on the original single for ones where the right number of times through the tune came closest to the magic three minutes, and to make things as interesting as possible within that. Since our 'Trad. Arrs' were very originally arr. we began our habit of changing traditional tune titles so we could justifiably claim the copyright on our versions. Thus *The Fiery Clockface* became *The Digital Watch*, our Bo Diddley-fied version of *The Dark Girl Dressed In Blue* (always our dance-off closer) became *The Duchess Dressed In Blue* and a sprightly Italian tune called *Sbrando* became *Smarlon*.

At actual ceilidhs, we eschewed the standard habit that many bands had of playing sets or medleys of tunes to keep up interest for the ten minutes of a dance and instead improvised the arse off a single one for the duration. It was a way of doing it that we only really shared with the Oyster Ceilidh Band (who became Oysterband) and a few other outfits of the day. Oh, and whereas the growing fashion among other ceilidh bands seemed to be to wear crumpled Hawaiian shirts on stage, Tiger Moth became a suits band.

In between the two Tiger Moth recording sessions, the English Country Blues Band did its last two gigs, a Towersey Folk Festival concert recorded and broadcast later by the BBC, and then a final celebratory one of our own at Farnham Maltings, with John Kirkpatrick & Sue Harris guesting. It was a grand send off, and then it was to be Tiger Moth all the way. Playing for dancing for three or four hours was so much more rewarding than playing at a seated folk club or concert audience for perhaps an hour.

There were other less happy changes around this time. After 14 years where we had spent most of them in each other's close company 24 hours a day on the road – probably more than most 'normal' married couples with proper jobs do in their lifetime – Maggie and I had separated as our interests diverged. But we remained good friends – to this day – able to be grown ups and make music together in company.

Maggie began a highly acclaimed solo career, evolving as a songwriter with later works like *A Place Called England* and *A Proper Sort Of Gardener*, both covered by June Tabor, the former winning song of the year in the BBC Folk Awards, and *Perfumes Of Arabia*, recorded by Martin Carthy. She also toured in a successful, sadly unrecorded, duo with Chris Coe, and took over Linda Thompson's role as singer in the National Theatre's production of *The Mysteries* at the Lyceum.

The *Tiger Moth* album caused quite a stir. The music on it got rave reviews, and its striking (and definitely not folky) cover by top fantasy artist Rodney Matthews – our old Bristol pal from Village Thing days – also grabbed people's attention. It won the main music biz trade press award for album cover of the year, all genres, all artists, beating anything on a major label. Rodney – who cultivated a resemblance to Frank Zappa – had to hire an evening suit and go and collect his award at a posh music-biz dinner from Jeremy Thorpe, leader of the Liberal Party. None of the band could afford the tickets.

At this point Jon Moore took himself off on a guitar course at a highly reputed music college in the USA and the band took a sabbatical. 1985 was the first year for two decades in which I didn't do any paid gigs, though I enjoyed occasionally sitting in on electric slide with other bands, including a couple of times with Oyster Band. Mostly I was involved with taking *The Southern Rag* monthly as *Folk Roots*, running Rogue Records and beginning to wear yet another hat as a radio presenter. Maggie's duo with Chris Coe toured as far away as Nepal, Thailand and the Philippines for the British Council. Rod Stradling joined another innovative band called Edward II & The Red Hot Polkas.

Jon returned and the Moth fluttered again. Our first festival of 1986 wasn't auspicious. We arrived at Trowbridge in the morning in order to get a sound check for our late night ceilidh. The disorganised evening concert vastly over-ran, so after waiting around the whole day we were an hour late beginning, through no fault of our own. We'd been on stage for barely twenty minutes and had just invited brilliant young Northumbrian musician Kathryn Tickell up to join us when the festival hit its curfew and the plugs were pulled. Much Grrrrr.

The next day I went to an early WOMAD festival being held not far away that same weekend, near Clevedon in Somerset. The music from the Bhundu Boys, Flaco Jimenez, Super Diamano, the Gambian National Troupe and many more was brilliant, the organisation exemplary (everything ran to time), and it became clear that something big was changing. The 1980s roots music brew was coming to the boil and what was about to be called 'world music' was infecting everybody who had open ears.

1987 began with a mighty bash. Billed as *English Roots Against Apartheid – The Hotttest Ceilidh In Town* and promoted jointly by *Folk Roots*, Cooking Vinyl Records and London listings magazine *City Limits*. Tiger Moth and Oyster Band joined forces for an epic night at the Town & Country Club in Kentish Town, at the time one of North London's major rock venues. In spite of heavy snow in the preceding days which caused a fair bit of nail biting, it got well over a thousand people doing English ceilidh dancing and an impressive list of guest artists who wanted to support this fundraising event for a key political cause of the time. And have loads of midwinter fun.

Both bands did their own sets, surprise guests popped up and played, Radio 1 DJ Andy Kershaw MC'd and the evening ended with a massive jam as everybody combined together for a roar through the hugest version of *Speed The Plough* ever known. It wasn't recorded, but Jak Kilby's iconic photo of the finale shows a couple of dozen people on stage including all of Tiger Moth and Oyster Band with Richard Thompson, Billy Bragg, Hank Wangford, Michelle Shocked, Rory McLeod, members of 3 Mustaphas 3 and the Boothill Foot Tappers and a huge sea of dancers. It raised a lot of money for Anti-Apartheid and people talked about it for years afterwards.

The next two years for Tiger Moth were mostly concerned with festivals and recording. I must say that I enjoyed that era of playing for dancing enormously, especially as we were soaking up musical influences from all over. I even briefly overcame my own self-conscious two-left-footed fear of ceilidh dance floors during the summer of '87 when my lithe and supportive dancing companion Katie Godfrey calmed my phobia and made it a pleasure. Until we got to Towersey Folk Festival and dance caller Taffy Thomas proceeded to take the piss out of me from the stage and my confidence instantly evaporated. Some 25 years later I reminded Taffy of this when running into him at the same festival, and he had the good grace to be mortified!

We'd regularly play tapes of music to each other in the van en-route to festivals, particularly Italian dance tunes from Rod and all sorts of Kenyan and Congolese music from me. Inevitably some of this would be absorbed by osmosis and elements would appear in that night's set, sometimes to stick. One memorable occasion was at Bromyard Festival when we were improvising away on favourite tune *The Sloe*. John Maxwell suddenly locked into the sort of bass drum and sizzling hi-hat groove that characterised Kenyan benga. The band picked up a gear, the dancers whooped and I grinned across at John and mouthed "Great!" He momentarily looked shocked and imperceptibly faltered for just a split second. At the end he needlessly apologised for this. His explanation was that he'd had a flashback to when playing in the Albion Band. He'd got enthusiastically carried away by something similar, but, he said, Ashley Hutchings had angrily shouted "Don't you *ever* do that again!" at him and fired him not long after. Tiger Moth was a much better home for his unruly playing.

By this time I'd become good pals with fine musician, world music producer and entertaining human Ben Mandelson (a.k.a. Hijaz Mustapha of the 3 Mustaphas 3 – more later!), so when we went into Topic's studio in January 1988 to record the second Tiger Moth LP, everybody was pleased to invite him in to co-produce and add some twanging. Chris Coe was AWOL at this time, so we added Ian Carter on keyboards (and in-house dance caller when playing live). Influences from Africa, southern Europe and the USA abounded, but all within the framework of English ceilidh tunes. With another eyeball-bending Rodney Matthews cover, it got uniformly rave reviews.

"The striking difference with *Howling Moth* is that they sound like a proper band and this is a proper album. One that is well balanced and carefully considered, with great depth and variety in the arrangement," reckoned Colin Irwin. A proper band, eh? That'll never do!

It lured *Guardian* writer Mark Cooper, later the long-time producer of *Later With Jools*, years of Glastonbury and much more on BBC TV, out to see us at a Buckinghamshire ceilidh. His resulting big piece probably captured the band better than any other press review.

"In the main hall the monthly ceilidh looks more like a riot... On stage, Tiger Moth, the vanguard of the New Wave of English Country Dance Bands alongside Edward II and Blowzabella, are changing gears, driven forward by the seated figure of Rod Stradling, a melodeon clutched to his chest, fingers working overtime and a maniacal stare on his face. He has all the intensity of a Vietnam veteran in a wheelchair. Behind Stradling, guitarist Jon Moore watches the tempo rise on the dance floor and then proceeds to throw in a few power chords to the delight of the band, while drummer John Maxwell drives the polka onward with frills and rolls that seem to spring more from Africa or the Caribbean than the English countryside. Somehow the soukous beat and the polka merge like they were made for another. The dancers have no time for such nice distinctions, only gathering themselves for another headlong rush as the beat picks up another notch." Yes, that was exactly what it was like. And Rod never lived down that description any more than the legend of his slippers!

Howling Moth was also notable for being the first record I'd ever made that came out simultaneously on CD, thus being the first one which sounded back at home like it had done in the studio rather than slightly, disappointingly, diminished through the medium of vinyl.

1988 was another good year for festivals, though we got our come-uppance at Sidmouth. In those days their main ceilidhs were held down in the town in a marquee on the Ham, where the big concert tent is these days. The day after ours, the local paper was full of complaints from the local residents about volume levels at the festival, something we'd experienced before from more conservative folk dancers and we'd accepted as a compliment, frankly. But it turned out that the offending event wasn't ours at all, but staid old M.O.R. TV-favourite folkies The Spinners in the open air arena. The shame! We were crestfallen...

It wasn't just folk festival ceilidhs that we were playing by then. That year we shared the bill at the South Bank with South Africa's Mahlathini & The Mahotella Queens, and at London's Astoria with Senegal's Baaba Maal and his band – experiencing the chaos that always seemed to surround Maal's shows. Their sound check was so prolonged that by the time we got a minimal one the doors had already opened.

Rogue Records were producing quite a few albums by the cream of touring world music artists at this time, and my final wheeze for the Moths as 'house band' was to put together a few collaborations with some of those musicians. One was with Tex-Mex squeezebox king Flaco Jimenez who dropped by Topic studio, listened to one run through, donned headphones and blazed through a take so exhilarating that nobody thought it could be bettered. So we all downed tools and went to the pub! Another involved Sierra-Leonian guitar king Abdul Tee-Jay. Most ambitious was with Gambian kora masters Dembo Konte & Kausu Kuyateh on a song called *Salt Of The Earth* that Maggie and Jon had created to the tune of Sandaly & Nmawa Kante's classic *Foudou*, originally recorded with seminal West African band Les Ambassadeurs. These all came out on a 12" EP, *The World At Sixes And Sevens*, credited to Orchestre Super Moth, and *Salt Of The Earth* apparently became a minor hit in London 'global dance' clubs.

An ambitious – though in retrospect terminally over-ambitious – project that I'd dreamed up failed to come to fruition when the sponsorship I'd been led to believe was forthcoming didn't materialise. If it had done, a van full of equipment – manufacturer donated PA, instruments and amplifiers – would have been loaded on a ship and sent out to the Gambia. Tiger Moth would have flown over once it had arrived and spent a month workshopping with local musicians on creating new music. When it was over and the results recorded, the van and equipment would have been donated to a local organisation and left behind for deserving musicians who had very little access to decent gear. One of those 'what if?' things it's easy to lie awake fantasising about.

After playing at the *Folk Roots* 10th birthday bash at London's 100 Club, where Abdul Tee-Jay augmented the band on guitar and animateurs Hijaz Mustapha and Bob Sinfield urged the crowd on, Tiger Moth called it a day in 1989 with a wild and memorable late night dance at that year's Bracknell Folk & Roots Festival. Once again, inevitably, it wasn't recorded but has another fine set of Jak Kilby's black & white photos, capturing for posterity that on this final show Maggie upstaged the band's suit wearers in a little black cocktail dress.

And from my point of view, apart from a few fun gigs with the odd scratch band (one being called the Harringay Modal Rounders and involving

Maggie, Ben Mandelson, Oyster Band's Chopper and Irish musician Ron Kavana), a reconvened Tiger Moth benefit for drummer John Maxwell who sadly was to die of throat cancer, and some odd recording sessions on slide guitar, my work load on other things pretty much prevented me from being a performing musician for the next fifteen years.

During the 1980s, the whole focus of live folk and roots music had moved away from the clubs, which kept decreasing in numbers and were pretty much exclusively the realm of the same generation who'd created them in the 1960s. The big growth area was now in festivals…

10.
Folk Festival Life

At the end of the 1960s folk boom years there were still hardly any folk festivals in England. Begun in 1965, Cambridge was soon established as the big broad-based one. Keele – later transferred to Loughborough – which had started the same year was the traditional one. Sidmouth was still mainly a folk dance festival, and a handful of others like Towersey were still in their infancy. The rock world had hi-jacked the National Jazz & Blues Festival which by 1971 had become the Reading Rock Festival, and the rock biz also tried its hand with the huge but short-lived Isle of Wight and Bath events. The latter inspired a Somerset farmer called Michael Eavis to run his own near Glastonbury from 1970 – see chapter 7. But during the subsequent decade there was an inexorable growth in summer folk events.

The UK's folk clubs – said to be over a thousand strong at their 1960s peak – had gone into a steady decline by the end of the 1970s. But festivals allowed people to see lots of artists with one weekend ticket, and as many in the audience were now reproducing they could take their kids rather than looking for weekly baby sitters in order to go to clubs. As the festivals grew they attracted dedicated regulars, and lifetime family friendships were forged from annual camping together. By the millennium, another generation of folk offspring who'd grown up going to the likes of Sidmouth and running round with the other folk kids would seed a rebirth in musicians and dancers.

There are those ancients who still think the folk clubs are the hub around which everything revolves, but in truth they've been out at the end of one of the spokes since the 1980s and the festivals, of all sizes, have long-since taken over that central role. Especially the possibility for artists to develop a career and their music while sustaining a living.

Drink driving laws had been tightened up in the '60s along with the introduction of breathaliser tests, so festival weekends also allowed folkies to indulge in their favourite sport of consuming vast amounts of real ale out of pewter tankards without needing to drive anywhere. The association of folk festivals with 'beer swilling' wasn't always a good thing, mind: the years that Cambridge was sponsored by Newcastle Brown saw a marked deterioration in crowd behaviour.

The rule-of-thumb seemed to be that successful events started small and grew organically. Fylde in the North West began in 1973, Trowbridge in 1974, Bracknell in 1975, and although they're all gone now they grew and flourished for a good many years. The few that tried to be massive from a standing start pretty much all fell over, though I'm not sure why the extraordinary Lincoln Folk Festival (or to be exact, Tupholme Manor Park Folk Concert) of July 1971 was never repeated.

A truly star-studded bill included the UK's Steeleye Span, Pentangle, the Incredible String Band, Sandy Denny and Carthy & Swarbrick mixed up with Americans like the extraordinary Buffy Sainte Marie, James Taylor, Sonny Terry & Brownie McGhee and Tim Hardin. The Byrds, in their line-up with guitar giant Clarence White, were booked to do an acoustic set which they did magnificently, finishing perfectly at sunset, when they came back for a fully electric encore of *Eight Miles High* as bonfires made from the toilet stalls blazed up around the site. One of life's more memorable festival moments.

Backstage, things were a little more bizarre. Tim Hardin, enhanced by certain substances, had to be dissuaded from attempting to fly out of a top floor window of the manor house, and unintentional comedy was provided by the arrival of American singer/ songwriter Tom Paxton. No doubt organised by his manager Jo Lustig, he swept up in a limo and emerged escorted by two fur-coated 'models', one on each arm, while Lustig bustled around him trying to attract attention. Cue mass attempts to stifle laughter and avoid eye contact.

On the other hand, everybody knows why Sussex Folk Jamboree at Goodwood Racecourse in August 1983 failed spectacularly, losing a number of people's shirts (and even houses). A massively over-ambitious event with a good but hardly startling bill topped by Christy Moore, Donovan, Incantation, Home Service, Albion Band, Peter Rowan and a sub strata of decent regular folk club names (with Renaissance, Georgie Fame and 'two headliners' still t.b.c even on their final, poorly designed adverts), it wasn't well promoted and didn't catch the public's imagination.

The audience numbered in their hundreds rather than the anticipated thousands, and had to be persuaded by the BBC who were filming it to all bunch up together in the stands for some tight shots to make it look like it had a good crowd. The observant would have noticed the same people applauding in the same way for whichever artist's performance their shots were cut into! One's heart went out to the catering and bar providers who were stuck with huge unsold stocks, having been misled into expecting many more customers.

By the late '70s, there were sufficient events, a choice on most weekends in the June to September high season when many folk clubs closed, that they almost became a travelling circus. The same popular artists waved each other goodbye on a Sunday evening, knowing that after doing their laundry and catching up on sleep, they'd probably see everybody again next Friday.

Much like folk clubs generally cloned the same format (two halves each with floor singers and a guest set, with a raffle in between), many folk festivals settled into a standard model: a couple of stages and maybe a dance tent, somewhere for some sessions, a space for morris dancing, lots of 'real ale' and a logo of a recognisable folkie stereotype or a cavorting, anthropomorphic creature. The more creative were the fore-runners of today's 'boutique festivals'. Things had gone from stages made of planks on farm scaffolding and primitive PA systems to decent infrastructure, lighting and sound (monitors even – virtually unknown at the beginning of the decade!). It was a good time to be alive and involved.

For a couple of years at the end of the decade I served as a roving English festivals correspondent for the Los Angeles based American magazine *Folk Scene*. Here's my 1979 report that they carried, which pretty well sums up how things were at that time.

Aaarrghh, it's festival lag, that dreaded disorienting disease which strikes annually around late summer when you've just spent nearly every weekend for a couple of months at a different event, often in the company of the same bunch of performers and friends from all over the country.

Lessons appear to have been well learned: there were newcomers to the 50 or more already established, but this year there were no big bullshit almost-pop festivals trying to be another Cambridge. Instead, lots and lots of comfortably sized ones where you could almost meet and say hello to everybody over the course of a couple of days (and sometimes it felt like you did).

Somewhere back in the early summer we loaded up our trusty VW and headed around to the North East of London for the first Epping Folk Festival. The admirable idea of the organisers was to involve the local community and hold all events in different halls and pubs in the centre of the small town. It almost worked, certainly well enough to convince them to try again next year. Friday night was just a nicely mixed concert with June Tabor & Martin Simpson billtopping, plus singer/guitarist Dave Evans making a triumphant return from self-imposed exile in Belgium, fine English traditional music from Pete and Chris Coe, blues from Dave Peabody and the ever energetic Albion Morris. Saturday it spread into town with several smaller concerts, Morris tours, pub sessions, music hall and a packed and sweaty ceilidh led by The Old Swan Band; on Sunday the whole event moved to a large pub two miles out of town where mini-concerts and workshops included banjo legend Derroll Adams, the superb Nic Jones, hot group Spredthick and the ever hilarious Fred Wedlock to round it off.

A few weeks later our festival bookings season started in earnest with the 10th Norwich Folk Festival, held on the University campus, which gives it the advantage of being able to hold its events indoors or outside depending on the famous English weather. Norwich, like Epping, has no fixed 'policy' but tries for a good mixture of the best of everything in the folk world: always succeeds, too. This year, a change from other English festivals in recent years where the melodeon has often held the fore, Norwich was very guitar-orientated. I found myself running a guitar workshop and trying to fit in Martin Carthy, Nic Jones, Chris Foster, Martin Simpson, Roy Bookbinder, Michael Chapman, Dave Evans and half a dozen more in two and a half hours...

Except when we played on them, we tended to miss the main concerts which ran the whole weekend, though they were reportedly excellent. Friday night had a subsidiary session of American music including Bookbinder, Jo-Ann Kelly and others; Saturday a folk quiz conducted by Pete Bellamy, workshops, open air sessions and one of the best jams the bar has ever heard, started by Bellamy playing blues guitar (!) and winding up around midnight with a vast horde going through the Ray Charles songbook with outbreaks of jiving. Sunday had probably the most memorable afternoon of any Festival this year when Taffy Thomas and Chris Foster brought a bus load of old traditional singers, musicians and step dancers up from rural Suffolk and turned the festival barn into a big English country pub. Many musicians usually more into contemporary stuff were instantly bowled over – the power of traditional music!

There was even more traditional music at our next festival, Loughborough, yet again in a university campus, and under the direction of Roy Harris. Low key and informal, it brings the cream of living traditional singers together with the best of the 'revival' and everybody is better for it. Of the older musicians, singers Fred Jordan, Willie Scott, Tom Brown, Bob Roberts with his ancient melodeon, Irish couple John and Julia Clifford and fiddle player Willy Taylor were all to the fore, whilst notable representatives of the younger generation included Pete & Chris Coe, Martin Carthy, Alistair Anderson, Tim Laycock (a fine, under-rated singer and duet concertina player), the Welsh group Ar Log and an entertaining Kent couple, Tundra.

That turned out to be a weird weekend; we were booked at two festivals, so after two days at Loughborough (no pressure, certainly no 'stars', mostly small, informal sessions, lots of song and tune swapping, jamming and real interest in the music) we drove 100 miles southwest to Trowbridge – another excellent event but in a very different way.

Trowbridge is held in an enormous tent set up in the big back garden of a pub. The Trowbridge philosophy has most of the performers booked as entertainment and is really a continuous concert stage for four days. All the artists do 'proper' sets, whip the audience into a frenzy and dare the next performer to follow them. That sounds awful but it's really not so: there's a great atmosphere, the crowd of 500 or so are all regulars who have been going for years and so it is good sociable fun.

This year's artists included Scotland's Tannahill Weavers, Seattle's own Jim Page with his talking blues and Guthriesque comment, comedians Derek Brimstone, Bernard Wrigley and Cosmotheka, the Dutch group Crackerhash, Dave Cousins of The Strawbs on his way back to the folk scene, songwriter Michael Moore, and the English country music band Flowers & Frolics (whose name – it's rhyming slang – does not give much warning of their exciting music and political commitment).

Where have we got to? Ah, yes – next came Bracknell. It has probably the most ideal venue – a park and country mansion converted to an arts centre – but they had a much bigger jazz festival there the preceding weekend which needed larger tent facilities. Hence the folk audience looked a bit lost in them. As ever, the highlight of the weekend came with the late Saturday night 'Rough Music' session led by Bill Caddick – the idea being that all participating artists must do something that they never would usually do in a folk club. This varied from songs sung while bicycle riding, a singer on stilts, an extremely loud and would-be offensive punk rocker, and closed with a massed New Victory Band (playing the wrong instruments), June Tabor, Cosmotheka, Martin Simpson, Caddick, ourselves, and lord knows who else, doing Rock Island Line and Save The Last Dance For Me. On the more sensible side, The New Victory Band once again conducted tremendous dance sessions, whilst among the more outstanding on the song stage were the har-

mony group Regal Slip with their complicated four-part vocal arrangements. Lots of Morris dancing, club singarounds, craft stalls, children's events and all sorts completed a splendid weekend (and it's only 20 miles from home so we could sleep in real beds!).

And so to Cambridge. We left last year crying "enough" after attending for 10 consecutive years. Overcrowding, too many drunks, too few toilets, bad sound and lots of playing hassles had finally done us in; as we drove away we'd joked to each other that "the only possible way they'll get us here next year is by booking Ry Cooder."

Guess what? They did... Not only Cooder, but Doc Watson, The Woodstock Mountain Revue (including Happy & Artie Traum, Bill Keith, Jim Rooney, John Herald, guest Jay Ungar and more), Rockin' Dopsie & The Cajun Twisters and Loudon Wainwright. The bastards! We couldn't miss all that, so off we went again. The insult was compounded by the fact that the English part of the bill was really crummy; apart from the New Victory Band holding the flag there was little to indicate how musically healthy the English folk scene is right now.

Cooder was superb. He appeared solo and yet years of listening to his music on record hadn't prepared us for how good he was, vocally as well as instrumentally. All the other American representatives were on form, too. And yes, it was just as overcrowded, under-toiletted and pop-festival like (it would have been impossible to see and hear anything if we were not in the position to get press enclosure passes), it poured with rain and everybody appeared to be having a wonderful time! But we won't go next year unless they book Charley Patton, Buddy Holly and Richard Farina...

Just for a change, the next weekend we popped over to Belgium for a festival. We usually manage one or two each summer and, particularly down in Flanders, they are always great fun. This year we were booked at Dranouter, a newish event in a tiny field just outside a little village between Ieper (or Ypres as you may know it) and the French border. There has been a huge folk revival in Belgium in the last decade so they still have a lot of the enthusiasm that has waned somewhat in Britain; the audiences are younger and the buzz from rediscovering their own traditional music is still fresh. Flemish groups De Snaar and 't Kliekske, their national folk giant Wannes Van De Velde (the equivalent in musical stature of Ewan MacColl and Martin Carthy combined), the brilliant young French guitarist Pierre Bensusan, French dance music trio Melusine, Balkans Pan-Ra and others all gave a very refreshing change to the continuous English and American music we'd recently been hearing. Flemish events are carefree, shambolic, always run late, involve a huge amount of drinking, eating and socialising and are absolutely wonderful!

And finally, Sidmouth arrived. Or we arrived there. It's all a bit hazy. Sidmouth is the grand-daddy of them all, 25 years old this year. It was predominantly a dance festival with teams from all over the world, but slowly the song and music side has reached an equal footing. The festival takes place in a seaside town at the height of the summer season. Music and singing fills all the pubs, the sea-front, and every available small hall. So many Morris dancers throng the streets that the 'normal' holiday makers don't notice the weird dress any more. It lasts a week and at the end you are totally exhausted, crying "no more festivals for another 10 years!" There is a saying on the English folk scene that everybody has to go to Sidmouth at least once in their lifetime, and it's certainly not an experience to miss (though "See Sidmouth and die" might be a more apt saying!).

It's odd: the music is not of a brilliant standard: apart from a few like Martin Carthy, John & Sue Kirkpatrick, Shirley Collins and Tony Rose, there are not a lot of 'names' on the bill. The rest is taken up by club performers, amateurs and newcomers, yet the informality and atmosphere is such that everybody has a great time. Each day culminates in a frenzied 'Late Night Extra' ceilidh where the dancing and singing (and drinking) continue until everyone collapses for a few hours sleep before starting again.

And that was just June to early August 1979. If I'd continued further along the calendar it could have taken in Towersey Festival that was already an established favourite on August Bank Holiday weekend, particular enjoyed by families who liked to camp. It was only in much later years that I worked out that their dead periods in programming twixt afternoon and evening were probably to allow the campers to go and feed their children (and themselves). And into September the season then drew to a close at Bromyard between Worcester and Hereford, with its strangely chilly microclimate to remind you that autumn was around the corner.

Fifty festivals seemed a lot then, but over the next twenty years the lists grew and grew and eventually sailed past ten times that number. Some came and went, the long-running ones evolving as audience expectations increased for that better sound, video screens, better catering, toilet and camping facilities. Later-comers had the advantage of learning from the good and bad points of those who'd figured it out by trial and error.

Some preferred to remain small, grassroots, and deliberately not aspire to growth – a good example being the English Country Music Weekends, almost entirely populated by musicians (and their camper vans), which have roamed the country since being founded by Rod & Danny Stradling back in the mid-1970s, about as far from any star system as you can get.

At the other extreme are things like Fairport Convention's annual Cropredy event with its single big stage, centred around one particular band and their mates, though I'm sure they don't classify it as a folk festival. It has a big, dedicated congregation, but I got a bit disillusioned by it after I went along with Martin Carthy & John Kirpatrick's band Brass Monkey in the mid-'80s to mix their sound and struggled to get a decent volume level. Soon after Brass Monkey's set, Fairport themselves took the stage and the rest of the PA was switched on. It wouldn't do to be upstaged by your support acts…

It was all pretty much a constant upward curve, adding more recent state-of-the-art events like Shrewsbury Folk Festival and Folk East, until the major crises of the 2020s – Covid, energy prices, climate change and huge increases in costs at the same time as audience's belts tightened. It remains to be seen if things will fully recover, though I suspect that folk festival going is now so engrained into the culture and habits of the massive audience that it ought to.

Back to those earlier days though. For years Cambridge Folk Festival became the biggest, the most influential, the one that got on TV and radio. It grew rapidly from its fairly laid-back beginnings. In those early years an artist or band could roll up, camp in the trees on the edge of the site, sign up for a spot in the Club Tent (the festival's open mic) and create such a buzz that they'd go away with full diaries for the coming autumn and winter's huge folk club circuit. Our Bristol pals the Pigsty Hill Light Orchestra had done just that and were able to turn fully professional as a result. Artists destined to be a bit lower down the main bill could seal the deal with the organisers by agreeing to do a stint MCing the club tent. Been there, done that! And if you weren't playing on a stage, jam sessions sprang up all over the site.

The main stage faced outwards onto the open grass in the daytime and then turned to face inside the big tent in the evening. After some six or seven years they added a *Grand Ole Opry* Country & Western/ bluegrass tent which reflected the very substantial Americana (as it's now called) subculture still in the region to this day, said to be a hangover from the WW2-and-after days of all the big American air bases in those parts. After a few more years that became Stage 2, and then nothing changed very much for four decades until they dumped the club tent in 2023 and renamed it Stage 3. The festival has a finite site bordered by roads and housing, so nowhere to expand to. (I only discovered quite recently, having moved to Cambridge in 2021, that the site actually looks much bigger when it doesn't have a folk festival superimposed on it.)

The upwards trajectory of the festival had many positive and a few negative points. With a bigger budget than any other folk event of the day, and considerable career kudos to be gained from doing it (think Glastonbury), they could have their pick of the top names. We were able to see many memorable performances by wonderful artists at their peak, particularly the American ones which Cambridge almost uniquely secured. Back then, Americans seemed much more polished and confident in their performances than many of us Brits (and often had better instruments too, before local makers changed that).

The downside was that self-importance brought out the worst in some artists, rather shockingly to those of us who were used to the supportive camaraderie of the English folk scene. Take Breton musician Alain Stivell, for example. One infamous year around 1974 he insisted that he'd only play using his own mixer desk for the main stage PA. This meant his crew driving his big white Mercedes tour bus through the audience seated on the grass to reach the front of the stage, holding up proceedings for the best part of an hour while they installed their gear. Then they reversed the process at the end, leaving the festival's crew to work out which of their microphones went back where. Several artists (including us) were bumped from the programme to allow the schedule to catch up. The Boys Of The Lough's following set was ruined as the sound crew struggled to identify the correct mics, with much random feedback or inaudibility. The usually mild-mannered Martin Carthy was so annoyed by his sound that, on coming off stage, he was seen to throw his guitar to the ground with an oath (though after carefully locating a pile of tarpaulins to soften the fall!).

Another incident involved Martin as well. After many years of trying, Cambridge succeeded in booking Joan Baez in 1982. I never could understand why they gave in to her (or maybe it was her management's) absurd demands though. Ms Baez would not leave her personal backstage caravan to walk on her personal red carpet to the stage which had been freshly decorated with her personal flower arrangements until the whole backstage area had been cleared, which involved even Martin Carthy, who'd just finished his set, being ejected. It was after that year that I stopped going so regularly! If you look on YouTube you can find 15 minutes of her set, complete with the flower arrangements. (As a footnote, years later she was introduced as a special guest by Waterson: Carthy at London's Barbican. "These people are my roots," she gushed sincerely...)

Sidmouth Folk Festival (or Folk Week) began a decade before Cambridge and was run in its first thirty or so years by the English Folk Dance & Song Society. Initially a folk dance festival, it slowly grew its song and music input and in spite of being imagined as rather traditional and staid by people who'd never been it, from the mid '70s onwards it actually became far more adventurous and subtly influential than 'the big one.'

It was at Sidmouth that the whole exciting 'new wave of English country music' ceilidh bands really evolved and took off, at the same time as the event was still hosting 'Dances For Dancers', full of couples in 1950s EFDSS uniform tracing intricate patterns on the floor at speed, while barely lifting up their feet, to the accompaniment of strict-tempo bands with large piano accordeons. Small wonder they were nicknamed 'music while you walk.' Those NWOECM bands and events got a whole new load of people from the folk club direction into social dancing, and from then on most festivals would have a dance tent, or at least clear a space for a ceilidh somewhere in the programme.

It was at Sidmouth where women's morris dancing took hold, and street theatre as an element of folk festivals, both having a marked effect on pulling in younger participants. It was Sidmouth, which had long included an international music element via its visiting folk dance troupes, that began to enthusiastically programme what would eventually be called 'world music' from the mid 1980s. It was Sidmouth who saw the value in presenting the older traditional players and singers, whereas some form of traditional music only really got a look in at Cambridge in the hands of those younger artists who had gained folk scene popularity, record sales and media coverage.

When we Hot Vultures began regularly going to Sidmouth in the 1970s, song events were held in what was called the Beach Store, a big folk club-sized room with a sand floor. It was actually where the council kept the deckchairs in the winter, but since Sidmouth's shoreline is famously pebbles, the oft-repeated joke was that it was where they stored the beach... As the festival grew in that decade, the Sidmouth Beach Store soon rivalled the Cambridge Club Tent as a place where folk club careers could be ignited.

In the 1980s, John Dowell took over the role of festival director, and Sidmouth continued to grow, to take over seemingly every venue and social gathering place in the small seaside town, as well as a large natural open air amphitheatre, adding enormously to the local economy.

It always had an anarchic creative streak. At one time there were ceilidhs in the Drill Hall on the sea front, and a themed one would be announced after the week had begun. One year it was a *Hitchhiker's Guide To The Galaxy*-themed *Ceilidh At The End Of The Universe* populated by people imaginatively dressed as characters from the recent hit radio show: legend had it that a couple of members of Flowers & Frolics did an overnight round trip to North London to nick a Hotblack Desiato estate agent signboard to erect outside the building.

In those days long before mobile phones and social media, such things tended to be plotted in the musicians' pub, the Dove, the one place where by general agreement no music took place. It was also where many subsequent musical adventures were catalysed. One night around 1987 much hilarity had ensued when a lubricated June Tabor and some women friends including Sarah Coxson, Anne Lennox-Martin and Debby McClatchy were burning an effigy in an ashtray of *NME* journalist Mark Sinker who had just given June's latest LP a stinker of a review, with much ribald waving of beer glasses. At this point several members of Oysterband walked in. "Is that June Tabor?" one asked, in mild awe: "I didn't know she was that much fun. Would you introduce us?" So I did, and the rest is English folk rock history.

An unforgettable experience was the 1986 appearance by the Gambian National Troupe which included fine musicians like kora master Dembo Konte. They happened to be in the UK at the right time so I was pleased to help broker their visit via Lucy Duran. They were the talking point of the festival, but what I remember the most is when the musicians did a wildly well-received interval spot in a late night ceilidh. As soon as they'd finished, the ceilidh dancing kicked in again and young folkie women seized some of the be-robed musicians and hauled them out onto the floor. The look of sheer panic on Dembo's faced as he whirled past in a frenzy of willow-stripping was memorable.

The festival became much bigger, budget-wise, at a time when the finances of the EFDSS were increasingly precarious, and it was realised that either organisation was capable of taking the other down in case of a shortfall. So in 1987 the festival was privatised, taken over by Mrs Casey Music's Steve Heap (then also director of the long-running Towersey Festival in Oxfordshire) and Haddenham Ceilidh organiser John Heydon. Alan Bearman, then organiser of one of the better London folk clubs, took over as Artistic Director and it continued to grow and thrive, soon adding a bigger out-of-town venue, the Bulverton Marquee, where younger people congregated for the Late Night Extras.

In spite of its huge benefits to the local economy, the council had always been reluctant to give the festival any financial safety net in the event of a year with terrible weather. Eventually, after the lively, televised 50th anniversary festival in 2004, Steve Heap announced that they were quitting as the personal risk was unbearable. Maybe it would have forced the council's hand if the festival had missed a year, so that they noticed the detrimental effect on the local economy, but instead a group of enthusiastic volunteers jumped in and continued it in a reduced way. After a shaky couple of years with dodgy direction, Alan Bearman was engaged to take over the helm again, and by the 2010s it was thriving as before (though without the weather-prone outdoor arena events that had been a big part of the previous risk). And so it goes... it survived Covid too.

Inevitably after more than a decade of playing festivals I got the bug myself. Where we were living in Farnham, the local community had rescued and renovated the old Maltings as a venue and by the late 1970s it was open for business. We'd already run occasional small concerts and big ceilidhs there, but eventually I had one of my lightbulb moments: a one day indoor event in the spring to kick off the season – to break the winter festival famine and set up a buzz for the year, but not requiring camping or putting up green field infrastructure.

Farnham Folk Day began on Sunday 18th April 1982 and ran every year until the end of the decade on the first Sunday after Easter, bar 1986 when the Maltings screwed up the venue booking. "The first annual Farnham Folk Day," was the hopeful but, it turned out, accurate description on the poster for what we described as "Eleven hours of the best national and local folk singers, musicians and groups in concerts, music sessions, barn dance, singarounds and workshops, plus... record and instrument stalls, morris dancing, food, bars. A day's delights." The 'national' part of the bill included Martin Carthy, Michael Chapman, the English Country Blues Band, Dave Evans, Maggie Holland, John Kirkpatrick & Sue Harris, the Old Swan Band, Spredthick, the Watersons and Peta Webb & Webb's Wonders, and to our delight it sold out, as it did every subsequent year, some 500 ticket buyers plus numerous performers, dancers and their guests.

As the decade progressed, the event gained a go-to reputation, not the least to album buyers who descended on the record stall in their droves to grab all the delights they'd been reading about or hearing on the radio over the winter months but couldn't find in record shops (remember those?). Before Amazon or Bandcamp, back when people used to buy music for their homes rather than expect it for free, the specialist customer had few other places to go for physical product, and stall operator Projection Records regularly reported individuals hauling off dozens of LPs, presumably after cashing in their grandmothers.

The '80s 'roots' explosion and interest in what later became known as 'world music' opened ears and possibilities, so we were able to expand the breadth of music to include the likes of the USA's Flaco Jimenez, Peter Rowan and Michelle Shocked, Italy's La Ciapa Rusa and Calicanto, West Africa's Dembo Konte & Kausu Kuyateh, Ali Farka Toure and Jali Musa Jawara and Morocco's Hassan Erraji. I saw no reason why these couldn't be programmed alongside proper job English traditional artists such as the Copper Family, Bampton Morris, Suffolk's Old Hat Concert Party and Northumberland's the Shepherds, and proved that to be right.

1985, the year we had the Shepherds (Joe Hutton, Willie Taylor & Will Atkinson) proved notable in another way. I'd booked them along with Alistair Anderson and then 17-year old piper Kathryn Tickell as a Northumbrian package. I interviewed Kathryn for *Folk Roots* on the day and asked her what her plans were. She told me she was going to turn professional as a musician rather than go to college. Apparently this was a spur of the moment thing on the "If I say it in print I'll have to go through with it" principle – she hadn't even told her parents! Luckily it turned out rather well for her, along with being the first sighting of a new young generation of English folk musicians. A veritable swallow...

There were many highlights of course but a particular personal favourite was a 1987 session I programmed into the smaller Barley Room, capacity about 150 though I'm sure we were well over the limit. Titled *Many Stringed*

Things From Far Flung Places, the bill was Dembo Konte & Kausu Kuyateh (koras), Sue Harris (hammered dulcimer) and Hassan Erraji (oud). I'd said to them that they could just do individual sets, but if they fancied collaborating together as well it would be nice. So they each did about 20 minutes, and then finished up with a joint set where each led a piece of music and the others improvised around it. It was extraordinary, music out of the sky, and the following week there were numerous hopeful 'phone calls asking if it had been recorded. Sadly, no...

The following year we struck lucky. I'd already booked Mali's great Ali Farka Touré, and had got to work on the publicity, when a late opportunity came to book Guinean kora player/singer Jali Musa Jawara (a.k.a. Djeli Moussa Diawara on his French releases) and his musicians. Charlie Gillett had licensed his utterly extraordinary first album for Oval Records in the UK and it had stopped the early '80s roots music traffic, leaving us gasping for breath with its sheer beauty and fearsome musicianship. Virtuoso kora and balafon were driven along by punchy 12-string guitar, and Jali Musa's soaring, soulful lead vocals were underpinned by a female chorus that could put goose-pimples on your goose-pimples. It had already taken up permanent residence in my theoretical *Desert Island Discs* so I was really looking forward to his appearance.

Come the day, come the artists... Instead of having wristbands for entry, every year we gave people badges with that year's festival logo on it, which had already been set as an image of Ali Farka Touré long before Jali Musa had been added to the bill. The latter took one look at them and demanded to know where 'his' badge was, before going into an enormous sulk and insisting that his musicians stayed in their dressing room all day, only emerging for a moody set. It took the shine off. I still love that album though!

Bracknell Folk Festival's founder Paul Dunderdale had moved away at the end of the 1970s. During the first half of the '80s it slowly lost attendees as it got stuck in a fairly narrow booking policy of mainly the sort of music you'd find in folk clubs. Not much of what was emerging from left-field in the '80s roots explosion, very little of the genuinely traditional, just straight up the middle. In late 1986 the management at South Hill Park Arts Centre held a meeting of all the local folk movers and shakers to debate what to do the next year: should they let it die, or try a reboot? If the latter, who should be got in to direct it? Everybody in the room pointed at me! Well, I wasn't about to turn down a challenge.

With a good budget and a really helpful South Hill Park team to look after the site infrastructure, technical matters, publicity and all the necessary Health & Safety stuff, I was left to get on with booking and programming the artistic side. Of course, expectation amongst the local pewter tankard wielders was that I'd ruin 'their' festival with its cellar bar singarounds and mass Sunday morris displays, but I was determined to keep everything that was popular and build on it rather than replace anything. Why wouldn't I?

For 1987 I was able to get some decent bill toppers including Billy Bragg, Irish folk supergroup Patrick Street, Brass Monkey, 3 Mustaphas 3 and others, as well as tried and trusted favourites from Farnham Folk Days including the Watersons, Kathryn Tickell and Alistair Anderson. Again, with Lucy Duran's help, I got lucky with the availability on a short tour of Mali's Sidiki Diabaté Ensemble which included young kora master Toumani Diabate on one of his first UK visits, and amazing singer Kandia Kouyaté. They were sensational, and only slightly alarmed on arrival to be confronted, as they got off their bus, by Shropshire Bedlams border morris side screaming past them in feathers, tatters and coal-blackened faces, waving sticks, as they scattered from their performance!

Among many other things, I got the Watersons and Swan Arcade to combine their voices together in a joint set, inaugurating an occasional grouping that would later record as Blue Murder, and Martin Carthy and Billy Bragg to do a guitar accompaniment workshop where they talked fascinatingly about practically anything but guitars! It really doesn't take much imagination to spot possibly intriguing collaborations once you've got an event full of artists who rarely have the chance to get together.

Probably the most talked about moment of that weekend was the summery Sunday afternoon spot by London based pan-African dance band Taxi Pata Pata. As they tore into their infectious, energetic take on Congolese soukous with horns and chiming electric guitars, it felt like the entire festival audience rushed towards the main stage from all over the site, took one breath and started dancing. Standing at the back by the sound desk, I suddenly found Brass Monkey's Howard Evans sidling up to me, who were due on next to finish the concert. He looked from the joyous spectacle to me and just said "Bastard!" He'd possibly forgotten how much fun I'd given them the night before by getting them playing for dancers in a ceilidh, something they rarely did.

It was deemed a big success and many of the doubters were graceful enough to admit that their expectations had been confounded, for the best.

I had three glorious years producing Bracknell Folk & Roots Festival before I had to quit while I was ahead and hand it on after I'd moved to North London and got far too busy with something called *Folk Roots*. 1989's was also announced as Tiger Moth's last dance for the same reason. I'd pushed the boundaries to stretch from the Mekons, Tymon Dogg, bhangra stars Alaap and Hungary's Marta Sebestyen & Muzsikas through folk scene greats like Archie Fisher, Peter Bellamy and Dick Gaughan to real traditional singers like the Copper Family and Horsham's great Gordon Hall, one of the most riveting singers of epic traditional ballads that I was ever privileged to encounter. Audiences doubled and seemed well pleased. Southern TV made a documentary of the 1988 one called *Two Thousand Folk* which can be found on YouTube.

My final Bracknell year in charge produced a couple of memorable moments. It was a bit wet, and after punk-folk band Blyth Power had done an exhilarating set, leader/drummer Joseph Porter slipped on the muddy stage off-ramp and landed noisily in a pile of drum stands and cymbals at the feet of Martin Carthy who was waiting to go on. Looking up at a clearly startled Carthy, he announced "You're my hero, you are!"

I'd also programmed UK resident Argentinian bandoneonist Teddy Peiro's Tango Orchestra, who were a big hit with their authentic 1930s music and Teddy's playing in particular. He'd not long retired from a life in 'variety' where, among other things, he'd been a star juggler. After their set he was being mobbed by some of folk's top squeezeboxers like John Kirkpatrick and Rod Stradling when he spotted a couple of standard issue festival hippy jugglers some twenty yards away. Teddy sauntered over, with us following curiously. He stood watching for a few minutes until one of the jugglers asked if he'd like a go. Playing the part of the innocent elderly punter perfectly, he took the offered balls and made a few failed attempts. Then just as the hippy juggler was asking him if he'd like to be shown how to do it, he went into overdrive – balls flying everywhere, behind his back, through his legs, round his head, at lightning speed. A small crowd gathered. After a few minutes Teddy let the balls fall, said something self-deprecating about beginner's luck, and ambled off to huge applause while the two hippies stood mouths open, dumbstruck, with "who was that masked man?" expressions on their faces.

I did one more useful thing at Bracknell. Also in 1988, after a few years of a peripatetic existence around venues in Essex, Somerset and Cornwall, the WOMAD festival – more on that later – was looking for a new home.

Bracknell Folk Festival had always been paired with a jazz festival on the adjacent weekend to share the site infrastructure costs, but after 1987 the jazz event had gone bust which threw the folk one into financial doubt. I was able to introduce my friends from WOMAD to Bracknell, where they ran in tandem with the folk festival for two summers – a worldwide festival in 1988 with such legends as Nusrat Fateh Ali Khan and Youssou N'Dour, and a more blues-oriented one in 1989 including Taj Mahal and Ali Farka Touré – before settling permanently in nearby Reading for many years.

Truly the 1980s were a golden age...

11.
The 1980s : The Juggling Decade

The 1980s were indeed a golden age and inspired me into more activities than now seem humanly possible. As the decade progressed, my growing 'day job' was the magazine *Southern Rag*, which remained quarterly up until changing title to *Folk Roots* and going monthly in 1985, later abbreviated to *fRoots*. I'll finally get around to all that in the next chapter. But there was so much more…

Looking back, I have absolutely no idea how I juggled my unfeasibly large number of other music-related roles and projects during that decade, as the folk and roots music scene in the UK blossomed. I was still playing and recording while editing a magazine, running festivals and a record label, organising tours, getting into radio and photography, field trips to West Africa and lots more. For somebody whose driving motivations are to do something properly or not do it at all, coupled with the constant fear of fucking up in public, it quite scares me now just to think about it (clearly far more than it did at the time!)

Joe Boyd once voiced the theory to me that everything started to fall apart once the fax machine became common. Up until then, working in an organised way was easier. You could put a letter in the post knowing that the very earliest you'd get a reply was a couple of days later, so you could put the file away and get to concentrate on something else. The moment the fax machine became ubiquitous, the answer could arrive within an hour. Then somebody invented email… I honestly don't think that, even if I still had the youthful energy, I could do now what I managed back then. Most of those balls that I kept in the air would constantly be bouncing around my feet. But luckily, that pocket calculator which had emerged at the end of Chapter 8 had freed up time for more creative activities.

The first new thing that I'd embarked on at the end of the '70s was photography. Just like nearly everything I've done in my post-school life including music, it was self-taught – by getting fascinated with the subject and trying to figure out a way of doing it myself, always intuitively rather than copying. It's much easier to learn a style of music if you can already hear what you're aiming for in your head, and with photography (and probably other forms of visual art too) there's nothing like being able to see the kind of finished image you'd like in your mind. The learning, with images as with music, can be as much from understanding what you *don't* like, and why that should be, as what impresses you. And striving for results from an untutored position can sometimes produce strikingly original end products by doing things 'wrong'. My later Blue Blokes 3 band colleague Lu Edmonds reckoned that was a major legacy of punk rock.

Nowadays it's easy to capture a technically decent image with a higher-end mobile phone, and some people are blessed with an innate sense of composition, but before all that came along I found it absorbing to read up on the theories and technicalities and then do lots of practising. I dug around for information on which camera bodies, lenses, basic darkroom equipment and lighting that I could afford. Then, as I slowly managed to acquire them, learning how to use it all without thinking, experimenting with the right film to use for different circumstances and how to process it. I soon got to photographing at gigs regularly, spent time wandering the locality, observing and shooting, and taking advantage of the patience of friends who were willing to model for me, sometimes surprisingly uninhibitedly, while I learned how lighting worked. I took, processed and printed a lot of photos…

With probably obsessive dedication I eventually got, looking back, adequately good at it. Musician friends started asking me to produce publicity shots for their posters and record covers. The magazine and the agency benefitted from original images, and for a couple of years I got to be the official *Melody Maker* photographer at Cambridge Folk Festival.

These days you see the obedient crocodile of snappers being escorted into the 'pit' at the front by security staff, restricted to the first three songs of a set (or less if the artist has a tantrum) before sitting out at the media facility editing their digital images on laptops for uploading immediately to photo agency web sites. All the while missing the rest of the music. That wouldn't have suited me at all! Back then, there were few photographers, no pit, no tiresome shooting restrictions that meant you missed the later highlights of a set. You were trusted to be unobtrusively professional.

I'd take quite a few rolls of 35mm black & white film over the weekend, then hare home on Sunday evening to process it all in multiple film drums late at night. Monday morning, after little sleep, I'd blearily take down the now dry negatives, make contact sheets, quickly go through them with a loupe to identify likely (and well-exposed) images, print up a dozen or so 10x8s, call up a bike courier and send them off to the *Melody Maker* picture editor 40 miles away in London. By Wednesday afternoon they'd be in the edition on the news stands.

That was all very exciting, but exhausting, so after a couple of summers I sensibly stopped accepting those particular commissions before the novelty wore off. But for another decade I'd rarely go to a gig or on a music trip without my camera bag. I only slowly stopped when, after moving into London at the end of the '80s, I couldn't easily set up a darkroom near running water, and magazine workload had got much more intense. I had more than a decade gap before re-equipping for digital but – partly because by then the magazine had several first class photographers on tap (one of whom somewhat less than subtly told me that she was a photographer, whereas I "only took photographs") – I never recaptured the thrill of those early days of live music photography. Mostly, everything else is too easy with an iPhone in the pocket to persuade me to drag a camera bag around…

The digital revolution has brought about another benefit though. Many negatives which I never could have printed well at the time, even allowing for the cost of materials, can now produce extraordinary results when carefully scanned and processed with Photoshop. That's another self-taught skill I've acquired down the years of slaving away at the Macface. If you already knew the principles of photography and darkroom work, Photoshop was quite easy to pick up intuitively. You knew what you wanted to achieve, so you just had to locate the process in a menu, experiment and improve. I've got many box files of black & white negatives to go back and re-explore for overlooked gems, some no doubt of historic value – when there's time…

The other thing that I finally learned how to do at the beginning of the '80s was drive. All the while we were Hot Vulturing throughout the '70s we had a left-hand drive VW bus, which wasn't ideal to learn on. Once we cut down on gigs and mostly cut out the ones that needed PA carried, we got a regular car. And having figured out that having Maggie teach me was likely to end in tears, our friend Caroline coached me in her battered VW Beetle, so garishly painted up in red and yellow flames that any sensible driver on the roads gave it a wide berth. I passed on my second attempt…

One skill that I'd evolved out of necessity since the late 1960s was booking gigs. My first experience of that had been the 1969 UK tour for Mississippi Fred McDowell. As well as the administrative side that I was cursed by finding easy, when you've been looking after your own career you're more aware of the stuff that some agents don't understand to be so important to artists. Geographical routing, avoiding dead nights, making sure technical requirements are followed, sorting out accommodation and catering – all the things that contribute greatly to the performer's well-being and ability to produce their best. We'd had years in the 1970s forced to take any and every gig that came in, either direct or via the various agents who put stuff our way, because every penny counted and we couldn't afford to do otherwise, and it had worn us out. For several years we'd been away from home in Europe for long spells, out of contact, so agents were a necessity. How on earth did everybody manage before mobile 'phones and email?

Eventually by the late '70s, when the UK folk scene had really opened up again for the latter day Hot Vultures and the English Country Blues Band, I'd gone back to completely managing our own work, making it nicer and building contacts. Databases? They were boxes of file cards and the search facility was thumbing through as efficient a filing system as one could devise. Research consisted of making sure I regularly got all the then numerous regional folk magazines, the invaluable annual publications like the *Folk Directory* published by the EFDSS, and the NUS college entertainments directory, constantly cross-checking new editions with the file cards and updating them.

All this was time-consumingly tedious but necessary, and when one of the main folk agencies of the day ceased operating at the beginning of the '80s, it suddenly became obvious that I had already built the resources, contacts and experience that could help a small selection of musician friends who were suddenly left stranded. I also had the basic office space, equipment and 'phone in the early home of the *Southern Rag*, and at that point I had the time. So at the beginning of 1981 I was flattered into being persuaded, got the necessary licence and announced the launch of F.M.S. – Folk Music Services – to be both an agency and a go-to place for promoters to find things like folk-experienced PA hire.

Southern Rag co-founder and graphic designer Lawrence Heath created a logo for it, a cartoon parody of the HMV dog, listening in folkie style with a paw to its ear. We soon had a compact but impressive roster that included Martin Carthy, John Kirkpatrick (and all of those two's spin-off projects like Carthy & Kirkpatrick's trio with Howard Evans that grew into Brass Monkey), the Watersons, the Old Swan Band, Michael Chapman & Rick Kemp, Peta Webb & Webb's Wonders, Dave Evans, and a few people coming in from abroad like French guitarist Pierre Bensusan and America's Debby Mc-

Clatchy. And ourselves of course. If you remember the detail in the last chapter, it was certainly no coincidence that this list bears an uncanny resemblance to the bill for that first Farnham Folk Day.

As it turned out, being an agent or tour organiser wasn't a lot of fun, let alone greatly financially rewarding. It could even have become a good way to ruin friendships, though luckily those mostly survived. Of all the hats that I've worn down the decades of 'doing stuff' in music, it was the one I've liked the least. I found engaging with uncomprehending, unreasonably demanding and amateurish promoters on behalf of others to be more depressingly stressful than I needed. With the magazine still only quarterly I initially had the time, but other projects came up that were much more enjoyable and engaging. By the end of 1983 I'd pretty much run the agency down again, other than for single artist tour projects in later years – Italy's La Ciapa Rusa in 1984, West African kora masters Dembo Konte & Kausu Kuyateh later in the '80s, and Madagascar's Tarika in the '90s

Other bright ideas were always getting me involved in side projects. In 1982 I'd noticed that BBC2 TV were inviting fresh applications for their *Open Door* series, a community access TV slot where organisations could make programmes about their causes. I'd allowed myself to be co-opted, and later elected, onto the National Executive Committee of the English Folk Dance & Song Society, where activists from the song side were trying to move the society away from what felt like a stranglehold by 1950s social dance members, so I put a proposal in to the BBC under the EFDSS banner. To my great surprise, it got selected.

Lawrence Heath was organiser of the local *Stagfolk* club, so we put together an evening at their regular venue, Shackleford Village Hall, that was designed to give a good cross-section of the sort of music you might find in one of the better folk clubs of the time.

The cunning plan was to pick musicians who, having each performed a song from their normal repertoire, could join together as a scratch ceilidh band for the finale when the chairs would be put away and a bit of dancing take place. Thus Martin Simpson, Maggie Holland, Pete & Chris Coe and Peta Webb & Webb's Wonders each did a song, between them showcasing guitar, banjo, concertina, cittern, melodeon and fiddle; the *Melody Maker*'s Colin Irwin and I had a short impassioned interval discussion in the bar while the room was cleared and then a joyous bit of social dancing finished it – Maggie switching to bass guitar and Chris to hammered dulcimer in the band as Eddie Upton called and the audience hit the floor with great enthusiasm.

The Open Door production team were incredibly helpful at facilitating our ideas on the night, and a few days later up at the BBC editing it all. It went out in May 1982 titled *The Not The Finger In The Ear Show*, a title parodying then popular comedy series *Not The 9 O'Clock News*, and resulted in some five hundred stamped addressed envelopes winging their way into the EFDSS asking for a leaflet about finding your local folk club. Needless to say there were a few whingers – "Why no folk club 'entertainers'?" "Why weren't the women wearing make-up?" – but it was largely considered a resounding success and my kudos went up a few notches. You can find a lo-fi copy on YouTube.

As an aside, a sad Stagfolk memory from a month after the broadcast. One of the popular local resident singers was Roger Nutbeem, a captain in the army medical corps. In June that year, during the Falklands War, the great Scottish singer Dick Gaughan played the club and gave a fine socialist diatribe about how it's only the footsoldiers who bear the brunt of wars, never the officer classes. The audience went very quiet. In the interval we had to take Dick aside and explain that Roger had just been killed in the sinking of the Sir Galahad at Fitzroy in the Falklands. To give Dick his due, when he went on for his second set he immediately gave a sincere apology for his comments.

I stuck it out on the EFDSS NEC for a couple of frustrating years before I accepted that I could do far more good for the folk scene in general sat at home working on the magazine, the festivals and other activities than in interminable Saturdays of stultifying committee meetings in the basement of Cecil Sharp House where little ever got achieved. The single thing that made it worthwhile was that when the rest of them realised that the important Gold Badge of the society hadn't been awarded to any traditional singers for some years, they asked me and my one 'song' activist ally on the NEC, Mel McLeod, to propose somebody. We quickly agreed on the great Norfolk singer Walter Pardon, and they nodded it through: it was obvious most of them had never heard of him but at least they took our word for it. Having clearly achieved the most I ever could, I resigned not long after.

By 1986 the EFDSS was in dire straits. There was a legendary fractious AGM at Cecil Sharp House when they were threatened with bankruptcy, and the Home Counties 1950s folk dance tendency nearly sank the whole thing, ignoring impassioned advice from respected society elders like Ursula Vaughan-Williams and the Rev. Kenneth Loveless. It inspired me to write an intentionally OTT piece in *Folk Roots* headlined *Doom Day At DEAF-ASS: Fear And Loathing At Cecil Sharp House* (DEAFASS was the acronym coined in the magazine's *Borfolk* cartoon for the Dance Earnestly And Forget About Song Society) which in turn spawned a rash of EFDSS Militant Tendency badges out there at the grass roots. And I got fan mail from both Ursula and the Rev. Ken!

It's a tribute to the hard work of many positive activists and inspired staff since those days that the Society somehow survived, to regain good health and forward-looking policies in the 21st century and for the building itself to become the excellent venue that few could have foreseen back then.

In 1983, a decade on from the end of Village Thing, I found myself running a label again. It started by accident. The previous year, Jim Lloyd of BBC Radio 2's *Folk On 2* had asked certain artists to nominate a piece of music they loved which most people might not have encountered. Maggie Holland had picked a track titled *A Lambkin Has Commenced Bleating* from an LP by Bulgarian singer Nadka Karadjova on the state Balkanton label. I'd found a copy in Collett's in London after having been introduced to her singing by Andrew Cronshaw. Radio 2 had to borrow our LP to dub off the track. When it was played, it got such a response that it was played again on Radio 4's *Pick Of The Week* where it provoked much listener excitement. DJ Terry Wogan's producer spotted this and Wogan then started spinning it regularly – all this from the tape off our LP!

Somebody at Polygram got wind of it, realised it was a potential hit and, enquiring at the BBC, was told that I owned the source LP. They mistakenly thought that meant I owned the rights and got in touch to license it for UK release, so we quickly decided to bluff it out and got a friend at the British Council to put us in touch with Balkanton in Sofia to set up a deal. The moment we had written agreement, rather than wait for tapes to wend their slow way to the UK, Polygram rush released it as a single coupled with another track from the album – all still mastered from our copy! – on a new label we called FMS. The LP came out later after the tapes eventually showed up.

If only we'd had email and file transfer back then. Sadly, the delay was too long: the week the single finally came out Terry Wogan went on several weeks holiday so it lost the crucial push and only scraped into the top 100.

Who knows what might have been? But I now seemed to have a label... In 1983 I renamed it Rogue Records and, having released Maggie's first solo LP and the singles I mentioned in Chapter 9, I set about trying to licence an album by Tex-Mex squeezebox legend Flaco Jimenez. Strangely, although he'd toured in the UK with Ry Cooder, he'd never had a release here and I had a great LP of his on a label from San Antonio, Texas, that I'd picked up on our US trip in 1980 and played solidly ever since. Surely, after the trials of licensing from Bulgaria, fixing up something from the USA ought to be a piece of cake? Turned out that the owner of the label only spoke Spanish, which I don't! But we got it sorted and with this the label was off and running alongside everything else I was doing.

Rogue was first and foremost intended to be a label for the artistic endeavours of the people who played in the English Country Blues Band and Tiger Moth, and kept being that. But it also allowed me to release all sorts of other things, the only yardstick being that they were records I'd like to own that I thought deserved a wider hearing. We also did one-off releases by Barnsley's Deighton Family, Texan 'nuclear polka' band Brave Combo, Milton Keynes based Anglo-French dance band Cock & Bull and the intriguing Mighty Clouds Of Dust who included various members or ex-members of the Pogues, Horslips, Oysterband, 3 Mustaphas 3 and Radiators From Space. But increasingly as the fertile 1980s following burgeoned for what became known as World Music (more on that later), the label headed in that direction.

Rogue benefitted from *Folk Roots* getting proper offices in Farnham in 1985, plus the first of its trusty and invaluable full-time staff. We'd found a place that had previously been occupied by a professional photographer and still had a proper plumbed-in darkroom with sinks, so my photography took a turn for the better as well. Mind you, I'd also added to my busy hours by getting myself a weekly programme on local radio station County Sound in Guildford.

I was increasingly going into London to see world music gigs as that scene exploded and more and more artists came on tour. My social circle expanded rapidly in that direction, though it was an old friend from Hot Vultures days who made the most auspicious introduction. Clare Cooper, who at this point was working for Visiting Arts, the organisation that sat between the Arts Council who funded local arts here and the British Council who promoted our culture abroad, had briefly been married to singer/songwriter Robb Johnson back in the days when he regularly booked us for the college folk clubs he organised. She'd helped in brokering the Nadka Karadjova deal and getting funding for FMS to tour the Italian band La Ciapa Rusa and was most insistent that I should meet a woman called Lucy Duran who was then curator of international music at the National Sound Archive, soon to become a lecturer at SOAS (London University's School of Oriental and African Studies).

I think Lucy was initially suspicious of this uneducated person who ran a folk music magazine and was wanting to find out as much as possible about West African music, the harp-like instrument called the kora in particular, but we eventually became good friends. It turned out that she'd spent some time living in the Gambia, knew many of the key musicians like Alhaji Bai Konte, Amadou Bansang Jobarteh and Jali Nyama Suso, had studied the instrument and been married to a Gambian. She was now living with her two children in a big flat in Camden that was a haven for visiting musicians and undoubtedly was, more than anybody else in the UK, responsible for the respect the instrument and the culture of the region gained in the 1980s, '90s and beyond.

Much later I properly interviewed her for *fRoots* and heard about her extraordinary life up to that point with an inspirational, artistic Spanish father and Anglo/American mother, times spent living in America, Chile, England and Greece as well as the Gambia. Before getting deep into West African music she'd studied the sitar with Imrat Khan and written a dissertation on Cretan mountain music. If I'd known all that then I probably wouldn't have dared approach her at all.

In the autumn of 1986 Lucy suggested I apply to book a place on a trip she was organising to the Gambia. Administered by the Commonwealth Institute, there were something like eighteen places available for the trip which was to take place for several weeks either side of Christmas and New Year, the numbers dictated by the capacity of the local bus they could hire. I didn't need any persuading.

Some days later I was at a pre-gig restaurant reception that Radio 1's Andy Kershaw had organised for the American street singer Ted Hawkins who he was championing. Kershaw looked run ragged, with bags on the usual bags under his eyes, so I mentioned that if he needed a holiday he might like to join Lucy's trip too. His eyes lit up at that idea, so the next day I rang her and found out there was just one place left. Could she reserve it for Kershaw? To my surprise she'd never heard of him – Radio 1 wasn't on her radar – but yes, OK. (Somehow in Kershaw's own autobiography this has become Lucy spending months of 1986 pursuing him, trying to persuade him to go!) And so we would both make our first footfall on the African continent.

A couple of weeks before the trip, everybody going was invited to an introductory talk in a library at the National Sound Archive. An amusing memory of that evening is sitting next to Kershaw waiting for it to start and him pulling a bound 1960s set of *Blues Unlimited* off the adjacent shelf to thumb through. He chanced on one of my *Blues In Britain* columns, looked at the cover date, looked at me, looked back at the magazine and then asked "How *old* are you?"

The trip was brilliant, a life changer. Met off the plane by Lucy who had gone on ahead, and kora master Dembo Konte who was to be our tour guide and musician finder, we travelled around the country staying in musicians' compounds and hearing the real roots music of many different ethnic groups – Mandinka, Wolof, Jola, Balanta.

One encounter that still sticks in my mind was with musician Bajawao Camara, one of the last players of the bolombato, a four string bass 'war harp' looking like a cross between a massive kora and a lyre. From an enormous calabash, a curved neck arched over his head terminating in a metal plate equipped with rattles. His amazingly complex music was accompanied by wives driving it along with metal beaters. There were times when you expected the ground to open up and ghostly legions of warriors to march out. He was also the spitting image of Mississippi Fred McDowell.

Regularly staying in the Konte family compound, Lucy and I had come equipped to 'field record' an album of the fresh new kora duo of Dembo Konte and his brother-in-law Kausu Kuyateh, partly as a calling card for a UK tour I was planning to organise in 1987 after having already seen Dembo in the Gambian National Troupe and heard some tapes of Kausu that Lucy had previously brought home. We set our equipment up in the compound late at night, after the omnipresent shoals of children had gone to sleep and with their wives plying the musicians with relays of strong, sweet gunpowder tea as a stimulant.

Kausu, who normally played a customised kora with 23 strings instead of the usual 21, had borrowed a 'regular' one so that the two could play as a duo, and he'd kick off each piece with often stunning improvisations. With constant calls of encouragement and approval, apparently revelling in each other's playing, the two continued for several hours – Dembo almost regal in his laid-back confidence and skill, Kausu hunched over the gourd and playing (so they say in Casamance) as if possessed by *djinns*.

Oddly, the only time I received any real culture shock around that, my first visit to a deprived third world country, was on returning to polite, white, middle class Farnham. I really didn't feel that I belonged there any more.

Rogue released the pick of those extraordinary duets on the album *Tanante* in early 1987. It received rave reviews in Britain and paved the way for a month's tour that the duo made in April and May that year. Perhaps luck was in the air, but nobody was really prepared for just how successful that tour was to be. With musical tastes in Britain being more open to sounds from other cultures than ever before, it took little effort to persuade live music promoters around England, Scotland and Wales to book the pair for a string of gigs where no kora players had gone before.

Certainly no kora players had ever opened a tour with a personal appearance at the big Virgin Megastore in London's Oxford Street. From here on, they progressed around a series of almost entirely sold-out dates in concerts, clubs, arts centres and folk festivals, charming and stunning all-comers with their singing and increasingly astonishing kora duetting. By the time they returned to London later in the tour, extensive press coverage and a number of important radio sessions had spread the word so well that the police had to be called to the Africa Centre to control the crowd who'd been unable to get in after they'd over-sold tickets – Britain's first and only kora riot!

By the end of this concentrated period of touring, their playing was reaching such heights on a rapidly expanding repertoire, much of it previously unrecorded material drawn from the less-documented Casamance region of southern Senegal, that we couldn't resist the opportunity to record the duo again, this time in Topic Records' studio near to where I would soon end up living in North London. Like the tour, the results exceeded our already high expectations – a beautiful mixture of more-than-accessible tunes, rhythms, and just stunning musicianship – and their second album *Simbomba* rapidly became regarded as a classic.

I went back to the Gambia the following three winters, each time taking Sarah Coxson as my travelling companion. She'd come to *Folk Roots* for a few weeks of pre-university 'work experience' and never left! In spite of our age difference we became an item for several years, bonding over shared musical enthusiasms.

The 1987 tour was again conducted by Lucy, most memorable for seeing Youssou N'Dour & Super Etoile De Dakar in the stadium in Ziguinchor in Casamance. He'd recently done a world tour with Peter Gabriel and it was the first time he'd brought a Western style PA system and lighting rig to West Africa. The big audience had zoned themselves into local ethnic groups and every time the band did something recognisably from one particular local tradition, that section of the crowd would jump to their feet, cheer and dance. It was one of the best gig experiences of my life!

Later that night, we sat talking at Youssou's hotel and another English person in the party told him how he hoped Youssou wouldn't go the route of Salif Keita's then-recent *Soro* album, which the Englishman considered 'Westernised' as it was full of synthesisers. Youssou politely, gentlemanly, put the guy in his place, saying that instruments don't have a nationality, only musicians, and that if a Senegalese musician played a synthesiser or an electric guitar, it became a Senegalese instrument.

I may have appeared to be seriously embedded with West African music at this time, but still jumped at the chance to produce some of England's most celebrated traditional singers, Sussex's Copper Family, for the *Coppersongs* LP on the EFDSS's in-house label in 1988. This was a snapshot of the generations of the day – patriarch Bob Copper, his son John and daughter Jill and their respective spouses Lynne and Jon Dudley, plus a cameo appearance by his grandchildren Ben, Tom and Lucy who have long-since sung in the family as grown-ups along with another generation again. It was a pleasure, and it has been a continuing delight to remain friends with the Copper hordes and watch their tradition continue to this day.

As 1988 progressed it became clear that being based in Farnham wasn't really working. The magazine often needed last minute artworks biked over by advertisers, and I was driving into London to gigs several times a week. Luck hit for once. One of the two elderly brothers who were the landlords of my Farnham flat had died, and to settle the estate the small Georgian block had been sold to a property company. They wanted to get vacant possession of the flats in order to renovate them (which they certainly needed – dry rot was rife) and were willing to offer sitting tenants a substantial amount to move out. To my amazement, when I asked for a figure that would provide me the necessary mortgage deposit for buying a house in North London, they promptly agreed it (leaving the obvious but forever thought "what if I'd asked for more?" of course.)

I contacted an estate agent near Topic's studio in Stroud Green, saying that I needed somewhere nearby that I could move into and start working from immediately. Sarah and I drove up to the appointment, her reading me the guide book on what to look out for when buying a house. To my annoyance, the place they'd lined up for me to see was part-gutted with no staircase – I didn't even set foot inside. Would I like to look at another house a mile away on the Harringay Ladder? I had no idea where that was, but it was better than wasting that day's journey so off we went. We had a quick poke around the area in the balmy September sun, discovering multicultural Green Lanes and the fabulous Yasar Halim patisserie just down the road. This looked promising…

The woman of the house welcomed us in. I noted that the big knocked-through front room, perfect for an office, had piles of LPs and a banjo. We progressed through the homely open plan dining/kitchen area into the garden. I was trying to remember the questions the book had advised to ask about the roof when her husband came home. During brief pleasantries I mentioned that I needed somewhere that could house my magazine office at home. "What magazine?" "Oh, you won't have heard of it – a music magazine called *Folk Roots*." "Yes I have, I've been thinking of subscribing. Do you know Robin Dransfield?" "Yes, he's an old friend…" "Well you just missed him – he always stays here when he's in London." He then took me to the record collection and pulled out one of my LPs. I think I'd already decided to buy the house before I'd even been upstairs. The first and only one I viewed!

I put in an offer the next day, including a lifetime subscription to *Folk Roots*. It was promptly accepted and we moved in two months later. I lived there for the next 23 years, though Robin never did come to stay.

Another thing Lucy Duran had turned me on to early on was an atmospheric local Senegalese cassette by the then-unknown (outside the region) Baaba Maal & Mansour Seck. In those days my morning alarm was a bedside cassette player that came on with a timer and that cassette lived in it for many months until I became completely obsessed by it. It slowly dawned on me that it might be possible to licence it for Rogue Records. Eventually I managed to organise a deal through a Gambian intermediary, and it reached the point where I had to take a deep breath and pay the advance on trust.

Then some six months went by and I found myself thinking I'd been conned, until Baaba Maal had his first UK gigs with his electric band Dande

Lenol and he and his manager Mbassou Niang turned up in London with some tapes. It turned out that the delay had been because the original stereo masters had vanished, but they'd eventually found the unmixed multi-track tapes of most of it, and of another similar album from the same time. So engineer David Kenny and I spent a week in the Topic studio cross-referencing from the cassette to the multi-tracks, trying to duplicate the mix and ambience of the original, and then improve on it with the better outboard equipment and effects we had at our disposal.

When the album *Djam Leelii* was released in early 1989, it caused a sensation in world music circles, hit lots of 'best of' lists, and was licensed on to Island's Mango label for the USA. Our UK release eventually shifted around 15,000 copies across the three formats of the day – this was the annoying era when old-skool vinyl and cassettes were thankfully on their way out, but not yet dead, and CDs fast rising, so all three had to be manufactured.

Baaba was so pleased with our remix that he proposed recording his next acoustic album in Dakar and sending David and I the tapes to mix. They proposed a deal where we'd pay him an 'advance' in UK manufactured cassettes of *Djam Leelii* at cost, which he could sell at a good profit back home where the music market was entirely cassettes. It seemed like a mutually beneficial deal so we duplicated a few thousand copies and shipped them out. Then… nothing, until his next album *Baayo* appeared on Mango, clearly the acoustic one we'd funded…

By then we'd recouped the 'advance' with continuing sales of *Djam Leelii* so nothing was lost, and with his growing reputation for diva-like behaviour I was fairly glad not to have to deal with them any more. And I'm still very proud of what we did with that first album, which many consider among his best.

Lucy stopped running the Gambia trips after 1987 but by then I knew the ropes and we kept going each winter, usually with a few others. In 1988 these included great friend Pauline Lalor who had tour-managed Dembo & Kausu and Flaco Jimenez in the UK, the former when trusty Gambian driver Jack Gomez was unavailable. That year, Lucy had given me contacts for Balanta guitarist/singer Pascal Diatta in Ziguinchor, so we took my Pro Walkman and some mics down there and recorded an album of Pascal and his wife, singer Sona Mané in a hotel room. It came out to some acclaim in 1989, though unfortunately bureaucracy prevented them from touring to support the release.

There was a very strange sequel to that year's visit. An English couple, Terry and Sheila, had been living at the Konte compound in Brikama and partly in the coastal village of Kartong which had a sacred crocodile pool. We'd visited Kartong on the first trip in 1986. The pool, between the village and the beach and shaded by trees, mysteriously stayed full of fresh water all year round, even through the hot, dry season. The villagers tended it and believed that the albino crocodile sometimes seen there was actually an ancestral spirit. We were warned that if we tried to photograph it, it would not appear in the image or, at worse, the whole film would be ruined. We did see it, which Dembo told us brought good luck, anointing us with green pond water, but several of our party found the photographic warning to be true.

This later year, Terry, a photographer, had become obsessed by the legend and had taken to going every morning to the pool and waiting with his camera. After they'd returned to the UK, Terry & Sheila had arranged to put on a gig for Dembo & Kausu on their imminent visit. Just as they were setting out on the tour a call came in from a distressed Sheila to say that Terry had suddenly and unexpectedly died. But she wanted the gig to go ahead as a wake for him, and they were still welcome to stay in the house.

When they returned to London later, Dembo recounted to me what had happened. After the gig, Sheila had produced a big stack of photos from their stay in Gambia and Dembo had been looking through before handing them on to Kausu. He'd suddenly slapped his hand over one and didn't pass it on, since Kausu was quite superstitious and sometimes haunted by those *djinns*. There in the picture was the albino crocodile glaring straight out at the photographer. "This shouldn't be possible," Dembo said. "I now know what killed Terry. He pushed it too far."

Also on this tour I'd had a call from a woman called Francesca who said she'd like to book them for a small house gathering: she was willing to pay their normal club fee. A few days before the date she'd rung again to say that they could bring along a few friends if they liked, so they'd feel more relaxed. A little group of us showed up to this clearly exclusive address in Holland Park, in a street lined with very expensive cars. The maid showed us in...

We slowly realised that we recognised some of the guests, including a famous footballer, a rock star guitarist and a former Doctor Who. We were introduced to Francesca's elegant mother, noting that the large oil painting on the wall was of her as a younger model. Francesca, it turned out, was

Francesca Thyssen (or as Wikipedia puts it, Francesca Anna Dolores Freiin von Thyssen-Bornemisza de Kászon et Impérfalva, the daughter of Baron Hans Heinrich von Thyssen-Bornemisza and his third wife, fashion model Fiona Frances Elaine Campbell-Walter, descendant of the Campbell baronets!) Industrialists and art collectors, basically. As Wikipedia also puts it, "After leaving Saint Martin's School of Art, she worked as an actress, singer and model. Her partying lifestyle in London in the 1980s earned her reputation as an It girl." We'd clearly momentarily become part of 'It', whatever that was! She'd apparently met Dembo previously at a house party given by writer James Fox (of *White Mischief* fame), a friend of Lucy's, hence the connection.

It was the custom with kora players to dash them with money by putting it into the sound hole, so I reckoned that if we set the ball rolling they ought to be quids-in this night. I slipped Sarah a fiver which she went up and posted, and Charlie Gillett followed suit. But then... nothing. Francesca told us later, in some amusement, that she knew and approved of what we'd tried to catalyse but none of her guests carried cash. We began to fantasise about installing a platinum card reader into the koras...

In 1989 we took Dembo & Kausu into the studio in London with the 3 Mustaphas 3, John Kirkpatrick and a bit of myself on slide guitar, to make their *Jali Roll* album, which hit all the world music albums of the year lists in 1990.

In West Africa, sales of anything hot soon fall prey to bootleggers, so we were determined to help Dembo & Kausu steal a march on them. In late December 1989, a month ahead of *Jali Roll*'s European release, Sarah and I went on the last of our winter Gambia trips, along with *Jali Roll* producer and guitarist Ben Mandelson and his partner Clare. We took a couple of suitcases full of cassettes and a few white-label vinyl copies to the Gambia, distributing the plastic to the radio stations while the musicians swamped the market stalls with original tapes.

Within a matter of days, you couldn't go anywhere without hearing tracks blaring at you from every ghetto blaster. Uniformed policemen would hurl themselves into the road to bring Dembo's disentegrating Peugeot to a juddering halt, but instead of "Let's see your papers" it would be "Konte, Konte, a cassette!" Tapes would be produced from within the voluminous folds of Dembo's robe, cash would change hands, and off we'd go again. To our great pleasure, Dembo would introduce Ben to people as the guitar player on the album and they'd fall about in exaggerated laughter, saying "No, no, you can't fool us, we know that's a Malian playing on there," which was greater praise to Ben's ears than they could have imagined.

Not only did the innovative sounds on *Jali Roll* amaze local music fans in the Gambia and briefly turn these two traditional players in their middle years into overnight pop stars, it continued to work its magic. Regularly since then, recordings have shown up from the region – not just Gambia but Mali, Senegal and Guinea too – showing that the special *Jali Roll* arrangements of old songs like *Alla L'aa Ke* and *Lambango* have been widely heard and entered local culture. The distinctive styles and instrumentation that the Mustaphas added to the kora kings' songs have been widely copied. Unwittingly, we corrupted a tradition in the nicest possible way, through cross-cultural creativity rather than corporate cultural imperialism.

And to complete the West African part of Rogue's releases, somewhere in among all that I'd become friends with Sierra Leonian guitarist Abdul Tejan-Jalloh, a.k.a. Abdul Tee-Jay, introduced by DJ Charlie Gillett. He was a brilliant player and arranger, the deputising guitarist of choice for any Paris-based Congolese band who arrived in London short of a player who'd failed the visa barrier. We released three albums by his excellent band Rokoto, and he took part in our Orchestre Super Moth sessions too.

Then I got distracted by the music of Madagascar, which I'll come to when we get to Chapter 14.

12.
Media Mogul : Magazines & Radio

When I co-founded the *Southern Rag* in 1979, I had no idea that it would turn into something so far-reachingly successful and influential, let alone dominate my life – eventually building up to sometimes hundred hour working weeks around monthly production deadlines – for the next forty years. There may be other music publications which have had the same Editor for that unbroken length of time, but I'm not aware of them.

Apart from *English Dance & Song*, the membership magazine of the EFDSS, folk magazine publishing had really begun in Britain in the mid-1950s. I wasn't really aware of all the earlier history until Eric Winter, the founding editor of *Sing*, kindly gave me his archive of folk magazines and memorabilia when he retired and moved back to the north in the mid-1980s. *Sing* itself was inspired by America's *Sing Out!* which had begun publishing in 1950.

Sing, like much of the immediate post-skiffle folk growth, was proudly left-leaning in its outlook and had connections to the early CND: early editions carried songs to be sung on Aldermaston marches. There were a few other short-lived titles like Reg Hall and friends' *Ethnic* and Michael Moorcock's *The Rambler*, but by the early 1960s it had been joined by a fair old swathe of tiny specialist publications. Some had a semblance of national distribution, via folk clubs, like the starkly titled *Folk* and later *Club Folk* under the auspices of the EFDSS, or *Folk Music/ Ballads & Songs* from serial folk magazine entrepreneur (and *Melody Maker* columnist) Karl Dallas. Others were more locally based like *Spin*, out of the big club run by the Spinners group in Liverpool, *Abe's Folk Music Almanac* edited by Bob Pegg, later of folk rock pioneers Mr Fox, out of Leeds University, and Oxford University's *Heritage* in which future *Guardian* writer and BBC *Newsnight* journalist, the admirable Robin Denselow, cut his teeth.

As recounted in Chapter 3, I first discovered *Sing* along with the UK's *Folk Scene* and the USA's addictive *Sing Out!*, *Boston Broadside* and *Little Sandy Review* on visits to Collett's Folk Shop in London from 1965. I was promptly hooked. I briefly contributed a *Blues In Britain* column to *Blues Unlimited*, then into the '70s began contributing reviews, the odd feature and, inevitably, bits of opinion to *Folk Review*, a monthly edited by Fred Woods throughout the decade. Others came and went – more Karl Dallas publications like *Folk News* and *Acoustic Music*, and other excellent specialised periodicals like *Traditional Music*, Keith Summers' *Musical Traditions*, Tony Russell's *Old Time Music* and Ken Hunt's *Swing 51*.

Around the country numerous local and regional magazines and newsletters grew for their local folk club circuit, some intelligently written and nicely presented, others little more than duplicated parish magazines. Many were simply produced via typewriter-cut wax paper stencils on hand-cranked Gestetner machines, the more sophisticated by litho printing. The better ones – I wrote a round-up feature on 15 of those for *Folk Review* in late 1978 – had a really beneficial effect on co-ordinating and promoting folk music in their region, making people feel part of a 'scene'. They were really useful resources for travelling folk musicians too, and a way of getting the word out for independent folk labels who were never going to get a sniff from the mainstream music press, let alone plays on national radio where the BBC's few regular folk programmes were always abysmal and restricted for 'needle time'. If you struck really lucky you just might get a Radio 1 play from John Peel, Alexis Korner or Bob Harris.

Somewhere around the end of 1978, Fred Woods was tired of running *Folk Review* (and it showed). He approached me and asked if I'd be interested in taking it over. Initially interested, I got together graphic designer/club organiser Lawrence Heath and friend Caroline Walker (then Hurrell) who worked as a typesetter in the print unit at Guildford University and we had a pub meeting where we quickly decided to give it a go. We got quite enthused by the idea until we saw the accounts: it was a complete stiff, too far run down and we'd have been paying to service the existing subscribers.

By then we'd got the magazine-running bit between our teeth though. We realised that although many parts of the country had those effective regional publications, there wasn't one for central southern England – "Surrey, Middlesex, Berkshire, Hampshire, Sussex and around" as we first defined it. So off we went. It was to be a quarterly and the name *The Southern Rag* jumped unbidden into my head. It was the title of a Blind Blake ragtime guitar record from the 1920s but hardly anybody knew that.

The first one, featuring a cover interview with the New Victory Band, was dated July to September 1979 and came out that June. In between our decision to start it and its appearance, there was another significant event out there in the real world: a certain Margaret Thatcher came to power, coinciding with an era in which folk music slowly began to gain its mojo again.

It took off immediately. The first year's cover subjects also included Nic Jones, June Tabor and a big round table discussion on "Folk: is it on the right lines?" We got subscribers from as far afield as Japan and the USA almost immediately, reviewed everything from the key LP releases from the folk scene of the day to concerts of Chinese traditional music, and in a surprisingly short space of time began to be regarded as the main UK folk magazine. This was helped not only by us – though I say so myself – doing it pretty well, but *Folk Review* and Karl Dallas' last magazines vanishing. Singer Bill Caddick had made one attempt at taking on and running *Folk Review* but threw in the towel after one issue.

For the first few years it was relatively simple, as a quarterly, to manage the production and admin during our spare time, though the content kept growing. From issue 13 in summer 1982 we changed from A5 format to a proper grown up A4, which made it a bit easier for me to take over the page layout as Lawrence finally had to reduce involvement. I was already familiar with pasting up artwork using Cowgum (later Spraymount and then hand waxers), Rotring pens, scalpels and cutting boards by then so the learning curve wasn't too steep.

It was issue 14 that autumn which I think was a gamechanger. The 1970s had shown the slow decline in quality, purpose, energy and creativity in the folk club world, but by late 1982 it was becoming apparent that this was changing, in the wider folk world if not in the folk clubs. We were several years into the Thatcher regime and political fires had begun to smoulder again as a result. The 1970s 'new wave of English country dance bands' had captured festival dance floors. Imaginary musical borders were being breached. Questing youth from the mid-'70s punk generation, who had been firmly ostracised by the folk world at the time, were still seeking something interesting, off the mainstream and of substance as pop headed into '80s synthesisers and haircuts: they were now finding their way in the back door. And actually, at this point even some mainstream music was showing hopeful signs – via Dexy's rootsy *Come On Eileen* topping the charts and XTC making albums like *Mummer* and *English Settlement*, sleeved in folk iconography.

It suddenly felt all rather exciting, so we tried – not very convincingly – in *Southern Rag 14* to give a label to it. It didn't stick, but it helped the conversation. And boy was there a lot of conversation: the letters pages of the day were packed and combustible.

In this issue, Colin Irwin – whose folk page had been dropped by his daytime employer *Melody Maker* and was very happy to be offered another outlet for his main enthusiasm – celebrated something we invented (but didn't actually exist, yet) called the "Rogue Folk movement." He gathered together the diverse likes of Moving Hearts, Jumpleads, Andrew Cronshaw, Oyster Band, Dick Gaughan, De Danann, Home Service, The English Country Blues Band and more, to make a point. And we pulled a sub-headline quote out of Cronshaw's cover interview: "If it's not exciting, it's not folk music, it's chamber music – it should scream a bit at you. There's no problem with what's folk music and what isn't – you can hear it, it's got a vitality." In the interview, he added that folk music "tends to be played by rather safe people these days. When I first encountered the folk scene… the people were alarming, a bit 'other'… there was an energy in those days because they *had* to play, not because they thought they'd impress a folk club."

The 1980s would go on to give us – whether you liked them or not – important catalysts like the Pogues, Billy Bragg and the hugely enjoyable Boothill Foot-tappers, the whole 'world music' explosion, the real growth of festivals, lots of frontline exposure on Radio 1 via John Peel and Andy Kershaw, and in young newcomers like Kathryn Tickell the first signs of a fresh generation of exceptionally high standard coming into traditional music. Importantly, too, we still had a fair number of the old traditional singers and musicians around to engage and inspire – Walter Pardon, Bob Cann, Gordon Hall, the Shepherds, the Coppers, Billy Bennington, Oscar Woods and lots more.

Billy Bragg was clearly a kindred spirit, even if he did say in his first interview with us in 1985 that "I never had any inclination to play folk clubs at all. Not in the slightest. Everyone used to say to me 'solo performer – you should be playing folk clubs'. They didn't understand that the only way I was gonna get what I wanted – which was scared and a lot of money – was by doing rock gigs. And standing down in a folk club playing to half a dozen people waiting to hear a 20-minute version of *John Barleycorn* wasn't my idea of a Saturday night out."

I think the Pogues and Boothills were quite startled to be welcomed with open arms by the folk scene. The former got booked early on by a folk club in Oxford and were clearly quite nervous before playing, disguising it with a 'don't give a fuck' bravado – only to find these expected 'purists' giving them a rave reception. It's something I've often seen repeated down the years, even well into the second decade of the next century with Stick In The Wheel. "But you're not supposed to *like* us, you're supposed to be offended, fuckit..." would be implied.

I nearly robbed the world of the Pogues' Shane McGowan's talent around that time. I was driving through Camden as he lurched drunkenly off the pavement right in front of me: luckily my braking reaction was good. I got a cheery wave of recognition as he staggered off. Strangely, later that day I was walking through Regents Park and was nearly run down myself by the legendary Ivor Cutler on his bicycle: my turn to leap out of the way. There must have been something in the air.

Looking back, I think we were right with the main thrust of that particular issue. If pushed, having experienced all the decades from the 1960s to now, I'd say that the 1980s were the most exhilarating. I'm not (entirely) making any claims for *Southern Rag 14* having had a particular effect, but I do think that it serves as a historical marker. From that viewpoint, you could justifiably say that the '80s start right there...

We hit a bit of a glitch with issue 18 in winter 1983 when Caroline changed her day job and we lost our free typesetting facility. For three issues we soldiered on with setting it on an electronic typewriter and camera-reducing the copy but it simply didn't work – frankly, it looked a bit shit – so come issue 21 in autumn '84 we took the plunge and bought our own Linotype computer typesetting terminal.

Once again it was a learning curve for me, this time massive. I'd never met a computer before. The screen was a green dot matrix display. Unlike later desktop publishing programmes you couldn't see your layout, no WYSIWYG. I needed to learn and properly understand the principles of typography in order to know which codes to input for font, font size and weight, line spacing, column width, kerning and so on. Then you took the information on a big floppy disk to an output bureau where you anxiously waited for rolls of beautifully printed type (if you'd done it right) on crisp, thin bromide paper to cut up and paste onto layout boards. But at least the magazine looked reasonably professional again and this worked right up until 1990 when we got our first of many Apple Macs, software like Quark XPress and Photoshop (more learning curves!) and went fully 'desktop.' I became a typography nerd and have remained so ever since: you can tell the later designers who never had to learn that stuff and so don't know why 'orphans' and 'widows' are Very Bad Form.

There was so much happening that doing it justice in a quarterly eventually proved impossible. And so it was that exactly six years after we started as quarterly A5 *Southern Rag* with a black & white cover we went monthly and onto the national news stands. Issue 25 came out with a full colour front (Richard Thompson had the honour, and Dave Peabody got the gig as the first of our regular cover photographers) under the new title *Folk Roots* – it being obvious that many potential readers stumbling across it for the first time would have no idea what a *Southern Rag* was.

I'd pitched it at a number of distributors and settled on Seymour who were one of the UK's main ones. They got rather over-enthused and although I'd told them that I estimated a sale of 12,000 – 15,000 might be reasonable, they'd pumped the first few monthly issues' print order up to twice that and then failed to monitor returns. By the time they'd discovered that my original guess was spot on, we were some six months of costly over-printing into it. Luckily that bank manager was understanding and we rapidly changed to firm sale rather than sale-or-return with the news trade. From then on there was very little wastage other than when we did the occasional promotion, and we clawed back the initial losses.

Those first six months of the 'new' format were the worst. Basically, we had learned all the necessary skills for putting together and publishing a magazine from scratch, mostly self-taught. Nobody was really prepared for the work load … 1985 was a heavy year!

By the time we went monthly we needed a proper office and were lucky to find that one in the middle of Farnham, right next to the postal sorting office, which meant that getting the monthly sacks full of franked-up subscription copies into the postal system wasn't too major an operation. Though as we were up two steep flights of stairs it did mean hauling all the boxes of copies delivered by our printers up there, and then carting the full sacks back down after stuffing the envelopes. Delivery day was all-hands-to-the-pump. Luckily we were younger then, though I don't think my back ever thanked me.

The reception to it becoming *Folk Roots* was exceptional. With the extra monthly capacity we were able to widen the range of music we covered, locally and internationally, without cutting back on our core roots in the UK folk scene. It was all guided by the twin principles of "anything from anywhere with roots in a tradition" and "inspiration to enthusiasm". It was a portal for us and everybody else to dive down into fascinating new musical wormholes – Tex-Mex conjunto music, Greek rebetika, Hungarian dance houses, music from Okinawa, Madagascar, Guinea, Cuba, all of West Africa and much more.

Not everybody was pleased of course, bearing in mind the tendency of folkies to whinge about anything which didn't conform to their narrow taste range. The second monthly issue had Flaco Jimenez on the front which delighted many but produced a frankly racist letter from one of the English folk club scene's 'entertainers' complaining about "funny foreign-coloured people" on the cover when we ought to be supporting the people who were supposedly the backbone of the folk clubs. Like him.

I've no recall what he made of it two issues further on when we celebrated our first African artist on the cover, Zimbabwe's Thomas Mapfumo, who I'd deliberately courted controversy by describing his band The Blacks Unlimited as the best folk rock band on the planet. His spleen probably exploded. But the description of their liberation songs from colonial rule clearly struck a chord with the great Pete Seeger who promptly sent us fan mail for introducing him to Thomas' music. Mind you, just a few months later I got a postcard from Pete bollocking us for introducing a Folk Albums Chart which he thought anathema to the whole non-commercial principles of folk music. Good old Pete, bless him!

It was Northumbrian traditional musician Alistair Anderson who later nailed it in a letter responding to an interview with Senegal's Baaba Maal. "In case there are still some readers who feel that the inclusion of features on foreign artists is irrelevant to a British folk magazine," he wrote, "may I suggest that they read Rob Prince's interview with Baaba Maal in *FR95*. Not only did it give a fascinating insight into his music but it included one of the most articulate discussions on using traditionally based music in a contemporary context that I have seen. Baaba Maal had a lot to say about building on the strengths of his tradition without swamping it. He did not pretend that such fusions of the old and the new are easy nor that one would not make mistakes along the way but the one thing that he returned to again and again was that in order to keep the energy of the tradition flowing through his new work he must know that tradition intimately and return to it repeatedy. This is surely of relevance to us all. As has been said before, the deeper the roots of the tree the further it can branch out without becoming unbalanced."

Somebody else mentioned that if you went through that feature replacing the words "Senegal" and "Senegalese" with "England" and "English", it would be the perfect manifesto for any home-grown traditionally rooted musician. And I also suggested around then that Oysterband and fellow Senegalese superstars Youssou N'Dour & Super Etoile De Dakar were in fact the same animal. Both were thoroughly grounded in local traditions, playing music which grew directly from those roots but on modern instruments, both addressing local political issues. The only difference was that Youssou had become the No.1 star in his country (he eventually ran, unsuccessfully, for President) whereas the Oysters could hardly get arrested in theirs!

This was not an entirely original thought, as it followed the thread from a piece by Tony Russell in an early '70s folk magazine. In it, he'd combined LPs by Mississippi John Hurt and Norfolk traditional singer Walter Pardon in one review, pointing out that although the music they played was completely different, they were in fact the same person – elderly gentlemen who had privately preserved the old music through years of disinterest by their community before they were fêted by a new young audience. It provided an instructive way of looking at musicians as what they were rather than in genre terms.

I now stare at my shelves bowing under the weight of bound copies of 40 years of the magazine, 425 issues in all, and do sometimes wonder whether, if I knew then what I know now about what I was letting myself in for, I'd do it all over again. Wouldn't it have been easier to leave it as a quarterly and have a life? There were many times, slaving away beyond knackered at 2am after another in a series of sixteen hour days and amidst one of its regular financial crises, when I would happily have walked away from it.

But I didn't, couldn't: I knew how much the always-fragile roots music ecosystem benefitted from its existence and how many artists had gained a leg up when no other media outlets were biting. I also had staff and freelancers who were dependent on their income from it. And on the personal plus side it gave me myriad opportunities to hear and meet amazing musicians and contribute a little to turning others on to them and their cultures, which was considerable compensation of a different kind.

To do the story of *Southern Rag / Folk Roots* and later *fRoots* any kind of justice would take a whole book, which may indeed have to be the case. All I can do here is give you a smattering of such snapshots.

All the contributing writers and photographers were always freelance. I never wanted to be an employer and I'm pretty sure I was often a crap one, but after 1985 it became necessary and I was blessed with a small, hard-working, engaged and loyal full-time staff who often went the extra miles down the years because they all understood that what we did was first and foremost for the good of the music out there, and for the paying readers. Almost all were existing friends, and those who weren't were recruited through the magazine's pages. The one exception to that (and coincidentally the only full-time male staff member) we found through a *Guardian* advert and it proved disastrous for the office environment. He didn't last long.

Co-founder Caroline Walker had returned as Assistant Editor when we went monthly, and Beverly Hill (yes, her real name!) stepped up from being part time for *Southern Rag* to managing subscriptions and sales through to the very end (and, realising that I wasn't a proper boss, would be sure to let me know whenever I was being a pillock…) When I moved the operation into North London three years later she bravely became a commuter, which I'm sure she never intended, only stopping doing that after the London tube bombings of 2005. Luckily technology had moved on by then and we were able to set up for her to continue working from home, well ahead of the trend.

Then we needed an advertising manager and were happy to find Lisa Warburton. She had no previous experience but understood the folk scene and its unique culture (she's a hammered dulcimer player), wanted to be part of it and evolved the role quite quickly. As soon as the London move came on the cards, Lisa said straight away that she didn't fancy the commute, but was willing to do it until we found somebody new who she could hand over to, for which we were very grateful. Meanwhile, Sarah Coxson who had come for work experience and never really left, had become part of the family, taking on the part-time role of News Editor. This suited her when she started studying at SOAS in London and gave her a home base for her first year there. Sarah would return to be Deputy Editor in later years, before becoming one of the UK's best respected folk agents.

After several interim advertising managers, culminating in me quickly needing to let the *Guardian* guy go, Gina Jennings stepped into the breach to help us out in the spring of 1992 – temporarily as a favour, she thought, as she had been off work for health reasons for quite a while. Like Beverly, she was still there when it all ended in 2019. Somewhere during those years she'd moved to just four streets away, become landlady to an Oysterbandsman and eventually married him. The *fRoots* extended family…

Having not only been a folk magazine junkie all those years, I'd always religiously read the mainstream music press, though by the mid-'80s it had become more of a chore. *Melody Maker* had dumped its folk section and the *NME* had completely lost the buzz of its mid-late '70s "hip young gunslingers" era of writers like Charles Shaar Murray. Interestingly, in the early days of our magazine I'd had an amicable correspondence (actual letters – remember them?) with then *NME* Editor Neil Spencer pointing out how much the folk scene had historically had in common with the punk ethos (DIY music, politics, fanzines, independent labels) and that they really shouldn't take the piss. It was interesting to find him eventually becoming the champion of folk albums in the *Observer*'s reviews pages in the next century.

And then in 1986 we saw the launch of *Q* Magazine, later followed by *Mojo*, *Uncut*, *The Word* and the other glossy dadrock monthlies, many of which seemed to involve that fine fellow Mark Ellen in their early stages. It was immediately apparent to me that *Folk Roots* had to stand up on newsagents' shelves alongside those, with their hugely greater resources, rather than compete with the other specialist folk and roots music magazines.

It took quite a while to up our self-taught, permanently cash-strapped standards, but we did eventually get there – covermount CDs and all, after a couple of vinyl compilations we made for sale. 1987's *Square Roots* was a general mixture from across our content with a good smattering of tracks specially recorded for it from the likes of Oysterband, 3 Mustaphas 3 and Billy Bragg, and 1988's *Tap Roots* a survey of the 'new wave of English country dance bands.' We inaugurated our highly respected annual Critics Polls, got our own dedicated *BIFF* cartoons, and by the '90s commissioned most of our own cover photo shoots so we would only rarely have to use stock shots that possibly could be seen widely elsewhere.

When I later assembled two double CD compilations – *Roots* and *Routes* – to celebrate our 20th anniversary in the late '90s, I was startled but secretly flattered when I heard that *Q* Magazine were refusing to review them as they couldn't promote "a rival magazine." Oh really?!

The mainstream music business's attitude was always to treat anything it didn't understand as a possible threat. In the late 1980s we were asked by trade publication *Music Week* if we could compile a monthly chart of folk, roots & world music albums for them to publish alongside their 'indie' one. We put together a national panel of some 50 shops with sizeable specialist racks, and laboriously assembled the figures every month. It was widely welcomed and also carried by *NME*. Then, suddenly in 1991, it disappeared from *Music Week* without warning. I eventually winkled out of them that they didn't like it because some records stayed in it for a long time, and it included many releases on specialist labels who didn't advertise in *Music Week*. I was actually told that they didn't want to encourage retailers to stock such labels. So much for accuracy in the face of commerce!

It was great in our pages to be able help artists, independent labels and events, especially those who appreciated it and became true friends along the way. They were the ones who realised that the main reason for the magazine to exist wasn't to make individual people famous and provide copy for their press kits. It was to support the whole ecosystem, to expand reader horizons to the benefit of everybody, to the best of our ability. To cover the music and musicians in a deserved depth that would rarely be found elsewhere.

As you can imagine, I took a pretty dim view of people like the notoriously abrasive agent – now one of the founding queenpins of a leading 'industry' organisation – who later refused to vote in our annual and highly respected Critics' Polls for the albums of the year because our rules quite reasonably asked people not to vote for their own products or clients. Her view was that a vote for anybody else would be a vote 'against' her own roster. And then there was the editor of a short-lived American world music magazine who was overheard saying at a trade fair that she couldn't understand why anybody would want to read the sort of 5,000 word cover features we regularly ran. Neither of them 'got it'.

We really appreciated the readers who trusted us year in, year out, with subscription renewals. Enough told us of the ways in which we'd changed their lives for the better that we had no choice but believe them. And those advertisers who knew that supporting the magazine helped the whole scene survive and prosper, not just their slice of it.

Whereas other music magazines always needed (they thought) to have a 'big name' on the cover to sell copies, or an artist with a new album on a label with a big advertising budget, we often ignored that. We knew that our readers and advertisers were loyal enough and our circulation was so solidly subscription-based that we could occasionally put fairly unknown artists on the front who simply deserved it. This was based on nothing more than gut feeling for years, until proved spectacularly around the millennium by two consecutive issues, one of which had Robert Plant on the front and then the next newcomer folk singer Bill Jones. They both sold the same number of copies and attracted the same advertisement load. After that we often went off-piste... We just increased our efforts to make it look nice, a proper grown-up magazine, and were pleased to give deserved leg-ups to quite a number of artists as a result.

It was particularly satisfying to realise, when I once went back and totted it up much later on, how good a record *Folk Roots/fRoots* had on diversity, both gender and ethnicity. Indeed, we did a number of issues where it just panned out that all the main features were on women artists, though we never labelled them as such. Hilariously, back in early social media days when the BBC had 'message boards', one entitled (male) singer/ songwriter was so annoyed about our reviews editor's decision that his album was musically irrelevant and wouldn't be covered that he launched a public diatribe against me and about how he couldn't get featured in *fRoots* because he wasn't a pretty young girl. Not only did he get roundly blasted by message board readers for misogyny and an inflated opinion of his own worth, but it was pointed out that the current cover feature was on 82 year old Cheikha Rimitti...

Meanwhile, I'd also got into radio...

Folk-related music has historically had a pretty poor deal on national radio in Britain. Since the BBC pensioned off the old Home Service and Light Programme in the mid-'60s, it has always been stuck on Radio 2, the home of M.O.R. The Light Programme's *A Cellar Full Of Folk* (produced by Ian Grant and mostly introduced by Cliff Aungier or Bill Clifton) gave way to Radio 2's *Country Meets Folk* (Wally Whyton) through *Folk On Friday* (Jim Lloyd), *Folkweave* (Tony Capstick), *Folk '79* (Johnny Silvo and Isla St. Clair), *Folk On Two* (Jim Lloyd again) and *The Folk Show* (Mike Harding, Mark Radcliffe), and horses have rarely been frightened, musically.

At any point you'd often have to look elsewhere for the cutting edge stuff – on Radio 1 via John Peel, sometimes Bob Harris and Alexis Korner in the '70s, Peel and Andy Kershaw in the '80s and '90s, or into the new century over on Radio 3, especially in the golden era of *Late Junction* in the 2000s when presented by Verity Sharp or Fiona Talkington. It was only in the 21st century that the BBC got constructively behind the annual Folk Awards, which – until budget cuts and Covid killed them off – had a really beneficial effect on the music being taken more seriously out there. Outside that, though, we still were only allowed an hour a week, a pittance compared with other genres like jazz or entire stations for classical music.

In March 1984 I somehow managed to blag my way into getting a weekly hour on Guildford's ILR station County Sound which ran for three years. It got surprisingly popular, no doubt due to my access to all the new releases via the magazine. Mainstream presenters on the station tended to take the piss out of me playing tracks from 'weird' African LPs until Paul Simon's *Graceland* became the new sliced bread, and then they wanted to borrow my records. They mocked at my occasional guests like Champion Doug Veitch (the reggae-inflected 'King of Caledonian Cajun Swing'), then were startled when Billy Bragg, who was in the Top 10 and on *Top Of The Pops* with *Between The Wars*, chose to come in and guest on my little folk show. They didn't usually get proper pop stars visiting the station. I got to be so much part of the furniture that they even entrusted me with a daytime Christmas show to play early '60s instrumental hits from the Piltdown Men to the Spotnicks as nobody else wanted to be on duty.

All was going fine until the Head of Music changed in 1987. The new guy called in the 'specialist' show people – myself, Bob Sinfield who did blues and jazz, the country music and classical presenters – and gave us a pep talk about how we were only to play the 'household names' from our specialities. He wasn't amused when I asked what I'd play the following week. I wasn't amused when he told me his idea of folk household names was the Strawbs.

It wasn't going to work and I was too busy to waste my energy on a fight. A few weeks of whinges later I went in early, dubbed a 10 minute track from Mali's magnificent Ami Koita onto tape, did my programme, thanked the listeners and announced politely 10 minutes before the end that it was to be my last show due to "musical differences". I put on the tape to run up to the changeover (having tipped off the following presenter) and left the building.

I was told later that the Head of Music had heard this in his car on his way home, done a U-turn on the A31 Hog's Back and raced back to the station in a rage, only to find I'd already gone. The next day he 'phoned and shouted at me apoplectically that I'd "never work in radio again". Right...

The following week I got called up by London's Capital Radio to ask if I could take over their folk slot for a month, which meant I got to studio hot-swap every week with the great Charlie Gillett, who was by then a good friend. Two weeks later I got called by producer Nick Freeth to headhunt me for a folk and world music show on the BBC World Service which I then did as *Folk Routes* for the next decade.

Nick duly became my 'Man At Radio' (and subsequently also mastered all the *fRoots* CDs and DL albums to the end). Via his independent production company he got me a couple of Radio 2 series – *Globesounds* and *Rooting About* – which were well received, other than by Radio 2's Controller Frances Line (by then married to folk perma-presenter Jim Lloyd). She apparently told the programme review panel that *Rooting About* may have been liked by them and the listeners but she didn't want it on her network...

Nick was also producing in the early days of London's Jazz FM. He called me up one Friday evening and asked a favour. Paul Jones, who did a 4-hour Saturday lunchtime blues show, had fallen sick: could I dep for him? Crikey! I'd got into the habit of meticulously preparing programmes with sequences worked out, track times ascertained and a few link notes jotted down to busk, but there was no way I could possibly do that for a 4-hour show at 12 hours' notice including a night's sleep. So I just slung all my favourite blues CDs into my box, added a handful of world music ones which had a bluesy feel that might appeal, and drove over the next morning for a quick workshop on how the desk functioned and what to do about adverts, news, live traffic reports etc.

It was a blast. Time whizzed by – it felt more like two hours than four – and lots of listeners rang in about things they were enjoying. The world music tracks by Ali Farka Touré, Cesaria Evora, Amar Sundy and others were particularly well received, and I heard a short while later that I'd cleared the Virgin Megastore and Stern's in the West End of Cesaria's CDs over the next few days. Jazz FM were pleased and so was Paul, so I got to do a couple more stand-ins for him shortly after. At which point I pitched for a world music show and to my great pleasure got one.

My slot on Sunday nights had been occupied by cheap live jazz recordings from Ronnie Scott's, sponsored by a whisky distillery, but the station had lost the sponsorship. It was considered a 'graveyard slot' as it was up against the weekly chart show on Radio 1, but world music was hot in London and I fairly soon gained impressive listening figures so they were very happy. I did it for the best part of a year and it was one of my favouritest things ever. The station had two studios that alternated so I'd slip into mine and set up, turn the lights down low, take over on the hour, and for the best part of the next one until the next presenter came in it would be just me and the security guard at reception in the station. Mostly I winged it with new releases and old favourites, talking to listeners, building up quite a rapport with the remote traffic reporter lady. Occasionally I'd have to do things like read out the Wimbledon results which I somehow managed to do with seeming authority even though I had not a single clue what I was talking about!

Towards the end of my tenure there were a few times that I couldn't do the show live, so rather than pre-record I got Charlie Gillett in to dep, who'd been off air in London for a few years since his Capital Radio days at this point. They'd let him go: ironically a few weeks before he'd won a Sony Gold Award as a broadcaster. I was very pleased that slipping him back on air led indirectly to him getting his subsequent and legendary BBC Radio London show.

Eventually I was a victim of my own success. Having boosted their Sunday evening listener figures (and been cited as an asset, ticking the musical diversity box in their successful licence renewal application), the whisky distillery wanted their sponsored jazz show back and I didn't have sponsorship. Money won. I was promised they'd find me another slot, but a few weeks later the programme controller left and his replacement didn't understand. That's radio, folks…

My other favourite radio experience around then was another short notice dep. I'd regularly gone to sit in the studio when Andy Kershaw was broadcasting his Radio 1 show, negotiating the tunnel maze from the Broadcasting House foyer to the building next door. One week when Kershaw was stuck on the Isle of Man and couldn't get back, his producer John Walters got me in to present in his place and I had a whale of a time, other than when the CD player refused to fire the Lenny Bruce I had cued up. At the end, I got to do a proper live-on-air DJ handover to the heroic John Peel which iced the cake perfectly. I was, for one night only, a Radio 1 DJ.

I became a bit of a rent-a-pundit, regularly getting invited onto Paul Jones' Radio 2 blues programme, and Janice Long's Saturday morning show on BBC London where I'd make knowledgeable noises co-reviewing singles. When they were desperate because somebody else had failed to show up, I would sometimes end up asked to be one of the talking heads reviewing the newspapers as well – which on one bizarre occasion also included Carol Thatcher. I once took my daughter along who sat patiently in the control room reading *Harry Potter*, a new thing then, until Janice spotted this through the glass and promptly asked her to comment on that on air too. Live radio was just so much fun, as I could always talk presentable bollocks out of my head in those days.

It all stopped in the late '90s. Around the time my years on the World Service came to an end, when they cut most of their music programmes to concentrate on speech-based ones, Jim Lloyd retired from his years presenting folk on Radio 2 which he'd done for nearly three decades. Frances Line retired as BBC Radio 2 controller at the same time. Jim was a very nice and enthusiastic man who had created the BBC Young Tradition Award but although at his instigation the programme had been willing to book artists like Dembo Konte & Kausu Kuyateh for sessions in the '80s, many felt that the style and content of *Folk On 2* was now dated and out of touch. For a brief period, the BBC Pebble Mill production department under Geoffrey Hewitt and David Corser continued to make a folk show presented by Ralph McTell, while the BBC put the contract for a permanent weekly hour out to tender.

I was approached by Pebble Mill to be the presenter in their bid to retain the programme. The decision came down to a final short list of two: the Pebble Mill proposal with me at the helm, and one from independent production company Smooth Operations with Mike Harding as the front man. Smooth Operations won it: I was told that the final decision rested on the facts that the BBC were leaning towards independent companies at that time, that Mike Harding was a 'household name' as he'd had a hit record, and that Pebble Mill had been seen to run a sinking ship with the Jim Lloyd programme (hardly fair when you can't remove a sitting tenant who is married to the controller!)

In early 1998, new Radio 2 controller Jim Moir hosted a lunch at Broadcasting House to announce the new programme, inviting a dozen or so movers and shakers from the folk scene of the day, keen to get the grass roots folk scene on board as they were aware that the previous programme had lost the confidence of the folk world. I was invited as *fRoots* editor, though obviously I felt very compromised – apart from Moir and his assistant I imagine I was the only person there who knew I was the failed candidate.

After the lunch came the announcement. Considerable surprise was expressed about the choice of presenter, with one major folk festival organiser openly questioning how in touch Mike Harding was with the scene at that time. John Leonard from Smooth Operations tried to allay those fears by saying that they'd be selecting the music, not Harding, which didn't help. I stayed silent throughout, feeling extremely uncomfortable. Eventually Moir turned to me and put me on the spot by asking who I thought would be the best presenter. ("You bastard," I thought!) I remember saying that it ought to be somebody with the equivalent knowledge and enthusiasm in the folk field as the late Alexis Korner had in his, but failing that perhaps it was time for a younger and maybe female presenter – I mentioned Catriona MacDonald who was doing a great job on BBC Scotland at that time.

When the new programme hit the airwaves, the *fRoots* mailbag promptly filled with letters in reaction, almost all of which were negative. Again, as both editor and losing candidate (though hardly anybody knew this), I found myself in an invidious position. I decided that the only thing we could do in order to maintain our integrity was print a proportionally representative sample. I heard through the grapevine from Radio 2 that Jim Moir was deeply displeased, and a familiar quote reached me that I would "never work on the BBC again."

As it happens, that pretty much turned out to be the case, though I don't actually believe that the folk show episode was the cause. Mike Harding and I eventually became reasonably friendly, as you'd expect from grown ups who share musical enthusiasms. After all, we were only pawns in their game.

13.
Let's Call It World Music

In marketing terms, World Music year zero was technically 1987, but it had been a long, slowly accelerating build up to that point. Leaving aside the millennia of immigration into Britain back to the Romans and beyond (I highly recommend Robert Winder's essential book *Bloody Foreigners* about such history) with all the multi-cultural influences that would have brought, the more recent 19th century had seen 'foreign' dances like the waltz and the polka gaining mass popularity in Britain, becoming naturalised. Morris dancing had entered from mainland Europe much earlier. Then recorded music from elsewhere became readily available in the 20th century, bringing crazes for everything from Argentinian tango to Hawaiian music in the 1920s and '30s, alongside the admittedly overwhelming American cultural overload.

In personal terms, that Miriam Makeba record which I'd heard in the Swahili in Weston-super-Mare in the early '60s and the odd 'exotic' hit record like Elias & His Zig Zag Jive Flutes' *Tom Hark* had attracted my curiosity. Davy Graham's early records had intriguing stuff that we were told came from expeditions to North Africa, and so had the Incredible String Band's. Then of course one couldn't miss the 1960s dip into Indian culture by the Beatles and, off the mainstream, experiments like Indo-Jazz fusions.

When my burrowings into roots musics led me to havens like Collett's, I'd occasionally impulse-bought albums on Lyrichord, Folkways or Nonesuch which had given me ideas which I didn't know how to follow up. But I was lucky: most people weren't aware of Collett's and if there was an 'International' section in their local record shop it most likely contained Johnny Hallyday, Nana Mouskouri, Dorita y Pepe (a UK duo, otherwise Dorothy and Peter Sensier, who specialised in Spanish and Latin American music on TV variety shows) and a Dutch fake Hawaiian called Wout Steenhuis. There wasn't much inspiration to enthusiasm in there.

But there were other underground routes to worldly delights. The American magazine *Sing Out!* was one. I first heard Alhaji Bai Konte's kora on one of their free flexi-discs in the '70s, little imagining that I'd one day visit his home compound in the Gambia and work with his son Dembo. Then, by the beginning of the '80s things gradually started to get better. The information revolution was growing and the world was getting smaller. Not long after *Southern Rag* started up, there was another short-lived but vital publication called *Collusion*, edited by David Toop, Sue Steward and Steve Beresford. Like *Blues Unlimited* in the '60s it brought the wonderful realisation that there were other like-questing minds out there, sources for import records and information.

Soon there were new labels and events springing up everywhere, and even new specialist shops like Stern's in London in which to buy records and meet the like-minded. In what now seems a relatively short time in African music alone there came Nigeria's King Sunny Ade, Senegal's Youssou N'Dour & Super Etoile De Dakar, Guinea's Bembeya Jazz and Jali Musa Jawara, Zaire's Kanda Bongo Man, Mali's Zani Diabate & The Super Djata Band, South Africa's Mahlathini & The Mahotella Queens, Kenya's Orchestre Virunga and Zimbabwe's Thomas Mapfumo & The Blacks Unlimited and the Bhundu Boys, all to play live before our very eyes.

We soon learned that we'd already missed a golden age of post-independence music in Mali, Guinea, Senegal and Zaire and were thrilled to catch up with it as re-issues multiplied. I got particularly entranced by the recordings of Guinea's Bembeya Jazz (not jazz as we know it!) featuring their epic guitarist Sekou 'Diamond Fingers' Diabate and was lucky to see them just once at London's Africa Centre before they disappeared from our vision for several decades.

Charlie Gillett later evolved a wiggy theory about why there were historically sudden bursts of musical creativity in certain small regions of the world – New Orleans in the 1920s, Memphis in the 1950s, Liverpool in the 1960s, Francophone West Africa in the 1970s for example. It was something to do with a space ship hovering above them beaming down inspiration. I was never sure if he was entirely serious!

The early and mid-1980s were a wonderful time to be involved with such music. Apart from the thrill of discovering it all for yourself, quite early on you'd realise you were standing at the back of venues in proximity to the same familiar audience faces. New social circles evolved – many of whom turned out to be the people who'd become enthusiastic activists in the following years, running labels, promoting, writing, broadcasting.

It seemed that music from Africa particularly appealed to people who came from the blues and R&B direction, Latin music – especially Cuban – grabbed jazzers (it was probably the trumpets), and sounds from Eastern and Southern Europe tickled the ears of those from the folk scene (where 'folk rock' had by now lost its mojo). Meanwhile the punk generation, dismayed with the awful manufactured state of 1980s synth pop, 'new romantics,' silly haircuts and trousers and proto-'yacht rock' with four-square rhythm sections battered by over-prominent snare drums, were looking for anything that seemed challenging and 'authentic.'

Initially all these tribes circled each other with a degree of suspicion, with a resistance from the wannabe 'cool' jazzers to what they saw as the deeply unhip folkies, for example, but most eventually got over it. It turned out that quite a few of the new African and Latin music fans had been youthful habitués of venues like Les Cousins in the 1960s. But whatever, it was a perfect time when supply and demand just about kept up with each other.

There were GLC shows, many a night at the Town & Country Club in Kentish Town or the Africa Centre in Covent Garden, gigs in Holland Park behind the Commonwealth Institute, club nights (where lots of Latin music held sway too) at the Mambo Inn in Brixton, DJ'd by Gerry Lyseight, Max Reinhardt & Rita Ray, or the Bass Clef in Hoxton by John Armstrong. Arts Worldwide tours showcased artists from Sudan, Morocco and Madagascar (including Mali's now near-forgotten Ousmane Sacko who brought with him a very young kora player called Toumani Diabate on his first UK visit). There was the birth of WOMAD festivals, and new UK labels sprang up like Earthworks, GlobeStyle, Hannibal and Stern's. It was initially very London-centric but soon spread nationally. Television series like Jeremy Marre's inspiring *Beats Of The Heart* documentaries and later BBC 2's *Rhythms Of The World* certainly helped in this as well as key radio DJs.

Before his tragically early death in 1984, Alexis Korner, ever broadminded, would play interesting overseas records on his Radio 1 show. When one of *Southern Rag*'s first Japanese subscribers had dropped me off copies of the early albums by Okinawa's Shoukichi Kina & Champluse, I'd taken it upon myself to get a few more copies of each and sent them to Alexis who featured them immediately, as did John Peel, the other recipient.

This was an early example of what became very common in the late '80s and '90s – supportive networking between radio and press people. We'd regularly tip each other off and pay attention to what the others were up to – press features or reviews leading to radio play and vice versa. Unity is power! Charlie Gillett coined the phrase 'world of mouth'. I have strong memories of returning from trips to West Africa or, later, Madagascar, and burning CDR copies of locally produced cassettes to bang around the other radio DJs, or picking up extra copies of CDs for them on record shopping trips to Paris. It was what we did. The important thing was getting this music which excited us to the widest possible audience. Sometimes in this way it would also reach label people or tour/ festival organisers who would join the chain. Everybody won.

Charlie Gillett and Andy Kershaw, who was recruited to Radio 1 not long after Korner's death, soon became converts to and proseytisers for an increasingly wide range of international sounds, and the 3 Mustaphas 3 popped up on John Peel's show. Our magazine was able to review more and more records because they were now becoming available on local release or import, and artists came here so we could talk to them.

Ah, the 3 Mustaphas 3! Whether they were a fez-wearing brethren of refrigeration engineers self-exported from mysterious Szegerely, somewhere in the Balkans, or a bunch of very world-musically literate UK funsters with long pedigrees disguised by improbable pseudonyms is now immaterial. Many years have passed since Billie Jo Mustapha jumped off the Szegerely bridge, but the Mustaphas remain unsurpassed as one of the greatest live bands of our time and the true godfathers of world music in the UK.

I first heard something on Peel's show from their 1985 debut mini-album *Bam! Mustaphas Play Stereo*, an early release on Ace Records' then new GlobeStyle imprint. Peel went along with the amusingly doubtful mythology and gave them live sessions. I was intrigued enough to ring up Ace to ask for an interview for an early *Folk Roots*. A hand was obviously clamped over the 'phone to muffle a hasty background conversation and then their press officer, the impressively named Vermilion Sands, handed it to a bloke with a dubious Balkan accent claiming to be their manager, a Mr Askadinia.

An assignation was made to meet in the legendary (in music business circles) Giaconda café in Denmark Street, London's Tin Pan Alley off the Charing Cross Road, on Mayday, 1985. And thus, in his guise as Hijaz Mustapha, I would first meet the inspiring, amusing, occasionally infuriating chap who would become my best pal and occasional musical accomplice over the subsequent decades, Ben Mandelson.

Ben's another of those, like Lucy Duran, who left an indelible under-the-counter mark on the shape of the 1980s music world, and as with Lucy I also eventually got around to interviewing him in depth about his remarkable musical adventures for *fRoots*. In brief, born in Liverpool he'd begun playing music in folk clubs but, like myself, was always curious about other kinds, be it Hank Williams, Billy Pigg or Ornette Coleman. He'd moved down to Brighton with his chum Rob Keyloch, and they played in a punk band called the Amazorblades who recorded for Chiswick, part of Ace Records with whose Roger Armstrong he'd eventually set up GlobeStyle.

But also he'd been in Howard Devoto's band Magazine, busked his way to Italy, played in the house band for the *Hank Williams: The Show He Never Gave* stage musical, travelled America by Greyhound bus hunting down roots music, fallen heavily for African music and spent time travelling and playing in Kenya, and been in one of the trailblazing early '80s London based African-style bands Orchestre Jazira. Later he'd be in Billy Bragg's Blokes and a main mover-shaker of what became WOMEX.

It was in Stern's in early 1986 that I'd picked up, on Mike Cooper's recommendation, an import LP on the French label Disques Esperance by a mysterious Malian guitar player called Ali Farka Touré and reviewed it in *Folk Roots*. A short while later Andy Kershaw would find the same album on a Paris jaunt and play it regularly on his Radio 1 show. In these ways, interest among roots, blues and West African music fans – a rapidly growing bunch at that time – was piqued. Debate ensued about whether he reminded us more of John Lee Hooker or Skip James.

The main UK tour organisers for interesting music from faraway places back then – a year before the marketing tag 'world music' was instigated – were Anne Hunt and Mary Farquharson at Arts Worldwide. Director Anne set off for Mali with the express intention of tracking Ali down and persuading him to come to the UK on tour. Meanwhile, Lucy Duran's flat in Camden was a buzzing hub where the door was always open. You could bowl up there and find Gambian kora masters or Cuban trumpeters ensconced in the sitting room, or Cretan musicians playing intense, intricate and apparently never-ending circular tunes at the kitchen table.

So it was that I showed up one sunny evening in 1987 to be greeted by Lucy with the biggest shit-eating grin imaginable on her face. "Ian! You'll *never* guess who's here!" Er, no… "Come in, come in…" And there, sat in the armchair by the window, was an impressively regal-looking African gentleman resplendent in a purple robe. "This," pronounced Lucy, unable to disguise her pleasure and excitement, "is Ali Farka Touré!" Anne Hunt had successfully found him. My flabber was extremely ghasted!

Also around that time, Anne had decided that they ought to start a label to record the remarkable artists that Arts Worldwide were bringing over, and thus the eventually mega-successful World Circuit Records, home of Buena Vista Social Club and all the rest, was born. She'd hired a young man called Nick Gold to run it, later augmented by Jenny Adlington, and one of his first duties was to pay visits to the people running some of the other little independent specialist labels putting out what was about to be called world music and ask how it was done. He came to visit our tiny Rogue Records set-up among the others. As Ben Mandelson, then at the helm of GlobeStyle, later commented, it was a good thing that he didn't take any of our advice!

World Circuit put Ali into the studio on that first UK visit, to record his eponymous first album for the label, which really launched his international career. The trust built up between Ali and Nick meant that another four solo albums for the label would follow over the next two decades.

Also on that visit, Ali made his first ever unadvertised UK live appearance at the Mean Fiddler in Harlesden. We reviewed it *Folk Roots*. I'd taken my camera, and nearly drove off the road later when spotting one of my photos blown up huge on posters advertising the South Bank debut double bill of Ali and Jali Musa Jawara. My shit-eating grin was probably as wide as Lucy's had been the previous year! It continued to stay plastered to my face when I was able to book him for our 1988 Farnham Folk Day. The following year, after I'd introduced my WOMAD friends to South Hill Park at Bracknell, he appeared with US bluesman Taj Mahal, one of his first cross-cultural collaborations.

Ali really loved my Thornbory acoustic guitar so I used to regularly lend it to him for his UK tours and recording, where he'd alternate it with his curious black Eastern European electric guitar. And so it came to 1994 when he was due to go to the States on the tour where he'd record *Talking Timbuktu* with Ry Cooder. Nick brought Ali round to my house a few days before they left, once again in his best regal robes, and he did the whole pantomime schtick of falling to one knee and pleading with me to sell him my guitar so he could take it to America. Regretfully, I explained I couldn't – it had been specially made for me to my specs and was far too personal (it's still my main instrument to this day). But I asked Nick where their first date was. Turned out it was McCabe's in Santa Monica, which just happened to be one of the best guitar shops in the USA. As I predicted, they sorted him immediately.

As well as Ali, that Thornbory guitar used to get borrowed occasionally by other visiting West African players like Baaba Maal, Guinea's Sékou 'Diamond Fingers' Diabaté from Bembeya Jazz and Mali's Djelimady Tounkara from the Super Rail Band. I fantasise that future guitar anoraks poring over photos will wonder what make of instrument – with its distinctive entwined serpents with vulture heads in mother-of-pearl on its headstock – was favoured by all these players, not realising it's always the same one.

Ali was just one of many astounding visitors in that glorious period in the mid 1980s when the world's roots musics exploded into our midst. In London, Ken Livingstone's GLC (before Mrs Thatcher had it abolished) were a key funder of cultural events including an annual Music Village held in Holland Park in conjunction with the Commonwealth Institute. 1984's African Music Village and 1985's Indian Ocean Music Village both included a group of musicians and dancers from the Bagamoyo College Of Arts in Tanzania, fronted by the extraordinary singer Hukwe Zawose. He was later signed by Real World Records though the early album *Tanzania Yetu* by the Bagamoyo Musicians (Triple Earth) remains an era classic.

I arranged to interview Zawose for *Folk Roots* at the 1985 festival, and took along my friend Clare Cooper from Visiting Arts. He was accompanied by a Tanzanian cultural attaché who translated, and it became apparent from the length of Hukwe's answers and the relative shortness of the translated versions that I certainly wasn't getting the full story, interesting though it was. At the end of the congenial interview, as hands were being shaken, Clare – who had remained quiet throughout – spoke to the pair in fluent Swahili. She had grown up there with her missionary parents, and the looks on their faces when they realised that all their interchanges had been fully understood were a picture.

It wasn't just African music that held sway, though it took the biggest share at the time. A series of import albums of Hungarian Dance House music, available via Collett's, had captured the imagination, and out of that movement came the band Muzsikas featuring the beguiling voice of Marta Sebestyen, soon taken to the hearts of UK folk audiences. They were signed to producer Joe Boyd's Hannibal label, along with Bulgaria's Trio Bulgarka who would later work with Kate Bush. Our minor success with Nadka Karadjova a few years earlier was a start, but it was an album titled *Le Mystère Des Voix Bulgares*, originally released in France in 1975, that really caught the public's imagination when re-issued on hip indie label 4AD in

LET'S CALL IT WORLD MUSIC

1986. That and (back to Africa) Paul Simon's *Graceland* opened the doors through which artists like Mory Kante and Ofra Haza would soon saunter to international chart hits.

This was all very well, and more and more was being played on the radio – often gloriously mispronounced by well-meaning presenters (who, me?) – but where the hell did you look in your High Street record shop for all this varied music that now had a burgeoning would-be buyer base but no obvious rack to browse?

It was my new pal Ben and Roger Armstrong from GlobeStyle who called the fateful meeting. At 7.00pm on Monday June 29th, 1987, what was initially described as an 'International Pop Label Meeting' was convened at the Empress Of Russia in St. John Street, Islington, then also the home of Islington Folk Club. "The main aim", began the suggested agenda, "is to broaden the appeal of our repertoire", and it listed various points for discussion such as identifying who the target audience were, how to reach them, how to deal with this at retail and, crucially, "adoption of a campaign/media title".

The minutes record who was there: Chris Popham, Ben Mandelson, Roger Armstrong and Ted Carroll from GlobeStyle/ Ace; Jonathan Rudnick from Crammed USA; Amanda Jones, Thos Brooman and Steve Hadrell from WOMAD; Charlie Gillett from Oval; Mark Kidel from Channel 4; myself and Lisa Warburton from *Folk Roots*/Rogue Records; Anne Hunt, Mary Farquharson and Nick Gold from Arts Worldwide/World Circuit; Scott Lund and Iain Scott from Stern's/Triple Earth; Joe Boyd from Hannibal and writer Chris Stapleton. Later meetings also saw participation from Robert Urbanus from Stern's, Gordon Potts and Simon Coe from Virgin Retail; Jumbo Vanrenen and Trevor Herman from Earthworks, Doug Veitch, Owen & Phil from the Bhundu Boys' UK label Disc'Afrique, Lucy Duran from the National Sound Archive, and quite a few others. But it's that first night bunch who you can blame for 'world music' as the catch-all that subsequently flew.

It wasn't a new name, just one of many that had floated around in the preceding decades. But the logic set out by Roger Armstrong was that an established, unified generic name would give retailers a place where they could confidently rack otherwise unstockable releases, and where customers might both search out items they'd heard on the radio (not knowing how to spell a mis-pronounced or mis-remembered name or title) and browse through wider catalogue to impulse buy.

Various titles were discussed including 'Worldbeat' (left out anything without drums), 'tropical' (bye bye Bulgarians), 'Ethnic' (boring and academic), 'International Pop' (the death-by-Johnny-and-Nana syndrome) and 'Roots' (left out Johnny and Nana). 'World music' seemed to include the most and omit the least, and got it on a show of hands. Nobody thought of defining it or pretending there was such a 'genre': it was just to be a convenient box in record shops, like jazz, classical or rock, all which you sort of knew what they were even if you couldn't agree on a definition.

The plot progressed quickly. The princely sum of £3500 was contributed by the participants, headed browser dividers were manufactured for distribution to record shops along with a co-operative starter pack of some 50 albums that were likely to be stout sellers, freelance press officer Suzanne Parks was hired for a short contract, press releases and information packs were written, Ben Mandelson assembled a compilation cassette for promotion and sale through the *NME*, and October was designated World Music Month. Somebody much later suggested that our £3500 eventually bought more worldwide column inches and airwave hours pound-for-pound than any other campaign in the history of the music biz. Suzanne Parks later got head-hunted by a major label as their press officer.

It was simply a great idea, followed up by a lot of unprecedented co-operation between enthusiasts (very few thought of each other as business rivals) who wanted others to have more opportunity to share their enthusiasms. Yes, it was good for business, but by being so it was automatically good for the incomes and careers of many of the artists too. But down the years, conspiracy theorists who weren't around at the time have regularly, perhaps wilfully, misunderstood the motivation and the point. Ideas of exploitation, exclusivity, cliques, ghettoisation, cultural imperialism, racism and all sorts of other nonsensical -isms have been chucked at the notion since, often by people who ought to have known better and in the end did little more than expose their own foibles.

Of course not everything was positive, but world music got way ahead on points. It sold large quantities of records that you couldn't find for love or money before. It let many musicians in poor countries get new respect (and houses, cars and food for their families), and it turned out massive audiences for festivals and concerts. It greatly helped international understanding and provoked inspiring cultural exchanges – people who found themselves neighbours in the same box or festival bill listened to each other and ended up making amazing music together.

As well as being irritated by people who now want to use the term 'Global Music' to get away from it (there's a difference?) I just feel a bit sorry for people with the thinking time on their hands to decide they hate 'world music'. After all, there never was any such thing – it was only ever intended to be a useful box in a record shop. And since there are very few of those left, it eventually gained inbuilt obsolescence all on its own.

Inevitably, there were a few early naysayers. London's *City Limits* magazine ran a knee-jerk featurette penned by Rick Glanville under the heading *Bullshit Detector*. "Anybody from the Third World is allowed to join through the paternalistic assumption of rudimentary, exotic and inaccessible qualities. What the punter-friendly moniker fails to do is sidestep the middle class white dominance which spawned it – *Folk Roots* magazine has tenaciously trumpeted acts like the Bhundu Boys and Youssou N'dour when such hi-tech contemporary synth bands have never worn an Aran jumper in their lives." Eh?

There were more serious unpleasantries. In 1989, black community newspaper *The Voice* was conned – their editor Steve Pope's own words – into publishing a grossly libellous piece by teenage UK musician Tunde Jegede suggesting that artists including Dembo Konte & Kausu Kuyateh were being exploited by "World Music slavemasters" like Ian Anderson, Lucy Duran and the WOMAD organisation. Dembo, who was here on tour at the time, was so livid that he immediately donned his best robe and set off down to the paper's office to bang on their front desk and remonstrate. Features editor Dotun Adebayo nearly lost his job: because the piece had said what they so imagined to be true, they'd published it without fact checking first. WOMAD sued. I ran into Dotun a few years later at a party and he was still apologising. We shook hands on it!

Also around that time there was an unruly public discussion held at the National Sound Archive. Members of Dade Krama, a group of Arts Council funded UK-based African musicians, declared that the only reason they had to search for their own gigs and self-produce their albums was that they were black in a white society. I, probably foolishly, pointed out that actually, virtually all English folk musicians also had to do the same thing, without any grant aid, but that if at the end of the day there were no gigs coming in we had to face up to the fact that maybe people didn't think our music was any good. Those guys never confronted that possibility. Needless to say, it wasn't a well-received message. But, while I, along with Lucy Duran, Charlie Gillett, Andy Kershaw and others, got roundly savaged again by Tunde Jegede and his English mother Galina Chester in the subsequent book *Storms Of The Heart*, edited by Kwesi Owusu of the associated group African Dawn, their lengthy diatribe about this meeting selectively failed to consider that point.

But these were minor ripples in the pond compared to how things panned out joyfully and internationally over the following decades. The notion spread around the globe, often festival-led, with WOMAD – formed in the early '80s by a collective led by Thos Brooman and funded by rock star Peter Gabriel – being the aspirational model. WOMAD – World Of Music, Arts & Dance – began by spectacularly losing shirts at Shepton Mallet Showground in Somerset (just a few miles from the equally loss-making origins of Glastonbury festival at Pilton), perambulated around numerous English sites from Mersea Island in Essex to Carlyon Bay in Cornwall, Morecambe in Lancashire and South Hill Park at Bracknell in the 1980s before settling on the outskirts of Reading and growing for many years. Eventually from 2007 (with a legendarily wet inauguration forever known as WOMUD) they re-settled at Charlton Park in north Wiltshire. Their HQ has long been at Gabriel's Real World studio complex at Box, not far away near Bath.

The Reading events in the 1990s and early 2000s always seemed to coincide with glorious weather (one year's BBC TV coverage showed me raving about how wonderful Orchestra Baobab were, looking every bit like a ranting tomato due to catching that sun.) The impeccable and never predictable booking policy of Thomas and booking queen Paula Henderson constantly produced thrilling surprises. My only ever complaint was that, compared with the great Canadian festivals where informal backstage sessions and jams between the diverse participating artists were an inspiring thing, they never happened at WOMAD. Indeed, the social backstage bar often had a DJ which prevented it – annoying, even when the DJ was the legendary Bristol character DJ Derek. But they became a statutory annual summer fixture in the social calendar, where the tribes met up and revelled in the music (not to mention the best range of festival food anywhere.)

Into the 1990s and onwards they licensed their team and expertise to partners around the world, with WOMAD events taking place in several dozen countries including Australia, New Zealand, the USA, Chile, Spain, Greece and even Russia.

Back in summer 1986, *Folk Roots* had hosted an interesting round table among the organisations then at the forefront of putting what was yet to be called world music out there. Arts Worldwide's approach was to go to a country and research the best representatives of a musical culture to bring over, and also attract that country's diaspora to their shows. As a result, their audience for a triple bill of Sudanese artists was rammed with not only Sudanese but also Egyptians and Ethiopians too, with white British in a minority. WOMAD's method was to check through artist submission demos sent in to them and then go on gut feeling as to what would work with their largely white UK audience. Often, with great artists like Nusrat Fateh Ali Khan, they struck gold. Both approaches turned out to be equally valid and successful.

The international dimension got even greater in the 1990s with the inspired founding of WOMEX (no relation – it stands for World Music Expo). At the beginning of the decade there were events called Berlin Independence Days (BID) held in the former East Berlin following German re-unification, promoting the work of independent labels and their artists. As part of these, Germany's Piranha organisation headed by Christoph Borkowsky – label, promoters and tour organisers – were involved in a dedicated world music section that was deemed so promising that when the main event fell over, Borkowsky and Ben Mandelson dreamed up WOMEX to continue it. This was to be an international conference, trade fair, showcase, meeting place and catalyst for the growing world music 'industry'. Other godfather Mustaphas like Lu Edmonds were much involved in the early days, and delegates (and showcasing artists) began coming from around the globe, particularly from France where 'musiques du monde' was as big and well-explored a concept as world music in the UK.

In 1992, in between those BIDs and the beginning of WOMEX proper, the Berlin organisers co-operated with those of the annual South By Southwest (SXSW) independent music industry bash in Austin, Texas and a whole collection of us early Euro world music botherers flew over to network with our North American counterparts, hang out in Austin music bars thrilling to local bands like Brave Combo and down large quantities of superior margaritas. It's probably the latter which explains why I don't remember much about it other than it being fun.

I do have really fond memories of the early WOMEXs held in the House Of World Cultures in Berlin though. The building in the Tiergarten housed everything that was needed for the five hundred or so early delegates –

rooms for seminars and discussions, a trade fair area, a large bar and café, small and large theatres and a suitable venue for club style shows. You could wander in from your hotel in the late morning and not leave until the small hours. The atmosphere was extremely convivial and in the evenings a circle of newly made friends could sit at big tables sharing tips, tales and enthusiasms. If there was a particular artist's showcase which caught your imagination in the programme you could leave your chair and your beer to be guarded while you checked it out, sometimes running back to gather up others. Lifelong friendships were made through this opportunity to relax and hear each other's life stories.

I used to explain the difference between WOMEX and big mainstream music business affairs like Midem in Cannes by saying that at Midem you'd probably encounter some pushy shyster in a satin tour jacket saying "my artist is going to be really big, best in the world, buy my artist, buy my records" while coming into WOMEX you were more likely to meet a fellow enthusiast who'd tell you "You ought to listen to that new band they've got over there, you'd really like them" and only later get around to mentioning their own activities.

Over the decades it grew bigger and bigger as it travelled annually around Europe, visiting some fifteen or more countries and eventually catering for up to three thousand at a time. Trade fair stands got bigger and more businesss-like as tourist and umbrella organisations gained sway over the smaller independents, and a tendency grew for 'fusion' artists to play something they called world music, which we all know isn't an actual thing. (In the early days, there was allegedly a rule – never actually invoked, to my knowledge – that the first delegate to ask the cliché question "what is world music?" in a panel or seminar would be taken from the building and hurled into the nearest canal...)

In 1997, a decade after the initial campaign, a Canadian musicologist called Randy Raine-Reusch wandered up to the *fRoots* stand at WOMEX, held that year in Marseille. He told us about how he was helping with a new event in Sarawak, Borneo called the Rainforest World Music Festival "What the fuck is 'world music' in Borneo?!" I cheekily asked. "Local music, not from here," was his instant response. This amused a few people, but since there wasn't ever actually a thing called world music to define, it had its flaws. From *fRoots*' viewpoint it certainly couldn't work as a content definition since 'from here' in the UK was a key part of what we covered (and was also music largely ignored by WOMEX down the years). So we modified it and adopted the cover tag line "Local Music From Out There."

"Out there" was deliberately enigmatic and could be interpreted not only as geographic – from out there in England to out in whole world – but also as out there beyond mainstream music, as in the old hippie "far out, maaan," or Lord Buckley's "Fargoneasphere." To the unitiated, much of what we covered was clearly by weirdos anyway. Lawrence Heath later worked out that an anagram of it was "Cool lute music from earth." So there!

The Rainforest World Music Festival grew into a wonderful thing which I was lucky enough to be invited to a couple of times in the next century. More on that later.

The best WOMEXs were those where the evening showcases and daytime trade fair were in the same place or at least in close proximity, where the showcase venues and sound systems were best suited to the range of artists appearing in them, and the opportunities for socialising without the need to shout over a DJ cacophony were there. I'd vote for Thessaloniki in Greece in 2012 as being peak WOMEX – a self-contained multi-purpose venue which was custom-built for an earlier Expo, a great selection of music and all the climatic and cullinary benefits of the host country.

Annoyingly, on the opening night in Thessaloniki, full of Womexical joys and greatly looking forward to it, I tripped and fell on the way in, badly spraining my ankle. But in spite of spending the next three days strapped up and in extreme pain, not to mention the following weeks back home, I still remember it as the best one ever. Age, costs and a promise to help the planet a little by giving up flying have conspired to prevent me from attending in more recent times, but in spite of my near disaster, Thessaloniki is still my favourite. Though the couple held in Essen in Germany in the early 2000s hold good memories too – for social reasons, a similarly compact venue and the fact we could easily drive there from England (shamefully, occasionally extracting awful received demo tapes from the car stereo and hurling them out of the window on the way back. Oops!)

By the 1990s world music had become part of the UK's national musical palette. By 1991 some naysayers were even suggesting that "the world music boom is over" – this at a time when all music was being battered by the Thatcher end-years recession (who remembers 14% interest rates?). So I wrote a *Folk Roots* Editorial pointing out that "by the time 'world music' was gaining its unsuitable but convenient and incredibly effective marketing tag on a couple of informal evenings in the Empress Of Russia some years back, world music was already on course to exactly mirror the late 1960s blues boom. Which started with nothing, was slowly built by a small bunch of dedicated enthusiasts working on shoestrings, gained popularity, suddenly became a media phenomena, sprouted a huge runaway bandwagon onto which clueless major labels and promoters jumped, peaked, and then sank back. But just remember: that the plateau at which it eventually levelled out was infinitely higher than before. Ever since, most record shops have had some kind of blues selection, artists have toured, specialist magazines and labels have thrived, it's been an established part of our national music scene. World music has followed the same route so far, and I see no reason to not expect it to follow the rest. It's here to stay, settling into its proper place as part of our musical landscape. Which is exactly how it should be."

I wasn't wrong. By then, any decent arts centre or theatre with a well-constructed music policy would automatically look for it as part of their standard, expected programming, like jazz, folk or classical music. Folk and rock festivals included it among their bills. Massive events like the multi-artist African Proms at the Royal Albert Hall in the mid '90s became common.

It became big business for major record labels too, in the wake of multi-million sales for Buena Vista Social Club, and plenty of one-off chart hits like Youssou N'Dour & Neneh Cherry's *Seven Seconds*, Mory Kanté's *Yeke Yeke* and Ofra Haza's *Im Nin Alu*. South Africa's Ladysmith Black Mambazo even got featured on TV adverts for Heinz baked beans. Though it should be pointed out that what got into the charts in the UK was skewed by the sources of the compilers' information – mainstream High Street record shops and chains on the whole. It was said that substantial sales of Bhangra records released by the UK's home-grown artists and bands were in such quantities that they'd have charted in the mid '80s if Asian corner shops where the bulk of their sales were made had been 'chart return' outlets rather than remaining under the radar.

The exemplary *Rough Guides* travel book series, co-founded by music fan Mark Ellingham, enthusiastically jumped in with *The Rough Guide To World Music* in 1994 which had contributions from dozens of the well-informed (and me – I penned the Madagascar chapter). By 2000 it had grown to a two-volume 2nd edition and in 2006 it had expanded to three small doorstops. Look what we started...

From a personal viewpoint, having had geography kicked away from me at school aged 12, I'd left education so clueless that, like undoubtedly many others, I probably thought there was one big country called 'Africa' where they spoke African. By the mid '80s I'd learned enormous amounts about the history and culture of the continent's individual countries, all entirely from getting interested in the music and a thirst to know what lay behind it.

Other parts of the world followed. The wormholes were now there to be wriggled down, and thus I was able to indulge little obsessions with Greek rembetika and its modern descendants, Texas Mexican border music, pizzica from Puglia, the music of Okinawa and much more, all off the 'Global Music' mainstreams of Africa-Cuba-India-Balkans. The gates were opened to the University Of Life campus, with CD booklets and magazine features as introductory text books.

The fabulous 1980s were the most fun, the most energising, where we all felt like part of a real community, largely outside of the 'music business'. This eventually got recognised several decades later when UK compilation label Nascente assembled a glorious 2-CD set titled *'80s World Music Classics –When The World Was Young*. Its 26 tracks were chosen largely by key movers and shakers from that decade, enthusiasts all. I'd recommend it to anybody who was or wasn't there as evidence for the defence.

14.
Tarika & Madagascar Eat The 1990s

Unexpectedly, my 1990s travels took me away from West Africa. While *Folk Roots* and Rogue Records carried on uninterrupted, I got sucked into the music (and politics) of Madagascar.

In May 1990 I got married again. I'd popped out one evening to a record label launch bash in North London and while there was introduced by Ben Mandelson and Roger Armstrong to Hanitra Rasoanaivo. She'd been their GlobeStyle Records guide, translator and musician finder when they'd done the epic Madagascar field trip which produced their four classic 1986 albums from the island, laying the foundations for the big Madagacar music focus in the next decade. We fell together and when her six month UK visa was about to expire, we sorted that in the Wood Green Registry Office.

On my first visit to the big red island in the Indian Ocean that summer to meet the new in-laws and family we'd been entrusted with wads of cash to pay due GlobeStyle royalties, which gave the ideal opportunity to meet a number of the best local musicians and find out about the musical – and political – history of the place. Little did I realise that I was about to disappear down a wormhole for a decade. We visited legendary *sodina* (flute) player Rakotofra – genuinely legendary as his image was etched on bank notes – and Hanitra's family laid on an outdoor party at their humble house to which many other musicians showed up and jammed. A grand day.

Music seemed to be in everybody's blood: I was astonished to discover that there was rarely a family occasion when singing didn't break out, with everybody reaching naturally for glorious vocal harmonies.

On my second visit I took my newly acquired DAT Walkman which allowed me to digitally record a couple of bands, the electric outfit of salegy king Jaojoby and the acoustic quartet Tarika Sammy, a version of which had appeared on one of the GlobeStyle LPs, both for broadcast on Andy Kershaw's Radio 1 show. And on these early trips I did a lot of digging in local markets for current cassette releases and scratchy old singles.

In the 1970s, there had been a thriving record industry in Madagascar, in the course of which hundreds of seven-inches of vibrant *salegy* and *watcha watcha* dance music were produced, some of which reputedly sold over 60,000 copies. But the last had been pressed by national label Disco-

Mad in the mid-1980s. The pressing plants had closed in Madagascar's deteriorating economic climate – by now it was one of the poorest countries in the world – and masters had been lost or destroyed. Even in the capital, you could barely find a few very scratchy, second hand copies on market stalls. Yet singles by Orchestre Liberty, Jaojoby, Jean Fredy or Abdallah had rivalled the recordings of famous bands from mainland Africa. Many had a distinct Malagasy style, a few directly absorbing East African and South African sounds that had flown in on the airwaves.

In 1991, Hanitra's younger sister Noro came to London for a six month visit in order to improve her English and potential work skills. While she was with us, Hanitra and Noro would regularly burst into harmony on old Malagasy traditional or family favourite songs around the house. I eventually got the DAT Walkman out and recorded them. Not long after this, my World Service producer Nick Freeth asked me to recommend tracks for a series on a capella singing being presented by Steeleye Span's Maddy Prior, and to my delight my recordings of Hanitra & Noro got accepted for it. And then a friend, Pete Lawrence, who'd previously been a co-founder of the Cooking Vinyl label, heard them singing while we were clearing up after a party and uttered the fateful words "they should front a band."

At the end of Noro's stay, they both went back to Antananarivo together, with the band idea in the back of Hanitra's mind. A week later she mentioned on a 'phone call that she'd just heard from Sammy, the leader of Tarika Sammy, who was desperate because his band had broken up – his girlfriend, who was one of the singers, had left him and the wife of remaining fellow musician, his cousin Tiana, was pregnant and couldn't continue as a singer herself either. Could we help him?

I foolishly suggested that maybe the sisters could team up with Sammy and Tiana for this new band idea. Actually, it wasn't the teaming up idea that turned out to have been foolish, but letting them retain the Tarika Sammy name rather than creating a new one was what ended up being a big mistake. But that only became apparent later, too late…

I decided that we'd take a flier on an album by this group for Rogue, and that if it worked we'd record it in London augmented by the 3 Mustaphas 3 rhythm section as we'd done so effectively on Konte & Kuyateh's *Jali Roll*. I also wanted to make a CD of Jaojoby, to be the first ever salegy band release outside Madagascar. To this end, while I stayed manning the *Folk Roots* office, Ben Mandelson went off to revisit Madagascar for the first time since his GlobeStyle trip, to record Jaojoby's album in a local studio and to work with our new band on rehearsing repertoire for their debut.

Both missions accomplished, I set about lining up a UK tour for Tarika Sammy which would include their album recording. At this point I only had demos to circulate but with the health of the world music circuit at the time, the hunger for new musical experiences, and no doubt a bit of trust from my track record, the tour came together quite well. So in April 1992, the quartet came to London, did a BBC Radio 1 Andy Kershaw session to introduce themselves to the nation's roots music fans, and then hit the road.

By then I was very confident about the music, but still nervous when we got to their very first concert at the Phoenix Arts Centre in Leicester. I'd volunteered to be their tour manager and sound engineer, partly to cut costs but mainly because I knew the music, what the numerous Malagasy traditional instruments they carried sounded like and how they should be balanced. Even the notion that there was often no 'lead' vocal but instead equally balanced harmonies was a stretch for sound engineers who were used to rock music values.

It would not only be their first time ever on stage together and playing through a PA system, it was their first time in front of an English-speaking audience. But I needn't have worried: Hanitra, who had been in amateur bands in Madagascar when younger, had by now taken in several years of observing others on the world music scene, learning what worked and what didn't. She'd drilled the new band in stagecraft in rehearsal, and instinctively knew how to introduce the songs with her fluent English, including just the right amount of charming humour. Even on this very first gig they came across more professionally than many homegrown folk bands with years of experience, and the audience were thrilled. When I revealed the truth of what they'd just seen to some of the organisers afterwards, they didn't believe me!

Twenty dates later, travelling all over the UK from Devon to Scotland and Wales and with a spell in the studio recording their debut CD *Fanafody* ("Medicine"), they finished up the tour at a WOMAD festival held on the old railway station at Morecambe in Lancashire. There they waved the musical flag for Madagascar alongside the famed Super Rail Band from Mali, Ethiopia's Aster Aweke, gospel legends the Five Blind Boys, the UK's Sheila Chandra and Benjamin Zephaniah and many others, as bona fide rising stars of world music. And I'd so fallen in love with the Renault Espace that I'd

Great grandmother Emily Agnes Stears who sang for Vaughan Williams in 1904.

Great aunts Elizabeth and Annie Stears & friend, Bonchurch I.O.W circa 1898.

Sheila Anderson (née Stears), 1945.

Sean Mayes 1983.

Photo: Ian A Anderson

Al Stewart 1984. *Alexis Korner 1970s.*

2007 re-union of some of the 1987 World Music 'inventors'. L to R standing: Chris Stapleton, Jonathan Rudnick, Robert Urbanus, Joe Boyd, Ben Mandelson, Phillip Sweeney, Roger Armstrong, Simon Coe, Ian A Anderson. Seated: Amanda Jones, Charlie Gillett, Mark Kidel, Thos Brooman.

The Old Swan Band 1981: Fi Fraser, Danny Stradling, Richard Valentine, Paul Burgess, Martin Brinsford, Jo Fraser, Rod Stradling. The new wave of English country dance bands.

Hukwe Zawose, Holland Park, 1985.

Ali Farka Touré playing IAA's guitar, 1987

Covers down the years. Above, Thomas Mapfumo (FR28, 1985) was the first African artist on the cover; Martin Carthy (fR186, 1998) marked the title change to fRoots.

  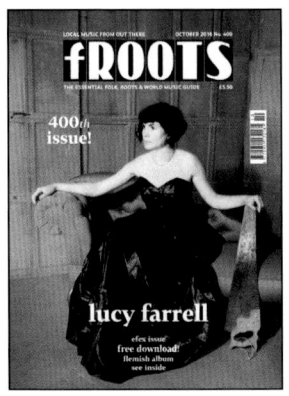

Dembo Konte & Kausu Kuyateh, 1991.

Lucy Duran & Sarah Coxson with local children, Bansang, the Gambia, 1987.

Folk Roots' early staff at Bracknell Folk Festival 1985: Beverly Hill, IAA, Caroline Walker.

Zuzana Novak, 2006. *Bob Copper, Peacehaven, 1984*

Some of 3 Mustaphas 3 at Yesterdays, Bristol, 1987. Uncle, Sabah Habas, Lavra, Hijaz...

Elizabeth Kinder, Sarawak, 2006.

Spider John Koerner, Green Note, 2009

Tarika 1995. Ny Ony, Solo, Donné & Noro, with Hanitra in front

Friends at Ethnoambient, Croatia, 2008. Mojmir Novakovic, Antonia Kavas, Kristi Stassinopoulou, Stathis Kalyviotis with IAA in front.

IAA (centre) getting his EFDSS Gold Badge, Cecil Sharp House 2015, with Ian Kearey, Shirley Collins, Alan James & Ben Mandelson.

hired for the tour that I ended up buying my first one and have never owned anything else since. An auspicious few months.

Somewhere on the road, driving through Wales, there was a lovely cultural misunderstanding. Mishearing comments about a flock on a hillside, one of the musicians had concluded that England's national dish was "fish and sheeps," which in Malagasy is "trondro sy ondry", pronounced sort of like "troonj sy oonj." We got the Mustaphas' tame artist Brak to doodle a little logo of a sheep with a fish hanging from its mouth, and the work of co-producers Ben Mandelson and I became "A Trondro Sy Ondry" production. We'd still be using that on our False Beards duo CD twenty years later.

The album came out that August in a triple Madagascar attack from Rogue Records along with Jaojoby's *Salegy* and Freddy De Majunga's *Tsinjaka*. The latter was an ace Malagasy guitarist long resident in Paris where he'd worked in the hi-tech Zairean soukous scene with other guitar stars like Diblo Dibala and Master Mwana Congo, before transferring those techniques to making a contemporary salegy record. All three were well-received, but Tarika Sammy's the most, and international interest began to flood in, particularly from America where the proto-WOMEX trip to South-By-Southwest had helped us establish good contacts.

One thing we'd learned on that first tour was that home-made traditional Malagasy instruments were fragile and hard to keep in tune under hot stage lights. So we set about getting versions made for the road, with built in transducer pick-ups. Guitar luthier Nigel Thornbory produced a couple of beautiful *kabosy*, the small, irregularly fretted 8-string instruments something like a cross between Arabic lutes and mandolins. My woodworking father – who had never considered making a musical instrument in his life and had no theoretical knowledge to work from – took up the challenge of making some *marovany*, the two-sided rectangular box zithers tuned (coincidentally?) not unlike the two courses of the West African kora. But whereas the Malagasy ones used unbraided bicycle brake cables as strings, nails to anchor them and moveable bridges to tune them, these were to have gauged steel guitar strings, fixed ebony bridges and hammered dulcimer tuning pegs.

It took a couple of prototypes to get them right but by the time Tarika Sammy returned for their autumn tour they were ready, installed in professionally built flight cases, as were the band's supply of *valiha*, the traditional zithers with strings around the circumference of bamboo tube bodies the diameter of small drainpipes. Those could only come from Madagascar, but we'd sourced some from the best maker to ship over. Sammy's home made ones, OK though they'd been, were honourably retired. To say that the musicians were excited by their new kit, augmented by a lovely small-body Lowden guitar, would be an understatement. To say that my bank balance was dented by getting it all together – ditto!

With this boost, their autumn tour went even better than the first, taking them to Germany and the Netherlands as well as around the UK and even gaining them niche fame from an appearance on the iconic, long running BBC children's TV programme *Blue Peter*. Though they were baffled when presented with their famous Blue Peter badges. No cultural references, you see.

Fine American tour agent Paul Kahn from Concerted Efforts came over to London to see them in action, and we did a deal with American label Green Linnet, until then known for Irish music but now expanding with a new world music imprint called Xenophile, to release *Fanafody* in North America. So in April 1993, a mere year after their formation, recording and first gigs, they headed off across the Atlantic for 25 dates around the country.

My own learning curve kicked in – welcome to the world of American work visas, expensive flight bookings and road managers. I went on the road with them for most of it – taking a week's break in the middle for a literally flying visit home to get a *Folk Roots* issue assembled and off to the printers, all juggled with the help of a lot of pre-planning and our truly reliable staff and freelances, without whom... Looking back – from a time when we're always permanently and easily in contact via the internet and smartphones to back then when we weren't – I can no longer conceive how this was possible.

That first US tour went really well, kicking off in California at the Freight & Salvage in Berkeley where the great Chris Strachwitz, founder of Arhoolie Records, came out to see them and say hello – we'd first met back in 1960s blues days. He was well impressed, but puzzled. "Are they something like the Madagascar equivalent to the New Lost City Ramblers?" he asked innocently. The NLCR had been at the forefront of the revival of old time country music in the USA from the 1950s, all young, keen and college educated. I had to explain that there was no equivalent to a folk revival in Madagascar, nor was it needed as music was just part of everybody's family life, educated or not.

They progressed up the West Coast as far as Vancouver in Canada, then headed down and across country. My short hop home meant that I missed their appearance at the New Orleans Jazz & Heritage Festival, to considerable regret, but I was back by the time they hit New England and then Symphony Space off Broadway in New York.

At that one I noticed a familiar-looking bear-like man lurking behind my sound desk – it was none other than legendary folk/blues recordist and collector Alan Lomax. We struck up a conversation and he invited us, the whole band, to join him for post-show dinner at a nearby Indian restaurant, where he and I got into spirited conversation about mutual musical enthusiasms. Me as fan boy: here was the guy who'd first field-recorded Muddy Waters. We got so animated that I failed to ask him the obvious question when he told me that normally he didn't like bands who deliberately mixed up a number of local traditions, as they did, but that ours were one of only two he'd ever encountered who'd pulled that off successfully. No, I didn't ask who the other one was.

What got me distracted was a discussion about the *hiragasy* from Madagascar – street musicians and entertainers whose music, instrumentation (violins, trumpets, etc), singing style and even some of the costumes they wore resembled a regional music from Mexico. I'd even played some on my Jazz FM show as a competition question asking where it came from, and nearly everybody had said Mexico. When I'd learned that all the vanilla in the world – one of Madagascar's main cash crops – evolved from a vine native to Mexico, it seemed likely to me that in order to cultivate it, the colonial administrators might well have brought Mexican labourers there to show them how to do it, and this might have included some musicians who mixed their styles up with the locals. Seemed really obvious to me – if it looks like a duck, quacks like a duck etc etc...

I explained my theory to Alan. He amiably shot me down in flames, citing his personally evolved science of 'cantometrics' (which I never did understand, to this day). We ended up agreeing to differ, but I was still completely convinced that I was right.

A few years later, I read Tim Ecott's wonderful book *Vanilla: Travels In Search Of The Luscious Substance*, the history of the cultivation of and trade in vanilla. Turns out that the vine was first taken to Europe, then to La Reunion in the Indian Ocean where in 1841 a slave boy called Edmond Albius discovered the secret of how to effectively hand-pollinate it. No Mexicans were ever involved in this discovery of how to cultivate a crop elsewhere (the fatal flaw had been that the European botanists had failed to realise that it needed a specialised Mexican bee), and all the commercial vanilla production worldwide ever since, including in Madagascar to where it was later taken, has been based on the method that Albius discovered.

So it turned out that Alan Lomax *was* right. Sadly I was unable to convey this apology to him effectively – or ask who that other band were – because by the second time I met him in Memphis at the 1998 Folk Alliance, he'd had a serious stroke.

Just because something looks like a duck and quacks like a duck and you'd very much like your evidence to prove it's a duck because obviously it's a duck…maybe it isn't always! Valuable life lesson.

There have been some great cosmic bad tricks played on me over the years, but high among them was when I herded the band to catch the overnight flight back to England. If you're lucky on those flights, there is a bit of space to stretch out, put in the earplugs and get some kip. This wasn't one of them. Portents were made ominous by a large, loud-mouthed bunch of American males of a forty-something nature gathered in our departure lounge. We had fingers crossed that they would be elsewhere on the 'plane, but of course they were in the three rows immediately behind us. Hardly had we got seated when I heard my name bellowed. Or did I? No, this bunch of charmers turned out to be a delegation of the Jethro Tull fan club making a pilgrimage to Britain. The entire flight was taken up by noisesome conversation that went "Ian Anderson blah blah blah. Ian Anderson blah blah blah…" in loud American accents. Never got a wink!

After a month back in the UK, France, Holland and Germany they headed off to North America again in July to hit the big Canadian festivals, returning to this side of the ocean for the better ones over here including WOMAD and Sidmouth Folk Festival in the UK and Dranouter in Belgium. Then they headed into the studio to record their second album *Balance*. This time we brought over a couple of top Malagasy players for the bass and drum seats, whilst I managed to keep my hand in by sneaking a bit of slide guitar onto one track.

Away on the road at the time of the first CD, they'd naturally fused the rhythms, melodies, harmonies and different instruments of the island's many tribes into something new, fresh, young and dynamic. Back home, some of those on the local music scene who'd got wind of it were inspired. Established pop stars used to apeing Western styles had begun knocking on their door asking for clues as to how to find their roots. Traditionally-based music didn't look staid and boring any more; you didn't have to use imported electric instruments and drum machines to be exciting!

Just a year on, after a further seven months of hard touring throughout Europe and North America as the flagship group for the welcome, long-overdue international boom in interest for Malagasy music, *Balance* went several more jumps ahead. On *Fanafody*, the focus had been on traditional songs and Sammy and Tiana's accumulated repertoire from the past. This time the material was to be virtually all new and original, mostly from Hanitra or Noro, following the creative surge that was driving them forward to forge a new young Malagasy roots music for the '90s.

Meanwhile, a sour note had crept in which became apparent right from the beginning of that otherwise wildly successful first American visit. Something odd was going on, though it took some time to reveal what was behind it. At around the same time that we'd been assembling our band, two Californian musicians had been in Madagascar, largely following GlobeStyle's lead, recording local musicians including the about-to-dissolve previous Tarika Sammy line-up for a compilation album on which the Californians also played. It was eventually released with the two Americans' names the most prominent, though not until after we'd completed *Fanafody* and the band's first UK tour.

What unfolded was that the two instigators and some of their acquaintances set about an unsubtle campaign to derail Tarika Sammy's success. It had clearly become apparent to them that the band's growing popularity meant that the pair weren't going to be able to stamp proprietory ownership on all Malagasy music in the USA and gain exclusive white saviour status for it. Further behind this was a particular disgruntled Malagasy musician who up to that point, supported by the dictator Ratsiraka, had been king of the roost but now was being sidelined internationally. He was apparently feeding these two charmers the sort of disinformation they wanted to believe.

Poison pen letters and faxes began to wing their way to promoters and potential audience members, then eventually the band's agent and record label, spreading outrageous fabricated rumours and lies – initially intended to derail their growing popularity, but also to sow dissent within the band. If they'd been subtle about it we might not have twigged so soon, but some of the accusations were so blatantly untrue that recipients who knew and trusted us were startled enough to forward copies on.

It came to a head in the late autumn of 1993 when my fax machine started deluging acreages of deranged messages, handwritten in capitals, from one of the pair in the small hours. I'd come into the office in the morning and find them strewn across the floor and the fax roll exhausted, so I had to start turning it off overnight. Then news came in from Madagascar saying that Sammy was telling people that he'd been fired from his group – or left it, depending on who he told – and that his money had been stolen by us.

Of course none of this was true. We'd invested so much work, finance, time, enthusiasm, creativity and energy in establishing the band who everybody was fully expecting to tour in 1994 in support of the new album. We were hardly going to wreck that. The money claim turned out to have been deliberately fabricated by one of the Californian pair as part of their disinformation campaign.

There is no doubt that Sammy did find the constant hard work of professional touring and rehearsal – five months on the road away from home including two North American tours in 1993 – extremely difficult to cope with and so was a ripe recipient for the untruths being fed to him by others. He later admitted as much. There had certainly been tensions: trouble had arisen for the group at home in Madagascar because some songs on *Fanafody* that Sammy claimed to have written turned out to have been authored by others. And I can quite understand how he may have become jealous that audiences and press alike tended to treat Hanitra and Noro as the focus of the group that for historic reasons bore his name.

At the end of 1993, exhausted from two years of non-stop work, Hanitra and I went for the only holiday we ever had, two weeks on the Caribbean coast of Mexico followed by Christmas with our new Green Linnet friends on freezing Cape Cod in the USA. But on a call home, word reached us of the Sammy crisis and it became apparent that we needed a Plan B if a band was going to tour in 1994.

Hanitra being Hanitra, she set to it. Having messaged ahead that she needed the best possible musicians, she flew to Madagascar, arriving just as the worst cyclone since the 1920s hit. Undeterred, she set off in a borrowed car around the rutted, flooded back streets of Antananarivo to check out those that she'd been recommended.

Her theory was that if she found them playing music at home when trapped indoors by the storm, they were suitably dedicated. And thus she located the three who would join her and Noro for the next seven years in a second, stable line-up whose name would from then on be simplified and depersonalised to just Tarika: 'the band'.

Multi-instrumentalists Donné and Solo came from real traditional music backgrounds, years of touring all over Madagascar in revered bands on the weddings, circumcisions and reburials circuit, but still with the energy of youth to try something new. Ny Ony was from the other direction, having played Madagascar's hot salegy dance music in bands where they naturally transfer the sound and style of traditional instruments onto electric guitar and bass. He was now discovering the real thing.

By the time I followed her a few weeks later, they'd gelled wonderfully and been hard at work rehearsing in a friend's house – not just learning old repertoire but creating new, along with tight choreography for an energetic stage show. By coincidence, a party of mostly French world music movers and shakers were in town for a jaunt organised by the European Broadcasting Union, and some of them dropped by the rehearsals. They were blown away by what they saw and said so. One great quote which we milked for a while was "virtuoso traditional music with the energy of punk rock..."

Meanwhile, on arrival I'd been hauled out of the immigration queue by police and sent to the Ministry Of Culture And Communications to explain to the Minister all the bad things that I'd reportedly done. These supposedly included signing them to contracts that were "indentured servitude," "sick and greedy" and that I'd set out to "fool little brown people," as relayed by the crazy Americans and the jealous local star. Luckily I had thought to bring the documents with me that proved the opposite. After carefully studying them, the Minister told me that they were in fact better agreements in favour of the artists than most he'd seen, and that he now suspected he knew who was behind this. I was welcome to continue my work promoting Malagasy music, which was much appreciated...

It was something of a relief when an early issue of *Mojo* magazine published a major feature on Captain Beefheart who, it turned out, had been subject of another public vendetta by one of our two Californian assailants. "[He's] nuts. He's obsessed. He's trying to make himself look good," quoth the good Cap'n. Phew, not just me then.

It was further relief when, after a few more weeks of bonkers accusatory faxes and the Californians putting up a fake lawyer to harrass me, who was suitably rebuffed, it all went quiet. There was another brief eruption in 1995 when one of their acquaintances got involved with a later band of Sammy's and trotted out the same stuff to our next US agent, the record label and the then growing internet newsgroups, but he got swiftly and publicly disabused.

It's a good thing that social media hadn't evolved back then as it did this century or I'm sure that it would have been much, much harder to quash the kind of fake stories and conspiracy theories that abound these days. Who'd be Taylor Swift? Meanwhile, I still hold a file the best part of an inch thick of distressing first-hand evidence of all that tediousness, just in case.

Re-energised and armed with demo recordings and a set of new photos of the band, I eventually went home to get the word out to our agents, promoters and US label partners that all was not only well but going to be better!

As indeed it was. The fully rehearsed Tarika came in June for gigs in the UK, Finland, Portugal and Canada, the latter their first visit to the wonderful Edmonton Folk Festival. This particular year, Edmonton added an opening Thursday night for Joni Mitchell to do her first Canadian festival appearance in more than a decade. Our old Scrub Jay Orchestra sidekick Martin Simpson and I found ourselves leaning on the side of the stage in the afternoon sun as Joni went through her soundcheck. Overwhelmed by being in such proximity to her, one of us turned to the other – we no longer remember who – and commented "wow, she sounds just like Joni Mitchell!" We knew what we meant: there were so many clones, but nothing approached the real thing.

The next day the sky fell in and it rained incessantly for the weekend, turning into a Glastonburyesque mudbath. Joni could quite easily have slipped off home but she didn't, spending the next few days sloshing around in her wellies (or whatever they call them over there) and enjoying all the music. At one point she agreed to a backstage press conference where she relaxed with her feet up, chain smoking. One clearly besotted journo asked with great respect what tuning she used for a particular song. "Ah..." she said, pausing for a long drag, "on that one I think I tuned the guitar to the coast of British Columbia..." Everybody gasped in awe. Afterwards, I shot off to the merch stall and bought a CD copy of *Blue* to replace my old vinyl, but never summed up the courage to ask her to sign it.

Also on that Canada trip they played the open air stage at Harbourfront in Toronto. We met up with excellent self-exiled Malagasy blues guitarist Madagascar Slim, who on discovering that I used to be a full-time musician asked "So why aren't you any more?" I explained how I'd got tired of life on the road with all its downsides and time wasting. "How come you're doing all that now with this band without any of the fun of playing?" he asked, quite reasonably. He had a point.

Between gigs that summer I got them into the studio in London and produced the first proper Tarika album *Bibiango*, which loosely translates as "hungry beasts, roaring lemurs"! Then we were off to the States, firing on all cylinders, for their first tour with new agent Herschel Freeman.

Herschel had managed a miracle of routing, a month that could all be done on the road. Tour manager Geoff, of biker stock, had picked up a hire van in Boston where the tour was to end and driven it down to meet us for the first date in Miami. By then it was obvious that this band were streets ahead of the previous line-up for on-stage energy and audience reaction, and as we progressed up through Florida to Alabama (where the gig in Birmingham was an African music club in a venue which had previously been the local Ku Klux Klan headquarters!), North Carolina and on to Washington, all the past hassles were soon forgotten.

On the way I'd squeaked when I saw a sign to Cumberland Gap: the band were suitably baffled, as they were again when I exclaimed loudly to Geoff that we were "on the New Jersey Turnpike in the wee wee hours!" In Washington DC the Malagasy ambassador came to their show and got up on stage to announce that Tarika were better ambassadors for their culture than he was! Then it was out to the Mid-West as far as the great Cedar Cultural Centre in Minneapolis where I paid my respects to Spider John, and back east via The Old Town School Of Folk Music in Chicago where I saw Big Bill Broonzy's guitar in a glass case... I sucked all this in, because I'd taken Madagascar Slim's comment to heart and had decided this would be my last long road tour with the band. It was getting impossible to juggle *Folk Roots* schedules, and by this point (the next chapter will explain) we had a daughter at home. From here onwards, English multi-instrumentalist and 'godfather of rogue folk' Andrew Cronshaw would get to roam the world, expertly looking after their sound and tour management.

Passing home via London they played the Royal Festival Hall with Zap Mama, followed by the Africolor Festival in Paris, and then that was it until the following summer when I did pull rank for a week in order to see the Canadian festivals again. This let me catch the reunion of Koerner, Ray & Glover and the unveiling of a new brass section by Quebecois giants La Bottine Souriante at another fabulous Winnipeg. Then Tarika and Cronshaw headed off for two months around Europe and a further two around the USA.

Artists complain these days about how they have to rely on gig merchandising because their record income has been decimated by streaming, but in the mid-'90s Tarika's merch side was already mighty. Their CD and T-shirt sales take could often be as big as the concert fee: there were occasions on North American dates when they shifted over 500 units. Arranging drops for merch re-stock en route became an important itinerary science.

While the rest of the band took a well-earned rest in 1996, Hanitra went off on a historical research trip back in Madagascar. We'd realised that 1997 was going to mark the 100th anniversary of the exile of Madagascar's last queen when the French took over as colonial power, and the 50th of a big uprising against them which had ended with a notorious massacre supposedly carried out by French African troops. Black Africans were known to the Malagasy as 'Senegalese' as a result, though most of them weren't actually from Senegal, and thoroughly demonised. As little children, Hanitra and Noro had been told that if they misbehaved, the Senegalese would come and eat them. But Tarika had met and become friends with Senegalese musicians at festivals while touring, overcoming their conditioning, and Hanitra wanted to dig out the truth, at the same time exposing post-independence corruption. And then write an album for 1997 release drawing all these threads together. Big Project!

Back home, I'd become friends with producer Simon Emmerson, then mastermind of Afro Celt Sound System, who'd recently worked on a Grammy-nominated Baaba Maal album. Would he like to produce this? He enthusiastically came on board, and he and engineer Martin Russell shipped digital equipment to Madagascar to do it. Returning to London, they added Senegalese tama drummer Massamba Diop and kora player Kauwding Cissokho from Baaba's band to the mix. The album was to be titled *Son Egal*, French for "equal sound" but also a pun on the Malagasy word for Senegalese, "Sonegaly." Hanitra and I put a lot of work into the notes and the package design.

On release in early 1997, *Son Egal* was their big breakthrough. By March it was top of the World Music charts on both sides of the Atlantic, rave reviewed and major featured in everything from the *Times* to *Playboy*. They were nominated in the 1997 Kora All-African Music Awards and won the AFIM Indie Award for Contemporary World Music Album in the USA. I was thrilled to get a call from Joe Boyd congratulating me on what we'd put together and achieved. In just three years they'd risen to the heights of the world music scene internationally, and their touring trajectory was ever upwards.

Better still was what happened in Madagascar, where until this point the band had hardly ever been able to play. But now broadcasting regulations had been relaxed and there were commercial radio stations as well as the state one. They all went crazy over *Son Egal*, particularly the song *Avelo* which expressed the hope that the ghosts of the ancestors would rise from their tombs and punish the corrupt politicians who had brought the country to its knees, all in a loosely trip-hop arrangement where Malagasy traditional instruments like the marovany jousted with the Senegalese. Nobody'd heard anything like it. And it was election time!

Possibly shamed by their historical role, the French Cultural Centre in Antananarivo, the only venue in the country at the time that had a Western-standard concert PA system, put them on for three sold-out nights. The first was televised and the press came. The following day the main newspaper carried the front page headline "Tarika Mania!" and editorialised that this was the band against which all future local ones must be judged, with veiled digs about the misinformation that had been circulated by that previous star's camp.

When I'd first visited in 1990, I'd been dismayed to find that traditional music was marginalised. TV had beamed in Western styles while the rich few, making their shopping pilgrimages to Paris, brought back synthesisers, drum machines and European fashion. *Vita Gasy* (Made in Madagascar) had become synonymous with 'worthless', and roots traditions were looked down on as associated with smelly people from the countryside. A new breed of rich-kid pop stars and artists with wealthy patrons had emerged, including Euro-pop chanteuses, bubble-gum salegy (all Mickey Mouse synths and drum machines); and embarrassing rock bands. All things Western and the standard multi-national hits soon found their way onto local radio.

Slowly the 1990s saw a considerable amount of international touring, recording by European and American labels, and festival appearances, spearheaded by Tarika, D'Gary, the Justin Vali Trio, Njava, Jaojoby, Rajery and Regis Gizavo. Back home, the message that the West liked all this music was helping helped to reinvest pride in the culture. Traditionally rooted musicians could, suddenly, not only aim to make a living from music (something almost unheard of before) but travel abroad as well. So the musical climate changed again, with one local newspaper pointing out that while Madagascar was in desperate economic straits, at least Malagasy musicians were achieving something in the wider world.

Son Egal lit a fuse. Within weeks of the onslaught of "Tarika Mania", Hanitra – who at the time was sporting a post-punk haircut with cropped sides and a pigtail – had become a style icon for rebellious young women, with growing numbers of imitators. And when their final album *Soul Makassar* included a song praising a rural delicacy called *Koba* (a kind of sweet pastry made out of rice flour with peanuts and honey in the middle, wrapped up in banana leaves and smoked over a fire), it soon moved from being something sold by impoverished roadside sellers to the menus of expensive hotels and restaurants. Vita Gasy became central to the campaign of Marc Ravalomanana who eventually defeated the old dictator Ratsiraka in 2002.

Propelled by the acclaim for *Son Egal*, 1997 would be their busiest year for touring yet, a lot of it spent in mainland Europe or North America. As I was no longer going on the road with them, trusting things in the care of Andrew Cronshaw and road managers George Cruze in North America and Bernie Parkyn in Europe, I no longer got to see so much of the action, but have a great memory of the 1997 UK WOMAD which just happened to fall on my 50th birthday. They already had a reputation for bringing the sun with them to festivals but when we arrived late that Saturday morning the rain was bucketing down. "Don't worry," I blithely said to the organisers, "they'll deal with it." And so it was that at the very moment the MC announced them on the main stage mid-afternoon, the sun burst out and seemingly the entire audience were up on their feet dancing.

I managed a good trip to Madagascar that winter of 1997/8 when we went on an epic voyage over often-unmade roads to the deep South West town of Tulear. On what was Boxing Day back in the UK, there it was 32 degrees of dry summer heat and we were bumping dust-caked along a sandy coast road bounded by baobabs, giant sizal and acres of impressively spiky cactus. Calling a roadside halt to get in some supplies we realised that something was going on in the village. Crowds of dancing people were legging it up the road, and half a dozen wandering groups of young kabosy players were sauntering in from the bush. A protesting *zébu* was being hauled off to meet its maker, ceremonial fish tied around its neck, and then from over the brow of the hill came the unmistakeable sound of an electric guitar cranked to 11.

By luck, we'd hit this village on the one day in every seven years when they held the *sambatra* circumcision ceremony and an all-night party was about to commence. Under the village shade-tree, the festivities were being led by Orchestre Rivo-Doza ('the cyclone band') comprising one probably Russian-made lead guitar, one 3-string bass guitar and a partly home-made drum kit. The fearsome music they were driving out was called tsapika and this was my first face-to-face experience of it.

Eventually in the market in Tulear I found a fairly raw-sounding cassette of them. Back home in England I dubbed a track off onto CDR and sent copies to Andy Kershaw and Charlie Gillett. Both opened their very next shows with it, clearly blown away. Joe Boyd heard it and immediately began planning a field trip recording project that sadly never happened.

The following year, for contrast, Tarika released *D*, code for Dance or *Dihy*, the Malagasy word for it. Classic songs from the 7" singles era of salegy, watsa-watsa and some new tsapika were re-arranged for traditional instruments while retaining their energy, and new ones were written in the style. The album was another hit on the international world music scene, and a slow dance track (what the Malagasy call a 'blues' but quite Polynesian sounding) titled *Raitra* became a massive No.1 hit at home. There were even mobile 'phones, an instant coffee brand and more named after it!

Another busy year of non-stop touring in 1998 finished in the UK with a headlining gig for the London Jazz Festival at the Queen Elizabeth Hall. After watching soundchecks, one of excellent support band Lo'Jo from France took Hanitra to one side and asked, worriedly, if she realised this was a jazz festival. Lo'Jo tried hard to be meaningfully jazz-like in their set, and the audience sat and enjoyed. Tarika came on for theirs and the place erupted, literally dancing in the aisles. Things were often like that!

Another project beckoned, like *Son Egal* from an idea seeded by me that Hanitra then ran with to create. The first settlers of Madagascar around 1,500 years ago were not from nearby Africa but of Malayo/ Polynesian origin, arriving from Indonesia either by a circuitous coastal route or directly across the Indian Ocean. They were related to the same people who, two thousand years earlier, had begun to spread out and eventually populate the Pacific, reaching Hawaii, Easter Island and New Zealand many centuries before European explorers. Similarly, ancient connections between Indonesia and Africa have been well documented and research had pointed to a catastrophic eruption of Krakatoa around 535 AD as a good reason for Indonesians to get on the boats and go west at that time. But hearing of dry academic research is one thing: encountering living evidence is another.

We'd both seen an early '90s TV travel documentary from Sulawesi that showed people who looked like her relatives involved in ancient burial customs that were startlingly familiar. Then we'd come across a bamboo instrument called the *sasandu* from the island of Roti near Timor which was a close relation of Madagascar's valiha tube zither, and records of music from far away Polynesian islands and even Okinawa, right on the other side of the Malayo/ Polynesian diaspora, that contained strong echoes of music made at home.

It became a burning ambition for Hanitra to visit Sulawesi and meet the descendants of their probably shared ancestors. In September 1999 she took a break and had an inspiring month's stay among the Bugis, Makassar and Torajan people, aided by sidekick Becky Morris. It was an experience which it's likely no other Malagasy had ever had. So many connections, similarities and ghosts – the look of the people, food, religion and beliefs, language, customs and rituals, clothes, rice cultivation – and extraordinary that they should still be so strong after 1500 years of mutual separation.

The central core of songs on the resulting album *Soul Makassar* came directly out of her Sulawesi voyage, and part of the recording involved Hanitra and producer Colin Bass (a.k.a. Sabah Habas Mustapha) taking the tapes to Bandung and Jakarta to work with musicians from other parts of Indonesia.

One of the reasons for Tarika's success was that every album they made was full of variety and always different from its predecessors, not common on the world music scene of the day where formulae tended to be adhered to. *D* had explored the energetic dance musics of the many regions of Madagascar while *Soul Makassar* focussed more on the musical roots of their own Merina people in the Malagasy highlands and its capital Antananarivo. Tarika were a shining example that taking strength from your roots and having pride in your culture can keep your head held high, wherever you come from or live.

Little did I know that in the process of sorting this album out I'd made a major error. BMG Records had launched a new world music label imprint called Wicklow, with Paddy Moloney of the Chieftains as its figurehead. They were making unrefusable offers to the major international touring world music bands and artists of the day (others included Finland's Varttina, Tuva's Yat-Kha and Scotland's Martyn Bennett) and in spite of my lifelong aversion to major labels, I forgot why it's never a good idea to break the rules of lessons learned the hard way. When they'd agreed to fund the $50,000 that the project was going to cost, we couldn't say no.

It turned out to be a very bad idea, but we wouldn't find that out until the 21st century dawned, and that's in Chapter 16… after everything else that happened alongside Madagascar Mania in the 1990s…

15.
The 1990s Otherwise...

It may seem from the last chapter that all I did in the 1990s was be distracted by Madagascar and look after Tarika's career, but in parallel with all that there was still an increasingly successful magazine to run and all sorts of other things to be involved in.

The decade opened with the roots music scene in the UK in rude health, with rapidly increasing numbers of CD releases, festivals, tours and gigs to report on in the news pages of *Folk Roots*. Readership and advertising were so buoyant that to our surprise we navigated through Thatcher's 1992 recession, the biggest since the 1930s and with interest rates soaring, without too much difficulty.

Mind you, it was hard in the off-mainstream record business, even after the years when it had been necessary to produce three formats for each release had passed. Mainstream media was (as ever) fond of putting up fake targets for controversy and there was a period when the myth that "CDs cost £1 to make but sell at £12 so the record companies are ripping everybody off for £11 profit" was the cry. Even the supposedly independent, investigative consumer magazine *Which?* jumped on the bandwagon that record labels had a licence to print money.

Of course, the truth was quite different. There was little escape then from the enormous cuts taken by the 'trade'. There were large discounts to the distributors who in turn gave large discounts to the shops (30% each in both cases), and the government took 17.5% VAT off the top. So independent labels only received less than half of what the customer paid, out of which they had to cover all studio recording, artwork, advertising and manufacturing costs (yes, a CD did indeed cost just over £1 to press), and artist and writer royalties. Even in those far off days when a successful folk or world music CD might expect to shift several thousand copies, there was very little margin to turn a profit for an independent who had to rely on the establishment to reach the public.

Small wonder that as the decade went on artists increasingly turned away from signing to labels and began self-releasing, selling direct to their fans on gigs. The post-gig merchandising table got well established during this era, and "doing the full country & western" bit of meeting and greeting the audience and signing their CDs became an essential for artists trying to scrape a living.

Another benefit after the '80s explosion was that it became rarer for the roots music scene, folk in particular, to be the butt of predictable mainstream media stereotyping. All those sneery comments about beards, sandals, cable-knit sweaters and "hey nonny no" slowly faded away.

In 1991, Mike Alexander's Pelicula Films (later the makers of the long-running *Transatlantic Sessions*) had a great wheeze with a programme that they conceived for Channel 4 TV titled *Beyond The Maypole*. It would never have been thought of, let alone made, a decade earlier. The conceit for it was that Biggie Tembo, front man of Zimbabwe's popular Bhundu Boys who'd conquered the rock circuit and Indie charts a few years earlier, was a folklorist coming to England so search out our 'exotic' roots music. And so he encountered Alistair Anderson with the Northumbrian Shepherds (Willy Taylor, Will Atkinson and Joe Hutton), Kathryn Tickell, Oysterband, the Barely Works, Billy Bragg, the Robb Johnson Band and more.

The crossover between the established folk scene's infrastructure and the new roots and world music ones was most noticeable at festivals level. At first, the longer-running folk festivals were slow to adapt, but with the growth of WOMAD and, as the world shrank, more artists beginning to bring back word of how events were being staged in North America and mainland Europe, things changed.

Personally, it was Canada which had provided the eye-opener. I'd never encountered events as well organised as Winnipeg or Edmonton Folk Festivals, or that attracted and used corporate sponsorship as well as the Montreal Jazz Festival. There were lots of lessons to digest that gave pointers for improvements here, bringing home how amateurish and lackadaisical UK promoters could be, how little they considered the needs (in terms of both stage presentation and personal comfort) of the artists. Going around the USA, Canada and Europe in the early '90s, there seemed to be a greater understanding that if you looked after the artists, they'd present a better show, the audience would be happier and the whole scene livelier and healthier. It was something that needed serious attention here, and over a few years things certainly bucked up.

The 1990s were the decade of phenomenal growth in folk festival numbers. We really noticed it when 1994's annual April festival issue of *Folk Roots* hit 116 pages. That growth would continue inexorably to its peak with April 2005's at 132 pages including 68 pages of advertising.

THE 1990s OTHERWISE...

In the mid-1990s we took things up a few more gears. Alongside being an early adopter of that new 'in' thing, a web site, *Folk Roots* was by then publishing ten times a year. The thick double issues for January/ February (in December) and August/ September (in July), came about because of the difficulty of assembling, printing and distributing issues over the year end holiday season and during the summer festival peak. We became even more like a proper grown-up magazine by starting to give free covermount CDs with those doubles, to let people hear more of the hard-to-find music that they were reading about.

We'd previously done that couple of 'various artist' vinyl LPs for sale via *Folk Roots*, and I discovered that I had a natural skill: compiling and sequencing them. It wasn't unrelated to putting good radio programmes together and I began to get asked to do them for others. An early one of those was a 1994 set for Topic Records that, to our astonishment, we got Arts Council funding for. Up to that point, virtually no English traditional recordings had appeared on CD, so Topic's Tony Engle, Veteran's John Howson and I brainstormed a set called *Hidden English* with tracks from most of the legendary English traditional singers and musicians who'd been recorded around the mid-20th century, performing, between them, many of the classic songs and tunes from the tradition. It was a snapshot of an era that was already pretty much over and even after Topic's later multi-volume themed CD series *The Voice Of The People* I think it still remains the best all-encompassing single sampler CD of the genre ever released, some thirty years later. So there!

By the mid-1990s, because of their superior sound quality, user friendliness and more economic use of storage space, the CD had justifiably taken over as the mass physical music carrier. In common with many people I'd found that my large LP collection was lying redundantly unplayed. There came a point around 1997 when I realised that both of my record decks no longer worked. Through disuse (the lids had largely become convenient places on which to pile things, like CDs!) the drive belts had perished. There was a lightbulb moment when I walked into the Wood Green branch of the Our Price Records chain and discovered that I could now get a mid-priced compilation CD of the works of Mississippi blues giant Charley Patton, once only available on rare, expensive but poor quality vinyl. If things even that 'obscure' were now appearing on CD, I really didn't need that massive weighty wall of lo-fi tarmac that was causing cracks to appear in the house...

I made an arrangement with an American record dealer to buy my thousands of LPs for a good average price. He came over, packed them into boxes and shipped them off to the USA. For a decade I hung on to a few hundred LPs in the two areas of music that I really didn't imagine would make it onto CD – local West African releases from the '60s/'70s classic era, and English traditional music – but eventually they mostly did too. So EBay beckoned…

But what happened to my old 'tarmac' collection? One answer was provided some 15 years later when I became friends with American guitarist/songwriter Steve Gunn. "How did you get into this area of music," I enquired, about his admiration for 1960s/'70s British psych folk and guitarists like Michael Chapman and Mike Cooper (and indeed me, as I discovered from a feature he'd done on 'crate-digging' for *Uncut* magazine where he'd highlighted one of my Village Thing LPs). "Well, there was this guy near where I lived who dealt in those kinds of records." Guess who…

There were also some big domestic changes. 1994 had begun with the Tarika line-up crisis. But at the same time as having to deal with all that, matters had come to a head of a more personal nature for Hanitra and I. She'd had a previous arranged marriage in Madagascar that had been disastrous and resulted in divorce, but not before she'd had a child. In those days in Madagascar, for a woman to get a divorce she had to give up everything including not only property but children, so her baby daughter Cathia had been surrendered to her now ex-husband's family before Hanitra escaped to the UK.

It had become clear on our visits to Madagascar that little Cathia was not being treated well by her father, sometimes locked up at home while he went out drinking, gambling and drunk driving, and often not sent to school. Eventually, in 1994 we'd gone to court and got custody. It was less difficult than we'd anticipated as we luckily got a three-women tribunal and the father turned up drunk in court. Our immediate plan had been for Hanitra's parents and extended family to take care of her in Madagascar in the short term, with our support, and not immediately yank her away from her family and culture. But word had come back that the father kept showing up and taking her away.

Tarika took a break from touring in the first half of 1995 so we decided that Cathia should come to the UK. While Hanitra was in Madagascar sorting everything out, I got builders in to put a loft extension onto the London house. Lesson learned the hard way: do not try to live in a house, let alone run a monthly magazine downstairs, while you're having that sort of major building work and the subsequent necessary redecoration done. Especially when the old loft has 100 years of London soot and dust up there just waiting to descend and find its way through every crack around every room door, regardless how efficiently you tape them up each morning!

I survived it, but only just. Advertising manager Gina was sat at her desk facing the office door at the time I tripped on loose carpet at the top of the stairs, bounced headlong down them, flew past and crashed in a heap against the front door. She assumed I was a goner, but amazingly nothing was more seriously damaged than my pride!

Cathia came that May and settled in far more easily than might have been expected, picking up English really quickly. We started her in the local junior school in September and she thrived, excelling academically. I'd never thought I wanted children – having no recollection of being one or experience around them – and had always half-jokingly said that I'd be fine with children if they could be born with fully-formed personalities so I could talk with them like small adults. By a stroke of great luck, this turned out to be exactly what I got. In later years people would congratulate me on my 'parenting skills' but I'd have to give all the credit to Cathia, who turned out brilliantly, for her daughtering skills.

She adapted to our music lifestyle with apparent ease and pleasure. That summer she came with us to Canada for Tarika's festival gigs. When people got up on stage to dance with Congolese superstar Papa Wemba at Winnipeg, she was up there like a shot, much to Wemba's visible astonishment and pleasure. And that autumn we took her to the epic African Prom at the Albert Hall, a lengthy show featuring Senegal's Youssou N'Dour and Baaba Maal, Algeria's Khaled, Mali's Salif Keita and South Africa's Lucky Dube with their respective bands.

An amazing event, filmed for TV, it was only marred by the behaviour of Maal who – as well producing overblown theatrics involving a giant throne being carried on stage for him to sit regally in – contrived to overrun by some 30 minutes which was clearly designed to result in his rival N'Dour's closing set being curtailed. We'd somehow managed to wangle a box for the *Folk Roots* staff, friends and refreshments so it had felt like a special deal. I think Cathia finally conked out and fell asleep on the way home, but it wasn't a school day the next day: we weren't that irresponsible!

In April 1995, just before Cathia arrived, there'd been a truly awful revelation from my cousin Sean Mayes.

Sean, as I mentioned earlier, had been a young prodigy classical pianist at school but blew most of his university grant on an electric organ, joining a college rock band. After graduating, he'd ended up back in Weston-super-Mare with my old Iveys chums Des and Mario in a band which evolved into classy rock'n'roll revivalists Fumble. He'd later toured the world in David Bowie's 1978 band (later writing the book *Life On Tour With David Bowie*) and joined Tom Robinson in his *War Baby* era.

Meanwhile his younger brother Ricky, a.k.a. Oscar, had been virtually written off by the family as less talented and a bit of a failure, which had become self-perpetuating as he fell into suspect company, depression and heavy drug use. These days his mental health issues would almost certainly have been recognised and perhaps addressed.

I'd last seen Ricky around 1971, and he'd been notably absent when we went back to Weston in April 1972 for my grandmother's funeral. When he never re-appeared over the following years, the story was that a week or two before the funeral he'd been called for by some of his disreputable friends, taken his sleeping bag and gone off down to Cornwall with them. As years went by, the supposition was that he'd later followed a dream he'd expressed of going on the hippy trail overland to India and perhaps met an unfortunate end on the way.

Eventually Sean and Ricky's grandfather, Uncle Tom, passed away, and their mother Joy had moved up to London where she too eventually died. My parents sometimes wondered if Ricky might show up on their doorstep one day, looking for her. Meanwhile Sean had enjoyed great success with Fumble, touring with rock'n'roll legends Chuck Berry and Fats Domino and being the house band in the West End *Elvis* musical before he'd joined Bowie and Robinson. Among other things he'd also played piano on Maggie Holland's first LP for Rogue Records.

He'd called me out of the blue one evening with two bits of shocking news, the timing being because the story was going to come out in the newspapers the next day and he wanted to forewarn me. The first was that he was dying of AIDs and probably had little more than a month to live. The second was that, faced with this imminent end, he'd presented himself at Paddington Green police station with a confession: that he'd covered up for more than two decades the fact that his mother had murdered his brother. He'd helped her and Uncle Tom bury the body a few days later, after he'd returned from a Fumble residency in Switzerland for my grandmother's funeral, to discover what had happened. He wanted to clear his conscience and, with his mother and grandfather now both dead, allow his brother to have a proper burial.

It turned out that Joy had written a confession for the eventuality of the discovery of the body, which came to me with Sean's papers after his own death. Writing "to whom it may concern" in Twickenham in October 1980, she'd said:

"My younger son Roderick was buried in the garden of 47 The Boulevard, Weston-super-Mare, on 7th April 1972. (Aged 23). Should his body be found during rebuilding, I wish the true circumstances of the death to be known so that no innocent person is implicated.

My much loved son Roderick had psychological problems in his teens (finding it difficult to relate to people socially), which were helped by smoking cannabis occasionally, i.e. at weekend parties. He was convicted and fined for possession when he was living in Chelmsford (a computer programmer with Marconi Ltd) and had a nervous breakdown, giving up his job and drinking heavily. Roderick came home to live and, unbeknown to his family, switched to the drug LSD – this being more difficult to trace than 'pot' (how I wish that cannabis had been legalised – he had been smoking this for years without harm).

Although Dr Hashim tried to help him and the staff at the mental hospital at Wells were very kind, Roderick refused further help and became quite out of his mind on LSD. When he was not on the drug he was suicidal and cried. I was working in London, but gave up my job and came home when my son Sean told me what was happening – the house, which Roderick shared with his grandfather Tom Thompson, was overrun with hippy friends. My father was leading a nightmare existence, unable to cope with either Roderick or his friends.

When I came home in March, a young nurse who had befriended Roderick came to see me and told me she had worked in a psychiatric ward and knew that Roderick would have to go to such a place. She could not help him and he would not see a doctor. (She was so upset that she left Weston-super-Mare.)

Taking into account that Roderick's life was ruined and that he would find being 'shut up' unbearable, I decided to end his life. While he was asleep I stunned him many times with an iron footscraper and then cut his throat. My father helped me to bury him between the shed and the wall in the back garden.

If I have had to endure hell living with this secret, I only hope that my son has found peace. My son Sean was in Switzerland at this time and only knew of the death when he came home."

Sean had naively hoped that he'd be able to achieve his aim quietly, but once he realised this would be impossible he'd rung the only remaining close family, my parents and I, to warn us. The story was indeed in many of the national and local newspapers the next day, some reported sympathetically, others more luridly. Nothing like the tragedy of a "gay rock star" with Bowie connections, dying of AIDs, involved in a brutal murder, to get the hacks slavering, accompanied by photos of grim-faced police officers carrying a body bag out of the property and details of the corpse being found wrapped in a sleeping bag…

In the *Western Daily Press*, police Detective Sergeant Mike Robinson who was in charge of the case appealed for anybody locally who'd known the family at the time to come forward, so my father did that. My mother later told me that the policeman had been very kind and respectful. Asking my father if he could think of any reason why Joy would be inclined to do such a thing, my father remembered that although, when they were children, she would never hurt a fly, there had been an incident when they were playing in a garden on the Somerset Levels. There was shooting going on nearby and an injured pigeon had fallen near them. Joy had unhesitatingly gone over and wrung its neck "to put it out of its misery."

There was an inquest and funeral within little more than a month, the police reasonably deciding there was no useful purpose to be served by prosecuting Sean as an accessory. He died shortly afterwards, much mourned by the Fumble family and his wide circle of friends. At his funeral, I met Sean's father for the only time: they'd fairly recently renewed contact. I can't begin to imagine what a shock this must all have been for him and wonder whether he felt any guilt for leaving the boys to grow up fatherless.

And talking of fathers… the attitude of mine to Hanitra and then Cathia was unexpected. Probably, like many *Express* and *Telegraph* (or worse) reading xenophobes, he'd had virtually zero personal experience of actually meeting people from other cultures and with brown skins. He somehow managed to ignore the facts and treat them as if they were any other white English born and raised, even discussing 'the immigrant problem' with Hanitra. And when Cathia did well in school and got her university place, he seemed as proud as if she were my blood daughter.

Somehow, around all this – there was no privacy when running a business from home with close friends as staff – life went on. The world out there did its best to confound things, often via Royal Mail who, when they didn't go on strike just as we were posting out subscription issues, did things like 'losing' a Special Delivery item containing the original transparency for the magazine's cover. They eventually admitted that it was in a van which had been stolen and its less obviously valuable contents recovered from a canal (shades of Transatlantic Records and Village Thing!) Somehow we got a replacement alternative to the printers in the nick of time.

Probably the worst mail-related crisis came in early 1996 when Flora Margarine decided to hold a big competition, running a special offer via a PO Box in London N4 whose number was similar to ours. The sorting office was inundated with their mail, having to take on extra staff, and literally hundreds of items of mail that were sent to us in the first months of the year were wrongly sorted. This was compounded by Flora then ending up with a large warehouse full of mail sacks and not getting around to opening them until long after receipt. They then simply chucked the stuff meant for other people back in the mail, badly torn open and roughly stapled together!

Adverts meant for the festival issue, invoice payments, subscription cheques, numerous press releases and feature copy simply vanished for several months. It upset a lot of people whose first assumption was that the fault was ours, and hit our already hard-pushed staff with a ridiculous amount of extra work, both sorting out the mess and dealing with irate 'phone calls. And of course there was a nasty dip in our cash flow, with all the headaches that causes.

Royal Mail's so-called 'Customer Services' categorically refused to consider compensation – but at least Flora kindly responded by offering to purchase a batch of WOMAD tickets to give away to readers in a competition.

One of my proudest achievements over the magazine's 40-year existence was that we published every single issue on time, which considering what the world constantly and unexpectedly chucked at us was truly remarkable!

We eventually extended the office back into the garden which allowed in lots of much-needed natural light, along with fresh air in the warmer months. Not to mention wildlife. You'd be surprised how much of that abounded in North London in an area surrounded by busy roads. Inquisitive squirrels, toads, baby foxes and birds frequently wandered in along with less-welcome mice. Pandemonium ensued one day when Gina returned from her lunch break, opened her desk drawer and a squirrel jumped out. But it wasn't just an animal sanctuary, it later provided the extra space for me to employ an assistant to take pressure off what was by now sometimes 100-plus hour weeks with the magazine, Tarika duties, radio and the tail of the record label. The first of those, Vanessa, arrived in the later '90s and, like her eventual successor Sofi Mogensen, proved indispensable.

Meanwhile, out in the international world of music, as well as the early touring I did with the band and the growth of WOMEX, I'd started attending the annual North American Folk Alliance conference/showcase events, affectionately known as 'Folk Aliens' to us Europeans. Now re-titled Folk Alliance International, they had begun in 1989 to provide advocacy, development and networking for the folk scene over there, soon extending abroad.

I've no idea what the earlier Folk Alliances were like but when I first went to the Boston one in 1994 the form was pretty well established. They'd book out one of those big North American conference hotels which allowed everything to be under the same roof: official showcase concerts, awards ceremonies, various sizes of presentations and seminars, panel discussions, a trade fair with stands from across the industry (artists, agents, festivals, record labels, instrument makers, magazines, regional organisations and all sorts) plus rooms for the many hundreds – these days thousands – of delegates.

Already well established by that first one I went to were private guerilla showcases that attending artists were allowed to put on in their hotel rooms, which being American were quite large when beds were upended against the wall. These were mostly acoustic but sometimes even with small PA systems. Mercifully, the accommodation floors were zoned so you could pick a quiet, showcase-free one where you might eventually get some sleep.

Nothing like it had ever existed in the UK: the only attempt had been a well-intentioned one instigated by Scottish singer Dick Gaughan and others in the early '80s to form an organisation called Perform, but it soon fizzled out. It wouldn't be until the mid-2010s that we'd get English Folk Expo, and even that, like WOMEX, has never been all under one roof.

I knew something rum was afoot as soon as I arrived in Boston and got on the FA shuttle bus at the airport. No sooner had it moved off than a be-denimed bloke got his Martin guitar out of its case and started serenading us, moving down the aisle handing out business cards. Then, entering the hotel lobby, it appeared that every surface including the walls of the lifts was covered with promotional fliers for private showcases and you could hardly walk a few metres without them being thrust into your hands. American folkies had always gained the reputation of being... pushy. But who knew?

It turned out that this particular Folk Alliance would go down in history as 'death by singer songwriter.' Over the following years, actual folk music, not only North American but from Europe and all over the world, would wrest control back. Just not this year. But it didn't stop me from meeting and making friends (sometimes for life) with many like-minded enthusiasts. The people from our American cousins, *Sing Out!* and *Dirty Linen* magazines were there and we hung out and did a panel together.

Most memorable that first year was a panel discussion that included myself, Jim Lloyd from BBC Radio 2 and others, titled "Opportunities in Europe." Jim and I decided we'd do the good guy/ bad guy routine in the presentation. He depicted the UK folk scene as wonderfully welcoming to everybody. I was delegated to point out that if you were a singer-songwriter with no perceptible roots, or bashing out Irish songs, or a white boy blueser with a National steel guitar doing the Robert Johnson songbook (for example), then not to bother as we had loads of those already. People kept jumping up and prefacing their question with "I'm a singer-songwriter and..."

Eventually one of our co-panellists from Scandinavia rose to his feet and declared loudly, with obvious irritation: "There is something you need to know. In Europe we do not consider that singer-songwriters are folk music." He sat down again, abruptly. There was a marked intake of shocked breath from around the room. For the rest of the conference you heard people at meal times, in the corridors and in the lifts asking each other "Did you hear what that guy from Europe said?"

In 1995 it went across country to Portland, Oregon, where folk music staged something of a comeback, and that process continued the next year in Washington DC. On one of those years, I'd taken my DAT Walkman to try to record some inserts for my BBC World Service show. Slightly the worse for drink, a friend from an American record label and I took ourselves into the lifts that ran between the private showcase floors, microphone in hand, saying to people "I'm from the BBC and I'm looking for the showcase that doesn't have a singer-songwriter." It's amazing, say you're from the BBC and people take you seriously, directing you down the corridors. An increasingly amusing sub-plot was that we'd occasionally stick our heads into the stairwell, to discover that somewhere in there was a didgeridoo player, but we never found him (or her) – they always seemed to be one floor above or below.

Before we collapsed into complete hilarity, we finally found ourselves on a basement floor where there was indeed a session where British people were singing traditional songs. As we entered the room, the person singing one was English singer-songwriter Steve Tilston, out of his usual zone!

In Washington there was a 'world music' discussion panel, again involving various Americans and Europeans. One American panellist stated that world music was so much easier for us Europeans because we "lived much closer to it." Other Americans pointed out his staggering lack of geographical awareness, even telling him that all he had to do was ask taxi drivers right there in Washington, possibly one of the most culturally diverse cities in the USA, what music they listened to in their homes. Or just head south of the border...

After a good one up in Toronto in 1997, it was in Memphis in 1998 that things got extraordinary. My dear friends The Copper Family from Sussex were doing a showcase/talk and afterwards we gathered on the landing outside. In this group mobbing them were – you'll have to take my word for this – Alan Lomax and his daughter, Pete Seeger, Woody Guthrie's daughter, Leadbelly's niece and Robert Johnson's nephew Robert Junior Lockwood. And at the point I realised this, one of them turned to me and asked for my advice on something. The ghost of my 16 year old self is still pinching himself ...

Later that night, walking down Beale Street (I'm not making this up!) Ben Mandelson and I got asked if we'd like to accompany Bob Copper singing some Sleepy John Estes songs at his 85th birthday bash coming up at the folk club in Lewes in January 2000, as he wanted to come out of the closet as a lifelong blues fan. We didn't need to be asked twice...

One advantage that I'd gained from moving close to the inaccurately named Green Lanes in North London was that there was the Greek record shop Trehantiri run by two brothers, Aki and Laki Pattalis, an Aladdin's cave heaving with Greek CDs, LPs and instruments. I soon learned not to take a wallet when I went in there as Aki's enthusiasms were so totally infectious. Among many artists he introduced me to, ancient and modern, was the great Greek star Eleftheria Arvanitaki. I got quite hooked into her music and we ended up doing a *Folk Roots* cover feature on her in 1997, in the issue which went into all the WOMEX delegate bags. This apparently had boosted her career outside of Greece, including quite a few WOMAD events worldwide.

We became good friends, but imagine my surprise when, as thanks, she then invited me, along with Hanitra and Cathia, to Athens at her expense, to see her in an extraordinary outdoor concert held in a big quarry. In what must have been a more than three hour show, she went through everything from her contemporary hits from her extraordinary album *Ta Kormia Kai Ta Maheria* (The Bodies And The Knives) with full rock band to traditional acoustic old-style *rembetika*, with some of Greece's best musicians – and quite a few impressive frock changes.

Later I was pleased to host her for dinner in London along with Ara Dinkjan, oud player from Night Ark and her Armenian producer of *Ta Kormia Kai Ta Maheria* and invite a delighted Aki & Laki from Trehantiri to join us.

The world definitely seemed smaller and easier in that pre-Brexit era. It was not unusual to be seized by the notion, every six months or so, to hop on an early Eurostar for a cheap day return to Paris, just to go shopping for the latest West African releases in the diaspora shops in Barbès and hit the big FNAC store in Les Halles to catch up on all the *musique du monde* delights the French labels were releasing. Then, if there was time, go and sit with a coffee and a *croque monsieur* and people-watch outside a favourite little café on the Place du Grand Réré, near to all the expensive little (window shopping only!) art galleries on the Rue de Seine in Odéon.

Back in the UK, we were spoiled. As the century drew to a close, things continued to be exciting. There was a series of sensational gigs at Camden's Jazz Café by women artists who were making extraordinary records. Emmylou Harris was there for two nights trying out the new band she'd used on her *Wrecking Ball* album, which was such a remarkable reinvention that ever afterwards somebody coming up with such a surprise would be described in our pages as "doing an Emmylou" (though in truth, there weren't many). There was the wonderful Canadian singer Lhasa who had just released her deservedly acclaimed debut CD *La Llorona*. I remember sitting next to an equally dumbstruck Charlie Gillett gripping the edge of the balcony in close proximity to her on the stage. And there was jazz singer Cassandra Wilson who'd emerged from a career in avant garde improv jazz to be signed by venerable Blue Note and produce the amazing *Blue Light Til Dawn* with its inspired mix of blues, pop, jazz, world music, and country.

And out in the folk world, Norma Waterson and Eliza Carthy had individually helped accelerate the newly hip acceptability of the music by getting Mercury Music Prize nominations in 1996 and 1998 respectively.

At *Folk Roots*, from the November 1998 issue, I'd had a brainwave and re-logoed it as *fRoots*. I'd just got tired of dealing with people's misconceptions about the 'F' word in the title. The American muzikbiz useage of the word to indicate anybody who wrote their own songs with an acoustic guitar meant, I thought, that anybody who was interested in all the traditional and world music that we covered might be put off by that word and never pick one up, whilst the people who were only interested in singer-songwriters would be annoyed that we didn't cover much of that any more. With so much good other stuff around, there just wasn't the space. And recently there had been the runaway success of Apple's new iMacs. If people had no difficulty seeing and pronouncing that as eye-Mac, why would they struggle with eff-Roots?

As it turned out, they did. I spent the next 21 years having to correct people who said it as "fruits" and even at the end in 2019, when it had been *fRoots* for more than half its existence, people still referred to it as *Folk Roots*. Even those who hadn't been born when it changed. Not the world's most successful rebranding then.

I'd been running into Neville Marten from *Guitarist* magazine as a fellow pundit on the Paul Jones Radio 2 show's annual round up of the year. *Guitarist* had started, like us, as an enthusiast-run independent and eventually been bought out by one of the UK's biggest publishing houses, Future Publishing in Bath. I asked him a while after this how they were getting on and he said it was the best thing they ever did: gave them massively more clout, distribution and security, and allowed them to get away from the boring business stuff and concentrate on the subject they loved, guitars. I expressed jealousy! He must have passed the word back because not long after this in 1999 I got a call from an executive at Future asking if I'd be interested in doing the same with *fRoots*. Well, yes!

We got some way down the negotiations, which included job security for our staff, working out of Future's London office rather than moving to their Bath headquarters, and a (what seemed) generous financial deal which would have cleared my mortgage. Brilliant. And then he upped and left Future. The person who took over his post didn't 'get it' and so it all vanished in a puff of mirage dust. Another of life's great 'what ifs'.

In spite of that, we ended the century on a reasonable high. The magazine was in good condition and growing, and the music we covered was going through one of its extended exciting phases again. As well as Britfolk now producing a new generation of artists, the rest of the world continued to shower us with new roots revelations. But it was quite startling when we suddenly thought we'd heard the future of folk and it came from… America!

The record that seemed to do that was *Songs From My Funeral* by a duo called Snakefarm. They were singer Anna Domino who, it turned out, had previously made solo records in the '80s that some said were a major influence on the gestation of trip hop, and her Belgian multi-instrumentalist partner Michel Delory.

It had been 30 years since Fairport Convention's *Liege & Lief* had forged a link between British traditional songs and the rock music of the day, proving that those old songs had within them the power to adapt and survive, and providing a blueprint for thousands who followed. For a while it even made folk music a fashionable youth movement. But there had been very few more such giant steps and what was current rock music in 1969 was now as far past its sell-by date as Glenn Miller was back then. That old folk rock format was very tired indeed, a predictable sub-set of pub rock along with formulaic 'blues bands'.

Skills in using computer generated beats and samples had been so well learned in the previous decade that the kit involved was by now just as valid a musical instrument as any of the older technology. There was no need to be surprised that Michael Delory was as good at keyboard and drum programming as he was at dobro, guitar and banjo – which is to say very good – or that Anna Domino's languid vocal delivery of *St James Infirmary* or *House Of The Rising* Sun floated far more perfectly and appropriately in a post-trip-hop landscape than it would if held in the straitjacket of a 'conventional' (i.e. old rock) rhythm section. For all its big beats, dance technology here restored a rhythmic freedom to songs that grew strange and assymetric little delivery habits along the way. The key to *Songs From My Funeral* was that the songs were the boss: they ultimately ran the show.

And they suddenly sounded very modern: the other thing that this album did was rehabilitate those Anglo-American folk songs like *Tom Dooley*, *Frankie & Johnny* and *The Banks Of The Ohio* which were jolly-sung to death from a million folk bandwagon songbooks in the late 1950s and '60s. The songs came alive again, letting you focus back on their qualities when wrested from the associations that had weighed them down. Their timeless relevance snapped back into focus once more.

A few months later they came to London to do a showcase. It was a bizarre gig somewhere off Tottenham Court Road in a venue called the Embassy Rooms, never heard of before or since, that looked like a de-frocked bingo hall. Unable to bring the session bass player and drummer, they'd filmed them performing their parts, projected on a screen between them by a VJ. It shouldn't have worked but it did, brilliantly. People still talk about it nearly a quarter of a century later. Folk-phobics like radio DJ Charlie Gillett became overnight fans.

And then they seemed to vanish again, for more than a decade before their next album and UK visit, when I was thrilled to put them on the cover of *fRoots* and host an acoustic gig at London's Green Note. Then they vanished again. Enigmatic or what? And they still may be the future of folk…

1999 marked the 20th anniversary of the magazine since we began as *Southern Rag* in 1979. I compiled two star-studded double CDs, *Roots* and *Routes*, of artists who'd appeared in our pages, released to great approval by Nascente Records. To mark the anniversary and promote the CDs we jointly hosted a mighty bash at Dingwall's in Camden, inviting a big horde of roots music industry and media mover-shakers, artists, writers, radio people, readers and good fRiends of *fRoots*.

A great variety of artists performed for us with contrasting sets from Tuva's Yat-Kha, Maggie Holland, Pete Morton, Abdul Tee-Jay's Palm Wine Trio, Tarika, the Copper Family and Afro Celt Sound System. The latter two groups seemed to form a mutual admiration society, seen to greatly enjoy each other's sets, which helped seed Afro Celt main man Simon Emmerson's 21st century project *The Imagined Village* later (more of that next chapter).

Having been tied down acting as host for the evening and MC for the live music, I'd just slipped into the catering area to hoover up any remaining food when an alarmed messenger came to find me. "Afro Celts are fighting on stage!" This turned out to be an exaggeration, but what I'd missed actually became the stuff of legend. Piper Michael McGoldrick really needed to catch the last train to Manchester and had arranged with the band's tour manager for a taxi to collect him at the necessary time. Inevitably with a multi-artist bill, things were running late and unfortunately, nobody had told Simon, who turned round to see McGoldrick packing up his pipes and walking offstage mid-set. There had been a brief but public altercation.

A few months later our stage manager for the evening, Becky Morris, a good friend of McGoldrick's, was asked by members of an Irish band about the big fight that had taken place among Afro Celts on stage at… the Albert Hall. So go Chinese whispers!

THE 1990s OTHERWISE...

Back in the real world, a mere four years after arriving in London with no English, Cathia passed the entrance exam for the sought-after (but non-fee paying) Latymer School in Edmonton, which nobody from her junior school had done in a decade. The 21st century was looking promising...

16.
Into The Noughties

The new century began with enormous optimism in our musical backwater. Britfolk had finally broken through the acceptability barrier. Norma Waterson had begun it with a Mercury Awards nomination in 1996, followed by Eliza Carthy with *Red Rice* in 1998 and Kate Rusby in 1999. Eliza got her second shout with *Anglicana* in 2003, and the process would continue via Seth Lakeman, the Unthanks and Sam Lee, though it was then followed by a decade gap – when folk-informed Colin Irwin and later Jude Rogers were no longer on the judging panel – before Lankum struck in 2023. Mind you, the mainstream media inevitably referred to them all as the "token folk record", as they also did with non-folk songwriters like Lou Rhodes (who'd at least had a folk club upbringing), Laura Marling, Beth Orton and Kathryn Williams.

On the creative fringes, if the '90s had ended with the musical promise of Snakefarm, the '00s began equally well with the re-birth of the great Joe Strummer and his band the Mescaleros, who included my old friend Tymon Dogg in their ranks. An invigoratingly original local mixture of world roots and rock, their second album *Global A Go-Go* from 2001 remains high on my 'desert island' list. They even captured 2002's Cambridge Folk Festival, where Joe did a cover photo shoot with Jak Kilby for *fRoots*. Unfortunately, Colin Irwin's planned interview to accompany it never came to fruition before Joe's shocking death at age only 50 that December. I'm still kicking myself for allowing overwork and bad weather to dissuade me from going to what turned out to be Joe and the Mescaleros' last gig at Acton Town Hall that November, where they were joined on stage by Joe's old Clash bandmate Mick Jones. And I'd even been put on the guest list by Tymon. What an idiot...

The continuing 21st century would finally, deservingly, see a wholesale sea change on the UK folk scene from the performer generations – mine! – who'd had a stranglehold since the 1960s and '70s. As well as those Mercury nominees, there were John Spiers & Jon Boden evolving into the mighty Bellowhead from 2004, Emily Portman and her trio with Lucy Farrell and Rachel Newton eventually joining with Alasdair Roberts as the Furrow Collective, the extraordinary Rheingans Sisters, the magnificent Angeline Morrison, Jim Moray and his sister Jackie Oates, Lisa Knapp (later to join Marry Waterson and the Dead Rat Orchestra's Nathaniel Mann in the inspiring

Hack-Poets Guild), Olivia Chaney, Bella Hardy, Julie Fowlis, Karine Polwart, Nancy Wallace, Telling The Bees, Kitty Macfarlane, Frankie Archer and too many more to comprehensively list. Predominantly younger women, though by the latter end of the 2010s there would be a satirically tagged 'New Wave Of Folk Blokes' like Jon Wilks, Thom Ashworth, Nick Hart, Sid Goldsmith & Jimmy Aldridge and more. Not that blokes had been inactive: one of the great English folk albums of the new century was Chris Wood's classic and influential *The Lark Descending* from 2005.

Young women also lead the way in a growing enthusiasm for Morris dancing, no longer the preserve of the unfit, bearded and beer-bellied. Prime mover among that was a human dynamo called Laurel Swift with her mixed-gender Morris Offspring side and organisation called Shooting Roots who grew a huge new community of folk youth. She also helped advise the wonderful 2009 film *Morris: A Life With Bells* On. By 2023, the sensational all-women Boss Morris were deservedly being feted everywhere, appearing in style magazines, on TV drama series and dancing with Wet Leg at the Brit Awards. They were part-taught by Laurel as well.

Although the focus had turned away from the USA, the 21st century brought us remarkable soloists like Devon Sproule, Sam Amidon, Anais Mitchell and Joan Shelley. And then there came a striking band called the Carolina Chocolate Drops, launching the later careers of Rhiannon Giddens, Dom Flemons and Leyla McCalla.

Another notable 21st century movement was the rise of English instrumental groups, spearheaded by Spiro and Leveret in particular. Outside of playing for dancing, instrumental folk had largely been the preserve of the Irish and Scottish in the UK, so this was a welcome development, as were all-women bands like Scotland's The Shee and Kinnaris Quintet, and more recently Bristol's Hedera. Indeed, Bristol led the way on the instrumental wave with both Spiro and Three Cane Whale (with musician Alex Vann in common). Not all were pleased, though, with one well-known Scottish fiddler stating that English musicians shouldn't be allowed in the Folk Awards as they "can't play folk music."

Along with positive developments in technology, world music and a growth in engagement from Arts funding, all of which I'll come to, this meant that the new century felt very buoyant and the content of *fRoots* reflected it. If the '60s were the first golden age and the '80s the second, then I'd pitch for the 'noughties' as being the third. So that was all good then… But sadly for me, disaster and complications outside my control were about to strike.

As mentioned, I'd over-ruled my instincts and signed Tarika to a major label deal. The band had made *Soul Makassar*, recorded in London and Indonesia and readied themselves for their biggest ever North American tour to promote it. But just a couple of weeks before the tour was due to start in June 2000, after air tickets had been bought and far too late to cancel the dates without us incurring the permanent wrath of major promoters, BMG closed down Wicklow without notice in a massive re-organisation, pulling the release and the crucial tour promotion support.

The tour had to go ahead anyway, but now without the benefit of either the heavy media coverage that flows from a new release or the new CDs to merchandise at the shows (which could double the profits on a concert). Worse, after years of touring on the basis of decent guaranteed fees against lower percentages of the door take (so you were sure of your income), on this tour with its anticipated massive buzz from the new album we'd finally gone for lower guarantees against higher percentages of the door, something that only well-established bands sure of their status can sensibly do. The carefully calculated finances were blown out of the water, and since all the travel costs, crew and band wages had to be paid anyway, I had to find the funds to cover it.

Meanwhile, Hanitra had met a new man, a very wealthy French benefactor, and begun separating from me as he poured money into her plans to build an Arts Centre back in Madagascar. So life became even more complicated, though at least he hired the lawyers who got BMG to sign over the master tapes of *Soul Makassar* in lieu of damages.

The one thing that, oddly enough, wasn't complicated was supporting Cathia's future. It hardly needed discussing. She'd adapted totally to English culture, got a great educational situation and a full social life with supportive school and friends. I'd mostly taken care of her single-handedly all the time the band had been away extensively touring and recording for the past five years. So Cathia would stay with me in London and her mother returned to Antananarivo. All three of us were happy with this arrangement and I became that rare thing, a single step-parent. That part all worked out fine – as I said before, Cathia had exceptional daughtering skills.

With the rights regained for *Soul Makassar*, I arranged a deal with a smaller world music label for North America, Triloka, who nevertheless had a good reputation in the field. We re-set the release for June 2001, but this time Tarika's tour wouldn't be scheduled until a couple of months afterwards, to allow time for the album to work its magic.

It did that very thing, surging to the top of the World Music charts in the USA and gaining copious rave reviews. CNN were due to start a dedicated World Music TV series and sent a crew to London to interview the band and film them live. Then the very week that the tour began, *Time* magazine ran a feature on "the ten best bands in the world outside the USA" (just think on the implications of that in a country which has a World Series in a sport hardly anybody else plays!). It included the likes of U2, Radiohead, Portishead... and Tarika.

The scene was set to recoup all the big losses from the previous year and make a lot more on top, beginning to repay the years of hard work and investment. In they flew, and played their first date of the tour at B.B. King's in Manhattan on September 10th. Or, as the Americans would write it, 9/10.

The next morning they woke up in their hotel over the water from Manhattan in Newark. It was 9/11 and they watched the buildings burn and collapse. The world had changed. George Cruze, their trusty American tour manager, came in and announced that they wouldn't be going to the airport to fly to Los Angeles for their gig that night as all flights were cancelled, (as they'd remain for several weeks). Instead of turning in the tour rentabus he'd keep it and they'd hit the road immediately to the following date in Tucson, Arizona, which would realistically be a two-day drive. They were advised not to get out of the bus across the south, except when really necessary, as the country was gripped with xenophobia. Their new sound engineer – Andrew Cronshaw had decided not to do this tour – was beside herself with worry as the venue where she usually worked was in the shadow of the World Trade Centre and close friends would have been there. It wasn't a happy trip.

They got to the venue in Tucson, where their previous visit had been a sell out, a wild success where they'd shifted hundreds of CDs – but hardly anybody came. America was staying home glued to its TVs. But not to see Tarika open the CNN World Music series: CNN pulled it, since Americans wouldn't want to be watching programmes about strange foreigners, would they?

The next couple of weeks continued in a similar manner, with expenses and losses piling up and income decimated. We could have cut our losses by stopping it and bringing them back to the UK but there were no flights. By the time we got them out the whole band were traumatised and most of them never wanted to tour again. They eventually returned to Madagascar where there was a near civil war going on, but at least it was in a culture they knew and understood.

The dire Madagascar situation, catalysed by the old corrupt dictator Ratsiraka's refusal to accept he'd lost an election, in Trump-anticipatory style, was woefully under-publicised by the West's media. I took to trawling their newspaper web sites with my rusty O-level French and paltry Malagasy, combining what I gleaned with news from family and friends there to produce an email newsletter every few days. It was subscribed to by some key journalists, broadcasters and diplomats: the only time I ever felt I was serving a useful role in world history.

On top of the losses from the previous tour, I was now many more thousands of pounds out of pocket. Foolishly, I now realise, and not being very good at seeking help, I sought to pay the extensive bills to cover the debts and losses in the short term by taking out and maxing out a lot of credit cards. But as I was to discover, there is no short term and it slowly spiralled out of control with ever-mounting interest adding to the debts. I'd have done far better to file for insolvency straight away at the beginning, but I had a magazine that required a home and a music scene that appeared to need it, staff who relied on me for their livelihoods and a step-daughter who deserved to get through her school years unscathed. And I suppose I'm stubborn – it's that old thing about not wanting to be seen to fuck up in public.

I spent a good part of the next decade consumed with the stress, at the same time as trying and eventually failing – my own fault entirely – to establish new relationships and keep a brave, sociable public face on it. Throwing myself into bonkers (over)work projects was my pain – and relationship – killer. I even tried counseling and consulting a healer to deal with what I dimly realised were growing mental health problems: both were excellent but I put up too much resistance.

By the time I finally admitted defeat and looked for advice in 2010, the debt had risen to £140K on some twenty credit cards and I'd paid a few hundred thousand pounds in interest. I sold the London house and moved back to Bristol in 2011, ending up renting a lovely big airy flat a few doors away from the Royal York Crescent one where we'd begun Village Thing in 1970. By then the technology was available for everybody to work from home, so the magazine kept going, the staff kept their income and Cathia had just finished university, landing an impressively decent proper job. Gallingly, by 2020 the house that I'd bought with that windfall deposit and sold for £500K in 2011 was worth over a million... Such is life when people fly aeroplanes into buildings.

September 11th 2001 didn't help the World Music scene either. There would be a big downturn in touring – drop in demand in America, plus worldwide complications over visas, baggage etc – all coinciding with a contraction in the record business because of its panic over downloading that led to a drop in record releases.

But in the shorter term everything had came up rosier in the UK, and I'd had a role in part of it. Somewhere around Christmas/New Year 2000/2001, pre-disaster, I'd been enjoying a long soak in my bath and had an Archimedes-like "Eureka" moment. The BBC Radio 2 Folk Awards had already been most beneficial to the new respect gained by the folk scene, and I dreamed up a scheme for what became the Radio 3 Awards For World Music.

By then Radio 3, under controller Roger Wright, had become the national broadcast home for world music, regularly including it in their ground breaking *Late Junction* series via enthusiastic presenters like Verity Sharp and Fiona Talkington, and eventually in presenting slots given to both Andy Kershaw and Lucy Duran.

It had become apparent that world music suffered because, although there were always great newly revealed artists bubbling under, none of them ever gained sufficient profile to make much headway beyond the dedicated outlets like WOMAD festivals and *fRoots*. To the mainstream media, when they were rarely interested, it was only ever for the same big names established in the 1980s – Youssou N'Dour, Salif Keita, Nusrat Fateh Ali Khan, Buena Vista Social Club. There needed to be a way to get limelight for new names as well as attention on the music in general.

After leaping dripping into a bath towel, I'd sat at the Mac and drafted out a fully fledged proposal for an awards scheme, based largely on geographical categories. I ran it by Charlie Gillett and Ben Mandelson for a bit of tweaking, submitted it to Roger Wright and to my great delight (and some amazement) it got accepted virtually unchanged.

Lots of meetings, brainstormings and the involvement of leading London promoters Serious later, it all came to fruition on January 28th 2002 at new state-of-the-art venue Ocean in Hackney. Radio 3 pulled out all the stops, including big financial ones, to make the Awards event a jaw-dropping success – possibly shooting itself in the foot by that first event being hard to top.

The *fRoots* Critics Poll was incorporated into the scheme for the Album Of The Year as our massive panel of more than 300 experts was as good as it could get, and so I was rung by the production team asking who I'd like to present the award to that first year's winner. "I don't suppose you could get Joe Strummer," I'd wondered. They rang back a couple of days later to say he'd enthusiastically agreed. Europe winners Taraf De Haidouks from Romania had apparently played at film star Johnny Depp's wedding – would he? Yes he would, resulting in a front page splash on the *Evening Standard* on the day of the event. TV star Sanjeev Baskar, Brian Eno and Blur's Damon Albarn were among others enlisted.

I got Cathia the afternoon off school, allegedly as an educational experience to see behind the scenes of a BBC TV production. Andy Kershaw took us backstage to meet Joe Strummer, who fixed me with an enigmatic smile and said "Yes, I know you." It would be a few years later, after Tymon Dogg had revealed that it was Joe who he'd used to bring to our 1970s Hot Vultures gigs, that I realised what he'd meant. And Djelimady Tounkara, who won the Africa award, followed in the footsteps of Ali Farka Touré by borrowing my beloved Thornbory guitar for his set.

The gig was sensational and the after-party was massive. There was a memorable moment during a conversation among a gaggle of people including Kershaw, Strummer, Eno, Martin Carthy, myself and others. The Manic Street Preachers had recently played a gig in Cuba and Joe admitted to Andy that he should have listened to AK's suggestion that the will-they-won't-they Clash reunion should have been that gig. Joe seemed quite crestfallen by this.

Andy told him that he'd just returned from the Babylon Arts Festival in Iraq and they were looking for a Western rock band who'd show a bit of solidarity. "That's it, that's it, we should do that!" exclaimed Joe. Much excitement ensued, with everybody involved in the conversation saying they'd like to hitch a ride on the bus across the desert!

Upon which Radio 3 boss Roger Wright appeared from across the other side of a room full of 500 or so liggers, all furiously knocking back copious amounts of license-fee funded booze and food, to enquire "What's this about Radio 3 broadcasting the Clash reunion live from the Babylon Arts Festival?" Jaws hit floors, and Kershaw was requested to go in for a meeting.

Sadly, this was already post-September 2001, and the growing push for the Bush/Blair war knocked that one on the head. And then Joe died. I still can't help thinking that in terms of history-making gigs, that would have been up there with the legends.

By the second year of the awards, the new BBC4 TV channel was involved: the first year it had gone out on BBC2 produced by BBC Knowledge. BBC4 became a crucial factor in exposure for folk and world music in its early years, much propelled by the enthusiasms of Mark Cooper who rose to be Creative Head of Music. Documentaries on artists like Martin Carthy, June Tabor and Nic Jones, the music of Madagascar, traditional customs, series like *Folk Britannia*, regular coverage of festivals like WOMAD, Cambridge and the 50th Sidmouth Folk Festival all flowed from his presence. Not to mention his work on BBC2 as producer of *Later With Jools* that slipped in many of 'our sort of' artists.

In 2003 the US invasion of Iraq was imminent and the early Audience Award category was hi-jacked by a little-known activist band called Seize The Day who seized the mailing list of the Stop The War organisation. They spammed out emails telling people – even if they'd never heard/ heard of the band, which clearly most hadn't – to vote for them in the Award to publicise the cause to the BBC. Even more annoyingly, they did this seemingly from the warmth of home on the very day when most of us were among the several million marching in the freezing cold on the largest protest march in living memory.

Quite reasonably, since this was seen as a scummy attempt at self-promotion by the band and clearly against the spirit of an award to celebrate the best under-recognised musicians in the wider world, the BBC disqualified them and pulled the category in subsequent years. So on the night of the 2003 event, several of the band or their supporters tried ineffectually to 'streak' their flabby arses naked on the stage for the TV cameras, to rapid security response and mass audience apathy.

fRoots had its own tiny way of taking a stand against George Bush, his policies and those who'd elected him. We instigated a partial cultural boycott of American music – not the traditional, grass roots kind but the products of major labels and production line music that was obliterating the world's endangered local forms. It was extremely well supported, particularly by Americans, oddly enough (though I did get a death threat from a Johnny Cash fan.) We mostly kept it up until Obama came to power. We wouldn't have another American artist on the cover until Devon Sproule blew us away in 2007. Tiny seeds...

My own contribution was to persuade Manteca Records to release a double CD compilation of great new roots music from all round Europe, from Scandinavia to Spain via a smattering of UK. I'd wanted to call it *The*

Revenge Of Old Europe but their focus group decided that *Nu Europe* was more saleable and less controversial. Annoying, but the music still stood.

The Awards For World Music ran through until 2008, after which the financial crisis forced Radio 3 to drop them and begin to cut back on their world music coverage. But they did enormous good while they lasted and helped many artists like Mariza, Tinariwen, Ojos De Brujo, Rokia Traore, Lhasa, Souad Massi, Amparanoia and Konono No.1 on their way to international stature. They were a Good Thing. But these days I prefer to shower rather than luxuriate in the bath, in case I do too much thinking!

Radio 3's *Late Junction* also became a very good thing for folk music: you'd quite regularly hear more quality English folk music on there over the course of a week than on Radio 2's Folk Show, especially via Verity Sharp who'd become a big supporter, attending Chris Wood's English Acoustic Collective workshops as a fiddle player. In March 2003 Fiona Talkington hosted a whole live evening on Radio 3, some six hours, titled *A Place Called England* (the name from Maggie Holland's song). It included a number of pre-recorded 'packages' on subjects like the Victorian song collectors and the 1950s 'revival': I got asked to put one together on where it was all heading.

I was rather pleased with myself for opening the segment with a 1950s field recording of East Anglian musicians, pointing out that neither the melodeon nor the hammered dulcimer were instruments originating from here, nor was the polka – and its title, *The Jenny Lind*, was named after a Swedish opera singer. But all had long been naturalised and were now considered English traditional. I'd discovered that many of the musicians who'd been involved in global dance fusion music in the previous decade were now investigating their own roots. Afro Celts' Simon Emmerson was working on what became *The Imagined Village*; David Muddyman (Loop Guru) was teaming up with singer Sharon Krauss on a traditional songs project called *Birdloom*; Tim Whelan from Transglobal Underground was digging into a 1930 *News Chronicle Songbook* for traditional and music hall songs. That proverb that "you can't know where you're going if you don't know where you come from" was casting a spell.

It was apparently one of the most acclaimed Radio 3 programmes of the time, one of the first where they'd encouraged listeners to interact live via email, and they'd done so in their droves. But in spite of that, when later that year Verity Sharp and I lodged a proposal with Roger Wright for a co-presented English folk programme – *Local Routes* to sit alongside Lucy

Duran's *World Routes* – it was turned down on the grounds that "Folk belongs to Radio 2". Where they had a sitting tenant.

I clearly wasn't going to get back on mainstream radio any time soon. But in 2002 I'd been invited by a new platform to produce a monthly, hour-long podcast that I called *fRoots Radio*, to showcase new releases in the areas of music covered by the magazine. At the time of writing it's still running, now called *Podwireless* since the 2019 closure of the magazine, and long-since expanded to two hours a show. There's always a way…

Sadly, in 2004 we lost long-time airwaves supporter John Peel. He'd played our sort of music among everything else from psychedelia to hardcore punk since the 1960s, and personally he'd given me my first Radio 1 session in 1968. On my birthday that July, by pure coincidence, he'd done a *Guardian* feature in which he picked his three favourite music magazines. "There's an excellent death metal magazine called *Terrorizer*. It's full of reviews of records by bands that I know nothing about. I've recently started getting the American magazine, *Maximum Rock'n'Roll*, again. And I get *Folk Roots*, or *fRoots* as it's now called." Talk about gobsmacked! To my great chagrin, I'd meant to drop him a postcard to thank him but busy months had flown by and before I'd done so the terrible news came that he'd died while on holiday in Peru that October, at the age of only 65. Another hero gone. It was just before that year's WOMEX and many there were in shock.

Plotting for what became the *Imagined Village* project had begun in earnest back around 2002. It had started in a conversation with headman Simon Emmerson who had become very conscious that the African and Asian members of his band Afro Celt Sound System as well as artists he was producing like Tarika and Baaba Maal were thoroughly in touch with their own cultural roots and traditions, but he didn't know enough about his own. When at school he'd enjoyed seeing Martin Carthy and he'd been a regular attender of Forest School Camps, connected with the Woodcraft movement, where a major feature was singing folk songs around a big camp fire – it later turned out that Bellowhead's Jon Boden had a similar background – but that was the extent of his knowledge. He was looking for an English project to reflect traditional roots in modern day multi-cultural society.

By 2004 it was coming together and Arts Council funding had been secured. Simon had asked me for suggestions and I'd mentioned a dream I'd long had of making a modern album of the songs of Sussex's Copper Family, whose traditional repertoire, often sung in harmony, had been handed down for hundreds of years. Simon liked the idea of starting from a capella sources since they wouldn't be presenting potential collaborators with preconceived ideas of accompaniments. He certainly didn't want to make a folk rock or 'fusion' record. So I gave him a set of Coppers recordings, but he soon realised that there weren't enough dark songs: their repertoire tends towards the bucolic. I introduced him to the records of the Watersons and Young Tradition, and then we decided to involve Martin Carthy as a further adviser.

Before letters went out to artists to explain the project and invite them on board, the three of us brainstormed it in Simon's house in Stoke Newington and things began to gel. I think it was Martin who suggested involving Benjamin Zephaniah. Others who ended up taking part included Paul Weller, Billy Bragg, Chris Wood, Eliza Carthy, Johnny Kalsi, Sheema Mukherjee and the Young Coppers – Bob's actually not *that* young grand children. All sorts of names who never made it to the project were proposed. Clearly Joe Strummer would have been a strong candidate if he hadn't died: others of my unfulfilled fantasies were to get John Lydon singing *Long Lankin*, and Sophie Ellis-Bextor, whose very English voice seems completely immune to standard pop music Americanisms, singing traditional songs.

One of my other early ideas was to get the three leading Anglo-Asian women singers, Sheila Chandra, Najma Akhtar and Susheela Raman, to do a harmony version of the Coppers' *The Banks Of Sweet Primroses*, but that never came together either (personality clashes, allegedly). Later, Simon told me that Sheila had recorded the parts solo so I thanked her for this when I saw her backstage at the Barbican's *Daughters Of Albion* concert. I explained that the song contains my all-time favourite English folk line, "Many a dark and cloudy morning turns out to be a sunshiny day." "Oh, I left that verse out," she replied, "I don't like songs that end on an optimistic note."

In the end it didn't make it onto the album anyway. Unfortunately neither did a mindblowing PJ Harvey version of *The Cruel Mother* which she pulled at the last minute for some inexplicable reason. I really hope that eventually sees the light of day somehow, somewhere. But not that truncated *Primroses*.

Simon took the multi-track tapes of Tiger Moth's late '80s *Sloe Benga* and remixed it, segueing the result into a new piece by Laurel Swift's ceilidh trio Gloworms, joining the generations. When the album was finally released in 2007, the Gloworms and I got to play on the launch gig at WOMAD, the very rainy year known forever as WOMUD. There are pictures of us all in a row, with Simon, Martin, Billy Bragg and myself apparently in Status Quo guitar formation in wellies, while Eliza Carthy fiddles up another kind of storm in hers.

Simon's quip at the time was words to the effect that if it was a success he'd get all the glory and if it was a flop I'd get all the blame! Luckily it was a huge success, generating several more albums and winning BBC Folk Awards. No blame!

There was so much promise. In 2000, Alan James, one of the WOMAD founders, had taken up the post of Head Of Contemporary Music at Arts Council England, and after many decades when folk music had been totally ignored by the establishment, things quickly began to change. Funding began to flow to Cecil Sharp House and the EFDSS (who previously had only ever received grants from the Sports Council for the supposedly beneficial health effects of folk dancing!), culminating in the society becoming an Arts Council National Portfolio Organisation under director Katy Spicer. Their level of professionalism and the House as a venue are improved to levels unrecognisable from the shambolic organisation I pitched into on their NEC in the early '80s.

It undoubtedly helped that Chris Smith, Minister for the Arts in the first Blair government, was one of the rare ones to be fully involved in his role. During the general election of 2001, Billy Bragg and I went and visited him and the two main opposition parties' shadow spokesmen – Michael Ancram for the Tories and Lembit Opik for the Lib Dems – for a *fRoots* feature on what we wittily called "the MP3". Smith was easily the most impressive. Of course, Blair promptly sacked him after the election. Opik achieved some sort of media notoriety a few years later for his affair with Gabriela Irimia of Romanian pop duo The Cheeky Girls, causing a ripple by bringing her as his guest to the Folk Awards. Former Bullingdon Club member Ancram, 13th Marquess of Lothian, who apparently used to sing *The Streets Of London* with his Martin guitar at Tory conferences, retired to the House Of Lords in 2010 and passed away in 2024.

Arts Council England also funded a professionally researched survey of 350 folk festivals in conjunction with the Association of Festival Organisers that was published in 2004. It showed that they generated £82 million a year, attracting a high proportion of younger people and women (52%) with a strong level of active participation and big benefits to local economies. It must have been a startling eye opener to the unaware.

And then there was technology. In 1998 Apple had brought out the iMac, which came fully internet connected and with a suite of intuitive applications installed including Garageband and iMovie, which allowed anybody to make reasonably professional quality recordings and videos in their bedroom. Suddenly, the means of creation and production were liberatingly democratised, affordable. If you had the talent you could probably now afford the tools.

Next, after the great file sharing scare of Napster, Apple's iTunes store came along in 2003 to establish a major market for legally downloadable music. MySpace, the first massively, globally adopted social networking site quickly became the place for artists and bands to upload and share their music and gain legions of fans. Suddenly, with the ability to record yourself well and make the product available without the suits being involved in the middle, the writing briefly looked like it might be on the wall for major record labels. Then by around 2007 Facebook took off. The world had completely changed.

Even though the suits and major labels eventually clawed their way back to mainstream control, the arrival at the end of the first decade of the new century of Bandcamp, a beneficial sales platform for independent artists to directly distribute their music and merchandise at low commission rates, kept the options open that had not existed in the 20th century. The later saturation of totally exploitative streaming via Spotify (creators of nothing, payers of virtually nothing) was soon hijacked in their favour by majors, but it still hasn't put that one back in the bottle.

It was said by 2007 that pretty much all the music that ever existed could be found somewhere on the web, either legally or dubiously. All these developments put a big dent in the market for physical products, leading to the collapse of familiar High Street record and book chains, failure of some of the vital distributors, and the growth of online traders like Amazon. What the changes in technology didn't achieve along those lines, the worldwide financial meltdown of 2008 finished off.

Another side-effect of the online world was that newsgroups and message boards and then full-blown social media killed the *fRoots* letters pages stone dead. What would often have been three solid pages each issue of heated, refereed discussion (with our famous award of a row of five pewter tankard icons for outrageous folkiness, the more unhinged the better!) dried up within a couple of years. Why wait for two months before you could get a letter published to make a pillock of yourself in public when you could do it instantly online? However, the benefits of creating a worldwide community of fellow enthusiasts far outweighed any downsides. Facebook became like a global café or pub where you could pop in for a break nattering with like-minded, far-flung friends, to exchange crucial information or engage in talking daft bollocks. A lifesaver for the more isolated. And it was a great resource for independent artists, like the earlier days of MySpace had been.

Back at *fRoots*, things had forged onwards and upwards, with so much exciting music to cover. The first few years of the decade saw the magazine looking better and better as advertising levels and ever-increasing sales finally allowed us to be perfect bound instead of stapled, to print in full colour throughout and regularly exceed 100 pages an issue. It finally looked and felt like a proper grown-up magazine, reflecting the authority of the scene it served. Readers even told us they liked the way it smelled when they removed their subscription copies from their envelopes – but then our readers always did include the weird.

Inevitably, others looked at our success and thought they could hijack it. They didn't comprehend that it was our many contributers' deep involvement in and knowledge of the grass roots, coupled with an instinctive grasp of the relationships between all the musics and the ecosystems in which they flourished, that partly explained our loyal following.

And so it was that in 1999 a magazine called *Songlines* had been launched by Haymarket, the big publishing group owned by Tory grandee Michael Heseltine. They initially tried to lure our established writers and set out to cover the same artists. One of their team apparently approached my assistant Vanessa at a concert and offered her a job if she'd like to bring all the computer files with her. Vanessa, who never used strong language, told us very proudly in the office the next day that she'd told him to fuck off. Then we began to hear from loyal advertisers that *Songlines* were telling potential clients that we'd gone out of business.

Haymarket soon dropped them and we thought that the irritation had passed. Vanessa moved on and was replaced as my office assistant by Sofi Mogensen, who grew indispensably into the role of deputy Editor by the time she left in 2011. But *Songlines* eventually found another publisher who proudly declared to their readers in 2004, when English folk records were getting nominations in the Radio 3 Awards For World Music, "Please, please let's stop pushing British folk into the spotlight. It's simply not relevant and not good enough, and diverting attention from far more interesting artists…

With the wealth of new music flooding over our borders, there's simply no need to include home-grown folkies who for some reason have been elevated to a status in world music scenes that bears no logic."

None of this endeared them to the folk scene one bit, and by then I was getting fed up. We'd worked stupidly hard for two decades to establish a magazine and scene where all this music could be covered together. At the very time when it seemed to have succeeded and become buoyant, so maybe we deserved a bonus from it all, they'd begun trying to cream off a share of it. This was at the time when I was fighting the growing Tarika disaster debts and really needed to be able to pay myself a realistic wage at long last.

I hated being confronted with the realities of the big bad business world, which I'd always tried to work outside of. I found myself doing big-booted things that I disliked greatly, like telling label PRs that we would only give their artist a cover feature if they guaranteed not to do one for the others for six months. That wasn't how things had ever worked in the folk world or the early days of the co-operative world music campaign and I hated having to do it. We were naively used to people being nice...

But all this had the benefit of making me up our game. If they were going to poach our writers, we'd find and establish new and better ones. Some came about after conversations with Charlie Gillett: "I wonder if so and so can write?" Turns out several could, really well, and so for example we gained Elizabeth Kinder and Jamie Renton who soon became exceptional interviewers and scribes. Others we found through our own folk scene grapevine, eventually bringing in people like Tim Chipping and Steve Hunt.

Songlines followed the predictable mainstream model of always having somebody established on the cover who had a new album to promote, so we made it our USP to put brilliant up-and-coming new artists on the front, sometimes (subsequent award winners like Catrin Finch & Seckou Keita or Olivia Chaney for example) even before they had a record out. And in my quest to stamp the magazine with a recognisable look I'd engaged brilliant photographer Judith Burrows in 2006, for whom every future cover shoot was a special creative project. We'd never again suffer the embarrassment of finding we were using the same stock PR shot on the cover as another magazine, even non-UK ones: you only got on the front of *fRoots* if you agreed to an original shoot and engaged with it. Many did. We weren't quite *Vogue*, but you get the idea!

The big bad business world's activities always seemed despicable when we came up against them. WH Smith were the nation's main news chain and distributors, and to get your title stocked on the racks in their top tier of stores you had to pay them big money. It felt a bit like the scandalous practice of having to pay to be the support band on a rock tour. We tried this a few times in order to widen our readership, only to find on checking around stores that *fRoots* still wasn't on the shelves. Oh, it's down to individual store managers to choose what actually goes on their shelves from what gets delivered to them, they then told us. Total scam. So we concentrated quite successfully on building our postal subscription base instead.

I'd first been introduced to Elizabeth Kinder by queen of world music PRs Sally Reeves at a BBC Radio 3 reception at WOMAD in 2005 and we immediately bonded, her becoming not only a key writer but an inspirational person to bounce ideas off and a wonderful travelling companion to far-off events as well. One of her best friends, occasional band mate and near-neighbour was Mark Ellen who I'd previously met socially. Mark, ex-*Old Grey Whistle Test* presenter and co-founder of many of the previous two decades' most successful music magazines like *Smash Hits*, *Q* and *Mojo*, was now editing the best one of all those, *the Word*. He was immensely helpful with advice to *fRoots*, as well as hosting a lively round-table discussion in his kitchen that we published in our 300th issue.

At the time, *the Word*'s major shareholders Guardian Media Group had been encouraging them to acquire other titles and they'd already taken an established rock magazine into the fold. Just as had happened a decade earlier with Future Publishing, we'd got a long, positive way down the business discussions about taking in *fRoots* when fate intervened. The 2008 financial crash came along, and the shareholders told them to halt acquisitions, go into their cave and pull the boulder across the door until it was all over. It never really was, and sadly *the Word* itself closed in 2012 after a long struggle of its own. Mark later told me that the sense of relief immediately after the pressure finally ended was blissful, something I'd eventually find out myself in 2019.

The 2008/9 financial crash hit everything in ways that the Thatcher regime's recession hadn't managed. The already confused and weakened mainstream music business models and the post-2001 international touring difficulties had made everything much more vulnerable, and world music CD releases fell off a cliff. For the first time I began to be really concerned about keeping *fRoots* (and by extension, myself) afloat.

In the meantime, I distracted myself with all sorts of amusement. *fRoots* was always known for being irreverent, right from its early days with Lawrence Heath's *Borfolk* cartoons and our scurrilous April Fool features and anagram competitions. We'd long had our own dedicated *BIFF* cartoon strips from the duo of Chris Garratt & Mick Kidd who'd previously reigned in the *Guardian*, and were pleased later to add David Owen's folk-warped popular culture images – his morris version of the Clash's iconic *London Calling* LP cover as *Bampton Calling* was a particular favourite. He'd later go on to organise the astounding 5000 Morris Dancers event on London's South Bank. And we were prone to adding fake albums into our new release lists. At the time when we were being swamped with new age Celtic sets we'd slipped in *Songs From An Ambient Celtic Rainforest* by the Dolphin Children (tipping off our American chums at *Dirty Linen* and *Sing Out!* who did the same). I'm sure many took it at face value and didn't even blink...

Side projects were also a blessing. David Owen designed the striking fronts for two compilation CDs which we did with Arts Council funding that allowed them to be widely distributed at appropriate trade fairs and conferences as well as to readers. *Looking For A New England: New Folk, Old Roots* (the main title with a nod to Billy Bragg, whose song of the same name had been a 1980s hit for Kirsty MacColl) was an 2009 sixteen-track CD featuring fifteen of the cream of 21st century English folk artists plus a vintage Shirley Collins piece – a key influence – as a scene setter. It was very well received, though not without attendant irritations.

The Arts Council introduced me to a character from an organisation called British Underground who up until that point had never had any involvement in the folk scene. At the meeting at the Arts Council offices he claimed to be most impressed with our work and wanted to put together a folk package under the *Looking For A New England* banner to take to South By South West in Austin, Texas, the next spring, for which the Arts Council would give BU funding. He asked me to select the artists and make their introductions to him: I was to be funded to attend the event and to head up a panel.

By the time the next year's SXSW came round, all *fRoots* involvement had been airbrushed from the promo and I was no longer invited, but I only found this out a few weeks before when *fRoots* and I were missing from the press release they put out: they hadn't even had the courtesy to tell me.

Straight after the event lots of the artists contacted me in considerable anger. They'd apparently been dumped in a hotel out of town with transport arrangements lacking, the gig was poorly promoted and tech requirements had been ignored. For them it had been a complete farce and waste of time. Meanwhile, British Underground's chosen few were apparently busily enjoying a good Austin jolly...

The next year we followed it with *Looking For A New England 2: The Other Traditions*, featuring artists originally or ancestrally from other cultures, now living in England or even born here. Again as a CD it was really well received – one reviewer saying it was their favourite world music compilation of the year, the more remarkable as everybody included on it lived here. But in its main purpose, to give a leg up to those artists, it was a non-starter.

We held a concert featuring a selection of the artists at Cecil Sharp House, which was well attended by a diverse audience except for most of the movers and shakers of the hip London folk scene who ignored it in their droves. We distributed the CDs and did a presentation to all the folk festival organisers attending the annual Association of Festival Organisers conference, pointing out that there were no airfare or visa issues involved in booking these extraordinary artists. As far as I know not a single one of them got a booking as a result. It appeared that all the enthusiastic barrier demolishing work we'd done so successfully in the 1980s had been for nothing. It felt like the biggest failure in my activist career, and still rankles.

It may sound from this chapter that the 21st century progressed as a series of personal disasters, setbacks and disappointments, which in some ways it did. But in lots of areas there were some fabulous experiences...

17.
21st Century : Live Music Again!

After being almost entirely absent from public gigging in the 1990s, I finally got back to it in the new century. The decade had barely begun when the invitation Ben Mandelson and I had received in Memphis to accompany Bob Copper as an unmasked blueser came to pass. Bob had been turned into a lifelong country blues fan way back in the 1930s when discovering a Sleepy John Estes 78, and reckoned that an evening being hosted by Lewes Folk Club to celebrate his 85th birthday would be a good time to go public.

Come the day, we spent an enjoyable afternoon working up some songs in Bob's old cottage in Peacehaven. The evening arrived, and the first half was filled with mostly unaccompanied singing of traditional songs from all comers. In the interval, Ben and I got out our instruments – a National steel guitar and an old Gibson mandolin – and tuned up. A few of the audience looked concerned: what unwelcome racket were these interlopers going to make?

Bob got to his feet and launched into an erudite introduction about how he felt that, although they sounded completely different, the music of farm workers from the southern states of the USA and the south of England came from the same place in the soul. We started playing. Some of the audience were looking perplexed: why was Bob still standing there? He launched into singing *Diving Duck Blues*. Jaws hit the floor. Shirley Collins, who was in on the secret, was beside herself with joy in the front row. Bob had a whale of a time. Realities were readjusted.

If you're still doubtful about Bob's theory, seek out his father Jim Copper's 1951 recording of *Lemany* on *You Never Heard So Sweet*, the Topic anthology CD of southern English traditional singers compiled by Shirley. If that's not country blues in spirit if not 12-bar form, I don't know what is.

A year or so later we were able to get Bob into a recording studio. Indeed the whole family came along: on Blind Willie Johnson's *Soul Of A Man* they got to overdub the chorus for the first and probably only time in their four hundred year career. And back at home, Bob had recorded a couple of things with his rarely-seen-in-public concertina, including a lovely version of Oscar Brown Junior's *Rags And Old Iron*. The results eventually got issued as the CD EP titled *Prostrate With Dismal*, the title being the famous 1930s quote from Bob's father about how the march of bungaloid building forms up the hillsides around Peacehaven made him feel. Really the southern English blues!

Things progressed, largely reunions initially. In 2002 a concert was organised in Bristol to mark 30 years since the closure of the Bristol Troubadour: Al Jones came up from Cornwall with Linda who would become his second wife, Elliot Jackson was coincidentally over from the USA where he was now living. So Anderson, Jones, Jackson got to twang again – after an hour's rehearsal in the hotel the night before. Sadly, this would be the trio's last time before, shockingly, Al Jones suddenly died in 2008, though Al and I did manage a few songs together at my 60th birthday bash the year before his passing.

Then in 2004 I got approached by Sidmouth Folk Festival, who were marking their 50th Anniversary, to see if Tiger Moth could be persuaded to flutter again. We didn't need to be asked twice, especially once it became apparent that WOMAD would be pleased to host us doing a ceilidh as well.

As drummer John Maxwell had, sadly, died in the '90s, we added Martin Brinsford from the Old Swan Band and Brass Monkey on the drum stool. Rod Stradling felt he wanted an extra tune player so we added excellent Stroud fiddler Fran Wade. Ben Mandelson and Danny Stradling joined full time, and Chris Coe was back on board on hammer dulcimer with Rod, Maggie Holland, Jon Moore and myself to make it a bigger, roaring unit, fronted by ace caller Gordon Potts, he of the black leather kilt.

Thus began the best ever run of Tiger Moth ceilidhs. At WOMAD, we found ourselves up against David Byrne on the main stage so were anticipating a thin turnout, but the big tent we were in was packed with, we were told, as many again dancing on the grass outside. Like events can sometimes be where younger, non-experienced folk dancers just throw themselves wholeheartedly into it, it was splendidly riotous. So was our Sidmouth Late Night Extra, where there had been a youth explosion since we'd last played it in the late '80s – much due to the activities of Laurel Swift's Shooting Roots events. The resulting energy coming off the dance floor was inspiring. Luckily it got filmed by BBC4 for their documentary celebrating the festival's big anniversary.

In 2005, there was a second big *Ceilidh Aid* event along the lines of 1987's huge anti-apartheid one, once again at the Forum in Kentish Town (as the old Town & Country Club was now known), to raise funds for reconstruction following the recent Asian tsunami disaster. Tiger Moth and Oysterband played again, repeating our closing amalgamated big band, along with Billy Bragg & The Blokes, Eliza Carthy, Hammersmith Morris, Morris Offspring and various surprise guests including Martin Carthy & Norma Waterson.

Then in 2006 we had one more Moth-go-round, including being invited back to WOMAD for a repeat triumph, and doing that year's Big Chill where once again a huge crowd of have-a-go dancers whooped it up, this time in the open-air afternoon sun. By now, Verity Sharp had swelled our ranks as another fiddler, and the photographic record shows that I'd – inspired by seeing Los De Abajo – foolishly acquired a pair of proper job authentic Mexican mariachi trousers, complete with fancy metalwork.

Those were a fun few years, being treated like a proper band on big festival stages rather than a side-show in some poorly equipped folk festival dance venues as had sometimes happened in the '80s. I think we rose to it and more than delivered. It was a great way to bow out, because after that the logistics of eel-herding what was now a 9-piece band spread over big geographical distances, coupled with some members' health issues, made it all impractical. Those few Tiger Moth revival years were among my favourite live gigging experiences ever: a classic of quitting while you're ahead, and a nice chance to strap on the old black Telecaster and make a loud noise again.

Occasionally Maggie, Ben and I would pop up as what we called the Hot Vultures 3, including at the event at Cecil Sharp House to pay tribute to Bob Copper after his passing, and at the Queen Elizabeth Hall on a big concert bill titled *Folk Roots, New Routes* 'curated' by Shirley Collins.

It would be Shirley herself, who holds responsibility for many notable things in my life, who directly caused my next phase of public twangery. Once again, it was something hosted by Vic Smith at Lewes Folk Club where it all began. Shirley had recently been awarded an MBE, and for an evening there in early 2007 to celebrate this, she had invited Ben and I to come and play. At the time, Lu Edmonds – Ben's fellow Mustapha and Bloke of Bragg (not to mention a Mekon and ex-Public Image Limited guitarist) – was staying at Ben's house while his flat was being renovated, so we roped him in as well and worked up a handful of songs.

I suppose our line-up of guitar, baritone bouzouki and Turkish saz or cumbus playing bluesy things was bound to catch attention, but I was unprepared when I was approached by Fledg'ling Records supremo (and later Topic Records director) David Suff at the annual BBC Folk Awards bash the following week. "I really enjoyed that," he said. "You should make a record."

"Well, who would be daft enough to put *that* out?" I responded. "No, you don't understand, I'd like you to make one for Fledg'ling." Undeterred by my protests that we only knew three songs at that point, and that even if we made an album we would be very unlikely to tour in support of it, he pressed the idea, so I took it to the others and – liking a challenge – they agreed.

We worked up a repertoire of songs led by Lu and I – Ben's a determined non-singer – and got Jamie Orchard-Lisle to record it. By then adopting the nom-de-disque Blue Blokes 3, we did a London CD launch gig in June 2008 and, inevitably, had so much fun that we found ourselves agreeing to do some festivals that summer and then a January 2009 tour. We were even more surprised when the CD *Stubble* entered the Top 10 of the World Music Charts Europe and we got rave press reviews.

The tour was a pleasure. I'm not usually a great fan of being trapped in a van with only blokes but they were all such great company. Sitting on stage between Ben and Lu, holding down a riff or the rhythm while they chucked improbable improvisations across me at each other or Lu burst into verses in Russian in the middle of blues standards, was just exhilarating. I'm sure my head must have swivelled from side to side like a Wimbledon watcher.

Our last gig was a sell-out at the Purcell Room in London, which was more like a house party as we must have known at least half the audience between us. We asked the venue to keep a bit of light on the audience so we could see their faces and, told by the South Bank authorities that we could only sell CDs post-gig at a commission reduced from their usual rip-off level if we agreed to do a CD signing, I suddenly had the brainwave of announcing to the crowd that this meant we had a CD and we wanted them all to come afterwards and sign it. I can recommend this to any band as a marketing ploy. It resulted in a long queue, massed post-show socialising and us selling loads of them too.

At some point in the last week of the tour I'd got a message via our My-Space that John Lydon was re-forming PiL and needed Lu back in the band, so off he went (that turned out brilliantly, by the way) and that was to be the last Blue Bloke-ing.

Some while later, Ben and I had volunteered to do a warm-up spot for veteran American musician Tom Paley at Camden's Green Note. It went rather well, and at this time Tom was attracting a new audience of young twenty-something old-time music fans. A couple of these, in their check shirts and old time music hats, approached us in the interval and asked, somewhat wide-eyed, if we'd made any records back in the olden days. Good grief, we'd become old and whiskery enough to be potential living legends, so we decided we could do worse than milk that.

By then I was living back in Bristol but we worked up another repertoire, calling ourselves The False Beards. (I'd suggested The False Brides, from the song of the same name that Cecil Sharp had collected from my distant Somerset ancestor, but Ben inexplicably vetoed that: I still prefer it!) In true Village Thing style, in my Royal York Crescent home studio, we recorded a CD titled *Ankle*, billing ourselves as "Old time English psych-folk blues world twangery," which was about the shortest comprehensive description we could dream up. Once again the critics and audiences enthused.

Ankle was the first release on my next and final label, Ghosts From The Basement (I'll tell you where that came from later in this chronologically challenged chapter!). GFTB just sells via Bandcamp or at gigs, and has mostly been devoted to re-issues including early stuff of mine, some classic Rogue and Village Thing material, a Rod Stradling anthology and of course that Bob Copper blues EP. You don't need to hunt for its releases in the few remaining record shops and it's definitely not on the loathsome Spotify.

We toured clubs and had festival fun, making it through to the end of 2013 before a nightmare Friday night motorway journey – eight hours from Bristol to Hebden Bridge to be in Yorkshire for a Saturday afternoon gig where we had to fight for a sound check – completely soured the process. I remembered why I had come off the road the first time round in the early '80s. So combined with the impracticability of living 120 miles apart, we called it a day. But never say never: at the time of writing in 2024 we've just done our first one in a decade and enjoyed it greatly.

2016 saw Maggie Holland and I get together for a short Hot Vultures re-union tour which was a pleasure, taking in nice summer festivals like Priddy, Shrewsbury and Sidmouth (where we got to play with Tymon Dogg again), and then I assumed I'd finally stopped. But no. I hadn't counted on Dave Kelly asking me out of the blue in January 2017 if I'd like to open for him and Paul Jones in Bristol. I probably hesitated, as I hadn't played completely solo in public since 1973, a mere 44 years earlier, but couldn't resist agreeing, if only to scare myself (which is never a bad thing).

To my surprise and relief it went well, and so for the next three years, right up until the pandemic lockdown hit in March 2020, I found myself doing an increasing number of enjoyable and well-received solo gigs, with a repertoire drawn from every stage of my musical career. And anecdotes. I found I was good at anecdotes. Made a new record and some videos even (gotta keep up with modern expectations) and compiled a couple of career-spanning anthology CDs. Restricting myself to clubs that were at sensible distances from home (i.e. my own bed) and the occasional festival, it was all very enjoyable and life affirming.

I was well-pleased to be invited to the Mekons' 40th anniversary *Mekonville* celebration, where I got to twang with Lu Edmonds again, and to feature among the massed psych-folk aristocracy on Terrascope's *Woolf 2* event. In the nick of pre-Brexit time in December 2019 I got to revisit Belgium for some really enjoyable joint gigs with my dear old friend and Belgian national treasure Roland Van Campenhout, staying with Danny Adams in Antwerp and Catherine Mattelaer in Gent and spending a day in Brussels where we met up with Dave Evans one last time before his passing. And shortly before lockdown I was booked by the splendid Fabulous Furry Folk Club at Glastonbury Assembly Rooms, 50 years after I'd done the first festival, for a guarantee of the fee I didn't get paid in 1970 as a humorous footnote for the local media. Strangely, Michael Eavis didn't show up!

The very last dates were a most agreeable short tour with Northumbrian concertina and small-pipes maestro Alistair Anderson (no actual relation: we billed ourselves as Not The Anderson Twins) which included a house concert for the hospitable Copper Family in Peacehaven, and then we all got locked at home alone and regular live music ended.

Outside of playing myself, there were lots of other involvements with live music. There's a line in a Si Kahn song that Dick Gaughan sang which really strikes me, about doing what you can with what you've got. If you have the ability to help people out at no cost to yourself, why wouldn't you? It was what Alexis Korner did for so many back at the beginning of my own career. So I was always very willing to share experience and contacts in helping people who I thought deserved it, and give them a leg up whether it be through the pages of *fRoots*, on events I was producing, or just via a bit of social engineering. One typical example was enthusiastically pointing the head of Nonesuch Records at Olivia Chaney who we did a cover feature on before she'd made an album: reader, he signed her.

I only came unstuck a few times through being taken advantage of, and one of those was entirely my fault. I'd been introduced to a London-based Greek singer and songwriter, and been very struck by her voice, songs and personality. Teamed up with a couple of first class musicians on bass and guitar, she was skilfully mixing her own material with arrangements of Greek traditional songs. It quickly got under my skin and I'm afraid I got somewhat besotted by her music. Why wouldn't I offer to help?

I was able to get her Arts Council funding that made possible a debut EP release and a two week tour in January 2006 that hit major venues. To help with costs I volunteered to tour manage, taking the trio, sound engineer Jamie Orchard-Lisle and all the gear on the road in my Espace with a roof box on, which was fun, cosy and sociable. The tour was notably well received, national radio and press coverage resulting in many of the venues being surprisingly full for a new artist. The EPs sold like the proverbial hot cakes on post-show merchandising where audiences were keen to meet and greet. The Arts Council were thrilled, telling me I'd ticked all the boxes and delivered in an exemplary way. It seemed she had major appeal and I began to wonder if we might be able to take on the music business…

I used up lots of personal goodwill by introducing her to a major producer and an important, well-respected PR. She went off into the studio to make a full album, and I set about fixing up a 20-date national tour for the following January. Everything looked rosy. And then she announced that she was ditching the Greek songs which were an important part of her audience appeal, adding a drummer, and wanting to take her sister on the road too.

This screwed up my carefully organised tour plan as I had to renegotiate technical requirements and accommodation with all those venues, and we had to hire a big Mercedes splitter van to fit so much more in instead of using my Espace for free. The budget was in tatters, and riding in a big noisy van killed the camaraderie of the road. My 540 mile drive back to London in it from Aberdeen in one day (as a gig to split that journey had fallen out at the last minute) was probably my least pleasurable road experience ever.

The album came out and wasn't as well received by the media as hoped, the audiences weren't so thrilled by the changed repertoire and the atmosphere on the road soon got frosty. Meanwhile, her father had decided to get involved by bringing in a non-music-business lawyer to renegotiate her still-unsigned contract with the producer, who quite reasonably walked away, scuppering chances of a US release by a prestigious label.

Clearly it was bound to be somebody else's fault that things weren't going so well this time round and you can imagine where the buck would stop. By now I'd probably used up all the goodwill and useful contacts I could provide, so I was dumped as soon as it was over. In the end it was quite a relief, though you can imagine why she's now known to some of the key people involved as "she who must not be mentioned."

That episode did provide one other eye-opener. Around then a divorced cabinet minister was taken apart on the front pages of the tabloid press for the 'inappropriate' behaviour of having dinner with a 29-year-old 'blonde' in a posh London club – which was set up as a press sting. Two weeks earlier, I'd been treated to dinner with my Greek friend, also a 29-year-old blonde, in the very same establishment. But being a person of no importance whatsoever (though I was exactly the same age and marital status as the supposedly offending minister), I wouldn't have been of the slightest interest to anybody in the media. There really shouldn't be different standards for so-called celebrities.

The other thing I came back into with a fresh enthusiasm in the 21st century was producing live music events which, unlike that episode, often gave great pleasure and satisfaction.

The first of these in 2003-2004 grew out of our association with Radio 3 over the Awards For World Music, though the inspiration for it certainly came from the George Bush administration's derogatory remarks about "old Europe." Collaborating with Radio 3's world music strand and BBC Radio London's Saturday night Charlie Gillett show, I created a six month series called *Europe In Union*, snappily titled to both reflect our admiration for the new roots musics evolving among our near neighbours and the fact that it was held in splendid Islington venue the Union Chapel. Promoters Serious, tour booker Katerina Pavlakis and Crouch End's popular Banners restaurants got involved too.

The headliners were artists coming in from mainland Europe including Italy's Eugenio Bennato & Taranta Power, Greece's Kristi Stassinopoulou and Ross Daly & Labyrinth, Belgium's Think Of One, and Spain's Ojos De Brujo and Mercedes Peon. The supports were UK-based world music artists while MCs included Charlie Gillett, Verity Sharp, Lucy Duran and Andy Kershaw. The usual form was that the main artists would come into the UK on the Saturday, do live guest interviews on Charlie's radio show, then be taken for a social dine-out at Banners On The Hill. By the time they got to the gig on Sunday, which was recorded for later broadcast on Radio 3, they'd recovered from travelling, met everybody involved and settled in. It was a very welcomed format.

Far and away the wildest one was by Ojos De Brujo, Barcelona's 9-piece flamenco/hip-hop fusion outfit who had stormed to success in Spain as well as wowing the delegates at WOMEX. Word had got out among the substantial Spanish youth population in London and it could easily have sold out twice over: the resulting crowd of disappointed ticket buyers and the volume from the gig itself probably contributed to the Union Chapel facing severe licensing restrictions the next year. Oops!

Next up was a collaboration with musician Andrew Cronshaw, Jamie Orchard-Lisle and the venue for a series of gigs at the Pizza On The Park in Knightsbridge. This was a lovely room, a satellite of Soho's Pizza Express Jazz Club, with good sound and sightlines, holding around 100. *Titled Half The World*, we put on a week of dates in August 2006 and a second one in February 2007. Artists included Belgium's Jaune Toujours, France's Moussu T e lei Jovents and Thierry Robin, Sweden's Ellika & Solo and the UK's Natacha Atlas and Eliza Carthy & The Ratcatchers.

The very first one headlined Senegal's Daby Baldé who came with his Belgian-based band. I was sitting at the back reading the newspaper while they soundchecked, so didn't notice that they'd been replaced on the stage by a young woman until she started playing the mbira (what we ignorant Westerners call "thumb piano") and singing Zimbabwean songs in Shona. I looked up and was startled to realise that this person was white…

She turned out to be Zuzana Novak, an English woman of Czech parentage, grown up in Yorkshire and having recently studied with Zimbabwe's Chartwell Dutiro at SOAS (after some gap years where she'd worked as a tree surgeon!) She'd done a spot at Baldé's gig elsewhere the night before and they'd been so impressed that they'd invited her along to our show as a guest.

I was equally impressed, and we repeated the process on our final Tiger Moth gig at Towersey Folk Festival later that month. Ben and I invited her along to do an interval spot on our Saturday night ceilidh and she went down the proverbial storm.

Zuzana subsequently became a true friend, not only part of our social scene but eventually writing for *fRoots*. She also occasionally put her tree surgeon skills to good use in my back garden, though we'd often just end up sitting on the bench under the tree putting the world to rights. On one occasion, a European festival organiser was staying with me and, having seen Zuzana do a solo gig at the Green Note the previous night, actually booked her for the festival while she was up my tree. That must count as a one-off!

The Green Note in Camden was the welcome home for my next series of gig productions, under the *fRoots Presents...* banner. Hosted by two wonderful, dedicated women, Immy and Risa, the Green Note is the nearest thing I've encountered this century to those great folk venues of the late 1960s: indeed, the performance room with its entry through an archway right next to the stage and the bar at the other end was very reminiscent of the Bristol Troubadour. Perfect listening atmosphere and, unlike those almost entirely acoustic rooms of the '60s, it had a good PA system – all the good things of the old brought into the modern world. Small wonder that they deservedly won *Time Out* magazine's publicly voted award for best London venue.

They gave me a free hand to programme everything from well-known to great up 'n' coming artists. The first one we did in 2009 was a dream gig for me: Spider John Koerner's first in the UK for 28 years, when he came and stayed for a short while. The last one in the *fRoots* series in 2013 was a fabulous acoustic gig by Snakefarm. In between we introduced many lovely nights including Olivia Chaney, the Emily Portman Trio, Nancy Wallace & Jason Steel, Kristi Stassinopoulu & Stathis Kalyviotis, Tucker Zimmerman, Telling The Bees, Duck Soup, all sorts of musical life from the wilfully obscure to legends like Tom Paley.

Outside of the specifically *fRoots*-produced evenings I enjoyed many other memorable ones there, including a revived Dr. Strangely Strange, an acoustic Mekons playing on what was, by pure coincidence, my birthday, to a date on the False Beards tour where I persuaded the great Shelagh McDonald to be our support as her first gig after effectively vanishing for some 40 years. We'd kept her appearance low key at her request but word still got out and it was packed, with some people even travelling from abroad.

Out of the blue I got approached by London's iconic Roundhouse. They were having amphitheatre-style banked seats installed for a winter theatre season and were looking for ideas for a week in January 2010 of seated music gigs before they removed them. It coincided with *fRoots*' 30th year, so I jumped at the chance, producing a celebratory fundraiser concert we called *Roots @ The Roundhouse*, a.k.a. *the fRootsenanny*, featuring lots of artists associated with the magazine.

With a big stage to work with, we were able to split it into two parts so solo artists or duos could perform on one side while bands were quietly setting up on the darkened other. After a long rest since my 1980s festivals, I found I was still a natural at this programming/ production lark, and coupled with a seeming ability to talk MC bollocks to the audience to smooth over changeovers we managed two seamless halves. Billy Bragg & The Blokes, Oysterband with June Tabor, Martin Simpson's band, Justin Adams & Juldeh Camara and the Ian King Band played sets on the band section of the stage; Kristi Stassinopoulu & Stathis Kalyviotis came from Greece, Devon Sproule flew in specially from the USA, and Jim Moray, Zuzana Novak & Pamela Wyn Shannon made cameo appearances.

Icing on the cake was the realisation that we had most of the members of the by now long-lost 3 Mustaphas 3 in the house in various guises, so they did a surprise, one-night-only reformation. And Laurel Swift did a stately solo morris jig, backed just by Will Pound on the harmonica, which took everybody's breath away, aided by large live back-projection screens.

"What are we going to finish up with?" I'd asked earlier and the unlikely idea had emerged to do an everybody-in version of *The White Cliffs Of Dover*, which Devon Sproule & Paul Curreri arranged beautifully. It was perfect! They later recorded a duo version for a *fRoots* compilation album so it's out there somewhere.

Maxi-kudos to Jamie for managing the sound – this was around the time he was also achieving what many had thought impossible by getting a decent PA system installed at Cecil Sharp House. In spite of several production meetings with the Roundhouse team and giving them the advance schedule of sound check times, we'd arrived late morning to find nothing set up, and a digital monitor desk that nobody in their crew knew how to operate. At one point in the afternoon we'd been three hours behind soundcheck schedule and I was considering driving off to Beachy Head. Somehow Jamie pulled it all together and we started (and finished) on schedule. Meanwhile all the artists were having a social whale of a time backstage.

I also learned a valuable lesson: do not expect to be on your feet for 14 hours in a brand new pair of Converse. By the time I was into the second half MCing my blisters meant I could barely hobble onto the stage and I ended up going to the after-party barefoot.

It was apparent that upping the production standard and programming something other than the predictable was the way to go. The folk world needed to keep pace with wider expectations. Later that year we celebrated the 40th anniversary of the launch of Village Thing with a very well-received label compilation CD titled – here's that name – *Ghosts From The Basement* and an all-day event of the same name at Cecil Sharp House. VT artists like

Wizz Jones, Steve Tilston, Dave Evans, Tucker Zimmerman, Ian Hunt and myself appeared, along with contemporaries like Keith Christmas plus a raft of younger artists inspired by the label's legacy including the Owl Service, Nancy Wallace, Pamela Wyn Shannon and Jason Steel (all assembled by the Rif Mountain label, who released a VT tribute CD *Echoes From The Mountain* as a marker).

That CD contains one of the few 'covers' ever recorded of one of my songs, by the Owl Service. Actually it should have included two as Sonic Youth's Thurston Moore also wanted to do one, but at the 11th hour a communication glitch with the label prevented it happening in time. Curses!

Over the next few years in *fRoots* you'd have seen my growing frustration with the lack of imagination being shown by event bookers. Every year the annual festival supplement had endless pages of identikit bills offering the same-old. Little chance was being given to the legions of extraordinarily good new British folk artists now regularly emerging or to the wealth of exciting music made by people from other cultures resident here. There was even a thing called Costa Del Folk which took one of those predictable bills to Spain for UK audiences to fly out to for a warm winter break, and never included any Spanish artists. It became nicknamed the UKIP Folk Festival. Meanwhile the BBC Folk Awards were getting christened the MOWOs (it'll make sense if you're aware what the MOBOs are...)

Following on from a panel I'd chaired at the 2011 AFO (Association Of Festival Organisers) conference, I'd written an Editorial questioning why successful festivals who came close to selling out every year through a combination of brand loyalty and astute picking of headliners couldn't be more adventurous lower down the bill, bringing in three or four new names or going off at interesting tangents.

"Can't take risks" was the common response from the festival bookers, but if the tickets were going to be sold anyway and there was an existing budget for non-headliners, where was that risk? My own long experience back to my '80s Farnham and Bracknell events was that audiences loved the opportunity festivals provide to discover new things and would thank you for it. Indeed, with now tightened purse strings and depleted household budgets, it had become difficult to get ticket buyers through the door for single concerts or club gigs by lesser-known, untested names, but the festival environment provided the perfect 'no risk' opportunity for audiences to check out new bands and artists – if they were booked.

The classic example to prove the fallacy of this attitude was WOMAD, where people bought their tickets and went every year for a bill where they'd almost certainly never have heard of most of the artists, and then spent their weekend rushing from stage to stage to investigate them all. Then they'd be off to the CD stall to take some of the experience home, and to watch the likes of *fRoots* for news of the artists touring again.

It seemed to me that when many of the long established festivals were in their youth, there was a thriving folk club circuit where artists established their names and built followings, which festivals then took advantage of. But by now there were many more festivals and far fewer clubs, so perhaps it was time to reverse that model and for festivals to shoulder more of the responsibility of helping new artists develop their careers, not simply leave it to the pages (and covers) of *fRoots* to spread the word. If we could take the 'risk', why not others?

Alan Bearman, directing Sidmouth Folk Week, was one who saw the point. In 2012 he asked me if I'd put together a week of afternoon double bills in a new venue that had become available, specifically to showcase new artists who weren't otherwise getting booked, plus a few living legends. And so began the annual strand called the *Cellarful Of Folkadelia*, which I produced for some five years – 50 artist sets in all – before handing the role over to Steve Hunt and Sarah Coxson to take onwards.

Included were some artists who'd continue onwards and upwards such as Lankum (billed as Lynched in those early days), Stick In The Wheel, Olivia Chaney, Leveret, the Furrow Collective (individually and collectively), the Rheingans Sisters, Lisa Knapp, Anna & Elizabeth from the USA, Three Cane Whale, and many more who just deserved to be seen like Chartwell Dutiro, Sproatly Smith, Telling The Bees, Amadou Diagne, Harp & A Monkey, Twelfth Day, Namvula and the Dead Rat Orchestra. Plus welcome re-appearances by Wizz Jones, Shelagh McDonald, Robin Dransfield, and Tymon Dogg. If they could have squeezed themselves into the often-packed room, other event bookers should have been inspired. But most still kept sticking beans in their ears, ignoring the evidence and saying they couldn't take risks.

The Roundhouse gig had opened my eyes to what you could do with imaginative production values, while my goat had truly been got by a big 2011 'tribute' concert to a much-loved folk artist at a major London venue which consisted of the entire cast of participants sitting on stage looking bored on a row of chairs until it was their turn to play, all under fixed lighting and through a low-budget house PA. Any sense of occasion was minimised.

My sense of "if you can't do something well, don't do it at all" came into play, so eventually I dreamed up another idea which I took to the Arts Council and was surprised, and of course thrilled, to get funded. This was 2014's *Bridges* at the Queen Elizabeth Hall, marking *fRoots*' 35th anniversary year. I invited half a dozen pairings of artists who had never worked together to each come up with a short collaborative set, and commissioned our photographer Judith Burrows (who was also an award-winning film maker) to produce creative back projection videos for each. The Arts Council funding paid for that and the artists' rehearsal time and travel/accomodation expenses; the QEH made sure we got excellent sound and lighting.

Bristol's instrumental quartet Spiro, who had never previously worked with a singer, teamed up with Croatia's shaman-like Mojmir Novakovic from the band Kries who they'd met at a festival the previous year. I put Eliza Carthy and Greek lafta virtuoso/ singer Martha Mavroidi together: they only met for the first time a few days before the concert. Lisa Knapp and partner Gerry Diver teamed up with instrumentalist Chris Morphitis and singer Katina Kangaris from the London-based Greek band Mavrika. Chris Wood and Ben Mandelson dreamed up some things with Brazilian percussionist Adriano Adewale, and Olivia Chaney was joined by pedal steel veteran BJ Cole. Welsh harper Catrin Finch and Senegalese kora master Sekou Keita had recently established a reputation together and just won the *fRoots* Critics Poll for album of the year for their debut, which gave an excuse to bill them and for a presentation by Radio 6 DJ Cerys Matthews.

It was a fabulous, sold-out night with a gratifying good reception. My only disappointments were that as MC I could only watch from the wings rather than immerse myself in it all from out front (I still haven't properly seen all Judith's gorgeous-looking film to this day!) – and that in spite of clearly proving how this sort of thing wasn't risky at all, virtually nobody else had the nous to follow up and develop any of the collaborations I'd catalysed. The exception was Eliza herself who fronted a 2016 event staged by the Sage Gateshead called *Generations: European Project*, which saw her collaborating with Martha Mavroidi again, plus Mauro Durante from Italy's Canzoniere Grecanico Salentino, three of Finland's Varttina and the Czech singer/violinist Iva Bittova. "It was part of a huge thing I wanted to do that didn't come to pass, and that was supposed to be the launch of it," Eliza told me more recently.

If I have to nominate the event I'm most maxi-proud of having produced, it happened the next year at Cecil Sharp House to mark the centenary of the birth of Bob Copper who'd passed away in 2004. Officially known as *Ten Thousand Times Adieu*, it soon took on the nickname *Bobstock* (with "Crackerjack"-style responses from the audience every time that name was mentioned on the night). With all profits going to the Vaughan Williams Library and such a much-loved giant to celebrate, it took little persuasion to assemble the artists for the line-up.

The overall theme was that everybody would sing a few songs from the famed Copper Family repertoire, including Bob's own or those collected by him on his travels for the BBC in the 1950s. But I certainly didn't want a staid succession of the obvious: it was mostly to be specially created teamings, long-unseen ones re-united, or new young performers.

By the time I'd got it all together no amount of pinching would quite let me believe what I'd managed. Martin Carthy re-joined with Maddy Prior and Rick Kemp for the first time since the early days of Steeleye Span. English country music pioneers Oak got back together, and Robin Dransfield came out of long retirement to perform with his two sons. Heather Wood, the last surviving member of the Young Tradition, came over from America (with an eyeball-searing psychedelic frock), while Bellowhead's Jon Boden put together the Bootleg Young Tradition with himself, Fay Hield and Neil McSweeney. Spiro composed a ten minute instrumental suite of Copper song tunes, which they later recorded for Real World. Olivia Chaney, Nancy Wallace and Lisa Knapp worked up a goose-pimpling little set of three-part harmony songs. Add to that Stick In The Wheel ("We never expected to spend Saturday night in a room full of Coppers"), Jim Causley, the startling duo of Stephanie Hladowski & C Joynes and Brighton's Long Hill Ramblers, plus a multi-generation massed Copper Family...

Even on the day the surprises kept coming. I was happy to introduce a little backing group featuring Ben Mandelson, John Kirkpatrick and Ian Kearey and "oh, a couple of chick singers." Shirley Collins and Linda Thompson, neither of whom had sung in public for years due to dysphonia problems, got a standing ovation even before they'd launched into *Soul Of A Man*, that Blind Willie Johnson classic which Bob had recorded.

We'd begun on time at 7.30 and had set a curfew for 11.10 pm after a grand all-Coppers and everybody else sing-up finale. With the invaluable assistance of Jamie Orchard-Lisle and his sound crew throughout, plus stage manager Carmen Hunt and the co-operation of all the artists (not a single wobbler was thrown, and we got more than sixty people on and off stage during the evening), Carmen and I looked at our watches after the final, rafter-raising applause had died down and it was exactly 11.10... Miracles can work!

At that point I was convinced I should be quitting while I was well ahead, but I still had a couple more project promises to keep in 2016. Alan Bearman had got me to put my reputation where my mouth was and produce a short season of all-instrumental concerts at London's King's Place under the series banner *No Voices*. I had Spiro supported by Three Cane Whale, Kathryn Tickell's band with all-women folk-inspired contemporary classical group Collectress opening, and Catrin Finch & Seckou Keita on with the pedal steel/cello pairing of BJ Cole & Emily Burridge. It sold out all three nights and the venue pronounced it one of their most successful folk events to date. Clearly all-instrumental folk concerts weren't a turn off.

That summer I helped create another internal Sidmouth Folk Festival event that already seems to have become a 'tradition', the annual Sidmouth Horse Trials – a daft competition for hobby horses and morris beasts for a trophy presented by *Wallace & Gromit* creators Aardman Animations. Sometimes I just have too many wiggy ideas.

I finally bowed out of big event production that autumn with a fiftieth anniversary celebration of the opening of the Bristol Troubadour. By this time the process had almost become like falling off a log. Get a good venue (in this case St George's in Bristol), re-assemble the battle-proven production team of Jamie Orchard-Lisle and Carmen Hunt, make it be in aid of a Good Cause, and assemble a mixture of veterans who played the club in the day along with younger West Country artists inspired by it. In the veterans camp were Michael Chapman, Wizz Jones, Jasper Carrott, Steve Tilston, Keith Christmas, Ian Hunt, Andy Leggett of Pigsty Hill Light Orchestra and friends, and myself with Maggie Holland and Elliot Jackson to kick it off. Among the young(er) ones were Three Cane Whale, Jim Moray, Jim Causley, Al Jones' daughter Emily Jones and Heg & The Wolf Chorus. Another sell-out, another ecstatic reception.

On the afternoon of the concert we held a public conversation about the days which birthed the club, also involving original organiser Ray Willmott, Joe Boyd, Dave Evans and the late Fred Wedlock's wife Sue, a.k.a. Flo. We put together more nostalgic back projections for the gig and a two-week photographic exhibition in the venue's vaults and somehow, in the nick of time, persuaded Bristol Civic Society to grant a blue plaque for the club's old location. That went up on the Sunday morning following the Saturday event. Most of the participants trooped up for the ceremony and photo opportunities, followed by a big fry-up in the café up the street.

Deed done. I'd promised myself that would be the last big one and so far have managed to keep to it. Debt served to society. Audiences and participating artists very happy. Reputation intact – I didn't fuck up in public. Enough banging my head on the proverbial brick wall: these events might not have inspired others to "take risks" but we all had a good time!

Actually, I probably should admit to the one where I blew it. Back in 2012, not long enough back in Bristol, I'd dreamed up an event called *Weirdlore*. What you might by now call the usual unusual suspects were due to convene early that summer at Bristol's Folk House for a day of "Psych folk and beyond, plus hobby horses, workshops, dancers and odd goings on." An ivy-encrusted horse skull featured on the poster advertising Telling The Bees, Rapunzel & Sedayne, Sproatly Smith, Johnny Kearney & Lucy Farrell, Mary Hampton, Sharron Kraus, Pamela Wyn Shannon, Boxcar Aldous Huxley, Three Cane Whale, Corncrow, Katie Rose, Kate & Corwen and something called Algernon & The Hawk (which was actually a figment of Jim Moray's imagination, dreamed up in our regular Tuesday night pub sessions).

Morris beasts were planned to roam among the audience and I'd even promised tickets to some of Glastonbury's finest Merlin cloak, wooden staff and Guinevere frock wearers to come and add visual spice to the proceedings.

It was just that bit too early in the growing wave of interest in such things, and I'd not been back in the area anywhere near long enough to know local promotion ropes. Early ticket sales were very low, and I lost my nerve and pulled the plug. Of course, too late, loads of people then jumped up and down saying they'd been going to attend. Folk Police Records had meanwhile assembled a compilation CD of all the artists, also titled *Weirdlore*, and released it anyway – it immediately sold like the proverbial hot cakes and soon became a collector's item. There are now people who believe the event really happened, and probably even some who have false memory of actually attending! Many of the artists who would have played it went on to thrill audiences in Sidmouth's Cellarful Of Folkadelia, so maybe that's what they'd be misremembering.

Oh, and I did do one more low key small one. 2017 marked the 50th anniversary of our old Folk Blues Bristol & West club, so we put on an evening at Folk House to mark it. Survivors Dave Kelly, Mike Cooper and I played. We later worked out that when we'd seen the legendary 1967 American Folk Blues Festival, the combined ages of the then seemingly ancient Son House, Skip James and Bukka White had been 192. Fifty years on, our own combined ages were 215. All things considered, we were quite sprightly.

18.
And The Rest...

Eyebrows had risen in the arts world at the widely reported 'price tag' of more than four million pounds per London 2012 Olympics medal gained after investment from Lottery funding. When the government made a raid on Lottery coffers to support participating athletes, we were told that this was a one-off and that other areas – particularly the Arts – would have their funding restored in due course. But the arts-sceptic Tories had come back to power from 2010 and this never happened.

My strongest memory of that election was driving down to Bristol to experience an amazing 'extreme world music noise' gig by a double bill of Congo's Konono No.1 and Omar Souleyman from Syria. On leaving in high exhilaration, I'd had that dashed when I turned on the car radio to hear that the Lib Dem's traitorous Nick Clegg had done a deal with the Tories to get themselves government suits, abandoning many long-held principles. They even got screwed on the vow to get the voting system changed to proportional representation, something I'd supported for decades. Never again: I subsequently joined the Green Party.

One of the very obvious benefits of all that extra sports funding was that being able to dedicate yourself full time to your chosen skill makes a massive difference to improving performance. Well, exactly the same thing applies to musicians. If they can concentrate on their playing, singing, writing, arranging and gigging without distraction from the need to clock in to an office or factory every day, the benefits are really remarkable. Don't imagine that being a musician is a cushy thing where you stay in bed all day and then turn up to play for an hour for loadsa money: there are actually years of hard work and dedication involved, plus the need to afford top line instruments and equipment (read 'bicycles' to continue the sporty analogy).

Then of course the country would eventually get such investments back through the enormous contribution the music industry made to the economy and exports, not to mention feel-good factors. Just like sport. Getting a fairer share of that funding pot can help musicians and musical communities blossom, evolve and thrive and give back so much well-being to this battered country.

Instead, the next fourteen years of Tory misgovernment chaos – topped by Brexit – gave a continual, debilitating series of blows to our music, already battered as the old record industry model had been murdered by the internet, and the economy crashed by American bankers.

As mentioned earlier, by the first years of this century we had finally shaken off decades of apathy, misconception and piss-taking for our alien folk music. For a while you could guarantee to see regular features and reviews in the 'quality' dailies and the dad-rock monthlies. The launch of BBC4 and all the gains from the new regime at BBC Radio 3 made a real difference. Radio 2 never increased its single hour ration per week for a specialist folk programme, but they put lots of budget and support into the Folk Awards and occasionally tracks into their general playlist. For quite a few years you could count on folk albums getting nominations in the prestigious Mercury Awards. As a result, UK folk and world music had become respected staples of programming for arts centres and concert halls, and festivals boomed.

Then everybody's advertising budgets crumbled and the BBC, always a political punchbag, were forced to slash costs. John Peel and Charlie Gillett died, Andy Kershaw vanished off air behind bars for a while, and 'must listen' radio habits ended with the coming of iPlayers. Content everywhere suffered cuts: eventually the *Guardian*, for example, would only allow one review each per month for folk and world music, the landscape covered by *fRoots* which might sometimes carry several hundred reviews in an issue. Everybody in the mainstream got conservative, squeezed and risk averse, and promoters followed suit.

The constant deluge of amazing new music didn't lessen just because there stopped being 'token folk' nominations in the Mercuries, but it got much harder to get its profile raised, given the ever-expanding haystack/needle ratio of the internet. And xenophobic Brexit rhetoric brought back some bad old days resistance to the musics of other cultures.

The new century wasn't all work and struggle, though: there was, miraculously, a decent amount of playtime that I could fit in among the often 90+ hour weeks. We'd had a wonderful social life in the early Bristol years and a second one while based in Farnham and being international folk ramblers. I'd had barely enough time to acquire a fresh London social circle before getting captured by Tarika and all things Malagasy for the whole of the '90s, but now I was single again, even though a single step-parent, so new things slowly evolved.

My London house had a small but comfortable back garden and nice neighbours, so sometimes in the summer months when the weather smiled we'd hold a Sunday afternoon-into-evening garden party, or an after-party for an event of the previous night. Usually these had impromptu music, anything from a jam by a grand selection of London-based African acoustic musicians to a small English ceilidh with a scratch band, much enjoyed by Cathia's enlightened teenage friends.

She'd hooked them into such things after getting the taste at Sidmouth, regularly taking some of them along to the monthly *Knees Up* ceilidhs at Cecil Sharp House. Somehow I'd become a 'ceilidh dad', dropping them off and collecting later, taxi-like, but that was marginally preferable to the chilling description I'd once overheard on the Friday after-school collection run where I'd heard one of her friends saying "Cathia's got a cool dad." Shades of 1960s 'trendy vicars'. Nooo!

At one party a friend had asked if she could bring Zimbabwean a capella group Black Umfolosi along as they were in town. As night fell they'd thanked us by assembling at the bottom of the garden and doing their spectacular, stomping, song-accompanied (think Ladysmith Black Mambazo) welly boot dance, to much applause from neighbours hanging out of their windows. In the next morning's light we discovered that the back garden wall had fallen down, Jericho-like, as a result...

I'd usually cook up a massive curry alongside a table loaded with salady things, pastries, dips and bread to die for from Yassar Halim's down on Green Lanes. And then there would be improbable quantities of my infamous killer margaritas. Much fun was had. It was once pointed out that a small missile aimed at some of these parties would have taken out many of the main activists on the UK roots music scene, since it was such a sociable, enthusiastic circle where many people involved were interconnected friends. It was a lovely world to be part of, so unlike the music business...

English festivals like Sidmouth and WOMAD had always been as much social occasions as musical honeypots, and since Cathia used to love going to those too there was no clash with my single step-parent status. Around the millennium we started adding the Whitsun morris dancing at Bampton in Oxfordshire to our regular annual calendar. Our ECBB/ Tiger Moth squeezebox maestro Rod Stradling had long been a musician for Bampton, but I'd been a late convert to the morris world itself, much too late in life and fitness to take it up if I was going to apply my 'do something properly or don't do it at all' principle. But you didn't have to be a leaping participant to appreciate the atmosphere and significance of Bampton's dancers on the picturesque lawns of its grand, wisteria-clad Cotswold houses. We started taking a little party every year: I retain a vision of Afro Celts' Simon Emmerson in his pre-Imagined Village days, sat buddha-like on the edge of one of those lawns, totally entranced by it all.

As well as the Awards For World Music that we were involved in, other annual social gathering high points were those BBC Radio 2 Folk Awards. In their earlier days the BBC lavished sizeable budgets on big, invite-only events with a dinner, lots of drink and a live, broadcast show in a London venue. All the nominees and celebrity award presenters, lots of luminaries and folk scene activists and their guests plus a good smattering of BBC wigs and assorted 'influencers' would have a great evening hanging out together. The result had been a real uplift in the profile and respectability of the folk scene, even though there were regular grumbles about certain 'household name' Americans of yesteryear being bestowed Lifetime Achievement Awards over more deserving (we thought) British ones.

We would get a generous allocation of tickets for *fRoots* staff and writers, though we were amused at how our table was always near the back, well out of the range of microphones to pick up scurrilous heckling or distance for bread roll lobbing at presenters. As if we would!

Eventually budgets got slashed and although the events got moved to prestigious venues like the Royal Albert Hall for a while, that was in order to claw back costs by maximising ticket sales to the wider public. The next few years, when guests realised too late that they weren't going to get a dinner to soak up the free booze, produced some 'interesting' social behaviour as evenings progressed! Eventually, the pandemic killed off the Folk Awards before the continual BBC cuts finished them.

In the '90s, as world music record sales had grown and events like WOMEX created international networks, journalists and broadcasters had increasingly been invited on overseas trips to experience artists in the context of their own home cultures, or to participate in festivals that hoped to boost tourism in their territories. Some became dab hands at positioning themselves for such offers – indeed, such free trips had become nicknamed 'sweeneys', entirely due to the prolific and successful activities of one of the champions, music, travel and food writer Philip Sweeney.

I remember the startled surprise shown by Phil when I decided I ought to tell him, at the London debut by Malian singer Rokia Traore, that he'd inspired both a noun and a verb. I'm not sure if he entirely believed me until 2007 when I was able to forward him the email approving successful submission of these terms to the online *Urban Dictionary*. "Noun: a free trip obtained by music journalists, usually paid for by a record company, artist's management or event promoter. Verb: the act of obtaining the above."

Personally, I'd mostly missed out on sweeneys up until the millennium, becoming just about the only world music person I knew who never got to Mali or Cuba when they were the two artist hot spots, nor to events such as overseas WOMADs or the likes of Morocco's Fez Festival. Tarika-wangling, production schedules, family responsibility and looking after the shop meant that the offers always had to go to others. But my famine broke in 2000 when Real World kindly sent me to Naples to do a *fRoots* cover feature on the splendid band Spaccanapoli, in the very street they were named after. My old pal Mike Cooper had long been living in Rome with his Italian partner Maria by then, so they came along for her to translate.

Next up came an invite to Zanzibar in 2002 to discover the music component of the annual ZIFF – Zanzibar International Film Festival – held at the old fort in Stonetown. British world music activist Yusuf Mahmoud had moved out there to run it as a VSO project, and Scottish promoter Fiona McAllister had become their press officer. If I'd run a music journalism workshop, they'd fund my airfare and accommodation. Well, of course!

It was a life-changing experience: I never even got out of Stonetown, which is saturated from centuries of multi-cultural occupation, the whole time I was there. I'd just finished reading Richard Hall's extraordinary book *Empires Of The Monsoon*, the entire history of the Indian Ocean, written like a can't-put-it-down page-turner novel, so it all came to life.

The music part of the ZIFF itself, focussed on the music of 'the Dhow countries', was amazing. The added thrills of encountering the late Zanzibar singing legend Bi Kidude up close in a small space or seeing the celebrated Culture Musical Club taarab orchestra in their own rehearsal rooms were gold dust bonuses. If it had been possible I'd have seriously considered packing up and moving the *fRoots* operation to the harbourside Dhow Countries Music Academy building! Eventually ZIFF's music section separated off to become the annual Sauti Za Busara festival at the same venue. Amazon's algorithms tell me that I've subsequently bought lots more copies of *Empires Of The Monsoon* to give to friends over the years, and I was doubly lucky to be invited back to Sauti Za Busara in early 2011 to experience it all once more, with a couple of trips to nearby desert islands thrown in.

Back home, not being a fan of London pubs, social life had begun to centre around the smaller of the two friendly cafés in Crouch End owned by Juliette Banner. The bigger one with its celebrated "Bob Dylan sat here" brass plaque on a table was right in the middle, whilst Banners On The Hill was up off Hornsey Rise. As well as just being a nice place to pop into, a regular group of us used to meet up the hill on Friday nights to talk about life, the universe and everything (indeed, quite often not about music). We even held a few bashes for *fRoots* staff and friends there, including one where we invited fast rising English folk duo John Spiers & Jon Boden to come and be heard by our radio and promoter pals. More "what you can do with what you've got" social engineering.

Much later, when I was back in Bristol in the following decade, I'd occasionally do some more social secretary work among a dozen or so who we fondly christened "the grumpy old men (and one woman) of world music," meeting up for dine-outs in the city. Such things were always rewarding, especially after people get to that certain age when, often for family reasons, they don't go out so much.

We knew the place so well that some of the staff became friends too, and Cathia ended up with a Saturday job there. Juliette herself, Andy Kershaw's partner at the time, was hospitable, big-hearted and caring, inviting myself and Cathia to their home for Christmas day on one of the first winters of our new domestic situation. She must have been a great employer to have.

At some point in what had by then become known as "Bannering", around 2001, Lucy Duran had brought along a Greek friend, Thalia Iakovidou, who it turned out was the best friend and manager of singer Kristi Stassinopoulou. Thalia and I got to be regular late-night workaholic email penpals and would meet up over the next few years at WOMEX to see all the showcases, as well as me going to Athens to interview Kristi for a *fRoots* cover feature. Then for some reason Thalia's regular emails stopped in July 2004, which I didn't immediately think strange as Greeks often get out of town in the hot mid-summer peak.

In September 2004 the gang were all up at Banners when *fRoots* contributer Paul Fisher, who tour managed Japanese artists in Europe, suddenly, out of the context of the conversation, mentioned to me that he'd seen Kristi and her band somewhere in the past week and Thalia, unusually, wasn't with them. He'd been told she was unwell. It was a weird moment at which the whole place had simultaneously fallen silent and I'd got profoundly spooked.

As soon as I got home later that night, I emailed Kristi to ask what was up. The next morning I was woken early by the 'phone. It was Kristi. "I can't believe I just saw your mail," she said. "Thalia died last night."

The story, I eventually found out, was that as recently as July, Thalia had suddenly become very ill and moved to her mother's to be cared for, not telling anybody what the problem was. It turned out to be terminal cancer, diagnosed only a short while earlier. On that day, Kristi and her partner Stathis Kalyviotis had wanted to visit her and been told she'd get in touch soon, when she felt able. They'd taken this as a good sign and were working on a recording of a new song, one of Thalia's favourites, which they planned to take over and play to her. They'd just finished the mix on their computer when there'd been a massive, brief power cut in their house. They checked that the mix had survived, then rang Thalia's mother to ask if they could come over, only to get the news that she'd died a few minutes earlier. It turned out that her passing and their power cut were both at exactly the same time as I'd got spooked in Banners...

Some six weeks later, I was busy at WOMEX setting up our stand when a woman I didn't know came up to speak. I couldn't give her my full attention but a while later I was in the beginning of the first showcase thinking how strange and sad it was going to be this year without Thalia joining our regular group when the same woman came up to me and mentioned Thalia's name. It was too noisy to talk, so we went out to the bar.

She turned out to be Antonia Kavas from the Ethnoambient Festival in Croatia, who had got in touch with me right back at the beginning of the year after reading my Kristi interview, to ask how to contact her with a view to a booking for the festival. I'd put her in touch with Thalia and, unknown to me, they'd become really good email and phone friends too. She'd been sad when Thalia hadn't been able to come with Kristi that July and meet her in person. It turned out that she too had been spooked in Zagreb at that exact time of Thalia's passing.

We stayed in that bar talking like long lost friends until it closed well after midnight, occasionally joined by her partner, Mojmir Novakovic of the band Kries, and then hung out together the rest of the weekend. They invited Cathia and I to come and stay in Zagreb over new year and I then became a regular visitor to their festival. This culminated in the False Beards playing it in 2013 and Spiro, who were also there, selecting Mojmir to collaborate with them for that *Bridges* concert in 2014.

When I told this story about Thalia's exit to my dear reiki healer friend and general spiritual believer Debby at the time, she wasn't surprised at all. It was obvious to her that on her way out Thalia had wanted to bring these friends together who didn't know each other. Up to that point I'd have said I was extremely sceptical about such things, but now I have a much more open mind as a result.

What I do know is that a photo I have that was taken a few years later of Mojmir, Antonia, Kristi, Stathis and myself all sat together on a wall at a later Ethnoambient festival is one of my most treasured, and although things like a pandemic and Brexit have conspired to keep us apart in more recent times, I still count them among my most loved friends. All thanks to Thalia.

In passing, a spin-off from my many late night email conversations with Thalia had been an awakened interest in 20th century history of the region, particularly the Smyrna tragedy of 1922 which we don't get taught about in the UK. Possibly the fact that our Lloyd George was partly to blame explains some of that. I'd encourage anybody to read Giles Milton's *Paradise Lost: The Destruction of Islam's City of Tolerance*, another can't-put-it-down page-turner history book written like a novel (and the real history in which Louis de Berniere's *Birds Without Wings* is set).

A little later, Debby asked me a favour. A friend of hers was sofa surfing and, knowing that Cathia had now gone off to university, she thought I might have some space. Could this person be my paying lodger for a few weeks? Well, OK... I'd never wanted a lodger, but why not? So she brought round Katie Rose, who turned out to be such a perfect house guest, a combination of a sunbeam and a church mouse, that she didn't leave for several years. Also a creative musician, she managed to record a whole album in her back bedroom without me even knowing. Friends beget friends. They all helped me hang on to some semblance of sanity during those strugglesome last years in London.

Travels got further afield. In 2006 I was invited by organiser Jun Lin Yeoh to visit the annual Rainforest World Music Festival in Sarawak, Borneo. Well-selected musicians from around the world and locally were to be enjoyed on one of the most spectacular sites, with a night time main stage that backed directly onto the rainforest, and daytime workshops in replicas of traditional longhouses. Since it's sponsored by the tourist board, us visitors got to arrive a few days early to acclimatise and were treated to cultural side trips, by boat across the local bay and up a river where flying fish might jump in, or into the jungle to see orang utan in their natural environment. And everybody got put up in a nearby hotel where post-gig unwinding around the skyline pool continued well into small hours.

I went with Elizabeth Kinder to do the *fRoots* writing while I took the photos, and we had a memorably good time. The entrance of Scotland's Peatbog Faeries, appearing through a cloud of dry ice as if from the jungle behind them, stripped to their kilted waists and painted in blue imitation woad while bagpipes and chiming electric guitar launched their high-energy set, was something unforgettable. The crowd, as they say, went wild.

Although based a long way away around the world, the energetic and unflappable Jun Lin was a regular WOMEXican and had a daughter at college in London so she too would also join our social gang from time to time. I was thrilled to get re-invited the next year (*fRoots* becoming a media sponsor may have helped somewhat!), and as Elizabeth sadly wasn't free this time I took Judith Burrows to do the photo coverage while I did the writing.

That second year there was an unfortunate coincidence. As Judith and I were setting out across the bay on the boat trip, my 'phone pinged. It was a text message from my parents' next door neighbour with the news that my father had died, which admittedly wasn't unexpected as Cathia and I had visited him in hospital a week earlier. Once we got back to the hotel that evening I called my mother to ask if she'd like me to fly straight home but she insisted I stayed: she had everything organised (that's where I get the gene from). I was just left with a feeling of guilt that I wasn't experiencing any grief, such had been my emotional distance from my father.

On my return, my mother commented that she wasn't really sure why she was organising a funeral at all as he'd been so non-sociable that probably nobody would come. This turned out to be nearly true: there were barely a dozen friends of hers there, none of his old colleagues or sailing acquaintances. Nevertheless, a few years later I was quite taken aback when she suddenly said to me, in the company of Cathia and that wonderfully supportive neighbour, "You know, I've come to realise that your father wasn't a very nice man..."

When I had my 60th birthday party not long after his funeral, the realisation that more than a hundred people had shown up from all over the world and many periods of my life was blessed confirmation that I had avoided turning into him.

AND THE REST...

How to have a great 60th birthday party at the Pizza On The Park, giving a nice meal and some drinks to that many people and with lots of fun, impromptu live music volunteered by guests? I left the music arrangements to Jamie and Ben so some surprises were possible, and called in the record dealer who occasionally cleared the *fRoots* office out of the leftover unwanted, unsolicited, irrelevant and mostly plain awful CDs that would slowly accumulate after we'd carefully gone through selecting the hundreds that could justifiably go out to reviewers. We felt no guilt about this, since we had always needed to put the time in to listen to them first, a thankless task and surely justifying the paltry £1 or so each we might get for disposing of the little blighters. Better that than them going to landfill too.

At this point we'd left it for quite a while and I was pleased to be handed a grand in cash for the accumulation. I think I only had to add something like another £20 to pay the party bill. On most other occasions this process simply defrayed our own necessary CD and book purchasing costs: creative recycling within the musical ecosystem. The only other treat I can remember from it was taking the cash stash down to Tottenham Court Road's Lombok store and buying what I still call my magic reading chair, a comfortable beauty with wide flat arms perfect for resting drinks and snacks on. You don't get such collateral rewards from unsolicited mp3 downloads...

Trips abroad wound down rapidly after the 2008 financial crisis, other than self-funded ones to WOMEX. I eventually realised that those costs were now hard to justify since what we did there increasingly became dominated by approaches from people wanting us to make their artists or events famous, without any reciprocation like subscribing or advertising. The notion that we were in a mutually supportive ecosystem was fading. I'd even skipped one year but then we were given the 2010 WOMEX Award ("for professional excellence") which was quite a thrill, the first time I'd ever got gonged for anything. Veteran journalist Robin Denselow kindly did their citation duties

By then, the recent financial crash had begun to hit the *fRoots* income and my worsening debt stress had got acute. Luckily my second Zanzibar visit in early 2011 was again sponsored by the festival but my mental state wasn't brilliant and in retrospect it was probably a mistake that I persuaded Clare, my supportive girlfriend of a couple of years, to come on the trip. My head was elsewhere, and I'm ashamed that I wasn't good company, which hastened our eventual break up.

Things had looked up by my next foreign music trip in summer 2012, a year after my move back to Bristol when things had stabilised somewhat. It turned out to be the best one of all. As well as Greek music, my other big Euro-obsession had been with Puglia, across the water in the heel of Italy. I'd made contact with various musicians from down there including astonishing singer Anna Cinzia Villani and the band Nidi D'Arac. Nidi D'Arac's energetic manager Flaminia Vulcano and Anna Cinzia got together to organise a spectacular week's visit where Elizabeth Kinder and myself based ourselves in Lecce and every day were taken on hair-raising drives around the region to meet and hear different traditional musicians in their homes or natural locations.

Music, food, culture, weather, landscape and the inspiring company of these three brilliant women combined for an unsurpassed experience. Once again I took the photos and Elizabeth wrote up the big *fRoots* feature. It came out so well that, having read it, BBC4's Mark Cooper recommended her to the producer of a film they'd just commissioned on flamenco as a researcher, but when they met her they were sufficiently impressed that they screen tested and hired her as the presenter. A bit special was our Elizabeth.

In 2013 a new annual autumn event began called English Folk Expo, originally in Bury and later migrating into Manchester. Positioned just before WOMEX in order perhaps to attract longer distance visitors to both, it concentrated professionally on the showcase and trade fair aspects, and was designed to mirror the Showcase Scotland programme at January's annual Celtic Connections in Glasgow. It was a joint concert by Spiro and Leveret at an early EFExpo which had conclusively proved that a whole evening of instrumental music wasn't a turn off for audiences, directly inspiring my *No Voices* season at King's Place a few years later.

English Folk Expo with its attendant Manchester Folk Festival became another good annual social meet-up with much late night talking of bollocks for England, only frustrating in that its definition of English folk didn't ever seem to include music from our home-grown ethnic minorities whilst a fake American bluegrass band could bag a showcase spot.

One of the specific reasons I'd moved back to Bristol in 2011, other than financial and, obviously, nostalgia, was that my elderly mother was now living on her own in Weston-super-Mare after my father's death, and her health was beginning to deteriorate. Being only 20 miles away meant that I could see her more often and be available if needed urgently.

AND THE REST...

In 2013, by then 88, her fandom for André Rieu's music took her on a dream trip to his castle venue in Holland for one of his orchestral spectaculars, but the effort had taken its toll and she'd picked up an infection. Early in 2014 her health took a nose dive and she was admitted to the local hospital, less than a mile away and built on fields where I'd explored as a child. Thus began a nightmare six months as an acknowledged-failing hospital (understaffed, underfunded, doctors and nurses demoralised, worn down beyond their capacity) made endless errors and continually compounded them.

She was admitted multiple times and often discharged too early, without making sure that the home care I'd arranged could snap back into place. On one occasion they even lost the clothes she'd come in wearing; on another the doctor on her ward admitted that he was very glad I was there to explain her recent medical history as he was the only one on duty when there should have been three and he wouldn't have had time to read through her now bulky pack of medical notes.

Eventually they reached the sad conclusion that her condition was terminal. I was very lucky to find her a place in a good local care home where she was comfortable and well attended for her final few weeks. She passed away mid-July, so I was now technically an orphan, down the very far end of a family twig. Her funeral was much better attended than my father's, and I got Cornwall folk hero John The Fish who had become a humanist funeral celebrant to come up and conduct the proceedings. Her old lady friends seemed to think that soft-spoken Fish in his long white beard (as per Michael Chapman's tribute tune *Fishbeard Sunset*) was a perfect choice.

As an only child I inherited the parental home but certainly didn't want to live there so I put it on the market. That September – in classic beautiful, mellow late summer light – I was introduced to the place they call 'the Folk Hogwarts', Halsway Manor folk centre nestling on the south side of the lovely Quantock hills, and was seized by the madcap idea of moving down near there, to the village of Stogumber. I probably would have seen sense anyway, but with my now partner Karen, Cambridge-based at the time, we decided on her moving back to Bristol where she'd also enjoyed living decades earlier, and us getting a place together. By luck, a flat came up just along Royal York Crescent from where I was then renting (and only three doors away from where we'd begun Village Thing 45 years earlier), and we got that together in 2015. So I stayed in Clifton Village for six more years and, alongside rejuvenating my gigging career, managed to pilot *fRoots* to its 40th anniversary.

I was also greatly honoured that year by being awarded the Gold Badge of the EFDSS for lifetime services to the music, pinned on me by none other than Shirley Collins, by then President of the society. As a special treat, she sang me a version of her *Death And The Lady*, set to a Muddy Waters-ish blues tune and backed by Ben Mandelson and Ian Kearey. This time Ben did the citation. It was all very heartwarming…

Those last few years of the magazine were a struggle, though in the process we produced what I think were our best ever issues, in both content and appearance. There'd been a surge in niche publications with higher end production values, much more desirable artefacts with heavier, better designed art paper covers that didn't need to be plastered with content lines, and sold outside of the mainstream news trade. I began heading *fRoots* in that direction.

It became apparent that life as a single-title publisher was finite. Indeed in the final few years I wasn't even taking any wages myself, just paying the staff and contributors as, having escaped from paying rent, I scraped by on the state pension which I could by now draw, and a bit of compensation for PPI payments on all those old credit cards.

In late 2017, with lots of goodwill and contributions from many supporters – particular kudos to Jo Breeze who set the whole thing up – we launched a "Help *fRoots*" Kickstarter fundraiser to pay off debilitating debts such as to printers and HMRC, give us a breathing space to devise a new strategy and hopefully attract acquisition by a bigger publisher with more heft. Many artists, labels and people in the business kicked in with rewards, from doing benefit gigs to valuable goods. To our astonishment it zoomed past its original £20K target and after all the costs of the campaign were taken into account we cleared half as much again. Space to breathe.

We held a really constructive meeting in early 2018 where more than a dozen friends, staff and very experienced people from all around the UK came together to brainstorm ideas. In Spring 2018 I made a radical change from it being a monthly to a big, thick (148 page) desirable quarterly on higher quality paper. For me it was the best editorial decision I ever made and the final six quarterly issues we published up to summer 2019 were easily the ones I'm proudest of: the best designed, produced and content-filled. It had been a long, self-taught learning curve but it had got there. Great latter-day thanks are due to Kitty MacFarlane who stepped in at the news desk, Steve Hunt administering reviews, Nancy Wallace on long-distance proof reading and Jon Wilks for helping update the original antediluvian web site.

AND THE REST...

Another personal boost came when I was invited by Folk Alliance International, which I hadn't attended for many years, to their February 2019 conference in Montreal, Canada, to receive a Lifetime Achievement Award (the other recipients included Buffy Sainte-Marie, Joni Mitchell and the late Leonard Cohen. Crikey!) I headed off across the ocean for a long weekend of manic showcases by lots of superb artists, many of whom were previously unknown to me. There was lots of socialising with North American friends who I hadn't seen for years or had never even met face to face, only over the e-waves. Who cares about jet lag when you're enjoying yourself?

I was getting a lot of helpful input on the potential rescue side, particularly from old early-WOMAD pals Thos Brooman and Alan James. For reasons never disclosed, Thos had been fired as director of his own festival in 2008, shortly before he was awarded a CBE, but we'd remained friends – something which obviously caused displeasure to his successor who didn't disguise his (eventually succesful) determination to ease *fRoots* and myself out of our close association with the event. And Alan had gone on to roles in the Big Chill festival, as head of contemporary music at the Arts Council, as chairman of the EFDSS board and as an artist manager. More to the point, he was a much-loved and respected person in the industry.

For years we'd been told by Arts Council people that they really admired what *fRoots* did and that we ticked every box for what they expected clients to achieve, but they didn't have any scheme or precedent for funding magazines. Alan set out to find a way through this and reported progress, but at the crucial point in spring 2019 he suddenly, unexpectedly, tragically died.

In the meantime I thought we'd found a publisher who understood and wanted us and, as we'd previously done with Future and *the Word*, had progressed discussions. But just as we'd published our huge celebratory 40th Anniversary issue that summer, word came through that they'd decided against it. I had no choice but to contact an administrator and put the *fRoots'* publisher, Southern Rag Ltd, into liquidation.

In many ways it came as a relief, and we'd gone out with a bang on a perfect issue, No.425. We'd been quitted while we were ahead. And rather amusingly, after forty years I'd finally made it onto the cover myself on that last one, albeit heavily disguised as a crow. I'd recently had the fun of inhabiting Alex Merry of Boss Morris' famous giant sheep, Ewegenie, a few times and had rather enjoyed morris beasting. It's quite intriguing how you acquire a new persona when interacting with small children and old ladies!

A little while later, but too late as it was all over, done and dusted, I was rung by somebody from the Arts Council who'd been away on a lengthy leave to say that they'd devised a possible funding scheme that Alan James' intervention had set in motion…

Jude Rogers wrote us a wonderful obituary in the *Guardian*. Such goodwill really helped. Another smaller crowd funder appeal raised sufficient funds to pay off the company overdraft that I was being held personally liable for by the bank as a guarantor from thirty years before. Our readers were truly supportive and understanding. It was quite an eye opener to find out how much we were really appreciated. I'd reached points over the last decade when I'd been doing endless long days, latterly without even being able to take any pay, but often seemed to get mean-spirited bashing in return from people who thought our only role in life was to make them famous. Our supporters deserve massive thanks for making a tired and cynical old bloke feel much, much better and to realise he was actually valued.

The fact that I was owed thousands by the company that I wasn't going to get back (that I'd had to inject from the sale of my house and later my mother's) at least allowed me to do a deal with the administrators. I was able to retain the old office equipment, physical archive and rights to the magazine name and past content. So they're theoretically safe for posterity and from marauders. I later donated the huge physical photo archive – eight filing cabinet drawers stuffed full – to the safe keeping of the Vaughan Williams Library at Cecil Sharp House. And so it passed.

As well as continuing to produce *Podwireless* I was looking forward to throwing myself further into solo gigging. By the end of 2019 Karen and I had decided to sell up and move to Cambridge where her grown up children live. Sod's law, within three months Covid came along, killed the gigs stone dead and lost us the buyer we'd found, so the move got delayed until 2021.

A parable! Somewhere in the mid-1970s when Hot Vultures were doing a folk club gig in the North West, Maggie Holland had noticed a shrivelled little plant on a darkened shelf in the middle of the smoky pub, with just a tiny hint of green. So she liberated it, wrapped it in damp tissue and took it home to Farnham. With a bit of rooting powder in a new pot with a polythene bag over it, it miraculously grew and grew.

By the time I moved to London in the late '80s, it had already become daughter of rescued cheese plant, propagated from a healthy leaf. By the mid '90s, this daughter of rescued cheese plant had grown so huge that it filled the entire bay window of my London living room, cutting out all the light. So I propagated another leaf and put a card in the local newsagents asking if anybody would like to give the big one a home. A very enthusiastic man soon arrived. "She'll love it," he exclaimed. "Your wife?" I enquired. "No, my python." He came back a day later with a mate's removal van and somehow extricated the monster monsterosa. I wonder if it now fills his entire house, where he's long since been consumed by his grateful reptillian chum.

Great grand-daughter of rescued cheese plant grew and grew, and eventually another propagation took place before I moved back to Bristol. I was determined to stunt the growth of this great-great-grand-daughter so put it in a relatively small pot. But grow it still did, until eventually it was so big that it was dominating our little Clifton conservatory. So I took the top two clean leaves with a bit of aerial root and started again. But somewhere between the time *fRoots* fell over and Covid lockdown began, the great-great-great-grand-daughter of the cheese plant that a folk club couldn't kill finally expired...

Actually I must admit that, unlike many more unfortunate people, I had a 'good' lockdown. Deserted, traffic-free streets in glorious spring weather, clean air and clear blue skies, the ability to walk up to nearby Ashton Court and enjoy lying in the grass below the singing skylarks, or sit undisturbed on a bench under trees in my favourite old Clifton cemetery while a fearless young robin came and ate out of my hand... It was actually a pleasure for a few months.

So we're here in Cambridge now, somewhat downsized into an unexpected semblance of leafy suburbia. Gigging's mostly been zapped by the fall out from the pandemic, but I like to do it whenever I'm asked. I'm still partly working away on that trusty old equipment, putting *Podwireless* together every month, compiling the odd CD sets for others, and excavating these tales from the archives and recesses of memory. Thinking fondly of lost friends – both Elizabeth Kinder and Spider John Koerner died within a month of each other as I was finalising this – and of scattered ones, and wondering what the future might bring.

I'll leave you with some thoughts...

19.
Conclusions & Wig Bubbles

Perhaps it was because I always had so many interests to chase down, so many metaphorical balls in the air, that I only ever tended to get as far as being 'good' at things but then was never motivated to go on and be the best. I don't think I was lazy, more that I could easily be distracted by the next interest, the next project, the next wormhole to wriggle down. Whether it was guitar playing, photography, typography, event or record production, or knowing about different genres of music or the cultures that made them, I'd get so far then... ooh look, squirrel! And I know I was crap with money and regret that I let my workaholic tendency kill some potentially wonderful relationships... Mea culpa.

Luckily at a time in the 'noughties' when I was having serious problems with self worth, the shrink told me that even though I considered myself an under achiever in most departments, the collective smorgasbord of skills and experiences I had to draw on made me unique and therefore of value, which was re-assuring and helped pull me through.

Over more than sixty years in this music, forty of them at the helm of *fRoots*, I had a lot of time to think and sometimes over-think. And things have changed so much down those years. Sometimes I wrote these passing thoughts down in my *fRoots* Editors Box. This final chapter rounds up a few of those, what Lord Buckley called "wig bubbles."

Starting with changes down the years. Back in ye oldene dayes at the beginning of it all in the mid-1960s, folk/ roots musicians didn't get to make records until they'd done a lot of gigs, which also helped knock things into shape and build a demand for when something finally got released. Indeed, it was almost impossible to get picked up by a record label unless you were out there gigging, as that's how word spread, sometimes via other musicians on the circuit.

The actual getting of gigs was mostly done by travelling around the country doing drop-in spots in folk clubs. If you 'went down well' you might be invited back for a paid gig and could then use that as a starting point for building your reputation in a particular area. But, of course, that was in the days when there were many hundreds more clubs than there are now, petrol was relatively cheaper and hitchhiking was common, safe and reliable.

Then there was an intermediate phase where things got a bit more professional. Promoters still needed to see you live or at least get the word-of-mouth from other shows, but they expected you, at the very least, to have professionally printed publicity posters to supply them with. Thus arose the phenomenon we first noticed in mainland Europe and soon spread here, of bands getting their promo photos and posters printed up when they'd barely started rehearsing.

Nowadays, it seems that you can't get a gig unless you have a record or video out there, so some musicians end up making them long before they're ready, and self-releasing has no A&R overview. The whole reality and economy has changed. Promoters won't consider booking you unless you can send them a CD or a YouTube link. Many in these austere times will no longer guarantee you a fee, and expect you to do all the promotional legwork, pushing out those Bandcamp and YouTube links to your friends, followers and fans via social networking sites to get people to pay at the door, of which you get a percentage, not a fee. Selling those CDs at the gig can then make the difference between scraping a living or not.

So the recording became the very first priority for hopeful 21st Century musicians, made possible – if not always advisable – by the democratisation of the recording process. I've been to open mic nights and young musician competitions where live performing skills were limited to a between-song mumble that "this is a song from my latest CD."

Nevertheless, I definitely prefer the idea that anybody can now get their music out to the world without the need to thumb it up the old A4 on a dark and stormy night. It became one of our main tasks at *fRoots*, searching the ever-expanding e-haystack for those increasingly buried needles, in order to help the deserving ones. Thankless, but still sometimes rewarding.

I probably get too excited about music for my own good. Those in my immediate circle of friends will know that I'm prone to pronouncements of great certainty that, at this moment in time, the band I'm seeing are the Best Live Band In The World, whether that's Guinea's Bembeya Jazz at London's South Bank or Swiss-based Orchestre Tout Puissant Marcel Duchamp in the bowels of a Bristol barge, definitely a BLBITW every time I've seen them. Because right then and there in that place and atmosphere and performance, they are and they transcend all others. It's quite possible that within weeks another band may gain a similar crown, but that's how it is. I've experienced this epiphany so many times and have never managed to build up a resistance. I love those moments! And I love sticking a CD in the player or finding a Bandcamp page and deciding within a few tracks that they're my new favourite artists. What's better?

If you believe the stereotypes, you're supposed to get more conservative as you get older. Your tastes are expected to atrophy: you'll know what you like and you won't approve of anybody messing around with it. You simply won't want to hear anything new. Not me, but I certainly encounter a lot of people like that, which is unfortunate if they've become so-called 'gatekeepers' – bookers of clubs or festivals, producers or presenters in radio or TV. I simply don't understand how people can be that way.

I'm the opposite. I get somewhat bored with musicians treading water, sticking to a tried formula, following rules. I like people who take risks; who play, sing or create without a safety net; who get lost in the movie that's going on inside the song or are captured by the thrill of the chase of the tune and don't want it ever to stop. Soloists who suck you into some vortex and obliterate the surroundings. Bands who stop being a set of individuals and become a higher life form via some kind of telepathy and alchemy. Sarah Coxson once described in *fRoots* how a particular band swooped and turned as one, like a flock of starlings – murmuration music. Hardly surprising that very band, Oxford's Telling The Bees, were one of those who, sitting a few feet away from them in the Green Note one night, I thought were another BLBITW at that point. They were too.

The other side of that coin, though, is that I can get really annoyed by stuff that doesn't move me. I've heard too many records that were too clean, too soulless, too correct, too indistinguishable from others. Would-be charismatic guitar slingers with mannered voices, concentrating entirely on the flash and the noise they make and the image they project but saying nothing. A plague of sexless blandness in faux folk voices that belong to no tradition other than the enclosed world of folk club 'folky'. Spooky twee is fine. Plastic twee is not. I prefer ramshackle to polished and boring. Life's too short for boring.

As you'll have gathered if you've got this far, I've been involved – 'worked' if you like – in so many aspects of our bit of not-the-music-business that I'm cursed/lucky (take your pick) to be able to see many points of view, the bigger picture, make connections, spot pitfalls, identify wheels that don't need reinventing. But sometimes I can get quite down and go "actually, who cares?"

For example, summer 2005 was a long, strange and rather depressing one so I was glad when it was over. It wasn't just that the English weather dampened certain festivals. Some of it was personal but there had been too much bad news out there in the real world. It seemed like there was trauma and death all over. Bombs in London or Iraq, planes falling out of the sky, devastating storms and floods or just the constant reporting of tiny individual tragedies – senseless murders, suicides of people pushed over the brink, deaths from diseases that we could probably cure if we didn't spend all that money on the tools to kill other people with.

At my lowest point, worn down by all sorts of sad silly stuff, I found myself sitting on a bench staring at the Adriatic and distant Croatian islands contemplating 'doing a Reggie Perrin'. It should have been a relaxing day – I was at a loose end, waiting for the start of what turned out to be a wonderful Ethnoambient festival – but I couldn't concentrate on the book I'd brought to read, the autobiography of a famous jazz singer who'd also had her share of downers.

The question I couldn't answer at the time was what on earth was I doing wasting my life on something as trivial and ephemeral as music? How could I justify spending my days putting together a magazine full of opinions on a bunch of people who – when it comes down to it – just twang things and hit things in pretty patterns and stand on stages largely spouting silly words? Or doing that myself. What, I wondered, was the point of it all? I had, I concluded, conspicuously done nothing of much value with my life. I really wasn't very good company for the rest of that day.

Coming back to London, it got more absurd. I did what I'd got into too much of a habit of doing – trawled through the internet message boards where people discussed this music. And what did I see? Endless trivia, pointless repetitive discussions, messengers being shot, opinions of taste being touted as ultimate truths, the dim doing battle with the dumb, all the while disconnected from the realities of life out there. I did the sensible thing I should have done ages before and went cold turkey on most of them.

But a few interesting things happened. A friend entrusted me with a CD's worth of her demo recordings and it had taken up residence in my car. Now I don't deny I was in a melancholy state, and her music tended towards the sad – no banging, jolly tunes to add unwelcome variety. But it did me tremendous good: the music matched my mood, but instead of dragging me to further depths it had a therapeutic effect, almost as if the heartfelt singing and words were coming directly to me and problems were somehow being understood and shared. Then at the end of that month I decided that a day in a sunny field with a bunch of badly dressed English people unselfconsciously enjoying dancing and singing to their roots music was what the doctor may be ordering. It was. I arrived with a small grey cloud still circling above my soul, but a day being buoyed up by the ebullient sounds of English dance music and the sight of young persons throwing themselves around to it quite blew it all away.

So that was alright then. Suddenly I could see some sense in all this game. Maybe this music that we treasure does have a real importance after all. It can work magic, it can heal and energise, bring people together, maybe even in its own small way it can change the world. And what we were doing with the magazine was trying our best to draw your attention to it, which might have some value after all. Especially if it improves your life too.

I wrote much of that for the next *fRoots*, which got the most extraordinary feedback. Well, I say I wrote it but I'm still not sure it was me, since it appeared to fall fully formed out of the sky onto the page. I'd actually had big doubts about publishing it at all, since in many ways it was like going naked in the rain, but two of my closest friends encouraged me. Then I got showered with the most amazing emails, 'phone calls and letters arriving, some from people I know well, some from complete strangers, some from quite well-known names who I wasn't even aware read the magazine.

They came from people who had also experienced a real crisis over the worth of what they produced, from people who'd had their lives turned round or even saved by particular music speaking directly to them, and from those who simply said "I've been there too." Somehow, perhaps because I deliberately left the personal crap out, it seemed to touch something universal that I honestly didn't anticipate.

Really, I'd expected little more than "there's no fool like an old fool" at best, since most people are rarely motivated to write to magazines unless it's to knock something. Instead, I was overwhelmed by the heartwarming, life affirming responses. I don't think I've ever been thanked by so many people for the simple act of writing something.

And then… there has been much debate and searching of souls in the mainstream media over the past few decades about Englishness; what is English culture and what does being English mean? There was a sharpening of focus brought about by the regaining of regional power by the Welsh and

Scottish: a feeling that we English should have pride in what makes us unique too, if only we could figure out precisely what it is. The explosion of cable TV and the internet brought with it a fast-rising backlash in some quarters against what felt like total obliteration of our culture by corporate America.

Identity became a much-discussed question among the large numbers born and brought up here from parents or grandparents who had been immigrants. And there was a real sea change in attitudes towards our multi-cultural society: percentages of those questioned in opinion polls who now feel comfortable with things like mixed marriages have soared in recent times.

But nothing's new. England has been a mongrel nation enjoying the multicultural experience for hundreds, perhaps thousands of years. Many things which we take for granted as being part of the traditional stock: the cup of tea and the potato, many words of our language, morris dancing, the polka and the squeezebox, are all the result of imports, an English spin on something which came from abroad, just like balti, bhangramuffin and jungle: something which could only flourish because of the particular fertility of English soil.

"Come all you at home with freedom, whatever the land that gave you birth. There's room for you both root and branch as long as you love the English earth. Room for vole and room for orchid, room for all to grow and thrive. Just less room for the fat landowner, on his arse in his four-wheel drive," as Maggie put it so well in *A Place Called England*.

Two books to read in order to find out about ourselves, both by the inestimable Robert Winder. *Bloody Foreigners* and *The Last Wolf*. You'll thank me.

Listening to a radio discussion on the subject, I was struck by how many similarities there are between how we think about Englishness and how we consider real traditional music. A traditional song had a creator once, but he or she is long forgotten. Down the years, many have added a different spin: new ideas, changed words, new instrumentation, new twists on rhythm and accent, but it's way past the point where we question that it's a proper English traditional song. There are other songs and tunes that we actually do know where they started, but they're already so far into the collective consciousness that they're nearly part of the traditional fabric: in another hundred years they will be totally assimilated. And then there are recent creations that we like very much and think might become traditional one day, but they still sound a bit 'different' at this point.

People are like that too. Those who the racists would think of as 'pure' English are in fact a big mess of genes from the migrating tribes of what we now call Europe, Scandinavia, the Romans and beyond, but their mixed origins are so long lost in the mists of time that we think – not that we ever think about it – of them as having been here forever. Then there are people who can trace their family trees back to elsewhere, often as refugees or economic migrants in past centuries, but enough generations have passed that they're indistinguishable from those who were here longer. And now we have the children of more recent settlers from the former colonies and beyond: already completely infused with the local culture from birth, just looking a little different to the eyes of some right now, but given time…

It was always the editorial stance of *fRoots* that we gain so much from knowing and enjoying the roots musics of other cultures whose mainstream popular music is much closer to the tradition than ours, be it Senegal or Ireland. This isn't so we can turn out English clones of those styles (though new ideas are always welcome), but to inspire musicians here to bring the whole panoply of English roots – of whatever vintage – back into our popular mainstream. That's if we ever figure out what they are…

We really need to draw a huge distinction between globalisation and multiculturalism. The former is the obliteration of local cultures by big business cultural imperialism, dictating the music people are allowed to hear by applying obscene marketing budgets that could quite literally help solve the problems of poverty, health, education and debt of some struggling small countries. The latter is just the 21st Century's extension of tradition, the folk process.

Before the days of recording and radio, traditions evolved slowly but evolve they surely did, otherwise we'd still be banging on rocks. A new instrument might come along, a new dance might find favour. Things we now think of as ancient and part of the fabric of tradition here – like the squeezebox or the polka – were once new-fangled and, crikey, foreign. Musicians always like to try new things: the good evolutions survive, the bad don't. There were possibly cries of "Judas!" when some morris dance side replaced their pipe and tabor with a concertina, and sniffy little-Englanders who tried to turn their back on the waltz and polka when they arrived.

Back in the last century (I still get a kick out of saying that!) the oral tradition got largely replaced by the aural as people gained access to record playing equipment, tape recorders and radio. Then, travel and communications brought horizons closer, and mass migrations mixed up large numbers of people at a speed never seen before. It's a different world, but the process is adapting to it. A few hundred years ago, an unknown sailor or traveller might have brought a foreign instrument to an island and over a period of time it could radically have changed a local tradition. But because of improved communication and recording, we know that in the 1960s, Johnny Moynihan and Andy Irvine introduced the bouzouki to Irish music and it is now pretty much standard kit for 'Celtic' bands everywhere. The djembe, a West African drum, spread worldwide over recent decades (because, like the guitar, it's portable and can be adapted to so many different musics). Digital sampling technology is just another instrument in the right hands, and rap is just another musical form sweeping the world like the polka and reggae did. If it works in a way that roots musicians like, it'll get integrated. Elements, speed and opportunity change, the process doesn't.

The thing is, nobody can *make* traditions do anything. They either evolve, mutate and survive of their own accord or they don't. Turning a deaf ear to where music is going in these interesting, multi-cultural times is as misguided as those old folk song collectors who ignored big chunks of the repertoires of their sources because, in their blinkered view, it 'wasn't traditional.' Sorry, in traditional music one of the only constant factors is that musicians have minds of their own!

In *fRoots*, there were often discussions about the 'right' sources. Back in 2004 Rod Stradling started one by regretting that younger musicians playing English dance music were not so versed in listening to the old traditional players who inspired the 1970s revolution, but were more influenced by the '70s/'80s bands themselves. Rod's view was that they would have more solid ground on which to innovate if they knew the foundations, which he considered to be the 'old boys'. It was a view which had cropped in our pages before when interviewing other English 'revival' artists like Martin Carthy, Shirley Collins or the late Peter Bellamy. "Don't copy me," they'd say, "go back to the traditional sources I learned from."

Others made a different and perhaps equally valid point. When Stradling was inspired by Oscar Woods, or Carthy by Sam Larner, they were in the physical presence of old, experienced carriers of the tradition in their own personal ways. But they weren't listening directly to the previous generations of players or singers whose musical changes to the shifting sands of tradition had in turn shaped these individual's styles. No, they were hearing them through one particular musician's idiosyncratic filter.

It may be hard to swallow, but to a twenty-something performer now, Rod, Shirley or Martin are that same animal, the old, experienced source, each a link to an earlier stage in the tradition but one who has pasted on their own experiences and variations. Your twenty year old can now only hear Oscar Woods or Sam Larner on record: useful, but only snapshots and hardly a substitute for the charisma of a living person. What are they supposed to do: continually refer back to one fixed point in the middle of the previous century, which is decreed to be 'the tradition', kept forever as a reference point in a frosted glass case? Or do what Rod, Shirley and Martin effectively did, go one step back in order to take several giant steps forward?

It must be a hugely difficult psychological adjustment for people who were once folk music's young guns to accept the senior role. I try to put myself in their shoes. When I was in my mid-to-late teens I sat at the feet of sixty-something blues legends Fred McDowell and Big Joe Williams and was massively inspired. Now I'm far older than those heroes were: an old boy too. The head spins at the thought, I reject it. No, surely not. Don't I still feel like I'm twenty-something inside my head?

Fred & Joe, Oscar & Sam, are long gone, ghosts in some digital file. Brilliant, inspiring ghosts – but from longer ago to the current younger generation of musicians than the era of 78s (and cylinders) was to mine. Our generation had dead heroes too – Charley Patton, Joseph Taylor – but only as reference points. We needed flesh and blood inspiration.

Of course today's musicians should try to listen to everything possible, especially if their desire is to keep their own old cultural traditions evolving. It's true: you can't know where you're going if you don't know where you come from. But today's young players also have so much more available to listen to, infinitely more than Oscar Woods or Fred McDowell ever had. As well as several generations of their own cultural predecessors, they can listen to the world – and every tradition out there is going through equivalent changes. Among all that, tradition forwarders like Rod, Shirley or Martin are much more significant than I'm sure they care to admit.

I don't have any trouble at all remembering what it was like being young. I well remember the late Bob Copper telling me in his eighties that he was still twenty nine in his head, and pretty much anybody over thirty will tell you that too. But it's almost impossible for me to put myself in the shoes of people growing up now with such a wealth of available information, who have easy and free access to every music ever recorded, who have so many inspiring cultures on their doorsteps, who have quality instruments and home recording facilities available at a reasonably manageable price, and probably their parents liking the same sort of music.

It's possible that it's exactly this easy availability of everything that's warping things. When I started out, if you discovered something which was really mysterious, fascinating, other, you had to go on a mission to find out more about it. And it was the post-war law that parents and teenagers hated each other's music. Before social networking, you often wondered if you were the only person interested in it. You seized on copies of rare records and arcane magazines, and if you ever did find a fellow fan of this weirdness, you excitedly shared your discoveries with them. If *fRoots* had existed then, I'd have been as happy as the proverbial pig in shit.

If you decided you wanted to go the next step and play the stuff yourself, the mission got harder. Affordable instruments were often fairly unplayable. There were no YouTube tutorials or DVDs and no college courses – you worked stuff out from records and, in the process of sometimes getting things spectacularly wrong, invented new and original ways of bending traditions. Meanwhile, all this was mixed up with, as Heather Wood said, "free beer and getting laid". Attitude.

Now you can easily find everything and get to play it if you want to, though usually in a club full of people your parents' (or grandparents') age, whose tastes have become conservative. But that's OK, because since there's no mystery about what's out there any more, there's no burning urgency to go looking. Web sources will keep you endlessly supplied with more of the stuff you already know you like, and steer you away from the stuff you haven't tried because you know you won't like it. Just like my late father with foreign food.

The first day of October one year, unbidden, Robin Williamson became an earworm with *October Song*, which is odd as I hadn't played that first Incredible String Band album for quite a while. Whatever, I could hear his voice in my head and it sounded like him alone. Like the late, great Peter Bellamy he had an unusual singing style, for sure, but was totally recognisably original and sang in a way which made you hang on to every word. Which somehow linked into an ongoing discussion we'd been having that 'the folk voice' was making a bit of an unfortunate comeback.

At the time I replied that I hadn't detected much of it. I thought that the iconic status among younger English folk artists of those who sang unaffectedly in their own voices – like Nic Jones and Shirley Collins – had rather done away with all those nasal affectations, randomly assembled faux-accents and general concentration on making a 'folk' noise with the mouth rather than the words of the song. Surely all those dreadful mannerisms were as discredited as clichés about fingers in ear and Aran sweaters from the same era?

But blow me down, I began noticing it more and more, to the point where I could see a danger of the easily piss-taken parody coming back to haunt us. "Why", Jim Moray asked, "would you want to invent a singing voice that doesn't sound nice, and conveys only how in thrall to a dead end of imagined authenticity you are?" Well, quite. One could also ask what the point is of singing traditional ballads if you maul the delivery so badly with mannerisms that it's difficult to comprehend the words.

Elsewhere, the Folkistanis were banging on about how they resented the popularity of the school of young women singers who, they sniff, sing in 'little girl' voices. Well, the good thing about them is that – like them or not – they are largely singing in their own natural voices and accents, and (it seems to me) are well involved in the stories of the songs they are singing. I'd rather hear a so-called 'waif' who believed in what she was singing and transmitted that to her listeners than some bawler concentrating only on making the folk noise. Since neither school, one suspects, has ever been near a coal mine, a naval battle or bit of poaching, incest or murder anyway...

It also made me wonder, though, about all the listening-without-responsibility that we do to singers from other cultures where we have no reference points. We often don't know what they're singing about, and we have no idea whether they may have vocal affectations that sound as gruesome to people of their own culture as some twerp channeling a Lincolnshire peasant while inappropriately wobbling the melody about might do to us. We can take it for granted, because of the home adulation they have, that the likes of Nusrat Fateh Ali Khan or Kandia Kouyaté weren't putting on silly voices. But who was to tell if the reason some of our 'wow' factor discoveries couldn't even get arrested on their home turf was that they sounded plain daft to locals?!

I suppose I understood the recent concerns that some had over changes to the Roald Dahl book texts (spoiler: I've never read one), though I did wonder if as a society we over-think and over-protect. I don't think many kids nowadays go off for hours at a time falling into rhynes and out of trees, grubbing around in all that germy dirt unsupervised as was normal for my generation, as figuratively in music as literally in life. But as a musician I do agree that if you become aware that certain old song lyrics are now uncomfortable to sing then there's nothing wrong with subtly changing them. But you should first and foremost do it for yourself, not calculating how you might appear to others.

Of course I don't mean that wholesale bowdlerisation which the Victorian collectors of traditional songs did, but small changes that you feel alright with. I'm OK with singing some murder ballads if they're telling a historic story, but definitely not songs that glorify misogyny and domestic violence. That was common in some of the old country blues lyrics I used to sing unthinkingly, learned off records as a teenager: makes me squirm to think about it now.

And that's all it's down to: thinking about what you're singing. Some people just concentrate on making noises with their mouths over a clever guitar (or whatever) part and don't really engage with the actual words. They're too concerned with style and perceived skill and don't see the pictures in their heads. But it's easy enough to tweak: as an example, I would never consider singing that old Muddy Waters/ Blind Boy Fuller line saying "I feel like slapping my pistol in your face" – but "I feel like snapping my fingers…" works just as well and allows the song to feel OK for me.

It's not just nasty stuff either. Once you start thinking about what you're actually singing, then perhaps you realise that as an English person you don't use dollars or walk on sidewalks or call your girlfriend "baby" (well not me anyway). Once you notice such things you can't un-notice them, and they're all easy enough to change. Becomes natural quite quickly. Ditto place names. Traditional singers have always done it. When I was a lad this was called 'the folk process', which isn't something you hear referred to very much these days, and not dismissed as 'wokeness'. Just get on with whatever feels good for you…

Which of course applies to other things that personally make me wince, like folk clubs where elderly (that's often younger than me nowadays) blokes in crumpled man shorts (on stage!), wearing hats to disguise their hair loss, strum expensive guitars while peering myopically at music stands. How did the latter become acceptable in folk clubs? But what right do I have to mock them and their audiences, who often resemble a contemporary equivalent to the Derby & Joan clubs of antiquity, when all they're doing is what makes them feel good? As the law used to say, "between consenting adults in private." I can always make my excuses, leave and let live…

There may be fewer opportunities for new musicians to get gigs via floor spots these days, it may be much harder as a promoter because of costly health & safety regulations, we may justifiably mourn the disappearance of record shops and the music press, we may rant on about how mainstream radio, TV and print media continue to ignore us... but beware of idealising the 'good old days'.

For both performers and audience, most venues have much better sound and lighting nowadays and most CDs have far superior recording and production values. I'd not want to go back to the first six or seven years of my playing career when you could rarely hear what you were playing on stage as monitors didn't exist, or when you were given just a day to make a whole LP with no say over the packaging because somebody who thought they knew better was in charge. I much prefer how venues are now smoke free and promoters far more likely to provide you with proper accommodation and even catering. I love the democratisation that technology has given us. Out there, the internet giveth and the internet taketh away (the likes of Spotify contributing to the financial devaluation of music), but overwhelmingly it giveth far more than it took.

Martin Carthy commented in a 1985 *Southern Rag* interview that "If the people who were listening to this music that they were just discovering twenty years ago – if they could have heard a record made in 1985, they wouldn't have believed it. How on earth do you get that from this?" And *that* was forty years ago! What would they make of all the music that I wouldn't want to live without today, the likes of the Rheingans Sisters, Spiro, Snakefarm, Orchestre Tout Puissant Marcel Duchamp, greekadelia, pizzica bands and much more.

As I've always signed off my radio shows and podcasts, probably to the irritation of many, "I've been Ian Anderson, and I shall be again, next time..." Though I just might come back as a crow...